MW01087945

ANTI-FANDOM

POSTMILLENNIAL POP

General Editors: Karen Tongson and Henry Jenkins

Anti-Fandom

Dislike and Hate in the Digital Age

Edited by
Melissa A. Click

NEW YORK UNIVERSITY PRESS
New York

NEW YORK UNIVERSITY PRESS
New York
www.nyupress.org

© 2019 by New York University
All rights reserved

References to Internet websites (URLs) were accurate at the time of writing. Neither the author nor New York University Press is responsible for URLs that may have expired or changed since the manuscript was prepared.

Library of Congress Cataloging-in-Publication Data
Names: Click, Melissa A., 1971– editor.
Title: Anti-fandom : dislike and hate in the digital age / edited by Melissa A. Click.
Description: New York : New York University Press, [2019] | Series: Postmillennial pop | Includes bibliographical references and index.
Identifiers: LCCN 2018020937| ISBN 9781479805273 (cl : alk. paper) | ISBN 9781479851041 (pb : alk. paper)
Subjects: LCSH: Celebrities—Public opinion. | Hate. | Social media. | Fans (Persons)—Attitudes.
Classification: LCC HM621 .A57 2018 | DDC 302.23/1—dc23
LC record available at https://lccn.loc.gov/2018020937

New York University Press books are printed on acid-free paper, and their binding materials are chosen for strength and durability. We strive to use environmentally responsible suppliers and materials to the greatest extent possible in publishing our books.

Manufactured in the United States of America

10 9 8 7 6 5 4 3 2 1

Also available as an ebook

For Gary Marlin Click

I will always be your #1 fan

CONTENTS

Introduction

Haters Gonna Hate

MELISSA A. CLICK

'Cause the players gonna play, play, play, play, play
And the haters gonna hate, hate, hate, hate, hate
Baby, I'm just gonna shake, shake, shake, shake, shake
I shake it off, I shake it off
—Taylor Swift

I twirl on them haters
—Beyoncé

It is commonplace today to see gushing fans lined up at movie pre-mieres, waiting for a glimpse of their favorite stars. Fan art created as homages to adored characters and fan fiction containing "will they or won't they?" fantasies abound in our social media feeds. In the twenty-five years since the publication of media scholar Henry Jenkins's *Textual Poachers* (1992), fan studies—and the cultural value and visibility of fandom—have come a long way. One of fan studies' enduring strengths is its focus on and valuation of affect, particularly its emphasis on fans' positive feelings of like and love. Yet examined less frequently are the equally intense, but opposite, feelings of dislike and hatred.

What is the opposite of fandom? Disinterest. Dislike. Disgust. Hate. Anti-fandom. It is visible in many of the same spaces where you see fan-dom: in the long lines at Comic-Con, at sporting events, in numerous online forums like Twitter, YouTube, Tumblr, and Reddit (never read the comments sections), and in our politics. This is where fans and fandoms debate and discipline. This is where we love to hate.

Why are some texts and fans targets of hate and anti-fandom more than others? What roles do digital technologies play in the development and practice of anti-fandom? What do anti-fans and anti-fan practices reveal about a text's construction, appeal, and reception? In their book *Fandom*, media scholars Jonathan Gray, Cornel Sandvoss, and C. Lee Harrington suggest that studies that examine "a spectrum of dislike, distaste, and hate" in fan and anti-fan cultures constitute one of six directions of the third wave of fan studies, the current iteration of the field, which has matured since many of its foundational texts emerged in the early 1990s (2007b, 15). An indicator of fan studies' maturity, they emphasize, is contemporary scholarship's interest in changing "the goalposts of inquiry and to broaden our analytic scope to a wide range of different audiences reflecting fandom's growing cultural currency" (2007b, 8). Demonstrating the possibilities and contributions of anti-fan scholarship, *Fandom* includes essays on dislike and anti-fandom, covering a range of topics from celebrity (Click 2007; Sconce 2007) and sports (Theodoropoulou 2007) to interactions with industry (Johnson 2007) and in families (Alters 2007).

A smattering of articles on anti-fandom followed the publication of Gray, Sandvoss, and Harrington's collection, including among them explorations of anti-fan reactions to celebrity (Claessens and Van den Bulck 2014), cheerleading (Jane 2014), online trolling (Phillips 2015), music (Giuffre 2014), professional wrestling (Hill 2015), television (Gray and Murray 2016), and the vampire franchise, *Twilight* (Gilbert 2012; Hills 2012; Pinkowitz 2011; Strong 2011; Williams 2013). While this work, and the necessity of studying anti-fandom generally, has been enthusiastically received, anti-fan scholarship has progressed only slightly in the last few years, which suggests the area of study needs direction and motivation. This new collection of fifteen innovative and original chapters aims to do just that, by providing a framework for future study through theoretical and methodological exemplars that engage the many questions about anti-fandom that remain.

As the frequent citation in this book (and elsewhere) attests, the description of anti-fans as "those who strongly dislike a given text or genre, considering it inane, stupid, morally bankrupt and/or aesthetic drivel," put forth by Jonathan Gray (2003, 70) in "New Audiences, New Textualities," has productively shaped scholarship on dislike, hate, and anti-fandom. Gray argues that the study of anti-fans (as well as non-fans) would help balance audience studies' nearly exclusive focus on the study of fans, and he also argues that this overreliance on fan populations has stunted scholarly knowledge of textuality, affective involvement, aesthetic and cultural value, and the relationships between text and audience. Although a number of the chapters in this collection, including Gray's new essay, endeavor to rework the atomic model Gray originally proposed (where fans/protons, anti-fans/electrons, and non-fans/positrons circulate differently around the text/atom), it has nonetheless served as a fruitful starting point for conceptualizing fans', anti-fans', and non-fans' engagement with media texts.

Gray later extended his exploration of anti-fandom through empirical examination of the website *Television Without Pity* (*TWoP*) and complicated his metaphorical conceptualization of the connections between fandom and anti-fandom, suggesting the two are not necessarily opposite in nature. He maintains that, "although pleasure and displeasure, or fandom or antifandom, could be positioned on opposite ends of a spectrum, they perhaps more accurately exist on a Möbius strip, with many fan and antifan behaviors and performances resembling, if not replicating each other" (Gray 2005, 845). This move, in combination with his use of *TWoP* to demonstrate three dimensions of anti-fan engagement with a text—moral, aesthetic, and rational-realist—offered useful frameworks for future studies of anti-fans' strategies and investments.

Nudging fan studies' attention beyond acts of viewing to the performativity of anti-fandom itself, Gray also suggests that community identification and participation can make anti-fandom pleasurable for the like-minded: "Hate or dislike of a text can be just as powerful as can a strong and admiring, affective relationship with a text, and they can produce just as much activity, identification, and meaning, and 'effects' or serve just as powerfully to unite and sustain a community or subculture" (Gray 2005, 841). Further, Gray observed the powerful extremes of group mentality in aggressive racist and sexist comments about *The Apprentice*'s Omarosa Manigault-Stallworth on *TWoP*. He warned that such comments, fueled by prejudice, resentment, and hatred, reflect the "darker dimensions of antifandom" (852), which require careful examination. Gray's observations in these areas have been useful for the anti-fan scholarship that has developed from his work.

Gray, of course, was not the first scholar to draw attention to audiences' strong negative emotions to media texts and figures; in fact, much of the first wave of scholarship on fans and fandom was positioned against the negativity and stereotyping fans endured from those who scorned their interests and activities (see, e.g., Jenkins 1992; Jenson 1992) and also illustrated that audiences and fans have different investments in the media texts and objects they enjoy (Fiske 1992; Grossberg 1992). Direct mentions of dislike and hate are present in a number of early studies of audiences and fans, including cultural studies scholar Ien Ang's (1985) study of the prime-time soap opera *Dallas*, which explored the variety of emotional attachments, including both love and hate, that viewers develop with media. Through an analysis of the forty-two responses to an ad she placed in the Dutch women's magazine *Viva* asking for descriptions of why people liked or disliked viewing the popular American drama, Ang asserts that describing one's relationship to a media text as either "love" or "hate" simplifies the complex and evolving relationships most viewers have with the programs they watch. She suggests that "what they say about *Dallas* is no more than a snapshot of their reception of the programme, an attempt to put a diffuse viewing experience into words. And when something is put into words there are always things which remain unexpressed and implicit" (Ang 1985, 14). Further, Ang argues that letter writers use an "ideology of mass culture" (92) or a belief that some cultural forms, specifically popular texts aimed at large audiences and typically American in origin, are "bad mass culture" (94) to rationalize and legitimize their personal and emotional positions on the program. Ang's work illustrates that, while discourses of hate emphasize aesthetics and critical distance, they also obscure the role pleasure plays in television viewing. Ang's study was one of the first to explore television viewers' different orientations to pleasure, and it remains a valuable exemplar for scholars wishing to study anti-fandom.

Media scholar John Fiske (1987) briefly mentions "haters" of Madonna in his discussion of the strain of television analysis developed from British cultural studies, emphasizing the way dislike of popular culture figures and texts is shaped by traditional gender ideologies. He observed that the hatred of Madonna "centers on her sexuality and—expressed as her presenting herself in whorelike terms—her painting and displaying herself to arouse the baser side of man" (274). Media scholars Laurie Schulze,

Anne Barton White, and Jane D. Brown examine hatred of Madonna in more detail, analyzing Madonna's "bad press" in the form of replies to a newspaper-sponsored letter writing contest and college students' writing about two of Madonna's videos. They found that haters' dislike was united around "a vision of her as the low-Other" (Schulze, White, and Brown 1993, 31) and resulted in an urge to challenge Madonna's status on aesthetic, social, and/or moral grounds. Through their emphasis on haters' particular dislike of Madonna's transgressive and carnivalesque displays of gender and sexuality, Schulze, White, and Brown insist that, while scholars typically praise audiences' resistive readings of mainstream texts, such readings may not always be socially progressive.

While some early fan studies scholarship focused directly on those who hate popular figures and media texts, other studies focused on the roles dislike and hate play in organized fan communities. Henry Jenkins (1992), in his ethnographic exploration of the practices and social institutions of media fandom, demonstrates that interpretation, evaluation, debate, and negotiation are integral parts of organized fandom and that fans' active and resistant readings of the texts they love can result in dislike, frustration, and anger. Through an account of fans' angry responses to the generic and character changes CBS made in the third season of *Beauty and the Beast* (1987–1990), Jenkins describes "how it is possible to remain a fan of a program while militantly rejecting producer actions that run contrary to one's own conception of the narrative" (1992, 132). These fans "scribble in the margins" (152) of their favorite texts, creating fan fiction, video, and music that move beyond simple replication of a text to "rework and rewrite it, repairing and dismissing unsatisfying aspects, developing interests not sufficiently explored" (162).

Echoing Jenkins's findings about fan frustrations with beloved texts, media scholars C. Lee Harrington and Denise D. Bielby found, in their study of soap opera fans, that the long-term relationships fans had with their favorite programs meant that sometimes "fans must actively struggle to locate and sustain the pleasure they find in soap operas" (Harrington and Bielby 1995, 154). While in the past fans may have at most written letters and made phone calls expressing their unhappiness to producers, or shared their feelings locally, the fans Harrington and Bielby studied were beginning to use more public forums like the daytime press and electronic bulletin boards to voice their disappointments more widely.

Although these soap opera fans were less likely to produce their own fan reworkings of soap opera storylines and characters, Harrington and Bielby observed that the most dedicated and loyal fans did believe that "they could tell better stories than do the writers and producers because they feel they know the characters and fictional community more intimately" (1995, 154). In her participant observation of soap fans on the rec.arts.tv.soaps online newsgroup, digital media scholar Nancy Baym (2000) similarly encountered fans' criticisms of the shows they enjoy and found that they continued to watch "despite the faults" (104) they saw in the shows. Baym's study demonstrates that, while fans frequently question the quality and realism of writing, acting, and props, they sustain their long-term investments in the soap operas they watch by fast-forwarding through storylines they dislike and by creatively reworking dissatisfying storylines. The presence of negative feelings in the fan communities studied in early fan scholarship, like the studies discussed above, suggests that dislike and hate play important roles in fan communities as well as outside them.

While the study of dislike, hate, and anti-fandom may not be new, it is even more important in the digital age, where the growth of online communication tools facilitate and increase the scope and speed of the participatory cultures that develop around media texts. As a result, audiences' engagements with media texts increasingly involve discussions in social media, including, for example, the use of Twitter for "hate watching" certain shows. Websites like *The A.V. Club* and social media platforms like YouTube often provide anti-fan perspectives on popular shows, and their comment sections are often full of criticisms, frustrations, and hateful declarations. While fan studies generally has examined fan spaces and practices online, few have explored the online communities, behaviors, and texts that have developed around hate and dislike. To demonstrate the important contributions scholarship on anti-fandom is poised to make to studies of online negative engagements about and around media texts, I explore in detail below the specific changes brought on by the development of the contemporary digital media environment that have led to the growth of anti-fandom, and I also explore the growth of the study of emotion and affect from a cultural perspective. These two areas of scholarship have proven fruitful and have much to contribute to emerging anti-fan scholarship.

Digital Media and Convergence Culture

The emergence of digital culture, or what Henry Jenkins calls "convergence culture," has facilitated the growth and visibility of public expressions of dislike and hatred as well as the growth and visibility of anti-fans themselves. Jenkins describes how convergence—or "the flow of content across multiple media platforms, the cooperation between multiple media industries, and the migratory behavior of media audiences who will go almost anywhere in search of the kinds of entertainment experiences they want" (Jenkins 2006, 2)—complicates the relationships between media producers and media audiences. In a digital environment in which the World Wide Web hosts multiple platforms offering a diversity of stories, and consumers have increased power to select, use, share, contribute to, and remix the media offerings that interest them (what some call Web 2.0), media producers have been forced to rethink their conceptions of the audience as a homogeneous mass and instead endeavor to build strong connections with consumers to keep their attention and build their loyalty. Television scholar Sharon Marie Ross, for instance, argues that, as early as the 1990s, broadcast and cable television networks began working to deepen their relationships with viewers by using "multi-platforming that gave television programs life in the worlds of film, print, the Internet, etc." (2008, 5). Aligned with Ross's description of TV industry efforts, in their book *Spreadable Media*, Henry Jenkins, Sam Ford, and Joshua Green argue that the media forms that most appeal to audiences include content with the potential to be spreadable or that encourage "audiences to share content for their own purposes, sometimes with the permission of rights holders, sometimes against their wishes" (2013, 3). To best design media content that is spreadable, Jenkins and his co-authors suggest that media producers should work to understand the motivations and practices of users who spread media content, warning that, "if it doesn't spread, it's dead" (188).

Nancy Baym and Robert Burnett's (2009) study of international fans of Swedish independent music offers a compelling example of fans' activities, and their value to producers, in a Web 2.0 environment. They argue that fans' online activities, ranging from low-investment activities like listing bands as favorites on social media profiles to more engaged media production like blogging, have created "an international presence far beyond what labels or bands could attain on their own" (Baym and Burnett 2009, 437). These fans' commitments to and investments in Swedish independent music, Baym and Burnett argue, cast them as "gatekeepers, filters, and influencers on a scale they never were before the Internet" (445–446), making them valuable to other fans and producers alike.

Baym and Burnett's (2009) study demonstrates the motivational and promotional power of fans' engagement with media that resonates with them. Jenkins (2006) argues, in line with this, that affective economics and brand loyalty are key to producers' reconceptualizations of the audience and to media production in a digital environment. Affective economics, "which seeks to understand the emotional underpinnings of consumer decision-making as a driving force behind viewing and purchasing decisions" (Jenkins 2006, 64), encourages producers to build networked communities around their media offerings by engaging consumers emotionally, and instructs that long-term brand relationships, a necessity for survival in the digital age, are built through such emotional engagements. Media producers' opportunities for observing and learning from audiences' existing emotional engagements with media content have increased in the contemporary digital environment because fan cultures and participatory practices have become more visible in the age of networked communication, as evidenced by Ross's assertion that "looking to past examples of how and why fans developed into social audiences" (Ross 2008, 7) has been a strategy used often by those in the TV industry.

Interactivity has emerged as one of the primary tools through which media producers can motivate audiences' affective engagements with media texts, and Web 2.0 is notable in large part for the growth in a range of interactive media offerings, from companion websites created to invite audiences deeper into media texts, to programming that encourages audiences to discuss and vote on outcomes. Tools of engagement, like interactivity, create media texts that offer multiple levels of participation and leave openings for audience members to share their perspectives, ultimately producing what Fiske (1989) has described as "producerly" texts and what Ross has described as "tele-participation" or "invitations to interact with TV shows beyond the moment of viewing and 'outside' of the TV show itself" (2008, 4). Such textual qualities

are more likely to attract audience members into participatory relationships with media content and other audience members as well and are
valuable to producers because "having something to do also gives fans
something to talk about and encourages them to spread the word to
other potential audience members" (Jenkins, Ford, and Green 2013, 136).
While these textual elements and audience practices may have once
been considered "cult," or outside of mainstream culture, the increased
production of producerly media content in our digital environment has
normalized fan behaviors once considered subcultural. The result is
that the increased mainstream offerings of producerly media texts have
moved subcultural fannish engagements, relationships, and practices
with media into the mainstream, opening the activities previously associated with fan cultures to mainstream culture. Such mainstreaming
has also "amplified and widened the scope of the activities of this already
socially networked and participatory audience" (167).

While convergence culture has normalized affective and interactive
fan practices typically considered to be cult or subcultural and media
producers have increasingly sought niche audiences to build long-term
relationships through media texts, audiences' affective engagements
with media texts have also led to the increasing visibility of fans' negative affective evaluations of media texts and media audiences. Two issues
related to the expression of anti-fandom in convergence culture stand
out as important to an exploration of anti-fandom: the divisive potential of the critical or "snarky" stances some digital audiences perform
online, and the privileges convergence culture offers to those groups
with greater online visibility. Media scholar Mark Andrejevic's (2008)
analysis of the user community on *Television Without Pity*—one of the
first online sites fully focused on the cultivation of skeptical and cynical
discussions of television programming—explores the enjoyment users
receive from the now-defunct site's mocking recaps of shows deemed
unworthy of praise and acclaim. Andrejevic also explores the pleasure
received from fellow users' recognition of their successful development
and performance of the kinds of ironic, sarcastic, and detached commentary the site promotes. The *TWoP* community in many ways embodied the kind of active engagement with media programming that
Jenkins encourages producers to seek in the era of convergence culture.
Participation on *TWoP* thus made watching television texts a prereq-

uisite for a more public and interactive enterprise—community review and discussion of television programming. As Andrejevic points out, the site's "real entertainment" involved users developing a deeper engagement with television texts, "which [took] the form of its online comeuppance: the gleeful dissection that takes place after it airs" (2008, 31).

Such a dissection required a healthy investment of users' time to develop the "critical, sarcastic repartee" so coveted on *TWoP*, and Andrejevic underscores that to successfully participate on *TWoP*, users had to carefully watch and rewatch the numerous programs under scrutiny on the site (2008, 31). *Television Without Pity* users also worked to develop the skills necessary to be critical viewers, thinkers, and writers; these skills were seen as so critical to successful participation on the site that those who felt unsure of their abilities refrained from commenting and lurked instead. While Andrejevic suggests that producers' use of *TWoP* users' uncompensated labor as market research constitutes exploitation, a topic also addressed by Baym and Burnett (2009) and others (e.g., De Kosnik 2013; Gregg 2011; Terranova 2000), Andrejevic found that *TWoP* users' investments of time and development of critical analysis skills increased their investment in and enjoyment of programming and the *TWoP* site.

While the development of the critical thinking skills necessary to participate in snarky repartee about television can be (and has been) seen as positive, Andrejevic's work demonstrates that the ironic and cynical stance that many *TWoP* users developed could encourage them to think that their savvy perspective sets them "apart from the rest of the audience" (Andrejevic 2008, 40). Through their scrutinizing focus on the intricacies of programs' production values and marketing strategies, Andrejevic observed that many *TWoP* users came to adopt a producer-oriented insider's perspective. They used this perspective to demonstrate that they were not dupes and to claim superiority over viewers whom they deemed less critical. Andrejevic argues that this insider's perspective turns the progressive potential of a "mediated interactivity" (24) with the power to rework the imbalance between producers and consumers into a kind of "participatory submission" (45). Andrejevic's work is useful for studies of anti-fandom because the complexities it demonstrates are associated with the ironic stance many *TWoP* users adopted. While users' critical analysis of television programming may warrant praise for the deep thinking it engendered, some used their critical skills to reassert the divide between producers and audiences by encouraging the development of an uncritical identification with media producers and of a dismissive differentiation from the mainstream media audience by positioning them as unthinking dupes. This identification could produce dangerous divisions among anti-/fan cultures on- and offline, and thus such orientations warrant further exploration.

While Andrejevic demonstrates the complexities of the snarky stance that has come to be associated with some forms of anti-fandom, other scholars have focused on the antagonism that has developed among fan groups, a partial result of the media industry's valuation of some forms of fandom over others. In *Spreadable Media*, Jenkins and his co-authors indicate that the increased number of media offerings and platforms in digital culture has fragmented media audiences, leaving producers with "uncertainty about how much value to place on different kinds of audiences" (Jenkins, Ford, and Green 2013, 116). Producers, despite their increasing dependence upon audiences in the convergence culture era, continue to view some audiences as more valuable than those they consider "surplus," or outside the target demographic. The dominance producers retain in this reconceptualized relationship means that they continue to be more eager to please the consumers that are most desirable to them, especially white, middle-class and college-educated males (Jenkins 2006).

Building upon such concerns, media studies scholar Suzanne Scott (2011) argues that new cultural and industrial visibility is available only to those fans the industry deems profitable and ideologically safe. These fans, whom Scott (drawing from obsession_inc 2009) deems "affirmational" fans, tend to uphold the sanctity of the text as produced and value relational ties with (and even pursue employment in) the industry and popular press; they also tend to be male. The convergence-era visibility these "fanboys" have received and cultivated overshadows "fangirls," whom Scott asserts are "transformational" fans, who develop orientations and practices that tend to involve resistive strategies of (re)reading against the grain of the text as produced. Through numerous examples from *Twilight*'s female fans "ruining" San Diego Comic-Con 2009 to *Supernatural*'s representation of fangirl character Becky Rosen, Scott demonstrates how fanboys have gained cultural visibility, commanded representational diversity, and accrued value to the media industry as desirable tastemakers. In contrast, fangirls, in part through their own strategic actions undertaken to stay off the industry's radar, have become more alienated and pathologized, and their work obscured and devalued. The resultant disparities are exacerbated by convergence-era discourses that suggest that digital technologies enable new fan-industry relationships and new depathologized portrayals of fans, in many cases producing antagonism among fan cultures. Scott's case studies demonstrate the importance of the ways "an understanding and interrogation of these boundaries between the mainstream and the margins, historically central to fan studies, is increasingly vital to any study of contemporary fan culture" (2011, 305). Gender is at the center of the dynamics Scott studies, which makes clear that explorations of race, class, sexuality, and nationality, among other identity categories, are crucial areas of investigation for future work in anti-fan studies.

The emergence of digital media culture, or convergence, has forced a reassessment of the traditional relationships between media producers and audiences, normalizing fan practices once considered cult or marginal, and encouraging producers to build long-term relationships with audiences by creating texts that encourage affective investments and inviting audiences to interact with media texts in a variety of formats. One outcome of these changes is the growth and increased visibility of anti-fan practices and cultures that both value and produce critical analyses of media texts and potentially also encourage antagonism among fannish groups. Digital media is only one contributing factor to the increased visibility of anti-fandom. Anti-fandom, as I explore next, must be understood as well through cultural approaches to emotion and affect.

Emotion and Affect

Whether seen as a "cultural turn" in emotion studies (Harding and Pribram 2009) or an "affective turn" in cultural theory and criticism (Clough 2008), the study of affect and emotion developed in the early to mid-1990s to address cultural questions not easily examined through the lenses of contemporary approaches such as poststructuralism and deconstruction (Clough 2008). But, despite its value for the exploration of questions involving identity and power, among others, cultural studies scholars Jennifer Harding and E. Deirdre Pribram (2009) argue that cultural scholars have been slow to examine emotions because of their association with the personal and experiential, with women and other "irrational" groups, and with biology and psychology.

Recognizing—and rejecting—such biases, cultural approaches argue against understanding emotions as only individual, as qualities possessed only by some groups, and as produced inside bodies; contemporary affect scholarship argues instead that emotions are social and cultural. Cultural studies scholar Sara Ahmed, in *The Cultural Politics of Emotion* (2004), asserts that emotions are historically rooted, performative speech acts. Instead of trying to understand what emotions *are*, Ahmed suggests scholars should investigate the circulation and impact of emotions—in short, what emotions *do*. Building upon Marxist notions, Ahmed describes emotions as a form of capital; she maintains that "affect does not reside positively in the sign or commodity, but is produced as an effect of its circulation" (253). This postulation means that, instead of being an "origin and destination," the subject, with respect to the circulation of emotion, is "simply one nodal point in the economy" (254). Ahmed also stresses that emotions do not circulate freely; some emotions stick, affix, and transfer more easily and powerfully to some signs and bodies (especially those with historical connections to particular emotions), and it is these attachments, repetitions, and accumulations of emotion that make individuals and collectives meaningful. She also indicates that frequency of circulation modifies signs' affect: "Signs increase in affective value as an effect of the movement between signs: the more signs circulate, the more affective they become" (253).

Underscoring Ahmed's assertion that "emotions are bound up with the securing of social hierarchy" (Ahmed 2004, 4), Harding and Pribram maintain that emotions work to create, and endeavor to fix, power relations and social identities. They suggest that "emotion relations, like power relations, are productive: they not only subordinate, they create" (Harding and Pribram 2009, 19). Further, emotions have no essence, no essential qualities; they shape and are shaped by the contexts in which they circulate. While emotions' cultural circulation and impact are "insufficiently understood" (19), Harding and Pribram suggest that the tactics and sites involved in struggles over the emotional investments that create and re-create gendered, raced, ethnic, sexual, and national identities are subject positions that are also likely locations where the power and impact of emotion can be challenged and reworked.

Crucial to the study of anti-fandom, Ahmed's discussion of hate and disgust illustrates how emotions work as forms of capital. Hate, Ahmed argues, is a response to feeling threatened and is wielded as a form of defense against potential harm. Hate differentiates among subjects (creating a "them" against which groups are positioned) and positions the other ("them") as a threat whose proximity endangers something that is loved (e.g., a media text, celebrity, or convention). She stresses that histories among and between subjects are present in such differentiations, and thus "some bodies are already encountered as more hateful than other bodies" (Ahmed 2004, 259). This does not mean, of course, that those seen as hateful are indeed hateful. Quite the contrary, it underscores that hatred has historically circulated around, and through repetition has stuck to, specific bodies or signs. Ahmed argues that individuals' opposition to the hated is simultaneously constitutive of collectivity: "How we feel about others is what aligns us with a collective, which paradoxically 'takes shape' only as an effect of such alignments" (260). The hated object, then, is crucial to the formation of the collective, and the expulsion or incorporation of the hated other is needed to maintain the collective identity.

While hatred produces powerful alliances and antagonisms, Ahmed argues that hate's economic or circulating nature makes it difficult to easily locate it in an object or figure. To sustain hate, expressions and acts of hatred must be continually repeated and recirculated, meaning that hatred is "a differentiation that is never 'over'" (Ahmed 2004, 255). Further, the collective, and the identities that compose it, are dependent upon the enduring association of hate and the othered "them." These collective identities built around repeated actions of hate form the basis for many anti-fandoms and anti-fan activities.

As with hate, Ahmed argues that the expression of disgust is permeated by power relations. While disgust involves feelings of repulsion assumedly provoked by the proximity of an offending object, disgust also involves an angered acknowledgment of vulnerability to that which disgusts: "Bodies that are disgusted are also bodies that feel a certain rage, a rage that the object has got close enough to sicken, and to be taken over or taken in. To be disgusted is, after all, *to be affected by what one has re-jected*" (Ahmed 2004, 86; emphasis in original). Further, the expression of disgust involves a desire to differentiate oneself from and position oneself above the disgusting object. Ahmed argues that objects are not inherently disgusting, but some are more likely to be seen as disgust ing because of connections with objects already framed as disgusting. She describes the act of calling something disgusting as a performative act that brings the object into being through its allegations: "To name something as disgusting . . . is performative. It relies on previous norms and conventions of speech, and it generates the object that it names" (93). Disgust, then, gains its power through its ability to relate, and sub-sequently bind, objects to each other, making it difficult to disentangle objects from these negative associations.

The successful positioning of an object as disgusting also requires others to repeat the condemnation, and Ahmed emphasizes that the community involving the shared desire to maintain distance from the disgusting object is built through this shared goal: "A community of witnesses is generated, whose apparent shared distance from an event or object that has been named as disgusting is achieved through the repetition of the word 'disgust'" (2004, 94). As with hate, Ahmed argues that expressions of disgust cannot fully or permanently eliminate the vulnerability the disgusted feels, and thus the act of naming the object as disgusting must be continually reiterated.

Although emotion and affect have always been crucial components of fan studies' interest in how feelings of love and like shape reception of media texts and bind communities of the like-minded, this scholarship has been less focused upon the circulation and effects of emotions than on the alliances and practices such feelings produce. Further, fan studies has neglected to produce an engaged examination of how negative emo-tions, like hate and disgust, are implicated in fans' expressions of love—both as tools for creating unity and for maintaining community borders. The cultural approach to emotion sketched here offers much food for thought for such explorations. A renewed focus on what emotions *do* in fan practices and communities would enable scholars to understand how fans' emotions are rooted historically and would allow scholars to address questions about how, why, and to what emotions stick. Further, the cultural approach's understanding of emotions as attempts to fix power relations and shape social identities is crucially important for fan studies scholarship that aims to understand fan practices and communities as intimately connected with identity categories, such as gender, race, ethnicity, class, and nation.

Media studies in general has been slow to engage with cultural approaches to affect (notable exceptions include De Kosnik 2013; Gregg 2011; Hills 2015; and Ouellette and Wilson 2011), but media scholar Emma A. Jane's (2012) work on "e-bile"—a term she employs to unite online texts and speech, including cyberbullying, flaming, and trolling—suggests that the critical analysis of hate is crucial to understanding, and maintaining civility in, our digital media environment. Based on the textual analysis of a range of material archived between 1999 and 2012, Jane describes e-bile as characterized by its "reliance on profanity, ad hominem invective, and hyperbolic imagery of graphic—often sexualized—violence" (Jane 2012, 3) that frames female targets through sexually violent language as stupid or hyperbolic and male targets as homosexual or effeminate. Despite evidence that "on-line hostility is getting more prevalent, it is getting uglier, and it has a number of distinctly gendered characteristics" (4), Jane argues that academic scholarship has tended to praise the creativity and resistance of e-bile producers while trivializing its impact on its victims. She asserts that scholarship must take such "textual sadism" (12) more seriously because its circulation affects users' willingness to participate openly online and thus may have serious consequences on the inclusivity of online cultures.

Jane further demonstrates how crucial an ethical understanding of e-bile and its impact are to scholarship on anti-fandom in her exploration of cheerleading anti-fans, a group she argues is composed of a diversity of social groups that simultaneously positions cheerleaders as "objects of derision and desire" (Jane 2014, 179). She points out that the digital environment has enabled anti-fans to directly contact their targets and their families, to target ordinary people, and produce commentary that is "hyperbolic, threatening, and misogynist in nature" (185). She critiques scholarship on anti-fandom that has characterized the objects of anti-fandom only as texts, and anti-fans themselves as only audience members, asserting that anti-fans are "powerful media producers, and their targets can include human subjects who may suffer real-life pain and suffering" (186). Thus, given that the targets of anti-fan ire may be the reputations and careers of public and private individuals as well as television characters or series, we can better understand the agency, responsibility, and impact involved in anti-fandom if we reconsider conceptions of anti-fans as critical thinking, resistive audience members. Insistent on the need to hold anti-fans responsible for the personal, social, and legal impact of their vitriolic expression, Jane maintains that, "when disgust and hate are expressed about a person or a group of people outside of media contexts (especially when this disgust or hate is based on a priori prejudices), it is usually known by other terms. 'Sexism', 'racism', 'homophobia', and 'hate speech' are a few that come to mind" (177). Although Jane's call to more seriously consider the ethical questions surrounding anti-fandom has been present in some anti-fan scholarship, particularly scholarship examining *Twilight* anti-fandom (e.g., Pinkowitz 2011; Strong 2011), her suggestion that scholars more carefully consider what anti-fandom *does* marks a crucial area of inquiry for anti-fan studies, and one with which cultural approaches to emotion can help. If indeed emotions are "investments in social norms" (Ahmed 2004, 261), anti-fan scholarship should seriously consider the goals and impact of such investments. Recent fan/anti-fan entanglements, like #GamerGate (e.g., Chess and Shaw 2015) and the harassment of Leslie Jones, star of the 2016 *Ghostbusters* film, on Twitter (Rogers 2016), suggest that scholarship on anti-fandom can—and indeed, should—contribute to and further our understanding of the circulation and impact of dislike and hate through digital technology. In fact, studies on dislike, hate, and anti-fandom, rooted in scholarship on digital media and in cultural approaches to emotion, have a crucial role in helping us fully understand the form and function of our contemporary media environment.

Anti-Fan Is the New Fan

The cutting-edge, previously unpublished research included in this collection explores anti-fandom and dislike through gender, generation, race, nationality, sexuality, taste, authenticity, electoral politics, and celebrity with a diversity of theoretical and methodological positions. This volume answers the call put forward in *Fandom:* Identities and Communities in a Mediated World, in which the editors argued that the study of hate and anti-fandom is an important direction to be undertaken by the third wave of fan studies, a wave that is charged to "tell us something about the way in which we relate to those around us, as well as the way we read the mediated texts that constitute an ever larger part of our horizon of experience" (Gray, Sandvoss, and Harrington 2007b, 10). *Anti-Fandom: Dislike and Hate in the Digital Age*, as a result, gives drive and direction to the study of anti-fandom and dislike in the contemporary digital environment, with a particular focus on the pleasures, performances, punishments, and practices that constitute anti-fandom.

Part I, "Theorizing Anti-Fandom," aims to broaden the study of anti-fandom by sketching the diversity and complexity of the topic and by offering theoretical frameworks to help ground future work. Jonathan Gray builds upon his foundational work in anti-fandom by examining a range of types of anti-fandom, many of which are discussed in the chapters that follow, and illustrates how exploration of a range of orientations to dislike and hate can fill gaps in media studies scholarship. The utility of anti-fan scholarship is the question Emma A. Jane raises through an examination of six case studies. She argues that changes in networked digital culture, as well as in anti-fans' threatening and violent discourse, require anti-fan scholars to carefully rethink their analyses of hate. Anne Gilbert examines the role irony plays in anti-fan cultures, arguing that snarky, sarcastic comments are less motivated by dislike than a desire to perform for an audience; in fact, Gilbert suggests such performances build anti-fan community. Focusing on the *Glee* Equality Project, Louisa Stein revisits Jenkins's suggestion that challenging and reworking beloved texts is a crucial component of fandom. Stein suggests that sharing dissatisfaction can help fans turn negativity into creativity. Matt Hills uses *Doctor Who* fandom to illustrate how lifelong relationships with enduring texts create generational boundaries around particular eras of texts that are policed with dislike.

The roles identity politics play in the expression of anti-fandom is the focus of Part II, "Anti-Fandom and Identities." Electoral politics is the focus of Cornel Sandvoss' chapter, in which he explores case studies involving politicians in the United States and Europe to demonstrate the ways anti-fandom can affect political participation and democracy generally. Holly Willson Holladay and Melissa A. Click explore *Breaking Bad* fans' gendered hatred of Skyler White and suggest that fans' feelings for the series' complex antihero Walter White, and their biases about gender roles, activated their strong negative feelings for Skyler and Anna Gunn, the actress who portrays her. Alfred L. Martin, Jr.'s interviews with black female viewers of Tyler Perry's films help reveal why these Perry anti-fans continue to watch his films. Despite their adamant dislike of the representations of African Americans that Perry produces, viewing these films helps anti-fans perform important familial, social, and political functions. The global anti-fan movement against reggaetón music is the focus of Michelle M. Rivera's chapter; in it, she demonstrates the complicated ways that gender, race, ethnicity, and nationality are inflected in anti-fan response to the Afrodiasporic musical form. Roberta Pearson's examination of anti-fan responses to programming changes at BBC Radio 3 demonstrates the importance of studying a range of cultural forms, including those considered high culture forms. The anti-fan comments she analyzed support her argument that "supracultural" fans are not always complicit with structures of power.

Part III, "Anti-Fandom in Real Life," explores a diverse collection of lived experiences of anti-fandom. Richard McCulloch examines the ways that European football fans criticize their own teams, arguing that, while expressions of anti-fandom may be regular discourse among fans, such expressions are governed by norms and expectations. Whitney Phillips investigates audience reaction to TLC's *Here Comes Honey Boo Boo* and argues that the show invites expressions of dislike that reinforce normative ideologies of race, class, and gender. These expressions challenge scholarly perceptions of anti-fandom as counterhegemonic. Bethan Jones argues that BDSM community members' negative reactions to *Fifty Shades of Grey* were bolstered by the subcultural capital they accrue as practitioners. While their experience bolstered their credibility with readers, it also affected the approaches they took to challenge the series' representations of BDSM. Understanding angry exchanges between fans and actors on Twitter structures Bertha Chin's chapter, where she demonstrates that the immediacy of social media changes the nature and tone of relationships between fans and celebrities. Fans' relieved reactions to the ends of television programs is Rebecca Williams' focus. She suggests that the creation and circulation of "rejection discourses" help fans cope with the psychological strains that come with cancellation.

Together, the chapters that constitute *Anti-Fandom: Dislike and Hate in the Digital Age* provide the emerging area of anti-fan studies with a productive foundation and demonstrate the importance of constructing a complex knowledge of emotion and media in fan studies. Love them or hate them, my hope is that the concepts and cases these chapters contain will generate new perspectives for understanding the impact of dislike, hate, and anti-fandom on our identities, relationships, and communities.

REFERENCES

Ahmed, S. 2004. *The Cultural Politics of Emotion*. New York: Routledge.

Alters, D. 2007. "The Other Side of Fandom: Anti-Fans, Non-Fans, and the Hurts of History." In *Fandom: Identities and Communities in a Mediated World*, edited by J. Gray, C. Sandvoss, and C. L. Harrington, 344–356. New York: New York University Press.

Andrejevic, M. 2008. "Watching *Television Without Pity*: The Productivity of Online Fans." *Television and New Media* 9:24–46.

Ang, I. 1985. *Watching Dallas: Soap Opera and the Melodramatic Imagination*. New York: Routledge.

Baym, N. 2000. *Tune In, Log On: Soaps, Fandom, and Online Community*. Thousand Oaks, CA: Sage.

Baym, N., and R. Burnett. 2009. "Amateur Experts: International Fan Labour in Swedish Independent Music." *International Journal of Cultural Studies* 12:433–449.

Chess, S., and A. Shaw. 2015. "A Conspiracy of Fishes, or How We Learned to Stop Worrying about #GamerGate and Embrace Hegemonic Masculinity." *Journal of Broadcasting and Electronic Media* 59:201–220.

Claessens, N., and H. Van den Bulck. 2014. "A Severe Case of Disliking Bimbo Heidi, Scumbag Jesse and Bastard Tiger: Analysing Celebrities' Online Anti-Fans." In *The Ashgate Companion to Fan Cultures*, edited by L. Duits, K. Zwaan, and S. Reijnders, 63–75. Burlington, VT: Ashgate.

Click, M. A. 2007. "Untidy: Fan Response to the Soiling of Martha Stewart's Spotless Image." In *Fandom: Identities and Communities in a Mediated World*, edited by J. Gray, C. Sandvoss, and C. L. Harrington, 301–315. New York: New York University Press.

Clough, P. 2008. "The Affective Turn: Political Economy, Biomedia and Bodies." *Theory, Culture and Society* 25:1–22.

De Kosnik, A. 2013. "Fandom as Free Labor." In *Digital Labor: The Internet as Playground and Factory*, edited by T. Scholz, 98–111. New York: Routledge.

Fiske, J. 1987. "British Cultural Studies and Television." In *Channels of Discourse: Television and Contemporary Criticism*, edited by R. C. Allen, 254–289. Chapel Hill: University of North Carolina Press.

———. 1989. *Reading the Popular*. Cambridge, MA: Unwin Hyman.

———. 1992. "The Cultural Economy of Fandom." In *The Adoring Audience: Fan Culture and Popular Media*, edited by L. A. Lewis, 30–49. New York: Routledge.

Gilbert, A. 2012. "Between Twi-Hards and Twi-Haters: The Complicated Terrain of Online 'Twilight' Audience Communities." In *Genre, Reception, and Adaptation in the "Twilight" Series*, edited by A. Morey, 163–179. Burlington, VT: Ashgate.

Giuffre, L. 2014. "Music for (Something Other than) Pleasure: Anti-Fans and the Other Side of Popular Music Appeal." In *The Ashgate Companion to Fan Cultures*, edited by L. Duits, K. Zwaan, and S. Reijnders, 49–62. Burlington, VT: Ashgate.

Gray, J. 2003. "New Audiences, New Textualities: Anti-Fans and Non-Fans." *International Journal of Cultural Studies* 6:64–81. doi: 10.1177/1367877903006001004.

———. 2005. "Antifandom and the Moral Text: *Television Without Pity* and Textual Dislike." *American Behavioral Scientist* 48:840–858.

Gray, J., and S. Murray. 2016. "Hidden: Studying Media Dislike and Its Meaning." *International Journal of Cultural Studies* 19, no. 4:357–372. doi: 10.1177/1367877915572223.

Gray, J., C. Sandvoss, and C. L. Harrington, eds. 2007a. *Fandom: Identities and Communities in a Mediated World*. New York: New York University Press.

Gray, J., C. Sandvoss, and C. L. Harrington. 2007b. "Introduction: Why Study Fans?" In *Fandom: Identities and Communities in a Mediated World*, edited by J. Gray, C. Sandvoss, and C. L. Harrington, 1–18. New York: New York University Press.

Gregg, M. 2011. *Work's Intimacy*. Malden, MA: Polity.

Grossberg, L. 1992. "Is There a Fan in the House? The Affective Sensibility of Fandom." In *The Adoring Audience: Fan Culture and Popular Media*, edited by L. A. Lewis, 50–65. New York: Routledge.

Harding, J., and D. Pribram. 2009. "Introduction." In *Emotions: A Cultural Studies Reader*, edited by J. Harding and D. Pribram, 1–24. New York: Routledge.

Harrington, C. L., and D. D. Bielby. 1995. *Soap Fans: Pursuing Pleasure and Making Meaning in Everyday Life*. Philadelphia: Temple University Press.

Hill, A. 2015. "Spectacle of Excess: The Passion Work of Professional Wrestlers, Fans and Anti-Fans." *European Journal of Cultural Studies* 18, no. 2:174–189. doi: 10.1177/1367549414563300.

Hills, M. 2012. "'Twilight' Fans Represented in Commercial Paratexts and Inter-Fandoms: Resisting and Repurposing Negative Fan Stereotypes." In *Genre, Reception, and Adaptation in the "Twilight" Series*, edited by A. Morey, 113–129. Burlington, VT: Ashgate.

———. 2015. "*Veronica Mars*, Fandom, and the 'Affective Economics' of Crowdfunding Poachers." *New Media and Society* 17:183–197.

Jane, E. A. 2012. "'You're a Ugly, Whorish, Slut': Understanding E-Bile." *Feminist Media Studies* 14:531–546.

———. 2014. "Beyond Antifandom: Cheerleading, Textual Hate and New Media Ethics." *International Journal of Cultural Studies* 17:175–190.

Jenkins, H. 1992. *Textual Poachers: Television Fans and Participatory Culture*. New York: Routledge.

———. 2006. *Convergence Culture: Where Old and New Media Collide*. New York: New York University Press.

Jenkins, H., S. Ford, and J. Green. 2013. *Spreadable Media: Creating Value and Meaning in a Networked Culture*. New York: New York University Press.

Jenson, J. 1992. "Fandom as Pathology: The Consequences of Characterization." In *The Adoring Audience: Fan Culture and Popular Media*, edited by L. A. Lewis, 9–29. New York: Routledge.

Johnson, D. 2007. "Fan-tagonism: Factions, Institutions, and Constitutive Hegemonies of Fandom." In *Fandom: Identities and Communities in a Mediated World*, edited by J. Gray, C. Sandvoss, and C. L. Harrington, 285–300. New York: New York University Press.

obsession_inc. 2009. "Affirmational Fandom vs. Transformational Fandom." *Dreamwidth*, June 1. www.dreamwidth.org.

Ouellette, L., and J. Wilson. 2011. "Women's Work: Affective Labour and Convergence Culture." *Cultural Studies* 25:548–565.

Phillips, W. 2015. *This Is Why We Can't Have Nice Things: Mapping the Relationship between Online Trolling and Mainstream Culture*. Cambridge, MA: MIT Press.

Pinkowitz, J. M. 2011. "'The Rabid Fans That Take [*Twilight*] Much Too Seriously': The Construction and Rejection of Excess in *Twilight* Antifandom." *Transformative Works and Cultures*, no. 7. doi: 10.3983/twc.2011.0247.

Rogers, K. 2016. "Leslie Jones, Star of 'Ghostbusters,' Becomes a Target of Online Trolls." *New York Times*, July 19. www.nytimes.com.

Ross, S. M. 2008. *Beyond the Box: Television and the Internet*. Malden, MA: Blackwell Publishing.

Schulze, L., A. B. White, and J. D. Brown. 1993. "'A Sacred Monster in Her Prime': Audience Construction of Madonna as Low-Other." In *The Madonna Connection: Representational Politics, Subcultural Identities, and Cultural Theory*, edited by C. Schwichtenberg, 15–37. Boulder, CO: Westview Press.

Sconce, J. 2007. "A Vacancy at the Paris Hilton." In *Fandom: Identities and Communities in a Mediated World*, edited by J. Gray, C. Sandvoss, and C. L. Harrington, 328–343. New York: New York University Press.

Scott, S. 2011. "Revenge of the Fanboy: Convergence Culture and the Politics of Incorporation." Doctoral dissertation, University of Southern California, Los Angeles.

Strong, C. 2011. "As Close to Worthless as It Can Get: *Twilight* Anti-Fans, Teenage Girls and Symbolic Violence." In *Fanpires: Audience Consumption of the Modern Vampire*, edited by G. Schott and K. Moffat, 73–89. Washington, DC: New Academia Publishing.

Terranova, T. 2000. "Free Labor: Producing Culture for the Digital Economy." *Social Text* 18:33–58.

Theodoropoulou, V. 2007. "The Anti-Fan within the Fan: Awe and Envy in Sport Fandom." In *Fandom: Identities and Communities in a Mediated World*, edited by J. Gray, C. Sandvoss, and C. L. Harrington, 316–327. New York: New York University Press.

Williams, R. 2013. "'Anyone Who Calls Muse a *Twilight* Band Will Be Shot on Sight': Music, Distinction, and the 'Interloping Fan' in the *Twilight* franchise." *Popular Music and Society* 36:327–342.

PART I

Theorizing Anti-Fandom

1

How Do I Dislike Thee? Let Me Count the Ways

JONATHAN GRAY

In 2003, I published an article about the control that fan studies had taken over audience studies and about my concerns that this had pushed under water greater and full consideration of distracted, sometime, and casual viewers—"non-fans"—and of those who dislike the text—anti-fans (Gray 2003). I was trying to rethink textuality and thus offered an "atomic" model of the text and its viewers, accounting for fans as positively charged protons in the very nucleus of the text, likely consuming all or most of a television show, for instance, plus a great deal of its various paratexts. Meanwhile, I described anti-fans as the negatively charged electrons, spinning around the nucleus and hence seeing less of it. As a visualization tool, and as a way of thinking about *textuality*, the atomic model had some utility. Thankfully, though, few who have cited the article have mentioned that model in particular. I say "thankfully" because it has its problems as a tool for thinking about *audiences*. On the one hand, the model and the article construct fans and anti-fans of the same text as opposites when they may not be. Inasmuch as fans and anti-fans are both highly "charged" viewers (i.e., they care about the text), we might instead expect them at times to have more in common with each other than with non-fans. On the other hand, the model crudely lumps various practices, motivations, and affective positions into one big undifferentiated mass called the "anti-fan." In the years since writing that article, I have come to regret not seeing more nuance and difference in anti-fandom.

As an exercise in speculation, therefore, this chapter aims to subdivide and taxonomize *some* forms of anti-fandom. It is not based on a specific audience research project and thus is not empirical. Rather, it gestures toward the rich and varied work that may lie ahead in studying anti-fans precisely because they are not all cut from the same cloth and because each form of anti-fandom therefore directs our attention to yet more realities and mysteries of media audiences (as of course do the other chapters in this collection, often with considerably more empiricism and detail). What does anti-fandom look like? How might we distinguish starkly different modes of disliking? And what is to be gained by examining each mode? This chapter offers preliminary answers to some of these questions, with a brief tour through several forms of anti-fandom. Occasionally, I enjoy the luxury of being able to point to work conducted by others that examines these forms of anti-fandom; at other times, I must simply ask for the reader's willingness to speculate with me.

Competitive Anti-Fandom

Although I wish to step back from a model that sees fans and anti-fans themselves as differently charged atoms, a good entry point to this taxonomization may be instances when the fan *object* and the anti-fan *object* are locked in a Manichean battle. As Vivi Theodoropoulou (2007) notes, fandom can easily lead to a form of anti-fandom when dislike (whether serious or playful) is directed at a perceived rival of one's beloved fan object. Theodoropoulou offers the clear example of sporting rivalries, in which certain fandoms practically require dislike of other teams: Boston Red Sox fans are expected to hate the New York Yankees, Liverpool fans "should" revile Manchester United, and so forth. However, we might apply Theodoropoulou's observation more broadly to all sorts of fandoms. Thus, for instance, we often see franchises pitted against each other: *Star Wars* fans and *Star Trek* fans will often perform dislike of the "rival" franchise, just as *Buffy* fans can at times offer *Twilight* or *Vampire Diaries* a chilled response, threatened in some way by the success of other vampire texts. Television texts that face off against each other in scheduling, or that replace one another on that schedule, may similarly be surrounded by anti-fans. Or entire media may be framed as locked into competition, such that cinephiles, for example, may feel compelled to grumble loudly about television and video games, and statements of love for a certain medium quite often involve straw-man invocations of other media.

A complex set of processes are in play with competitive anti-fandoms. Analysts could ask, in particular, about the choice of rival, what this says about the beloved object that is being "defended," and what perceived threat exists to the beloved object in the first place. Sport rivalries may seem relatively simple, inasmuch as many key rivalries develop when teams must commonly defeat each other to advance. So, for instance, in the National Hockey League a rivalry developed between the Colorado Avalanche and the Detroit Red Wings after the two teams met each other numerous times in the Stanley Cup playoffs throughout the 1990s and 2000s. Manchester United and Liverpool, too, have vied for supremacy in the English Premier League many times, thereby commonly pitting them and their fans against each other. But as is the case with this latter rivalry, sporting competitions can be about much more than just wins and losses, as geographic rivalries are often superimposed onto the realm of sports. Theodoropoulou examines this in the case of Greece's two elite soccer clubs, Panathinaikos and Olympiacos, the former of which has become articulated to urban and upscale Athens, the latter to the surrounding, working-class areas, such that matchups between the two teams become grand dramas of two classes and two regions at war with one another. Or one need only think of national sports rivalries to see plenty of instances when sporting matches are seen to be competitions of ways of life, as with Cold War–era rivalries between the United States and East Germany or the Soviet Union (witness the ideological reading of the so-called Miracle on Ice in 1980). In this respect, sporting anti-fandoms can tell us a great deal about the values that a community or individual hold dearly and about the cultural geographies and moral economies being created around teams.

Rivalries outside the realm of sports or scheduling conflicts add extra complexities, for when two texts are not involved in leagues or competitions against each other, or are not vying for audience attention in a specific time block, we as analysts must ascertain why it is that this or that text is perceived as a rival. What threat, for instance, does *Star Wars* pose to *Star Trek* such that some fans feel the need to choose between them? Or why might a *Buffy* fan find *Twilight* especially egregious, but not any number of other films or television shows? As with these two examples, sometimes we should expect competitive anti-fandoms to exist within genres, with anti-fandom being a performative form of distinction. Perhaps Freud's narcissism of small differences is at work when *Star Trek* fans, wary of being lumped in as generic science fiction fans, feel a need to delineate how their beloved object differs from other texts in the genre, as with the prominent *Star Wars*. These competitions may also tell us, therefore, about what genre fans find important about a genre and about what they most want from it. Some *Buffy* fans' disdain for *Twilight*'s Bella, and stated preference for Buffy, might tell us a great deal about those fans' expectations about the role and status of women in the vampire genre. It might also tell us about audiences' lack of comfort with public genre classifications writ large, whereby one rejects the label, and the generalization implied, that is attached to a beloved object and performs and articulates a dislike for others in that genre to argue for uniqueness—un-generic-ness—in that object.

Bad Objects

What, though, of one-way rivalries? Here one might think of a general, popular dislike of the New York Yankees in baseball fandom, of Duke in college basketball fandom, or of Manchester United in soccer fandom. As with two-way rivalries, these may reveal something about cultural geographies, as, for instance, the New York Yankees are commonly derided for having more money than sense and/or for having an unfair advantage in a way that quite clearly voices a concern about New York City in general having inordinate power. Duke's status as an elite private school similarly compounds its dislikeability, especially when voiced by fans from public institutions such as the University of Kentucky. These may have little to do with geography, indeed, but will often have a great deal to do with power. Manchester United anti-fandom, for instance, should hardly be read automatically as an indicator of concerns about Manchester's power within the English cultural economy (although we might expect that those in Manchester's suburbs or outlying towns may feel such power), and we might more appropriately expect to see dislike of London-based teams. However, Man U anti-fandom says a lot about fans' concerns about money taking over the sport, as expressions of this anti-fandom regularly focus on the team's proclivity to pay extravagant sums to buy the very best players from around the world.

Bad objects abound in anti-fandom, not just in sports. *Twilight*, for instance, may have its rival vampire genre anti-fans, but it has also more generally been constructed as a bad text, as have texts such as *Keeping*

Up with the Kardashians, Titanic, Miley Cyrus, Nickelback, and Celine Dion (see Wilson 2007). Of course, we all have our own personal bad objects, but here I refer to popular bad objects. In simple cases, they may be based on a widespread agreement—whether moral, aesthetic, affective, or political—about what is inappropriate in the media world. But we should also expect that bad object anti-fandoms are coalitional and intersectional, as the object finds itself at the crossroads of multiple types of anti-fandom. To take Miley Cyrus in Fall 2013, for instance, it would be insufficient to suggest that she became such a lightning rod for dislike within popular culture simply because a nation (and more) shared moral approbation for her behavior, or a gendered disdain for pop culture icons, or an aesthetic disapproval of her style of music. More likely, these various reasons, alongside many more, intersected and in doing so strengthened the resolve of any one "entryway" to the Bad Object anti-fandom. If one hates pop music, therefore, one has any number of options of figures and bands to dislike, but when Cyrus is so widely reviled by others for other reasons, it simply becomes easier to nominate her the representative of pop music and to focus one's dislike in her direction.

As with all coalitions, though, Bad Object anti-fandoms unite groups that may otherwise not work together, and they may even lead to awkward compromises of group values. In the case of Cyrus, for instance, a group may have nonsexist, nonelitist reasons for reviling her but may find themselves embroiled in an anti-fandom that often takes a virulently sexist, elitist form. Anti-fandoms are thus key sites to examine how and whether hegemonic values are maintained or challenged through coalitional dislike. One could hypothesize, for example, and as with the case of Cyrus, that, in a patriarchal society, female figures and texts aimed at or otherwise coded as designed for women will prove easy default bad objects, as even those consumers with feminist values may find anti-fan coalitions easier to come by when they are directed at female figures or texts. Pierre Bourdieu's theory of cultural distinction (1984) may prove central to an understanding of why certain types of texts are popularly derided, but it rarely tells us everything, as one is still regularly left with questions of why *this* text, performer, or celebrity is hated more than others of their ilk. Carl Wilson's book-length journey into and analysis of his own dislike of Celine Dion is illustrative here, for while he diagnoses himself in Bourdieuian terms as something of a snob, as he elaborates upon his dislike one can see its complexities, part classed, part gendered, part national, part linguistic, part generational. At times he finds his dislike echoed by others, while elsewhere he bristles against other's stated reasons for disliking Dion (Wilson 2007). As cultural critics, we, too, must be willing to go beyond Bourdieu and ask about the various reasons for dislike and about how it moves and who it connects. Henry Jenkins, Sam Ford, and Joshua Green (2013) write of "spreadable media," rejecting the notion of "viral content" to ask instead about the agential decisions made to spread media. Their model focuses on content that is enjoyed, but we could and should just as easily ask about the coalitional, collaborational, and contestational work that is required to spread anti-fandom.

Disappointed Anti-Fandom

Above, I discuss anti-fandom as opposed to fandom, or as directed toward one object as an outgrowth of fandom toward another object. In truth, however, we will often find anti-fandom and fandom working in tandem, an inseparable pair. Certainly, a great deal of fan studies has examined processes that are remarkably close to anti-fandom. Henry Jenkins's famous *Textual Poachers* (1992) catalogues and theorizes multiple instances in which fans like a text *to a point* but reject parts of the text and feel the need to renovate or cure those parts. In other words, they are fans of the text as a whole yet also anti-fans of specific parts. Jenkins's exploration in *Textual Poachers* of *Star Trek* slash fiction suggests as much, for instance, as it discusses women who love the science fiction frontier of *Star Trek*, rich with the possibility of new ways of aligning social structures, yet they find the hypermasculinization of Kirk and Spock disappointing. Kirk conforms to one hypermasculine stereotype as the always-active man in charge, while Spock conforms to another as the coldly rational, unemotional Vulcan. Through slash fiction that endows each man with traits often labeled as "feminine"—and hence that makes them a loving, caring couple—fans poach on the text and force its hypermasculinity to conform to their more progressive, preferred image of *Star Trek* as text. That desire to cure and rectify ills may be implicitly fannish, but the seed of dislike is inherently anti-fannish. It is a seed, too, that may grow over time and eventually come to dominate, as explored by Rebecca Williams (in this volume). And it is unsurprising that anti-fannish moments and practices have often been those that fan scholars find most fascinating, since it is at these sites—where the text is at risk of unraveling or is seen to have recently done so—that the analyst can find out what it is that the fan truly likes or liked, what the text's best self should be according to the fan(s), and hence what has gone wrong.

Not all such sites of dislike are repaired through fandom, however, nor will all audiences respond to disappointment by poaching and creative transformation. Some audiences may be otherwise inclined to like or love a text, but something key in the text may alienate, annoy, disgust, anger, or disappoint yet other audiences. Celeste Condit (1989), in a response to active audience theory, notes that, while all of us are capable of being active audiences—and hence while all of us *can* poach—this takes time and effort, and some audiences will not find that labor enjoyable or worth it. If media and cultural studies has already catalogued well the process in which fans aim to mend things within a text that are perceived to be wrong or broken, let us also extend that work to comprehend better the points at which audiences can no longer in good conscience even try to fix a text, at which point they simply tune out and/or at which point they do not have the desire to bother fixing the text.

Or we could slide the other way along a spectrum of anti-fan volume and inquire into moments when part of a text is disliked but when the audience is still content on balance to keep consuming it as is. Fan studies have proven that fandom never requires that one loves absolutely everything about a text, and thus we should expect that many people who watch this or that television show, for instance, and who like it and who are engaged in no productive repurposing of the text, may still have parts of the text that they abhor or dislike. Speaking personally, I greatly enjoyed *Lost* as a television show and watched it faithfully till the end. I was always uncomfortable with its gender politics, however, yet save from drawing attention to them in classes when teaching *Lost*, I never engaged in productive activities to repurpose the text's gender politics. I kept watching. One might expect that as a man I had a certain privilege here—or, moreover, as a straight, white, middle-class, middle-aged man, and hence as one who is regularly invited and allowed to watch television from the center, I have all sorts of privilege. And thus it might be interesting not just to examine when audiences' disappointments must be addressed, or when they cannot be addressed and lead to leaving the audience, but also to see how and whether these options are in some way related to one's experience of marginalization (see Gray and Murray 2016). As legitimate as poaching and transformative fandom is as a response to objectionable, disappointing media, we also need a theory of *cultural exhaustion* to explain the frustration, anger, alienation, and hence anti-fandom that arise when an individual or community is constantly being misrepresented, not represented, insulted, and/or left out by media. There is an important empirical question to be asked here, too: Are poaching and anti-fandom similarly motivated, two "equal" responses to a similar objection? Or are there important differences between the two and between the motivations and experiences that lead to either response?

Anti Fans Anti-Fandom

Assuming that the anti-fan object is primary, though, is dangerous, as we should also expect to find anti-fandom that is directed towards *fans* of the nominal anti-fan object, rather than to the *object*. Once more, sports anti-fandom proves a helpful site for illustration, as perennially successful teams may engender proud fans who rub other viewers the wrong way. But this form of anti-fandom is evident across media. Criticisms by self-proclaimed "transformational" fans of those dubbed as "affirmative," for instance (see obsession_inc 2009), may lead to the former disliking certain texts that serve as magnets for the latter. Or, alternately, "affirmative" fans who do not engage in fanfic, vidding, or other productive acts may pathologize those who do and thus feel a need to stay clear of—and to dislike—the texts that attract productive, "transformational" fans. *Supernatural*, for instance, may become "one of those shows" to such viewers, based largely on the activity of its fans. Shortcuts about which media to consume are required in an era of countless options, and so we should expect the visibility of some texts' fans to serve as a "trailer" of sorts for the text, leading to judgments passed on the texts by virtue of their fan behaviors or simply by who is a fan.

At times, anti-fans will find no specific activity of the fans to be objectionable but will instead find the fans objectionable owing simply to their identity categories. Those who hate "young people today" will likely hate everything they're known to watch and might even hate those beloved texts *in lieu of* voicing public disdain for the viewers themselves. Certainly, in a "postracial," "postfeminist" world in which racism and sexism have supposedly disappeared, we should expect to find all sorts of racism and sexism taking the more publicly acceptable form of denigrating texts associated with people of color and women. We should also expect more complex (and some more progressive) dislikes of people to be voiced as dislike of "their" texts. The disliked fan in question may even be one person alone. John McCain's stated preference for *24*, for instance, waved a red flag to many with leftist politics, so that a 2008 *Nation* article's critique of the show condemns it from the outset by opening with the information that it is McCain's favorite series (Wiener 2008). Just as spokespersons are hired in the hopes that positive regard for them will rub off on the product or cause bankrolling of the spokesperson, so, too, can public figures' fandoms have a toxic effect for some could-be consumers. And such decisions need not be communal or public, as they may be made at the very personal level of disliking shows for which an enemy, ex, or rival professes adoration.

Exploring such anti-fandoms could tell us a great deal about normative expectations of viewing or listening practices. Indeed, there is still very little work that examines fans' and other viewers' images, constructions, and understandings of other viewers or that examines how various groups interact with each other. Derek Johnson's essay "Fan-tagonism" (2007) offers a rare glimpse, though, of the kinds of skirmishes between groups, as he examines heated exchanges between *Buffy* fans. Johnson's later "Participation Is Magic" (2013) also productively illustrates how such skirmishes—here, between fans and detractors of *My Little Pony: Friendship Is Magic*—can be mined to understand the hierarchies of identity and power that play into consumptive practices. Such work could thereby tell us what sorts of variables commonly lead to anti fans anti-fandom. How deeply political might some choices *not to watch* be, we might ask? Or how much of a barrier do others' fandoms place to our own viewing? If we are watching *Show X* on the television, but not *Shows A–W*, *Y*, and *Z*, how purposive and principled are those acts of not watching, and how many are tied to suspicions of who else might be watching? How much do fandoms or viewing groups become imagined communities, whose memberships matter to our daily decisions of what not to watch? Or why do some groups of fans become hated?

Another type of anti fan anti-fan is one whose anti-fandom is either generated or amplified by perceptions of the text's importance. Precisely because something is important to others and/or is popular, this individual dislikes it. This is a deeply performative form of anti-fandom, for even when the performance is silent, to oneself, it is a way of enacting distinction, of announcing difference. Joli Jensen (1992) posits that the pathologization of fandom finds its roots in an unacknowledged fear of modernity, whereby concerns that we are watching too much and losing ourselves in the process are tempered by regarding fans as those who watch way more than us and who are utterly lost in the system. The supposed abnormality of the fan, Jensen suggests, constructs the rest of us as blessedly normal by contrast. Similarly, we regularly see individuals announce their supposed freedom from the trappings of trendiness and the popular by proclaiming their utter dislike of that which is trendy and popular. Whether it is *Star Wars* or the latest Pixar film, *Twilight* or an Emmy Award winner, many texts gain cadres of detractors as soon as they become widely popular. Here, we could consider the cultural cachet of the designation "indie," as it announces distinction from, and at times avoidance of, "the mainstream." One may not even have a particular grievance with the mainstream, other than that it is the mainstream, and hence an anti-fandom of that which is popular can serve as a way to announce "I am not like other people."

Hatewatching

In discussing various forms of anti-fandom, so far I have said little about *how* one is an anti-fan and about what this position involves. Often, we should assume, it will require tuning out, turning off, and walking away in disgust. Certainly, the notion of cultural exhaustion seems to dictate and require a decisive act of turning off. But anti-fandom and exhaustion can also involve further consumption, as in the prominent case of hatewatching. *Urban Dictionary* (beatnikherbie 2013) defines "hatewatch" as

> watching a TV show or movie that you hate because you hate it.
>
> Usage note: hatewatching is distinct from enjoying a guilty pleasure, wherein you like something despite its obvious badness. A hatewatched

show is one the viewer genuinely despises but cannot stop watching. This could be because it is so "important" they feel they have to, because it has enough promise that they hope it gets better, because it's so well-crafted in it's [sic] terribleness that the badness itself is noteworthy, or because they enjoy the adrenaline that pure revulsion can bring. Whatever the reason, the hatewatcher can't look away from the trainwreck.

As this definition suggests, some forms of hatewatching tell us both about expectations one has of the media ("because it has enough promise that they hope it gets better") and expectations others have of us as viewers ("because it is so 'important' they feel they have to"), while other forms mix dislike and pleasure in interesting ways ("they enjoy the adrenaline that pure revulsion can bring"). Let us take each in turn (although for more on hatewatching, one should obviously also consult Anne Gilbert's chapter, in this volume).

Throughout this chapter, I have argued that anti-fandom can tell us a great deal about people's expectations and hopes of the media. We can see this in Disappointed Anti-Fandom in particular, in which the text offers other pleasures but a key expectation is frustrated. What we might call *hopeful hatewatching* (when it's hoped a show might get better) is somewhat analogous—such that Disappointed Anti-Fandom could easily lead to hatewatching—but it suggests a greater overall absence of that which is expected. We will likely see hopeful hatewatching only in cases in which the premise of a text was enticing, enough to get hopes up, yet ultimately in which the execution of the text is utterly disappointing to a viewer or viewers. *Glee* had multiple LGBTQ hatewatchers, for instance, who recognized its rarity as a show with several LGBTQ characters and with storylines surrounding LGBTQ issues, and yet they found it a failure as a show. Hopeful hatewatching tells us that a text's concept is appealing, the follow-through a letdown. And we might expect that letdown to be stark, for we will likely only find hopeful hatewatching when that which is being hoped for is (perceived as) so very absent from the media at large. After all, if that which is hoped for can be found in many better texts, one would expect to see hatewatchers decamp from the hatewatching and enjoy the more unmitigated pleasures of texts that don't suffer from the hatewatched show's problems. In the case of *Glee*, if thoughtfully written, interesting LGBTQ characters could be found

far and wide across television, and if LGBTQ representation was habitually handled with cultural sensitivity and intelligence, *Glee* hatewatchers could simply change the channel to a better show. But since they
could not, and since *Glee* promised more than do most shows, some
hatewatched. Hopeful hatewatching, in short, is a resigned, begrudging
form of viewing that tells us about audience needs that are categorically
not being met.

Similarly resigned in mode is what we could call *monitorial hatewatching*, in which the hatewatcher feels as though he or she *must* watch
the show. I suspect this is common with media studies academics, as our
jobs require us to be more broadly aware of what is popular than our
personal pleasures may otherwise dictate, frequently leading to dutiful
watching. But monitorial hatewatching is ubiquitous, and it would be
interesting to see what compels people to watch that which they dislike.
As with hopeful hatewatching, we might expect to see minority audiences who are poorly represented by the media as especially inclined
to engage in monitorial hatewatching of rare yet botched instances of
representation. *Glee*, then, may also have been monitorially hatewatched
by some LGBTQ audiences who felt an urge to survey and keep up with
what the show was doing and what it was saying about LGBTQ identities. And Fox News is monitored by some liberals just as the *Huffington
Post* and Rachel Maddow are monitored by some conservatives. Watching has long been assumed to involve and require pleasure, but this is a
highly problematic assumption that radically narrows an understanding
of the many complex interactions between individuals, communities,
and texts. More examination of monitorial hatewatching might enable
us to better theorize viewing as *duty*, as aware of the importance of some
narratives, and as a conscious act to broaden one's horizons.

Jeffrey Sconce has provocatively suggested another type of *cynical
hatewatching*, observing that

> there would seem to be an audience today that appears to go to the mov-
> ies, not out of an expectation of actually being moved, engaged, or even
> remotely entertained in any conventional sense, but rather to wallow in
> the cinema as a faltering medium in a failing culture. Often, the goal is
> less to watch an individual title than to bear witness to an entire cultural
> institution in collapse. Almost every title is to be met with suspicion, and

if there is any pleasure to be had in a day at the theater, it is rooted either in masochism or a radical reframing of what constitutes *interest* in the cinema (or perhaps both). [Sconce 2007: 276–277; emphasis in original]

Sconce likens the attraction of "cine-cynics" to this "cinema of negative guarantees" to a form of camp, yet he is careful to dub it a perverted camp "without empathy or historical distance, a once playful dandyism decayed, through years of despair and disappointment, into the giddy nihilism of the bored libertine" (Sconce 2007, 278). Camp, after all, is loving, transgressive, and contains an implicit challenge to evaluative schemas that classify good and bad in the first place. Many scholars have thus noted camp's productivity as a queer strategy of viewing and of performance (see Cleto 1999; and Meyer 1993). Sconce and others have also noted a form of fandom of "bad films" and exploitation cinema, in which something is *loved* because it is bad (see also Jancovich et al. 2003; and Mathijs and Mendik 2007). He suggests that the key pleasures of these genres of text and fandom are meta, as they are read as commentaries on the act of creation itself and/or as statements about film production as process (Sconce 2007, 288). With cynical hatewatching, though, the "pleasure" lies in the criticism and in confirming that, yes, the film or film culture in question is horrendous, and as opposed to camp or "bad film" fandom, there is no attempt made—either explicit or implied—to challenge existing taste hierarchies and criteria for evaluation. As an example, Sconce points to *The Onion A.V. Club*'s feature "DVD Commentaries of the Damned" and the critic's interest in David Spade's *Dickie Roberts: Former Child Star*, an interest that exhibits not a hope to enjoy Spade as performer, but rather a desire or need "to sample the cultural symptom of a David Spade film" (Sconce 2007, 298).

As I have done with other forms of anti-fandom above, Sconce ultimately diagnoses unmet expectations as key to cynical hatewatching, as he sees cine-cynics as simultaneously reaffirming for themselves the supremacy of a prior era of filmmaking and noting a perpetual failure of film to shake its industrial trappings and live up to the promise of being a true art. These observations are not, however, based on empirical work, and thus we might read them as a hypothesis to be tested: What *does* the ascendancy of snark—and not the snark that masks sincere fandom, but a snark that exhibits contempt—say about viewing? What is snark or "cine-cynicism" as a reading formation? Although Sconce sees cine-cynicism as practiced most clearly by cultural critics ready to snark about the awful DVD bonus features of an already awful film, for instance, he detects in many of us a "defensive posture" (Sconce 2007, 294) carried into our moviegoing, in which we brace for the bad and may, mothlike, constantly fly toward that flame. This may be a common mode of viewing, in other words, one that demands further study.

Finally, we might posit a form of *visceral hatewatching*. Here I allude to hatewatching that is devoid of camp pleasures or smug affirmations and that makes one angry or upset yet that is consumed all the same. A form of masochism is at play here, in which one knows that consumption will be painful, yet one still engages. To invoke masochism is to risk suggesting pathology, but I would rather focus on visceral hatewatching as telling us something about boredom and the media. Surely, many have had the experience of renting a sad movie or clicking through from Facebook to a tragic tale knowing that it will likely make us cry, yet doing so with a certain degree of relish. Media give us corporal pleasures, affective jolts, not just characters to identify with or against and narratives and themes to ponder. Visceral hatewatching reminds us that sometimes we just want to *feel*, even if that feeling is anger, annoyance, or dislike (and even though that anger is, of course, socially constructed). Again, as with hopeful hatewatching, visceral hatewatching may serve as a condemnation and judgment upon what else is on television, available on the Internet today, or at other sites of consumption. Just as Anna McCarthy (2001) reads waiting-room television to suggest a fundamental boringness of much media, visceral hatewatching similarly castigates its nonhatewatched peers.

Any one of the above forms of hatewatching might overlap with one another. A left-leaning viewer may tune in to Fox News with mixed motivations, hoping to monitor what the political right is thinking but also to seek a visceral pleasure. Another viewer may feel compelled to watch a show that she finds awful but finds pleasure in how very awful it is. Various other permutations exist. And another dimension that may transform or augment hatewatching is whether it is done alone, with others who are not similarly hatewatching, or with hatewatchers-in-arms. Hatewatching may be a coping strategy for family members or roommates forced to watch each other's favorite shows, for bar patrons or anyone sitting in a waiting room with a television. In turn, that hatewatching could take silent form or could be performative, as one engages the television and one's fellow watchers in dialogue while watching. And the performativity of hatewatching will in some instances lend itself well to being a communal activity, in which a group of friends unite to watch something they know will be gloriously bad, that they feel compelled to monitor, and/or that they feel they must watch. Such sites could prove rich for studying, as we might then hear articulated the expectations, desires, frustrations, and camp pleasures of watching something that is seen as "bad" while also hearing how "good" and "bad" are being constructed communally in the first place.

Deep or Fleeting Anti-Fandom?

Of all anti-fandoms, we should ask another question: whether the anti-fan object is fleeting and a stand-in and the latest gestalt for a larger concern or displeasure, or whether this is deeper, hard-wired anti-fandom. If we return to Miley Cyrus, for instance, her appearance at the Video Music Awards in 2013 led to her becoming a lightning rod for anti-fandom and to her becoming a Bad Object. But surely some of the resulting anti-fans were relatively new to disliking Cyrus and soon moved on to other dislikes, whereas others were ahead of the curve, with 2013 by no means the beginning or end of their anti-fandom. Fleeting anti-fandom is likely indicative of a larger anti-fandom or concern, in which the momentarily disliked object serves largely and perhaps only as an instance of something grander that is disliked. By contrast, we should ascertain whether more is at stake in disliking *this* object specifically and work out precisely what the true object of dislike is. If one hates pop music in general, for example, one's momentary dislike of Miley Cyrus in 2013 is to be expected, and an analyst who dedicates too much time to examining "Why Miley?" may have missed the point. If one has disliked Cyrus for years, the question of "Why Miley?" is key.

Conclusion

There is little to say to conclude this chapter, since I have tried to offer a variety of anti-fan types. The list is not intended to be exhaustive, nor are grand conclusions or summations possible prior to the empirical work that could add flesh to speculative skeletons and that would require new taxonomies. Instead, then, I have written this chapter relieved to know both that it will be preceded by Melissa Click's introduction which offers theoretical heft and direction to the project(s) of anti-fandom where I have not—not least of all by productively proposing an embrace of affect theory (Click, in this volume)—and that it will be followed by empirical studies and by a combined, concerted attempt to make sense of anti-fans. Dislike may appear to be (and often is) a negative, ugly emotion, and in the wake of Bourdieu (1984) and Fiske (1989), media and cultural studies often operates with an automatic distrust and suspicion of dislike as snobbery, as ill intentioned, and as a cultural weapon. But at the very least the meaning of dislike should not be assumed. At the most, we should expect anti-fandom to at times be productive, progressive, and nuanced, to tell us about audiences' hopes and expectations for the media writ large, and hence to be a key site for understanding why, how, and when the media matters to us and why, how, and when it doesn't.

REFERENCES

beatnikherbie. 2013. "Hatewatch." *Urban Dictionary*, July 15. www.urbandictionary. com.

Bourdieu, Pierre. 1984. *Distinction: A Social Critique of the Judgement of Taste*. Translated by Richard Nice. Cambridge, MA: Harvard University Press.

Cleto, Fabio, ed. 1999. *Camp: Queer Aesthetics and the Performing Subject—A Reader*. Ann Arbor: University of Michigan Press.

Click, Melissa A. In this volume. "Introduction: Haters Gonna Hate."

Condit, Celeste Michelle. 1989. "The Rhetorical Limits of Polysemy." *Critical Studies in Mass Communication* 6, no. 2:103–122.

Fiske, John. 1989. *Understanding Popular Culture*. London: Unwin Hyman.

Gilbert, Anne. In this volume. "Hatewatch with Me: Anti-Fandom as Social Performance."

Gray, Jonathan. 2003. "New Audiences, New Textualities: Anti-Fans and Non-Fans." *International Journal of Cultural Studies* 6, no. 1:64–81.

Gray, Jonathan, and Sarah Murray. 2016. "Hidden: Studying Media Dislike and Its Meaning." *International Journal of Cultural Studies* 19, no. 4:357–372.

Jancovich, Mark, Antonio Lázaro Reboli, Julian Stringer, and Andrew Willis, eds. 2003. *Defining Cult Movies: The Cultural Politics of Oppositional Taste*. Manchester: Manchester University Press.

Jenkins, Henry. 1992. *Textual Poachers: Television Fans and Participatory Culture*. New York: Routledge.

Jenkins, Henry, Sam Ford, and Joshua Green. 2013. *Spreadable Media: Creating Value and Meaning in a Networked Culture*. New York: NYU Press.

Jensen, Joli. 1992. "Fandom as Pathology: The Consequences of Characterization." In *The Adoring Audience: Fan Culture and Popular Media*, edited by Lisa A. Lewis, 9–29. New York: Routledge.

Johnson, Derek. 2007. "Fan-tagonism: Factions, Institutions, and Constitutive Hegemonies of Fandom." In *Fandom: Identities and Communities in a Mediated World*, edited by Jonathan Gray, Cornel Sandvoss, and C. Lee Harrington, 285–300. New York: NYU Press.

———. 2013. "Participation Is Magic: Collaboration, Authorial Legitimacy, and the Audience Function." In *A Companion to Media Authorship*, edited by Jonathan Gray and Derek Johnson, 135–157. Malden, MA: Wiley-Blackwell.

Mathijs, Ernest, and Xavier Mendik, eds. 2007. *The Cult Film Reader*. New York: Open University Press.

McCarthy, Anna. 2001. *Ambient Television: Visual Culture and Public Space*. Durham, NC: Duke University Press.

Meyer, Moe, ed. 1993. *The Politics and Poetics of Camp*. New York: Routledge.

obsession_inc. 2009. "Affirmational Fandom vs. Transformational Fandom." *Dreamwidth*, June 1. www.dreamwidth.org.

Sconce, Jeffrey. 2007. "Movies: A Century of Failure." In *Sleaze Artists: Cinema at the Margins of Taste, Style, and Politics*, edited by Jeffrey Sconce. Durham, NC: Duke University Press.

Theodoropoulou, Vivi. 2007. "The Anti-Fan within the Fan: Awe and Envy in Sport Fandom." In *Fandom: Identities and Communities in a Mediated World*, edited by Jonathan Gray, Cornel Sandvoss, and C. Lee Harrington, 316–327. New York: NYU Press.

Wiener, Jon. 2008. "McCain's Favorite TV Show, '24,' Brings Torture Back Sunday." *Nation*, November 18. www.thenation.com.

Williams, Rebecca. In this volume. "'Putting the Show out of Its Misery': Textual Endings, Anti-Fandom, and the 'Rejection Discourse.'"

Wilson, Carl. 2007. *Let's Talk about Love: A Journey to the End of Taste*. New York: Bloomsbury.

2

Hating 3.0

Should Anti-Fan Studies Be Renewed for Another Season?

EMMA A. JANE

Introduction

We live in the age of the anti-fan. Yet anti-fan studies may not be the best lens for analyzing this age and these anti-fans. This is the seemingly paradoxical argument at the heart of this chapter. My case is that, while anti-fan scholars have done excellent work texturing understandings about the audienceship experience, it is precisely this audience centricity—this continuing focus on the "realities and mysteries of media audiences" (Gray 2018, chapter 1 in this volume)—that raises questions about the viability of anti-fan studies going forward.

Audienceship in digital media cultures has changed. It is so radically altered that what fills the spaces previously occupied by audiences now seems qualitatively different. To deploy a *Star Trek*–ism, it's audienceship, but not as we know it. While this has ramifications for disciplinary approaches well beyond anti-fandom, the problems it presents for anti-fan studies are particularly pressing. Anti-fan activity has become more complex and forceful as a result of the monumental changes that have occurred and that continue to occur in the networked digital mediasphere. Yet, by my account, the anti-fan model is shot through with legacy media orientations, even when the increase in and diversity of anti-fan activity online is recognized. These legacy media orientations relate to two assumptions: first, that it is still possible to make meaningful divisions between media producers, texts, and audiences in a way that lends itself to anti-fan analysis, and second, that the collective force of anti-fans does not constitute a particularly strong or problematic force. As I show, anti-fans have become extremely powerful. And increasingly this power is being deployed in ways that evince bullying, prejudice, hate speech, oppression, and violence.

I begin this chapter with a literature review to support my contention that the anti-fan model may be approaching its use-by date because it was designed to analyze a different sort of discourse in a different type of context. I then illustrate my central points with six case studies that have played out in the Web 2.0/Web 3.0 era.[1]

The six case studies in this chapter involve anti-fan activity ostensibly in response to (1) British bank note design, (2) a blogger's photograph of her twins, (3) the Australian television personality Waleed Aly, (4) the 2016 remake of the film *Ghostbusters*, (5) the online encyclopedia *Wikipedia*, and (6) [this space intentionally left blank]. (As I explain below, the anti-fan targets in case study no. 6 are too ambiguous to neatly capture in a short list such as this one.) Together, these case studies demonstrate a number of key features of contemporary anti-fan activity, including marked increases in the sophistication and audience reach of anti-fan texts; the explicit, violent, and directly threatening nature of anti-fan discourse; the number of anti-fan mob attacks on individuals; and the number of anti-fan targets who are not "traditional" celebrities but "ordinary" people (considered fair game for scathing "reviews" from anti-fans because anyone with an Internet connection is potentially functioning as—or at least is regarded as functioning as—a media producer and/or text). The starkly misogynist and racist rhetoric apparent in a number of these case studies is used to illustrate the potential harm this discourse can cause not only to its immediate or putative targets but to broader communities of marginalized people as well. That anti-fan discourse is increasingly being used as a sort of metaphorical fig leaf for preexisting prejudice and bigotry is also discussed. After examining first the logistical issues and then the political and ethical issues raised by these case studies, I then direct my attention away from anti-fan producers and toward anti-fan analysts to consider some possible ways forward for the field.

This chapter is based on data collected as part of an ongoing series of research projects focused on what I have previously called "e-bile" (Jane 2014a, 2014b). I have been mapping, archiving, and analyzing vitriol online since 1998. My methodologies vary and include approaches from the emerging field of Internet historiography, as well as textual analysis and qualitative interviews. While my most recent work has focused on misogyny online (Jane 2017), the origins of my research were broad, and I continue to track and study a wide variety of vitriolic discourse in digital media contexts. The six case studies in this chapter were selected because they capture some key variations and similarities in contemporary anti-fan discourse. Case study no. 1, for instance, is a violent, misogynist mob attack against a noncelebrity, whereas case study no. 6 involves no hateful discourse and targets only high-profile individuals. Despite their differences, all six examples have two important commonalities: First, their media protagonists and texts are complex and difficult to categorize, and second, the anti-fan activity observable is *powerful* activity.

Theoretically, my hermeneutic is eclectic and works across feminist and gender theory, critical race theory, philosophy of law, philosophy of language, literary studies, and cultural and media studies. Particularly relevant to this chapter is my use of Michel Foucault–inspired genealogy. Given that Foucauldian genealogy requires moving beyond the ahistorical unearthing and examination of artefacts (Foucault 1976, 1980, 1984), I study not only manifestations of cyberhate but also the conditions of possibility for the prevalence of such discourse. This has required scrutinizing the various interpretative apparatus used to frame and make sense of negative affect and hostility online. In particular, I have explored the potential connections between these sense-making frameworks and the documented failures of various institutions and authorities—such as police, policy makers, and platform operators—to adequately respond to harmful cyberhate (see Jane 2015, 2017). As such, this chapter is not intended to imply that anti-fan studies constitutes a special case in terms of its potential to underplay hateful discourse online. Instead, following Foucault, understanding the way a cultural phenomenon is talked about and rendered intelligible requires "dealing less with *a* discourse . . . than with a multiplicity of discourses produced by a whole series of mechanisms operating in different institutions" (1976, 33; emphasis in original). This chapter, therefore, recognizes the anti-fan model as just one mechanism in one institution producing powerful discourse and knowledge in relation to vitriol online.

Legacy Media Orientations

Like fan studies, anti-fan literature sits squarely within the domains of audience research and reception studies. Thus Jonathan Gray's foundational work (2003, 2005) figures anti-fan activity primarily in terms of decoding and meaning making (Jane 2014c, 176). This makes sense given that fan studies and, to a lesser extent (because it is a newer field), anti-fan studies emerged at a time when it was relatively easy to identify who was who in various media scenes. The archetypal producer was usually a media behemoth broadcasting or publishing texts mostly on its own terms, while the archetypal consumer was typically part of a readily identifiable audience and typically did not multitask as a producer.

Further, members of this audience tended to be framed—at least in early cultural and media studies—as underdogs in need of allies and advocates. This was a response to reductionist Frankfurt School–style depictions of media spectators as passive automatons being brainwashed and manipulated by the mass culture industries. Conceptual interventions such as Stuart Hall's "encoding-decoding" model (2005) have drawn much-needed attention to the agency audience members can exercise in terms of reading media texts in an idiosyncratic, creative, and potentially transgressive manner that potentially speaks back and up to power. For Hall, "the people versus the power bloc" is the "central line of contradiction around which the terrain of culture is polarised" (Hall 1981, 238). Early work on fandom (see, e.g., Jenkins 2013) also positions fans very much in opposition to "The Powers That Be" (Hellekson 2009).

We can see, therefore, that historically the agency of anti-fans has generally been assumed to be contained within the domain of individual experience in the form of actively reading media texts. If directed outward, audience power has tended to be understood as lateral force (in the form of intra- or inter-fan group friction) or a force that "punches up" (in that underdog mass audience members are "talking back" to powerful hegemons such as multinational media corporations). The idea that anti-fans are speaking a sort of personal truth to hegemonic power might help explain why anti-fan discourse has, for the most part, not been a candidate for rigorous ethical interrogation, even when the discourse has been extremely negative and hateful.

Initially, this conceptualization of fans and anti-fans as having power, but only power of a particular and delineated kind, was apt. En masse, members of audiences could obviously wield strong force if enough of them embraced or rejected, for example, a television series in that the series might be renewed or canceled. For the most part, however, agency was exercized at the internal, the individual, and local level. Before the Internet—and particularly before the Web 2.0 era—audience members were especially restricted in terms of the type of response text they could produce and publish and the audiences these could reach. For example, early fan and anti-fan cultures were transmitted mostly orally and in person (e.g., at conventions).

Now, however, the extraordinary growth and accessibility of networked digital media technologies have dramatically changed the ways audience members such as fans and anti-fans can express themselves. Indeed, as I argue, these changes are so radical they call into question the very category of "audience" itself. Cogent here is the fact that television—the central media associated with early anti-fan studies—has altered to the point where media reports of "the death of television" have become commonplace (Barker and Jane 2016, 452–453). In place of the broadcasting network model of television is a fractured new marketplace of on-demand entertainment in which fans "see themselves as customers, not devotees" (Miller 2011) and are increasingly calling the shots. The use of technologies such as ad blocking, for instance, are having a profound impact on the monetization strategies deployed by content providers (Barker and Jane 2016, 454).

This edited volume is testimony to the fact that anti-fan scholars are not neglecting the rising visibility and productivity of fans and anti-fans in digital domains. In her introduction, for example, Melissa Click emphasizes the importance of studying the way social media platforms support anti-fan practices such as hatewatching (Click, in this volume; see also Jenkins, Ford, and Green 2013, 167). A degree of attention has also been paid to what Gray refers to—although initially only in passing—as anti-fandom's "darker dimensions" (2005, 852). Other scholars note that audiences' resistive readings of mainstream texts may not always be socially progressive (Schulze, White, and Brown 1993) and may uphold normative ideologies relating to race, class, and gender (Phillips, in this volume). Click, meanwhile, calls on anti-fan scholars to bring more critical attention to the circulation and impact of dislike and hate through digital technology (Click, in this volume). Yet Gray's observation that "in a 'postracial,' 'postfeminist' world . . . we should expect to find all sorts of racism and sexism taking the more publicly acceptable form of denigrating texts associated with people of color and women" (2018, chapter 1 in this volume) is mostly just that: an observation. While this is congruent with Gray's stated aim of using his essay in this volume to rethink anti-fandom from a taxonomical perspective, my case is that, while noticing and categorizing conspicuously hateful speech in anti-fan discourse is an excellent start, such discourse should also be subject to rigorous interrogation.

Further, the changing contours of anti-fan activity invite a sort of epistemological inversion by which the original objects under investigation can be used as lens through which to view our conceptual model. The virulence and violence of contemporary anti-fandom, for instance, raises significant questions about the parameters of the field. Given that media studies permits anything to be analyzed as a text (McKee 2003, 4), does it follow that anyone who dislikes any thing can be considered an anti-fan? Surely the answer is "no" (the reductio ad absurdum being the decision to classify a killer first and foremost as an anti-fan of someone's life). I return to these issues presently. For the time being, I offer six case studies exemplifying the ways media producers and audience members in contemporary digital cultures are in constant and radical states of overlap and flux. These case studies also illustrate various aspects of the force wielded by anti-fan activity, paving the way for a discussion of the political and ethical issues raised not only by this force but also by the way this force is investigated (and not investigated) by scholars.

Urns of Cremated Babies and the "Ass Fuck Gut Punch"— Contemporary Anti-Fandom

Case Study No. 1: Anti-Fans of a Bank Note Design

In 2013, the Bank of England announced it would bring forward the introduction of a £10 note featuring the face of Jane Austen. This followed a feminist campaign led by the activist and student Caroline Criado-Perez. In the aftermath of the bank's decision, anti-fans subjected Criado-Perez to a deluge of sexualized violence over Twitter.

Representative examples include "Open that cunt wide bitch . . . you about to feel da pain"; "I have a sniper rifle aimed directly at your head currently"; and "FIRST WE WILL MUTILATE YOUR GENITALS WITH SCISSORS, THEN SET YOUR HOUSE ON FIRE WHILE YOU BEG TO DIE TONIGHT. 23.00" (cited in Criado-Perez 2013). At the peak of the fortnight-long attack, the messages were arriving at the rate of around fifty an hour. Public supporters of Criado-Perez—such as the British Labour MP Stella Creasy—were targeted for similar abuse.

Case Study No. 2: Anti-Fans of a Blogger's Photograph of Her Twins

In 2015, the Australian blogger Annie Nolan was waiting for a train with her two-year-old twins when she wrote a list of what were intended to be funny statements on the back of two large envelopes. She then placed these on her children's pram and photographed them. These statements took the form of a series of answers to questions strangers frequently ask Nolan about her twins. They included "CONCEIVED BY F***ING," "BORN VIA C-SECTION," and "YES, MY HANDS ARE FULL (SOME-TIMES WITH 2 GLASSES OF WINE JUST TO GET THROUGH)" (cited in Tran and McNab 2015, asterisks in original). Nolan says she wrote the signs because she feels like a "broken record" when strangers repeatedly stop her to ask the same, twin-related questions (Tran and McNab 2015). She uploaded the photo to her blog's public Facebook page when the latter had only about two hundred followers. The post, however, went viral and was viewed more than two million times over two days. Anti-fans of the image inundated Nolan with abuse and death threats, including someone saying they would shove a broken glass into her face if they saw her on the street (A. Nolan, personal communication, July 31, 2015). Others bombarded her with photos of their dead children and the urns of their cremated babies alongside messages accusing her of being a bad mother ungrateful that her children were alive (ibid.).

Case Study No. 3: Anti-Fans of the Australian Television Personality Waleed Aly

Waleed Aly co-hosts the popular Australian current affairs program *The Project*. He deliberately avoids social media because he does not want to worry about "what Twitter is going to say" when he articulates his political positions on air (Aly, cited in Willis 2015). Anti-fans are, however, still able to target Aly for abusive tweets via the hashtag #waleedaly and via his family and colleagues. One man, for instance, directed a #waleedaly tweet at Aly's spouse, the academic Susan Carland, as well as to the Australian Muslim lawyer Mariam Veiszadeh (both of whom *do* hold Twitter accounts). The tweet read: "This is my death threat to you and Waleed and his hijabi scumfuk floozie. I hope you all meet with natural accidents" (A. Lattouf, personal communication, May 27, 2016). Other anti-fans have used online platforms to call Aly a "RACIST Muslim CUNT" (@BELIMBLA4 2015), a "muslime cunt," and "Muzzie prick" (*LiveLeak*, n.d.).

Case Study No. 4: Anti-Fans of the 2016 Remake of Ghostbusters

Anti-fan activity around the 2016 "reboot" of the 1984 film *Ghostbusters* commenced well before the film's release and focused primarily on the fact that its four male leads had been replaced by female characters. The film's trailer rapidly became the most "disliked" movie preview in YouTube history, leading to media speculation that the negative response was not organic but "part of a coordinated attack on the film" by angry anti-fans reportedly using "bots to artificially drive up the 'dislikes'" in an attempt to "downvote [the film] into oblivion" (Sampson 2016). After the film's release, one of its leads, the African American actress Leslie Jones, was targeted for savage racist and sexist abuse online. She received material comparing her to a gorilla, as well as photographs of her from the film's premiere "splattered" with semen (Stein 2016). Jones' public declarations of fear and distress about the abuse were greeted by "positively gleeful" and "triumphant" anti-fan gloating that the actress appeared to have "melted down . . . probably to the point of no return" (@foghornl33, cited in Romano 2016).

Case Study No. 5: Anti-Fans of Wikipedia

Encyclopedia Dramatica is ostensibly a "snarky Wikipedia anti-fan[site]" (Dee 2007), and it claims it intends to parody "the supposed objectivity and accuracy, elitism, and stupid edit wars" of "a much less funny online encyclopedia" (*Encyclopedia Dramatica*, n.d.-a). In addition to explicit, sex-related images, *Encyclopedia Dramatica* brims with hyperbolic misogynist, racist, and homophobic content that rhetorically is very different from the "critical, sarcastic repartee" and "snarkastic" comments (Andrejevic 2008, 31) usually cited or described in anti-fan literature. Its thirty-two-thousand-word "List of Sex Moves" page, for instance, describes in unequivocal detail thousands of demeaning and/ or violent sexual acts. A representative sample is the "A.F.G.P." or "Ass Fuck Gut Punch":

> While fucking a girl in the ass from behind (and timing is everything on this move), you quickly punch the bitch in her gut. This must be done without warning for full effect, as it will cause her to flinch with pain, thus tightening her anus as you pull out with a fresh, clean dick—free of shit thanks to the A.F.G.P. [*Encyclopedia Dramatica*, n.d.-b]

Encyclopedia Dramatica's page on the indie video game developer Zoe Quinn calls her an "internet whore," "cunt," "faggot," "molester," and "rapist," who "sucks the dick of anyone willing to suppress negative publicity about her" and who successfully prosecutes "e-begging scams" owing to the "sheer number of cocks" she "has had inside her" (*Encyclopedia Dramatica*, n.d.-c). The page includes a detailed table of people Quinn is accused of sleeping with in order to advance her career, as well as nude photographs of her with captions such as, "Seriously someone went out of their way to fuck this pink-haired fugly cow?" (*Encyclopedia Dramatica*, n.d.-c).

Case Study No. 6: Anti-Fans of [This Space Intentionally Left Blank]

Since 2011, the YouTube channel Bad Lip Reading (n.d.) has been satirizing short clips from films, television programs, songs, sports broadcasts, political news stories, and other media by overdubbing vocals that roughly match the lip movements of the people on-screen but produce surreal word salads (Barker and Jane 2016, 594). Despite being the work of an anonymous, "citizen" producer, Bad Lip Reading attracts audience numbers legacy media companies would metaphorically kill for: At the time of writing, it had nearly 7 million subscribers.

These figures—combined with the sophisticated production values of the clips—show that Bad Lip Reading is hardly the work of a disgruntled fan scribbling "in the margins" (Jenkins, Ford, and Green 2013, 152) and is far from the sort of "producerly" media text described by John Fiske (2011). By any measure, it is a powerful, mainstream media text in its own right. The complex and ambiguous nature of the objects and subjects of the channel's anti-fandom is discussed below.

It's *Complicated*

These case studies draw attention to two sets of problems with the anti-fandom model as it stands: logistical problems and ethical problems. The former raise questions about whether the complex tangle of players and texts in contemporary media scenes are still conducive to meaningful analysis using anti-fan approaches. Networked digital media culture (which increasingly is *all* media culture) is dialectical, iterative, collaborative, and user-producer driven. It is a truism to state that this has resulted in a radical collapse of traditional distinctions between broadcasters and receivers, producers and consumers, professionals and amateurs, and texts and audiences. At any given moment, a single person might simultaneously hold many roles, including that of content producer, fact-checker, editor, curator, aggregator, broadcaster, publisher, audience member, reviewer, devoted fan, vitriolic anti-fan, citizen surveillor and regulation officer, whistleblower, saboteur, digilante activist, hate speech producer, hate speech recipient, lynch mob member, stalker, committer of crime, victim of crime, or aspects of all these things at once. Indeed, at any given moment, people might suddenly find they are circulating as media texts themselves. This complexity makes it extremely difficult to determine who and what are playing which roles in any single anti-fan scene.

In the first case study, for instance, the primary media texts are androcentric bank notes, and the primary anti-fan is Criado-Perez. Criado-Perez, however, rapidly becomes a text herself and draws the ire of anti-fans of her bank note activism. Next come anti-fans of this second set of anti-fans in the form of individuals such as Creasy, whose public declarations of her own, particular anti-fan position quickly render her an object/subject of anti-fandom herself. In case study no. 2, the originary media producer is Nolan, whose own work is a sort of anti-fan response to strangers who slow her down with predictable questions when she is attempting to travel via public transport with her twins. Nolan's anti-fans object not only to the photo but also to Nolan herself. Case study no. 3 also involves multiple "bad objects" (Gray, in this volume), including *The Project* (dismissed by one of Aly's detractors as a "libtarded Tv Show"; see *LiveLeak*, n.d.), specific views Aly has expressed on the program, Aly's performance as a talk show celebrity, and/or Islam and Muslims in general.

The complexity of case study no. 4 is partly due to the fact that, while the originary text was the 2014 announcement of the remake of *Ghostbusters*, other texts—such as the trailer and the film itself—also have primary text status. As with case study no. 1, wave upon wave of anti-fan groups are identifiable. First came the original anti-fans of the film's female lineup, then anti-fans of these anti-fans, then anti-fans of these anti-fans of the anti-fans (and so on). Close observation of the exchanges reveal that this is not simply a case of group A arguing with group B about text X (or even texts X) over time. Instead, the objectors and counterobjectors and objections and counterobjections vary, moving well beyond the *Ghostbusters* franchise to cover (and this is not an exhaustive list) debates around the integrity of film remakes, 1980s nostalgia, the role of politics in popular culture, free speech, feminism and gender equality, social justice agendas, and "the supposed marginalization of the American male" (Griner 2016).

Case study no. 5 typifies many aspects of contemporary anti-fandom in that *Encyclopedia Dramatica* is the work of individuals who are archetypal media producer-broadcaster-consumer hybrids and whose discourse is hyperbolic, vitriolic, sexually explicit, and arguably threatening in nature. It also illustrates the way the putative objects and subjects of anti-fan activity seem to be serving as a cover for broader prejudices such as misogyny, racism, religious and cultural intolerance, homophobia, and so on. At the very least, *Encyclopedia Dramatica* looks less like an anti-fan response to *Wikipedia* than a response to phenomena such as political correctness, sincerity, earnestness, social justice politics, identity politics, Internet newcomers, naïveté, and various epistemological orientations. Further, the entry on Quinn is suggestive of a disavowed obsession in that she is derided as unworthy of attention in a manner that involves paying her a great deal of attention. This dynamic chimes with Click's use of affect scholarship to note that hate tends to involve grabbing and entangling, as well as rejection (Click, in this volume).

The objects and subjects of Bad Lip Reading's anti-fandom are ambiguous. The channel's title suggests it could be a parody of those who read lips badly, yet Bad Lip Reading also seems like an anti-fan response to celebrity hubris, political pomp, and the monotony and predictability of certain pop cultural conventions and tropes. By the same token, it could also be categorized as the work of a fan's exuberant reveling in surreal humor and the extent to which it has become possible to repurpose and subvert "traditional" media texts, genres, and celebrities.

As we can see from the six case studies above, the dynamic and liminal status of key players and texts can make it extremely difficult to answer fundamental questions such as, "Who is the primary media producer?" "What is the primary text being offered for consumption?" "Who is the audience?" "What is being objected to?" "Are these objectors best classed as anti-fans of one thing or fans of another thing?" and "How should we proceed when anti-fans produce powerful new primary texts or suddenly begin circulating as primary texts themselves?" To add to the confusion, the sedimentation of in-jokes and the ironic, palimpsestic humor so common in online domains can make it extraordinarily difficult to divine whether a given text is a form of fandom, anti-fandom, both at once, or neither.

The takeaway point? It's *complicated*.

Forceful and *Problematically* Forceful

If toxic and violent anti-fan discourse circulated infrequently or only in niche forms in niche domains, a case could be made that, while such discourse is somewhat problematic, it is not extremely problematic because it is not particularly powerful. This section discusses the second set of problems (the ethical problems) mentioned above and shows that contemporary anti-fandom does wield significant force because, among other things, it is prevalent, it involves sophisticated texts, and it can reach huge audiences. Further, I argue that this force is a problematic force because frequently it is threatening and violent, it directly reaches targets, it causes real people real suffering, its targets are "ordinary" people, it manifests in large mobs piling onto lone targets, its marks are members of traditionally marginalized or oppressed social groups, and/ or it disavows its bigotry, prejudice, and hatefulness.

The self-publishing and multimedia production opportunities afforded by digital and networked technologies mean that "ordinary" people are now able to comment on and produce mass popular entertainment in a manner that used to be reserved for experts and corporations. As is illustrated particularly clearly in case study no. 6, anti-fans are creating sophisticated texts that have high production values, are circulated for mass consumption and critique, and may achieve audience shares that rival or dwarf those associated with the original text to which they are responding. While there still exist many mass media texts produced by large corporations, the terms of engagement have changed. "On demand" is now the default position for electronic entertainment provision. Media consumers are accustomed to watching what they want, when they want it. They are used to having their preferences catered to and their loud objections heard and answered. This is why it could be said that this is very much the age of the anti-fan. For David Ayer, the director of the 2016 film *Suicide Squad*, navigating contemporary audiences is like a "Roman arena" where a show of thumbs-up or thumbs-down can leave a film "executed in the sawdust" (cited in Martens 2016). The media commentator Todd Martens, meanwhile, notes fans' strong sense of ownership over pop cultural texts, as manifest in sometimes vicious campaigns demanding changes to plotlines and to the gender, sexual preferences, and race of characters (2016).

In recent years, antagonistic anti-fan campaigns have been directed at the novelist George R. R. Martin (who received death threats for not writing a new *Game of Thrones* novel quickly enough), the filmmaker Joss Whedon (who received death threats for including a romance between Black Widow and Bruce Banner in *Avengers: Age of Ultron*), the actor Brenock O'Connor (who received death threats after his fictional character killed Jon Snow in *Game of Thrones*), and the nonfictional U.S. prosecutor Ken Kratz (who received messages from people saying they hoped his daughter would be raped in front of him after he appeared in the Netflix docuseries *Making a Murderer*; see Bacchiocchi 2016; Martens 2016; and Roberts 2016). An insight into anti-fans' sense of entitlement to abuse celebrity targets in this way can be found in one man's tweet—about Creasy during the bank note incident—which read, "If you can't threaten to rape a celebrity, what is the point in having them?" (Nunn, cited in Carter 2014).

It is certainly not my intention in this chapter to suggest that all forms of online "hating" are oppressive or cause harm to targets. (Indeed, Bad Lip Reading's fan base includes some of the celebrities it so mercilessly pillories; see Barker and Jane 2016, 594.) What I am arguing, however, is that more anti-fans are causing more harm, more often. This is partly due to the fact that the cybersphere lends itself to the rapid formation of snowballing anti-fan mobs whose members can attack with extraordinary brutality. While these mobs may disperse quickly, the nature of the Internet means that their anti-fan texts often live on indefinitely. That naked photos and character assassinations of Quinn are still readily available on *Encyclopedia Dramatica* two years after she was first attacked during GamerGate in 2014 (see below) is testimony to the fact that—once uploaded—compromising material online is all but impossible to remove.

The networked nature of the cybersphere also means that anti-fan abuse has the potential to "land"—both in terms of arriving literally in targets' homes as well as in terms of causing real torment, not only to targets, but to targets' family members, friends, and allies as well. The collateral damage caused by cyber mob attacks includes job loss, ongoing employment difficulties, social stigma, and severe emotional distress (Citron 2014; Jane 2017; Ronson 2015). Criado-Perez, for instance, "broke down completely" during the attack described in case study no. 1, saying she struggled to eat, sleep, and work (2013). While Nolan was able to shrug off most the abuse, she says she believes the enormity and hatefulness of the attack would have prompted a suicide attempt if she had received it when she was younger and more emotionally vulnerable (A. Nolan, personal communication, July 31, 2015). She says her mother, meanwhile, was "really traumatised" and lost several kilograms of weight during the incident (ibid.).

While there is no evidence that *Encyclopedia Dramatica*'s putative target, *Wikipedia*, has been negatively affected by the site, Quinn's personal suffering as the result of this sort of anti-fan material is well documented. Quinn, after all, is "patient zero" (Stuart 2014) of GamerGate, the extraordinary, ongoing attack on women in gaming that began in

2014 and that perfectly demonstrates the slippage between contemporary anti-fandom and outright misogyny, harassment, and violence. During GamerGate, Quinn received more than sixteen gigabytes of abuse (Jason 2015) and fled her home after anti-fans began circulating her home address alongside their threats of rape, mutilation, and murder. Quinn's concern was that it would only be a matter of time before one of her anonymous detractors eventually followed through on their vows to kill her (Quinn, cited in Stuart 2014).

As we have seen, contemporary anti-fandom often involves "ordinary" people directing explicit, ad hominem invective toward other "ordinary" people who may be more vulnerable to anti-fan campaigns than seasoned celebrities. Case study no. 4, however, shows that celebrity targets may also suffer significant fear and distress (see Jones, cited in Stein 2016). When militant cyber mobs "pile on" an individual such as Jones, it looks more like bullying than anti-fandom. And when that individual also happens to be a woman of color, it looks very much like the sort of hate speech considered entirely unacceptable—if not illegal—in other contexts. Certainly in both case studies nos. 3 and 4, the anti-fan activity directed toward Aly and Jones seems less about these celebrities qua celebrities and more about religious intolerance, racism, and misogyny. As such, Aly and Jones are being used as vehicles for the articulation of noxious a priori prejudices. The power of such hate speech lies in its ability to harm broader communities as well as individuals. In the context of anti-fandom, its power also lies in its insidious insistence that it is one thing (e.g., harmless commentary on a film) when it is actually something else (e.g., violent misogyny and racial vilification). Engaging in violent hate speech and then telling distressed targets they're imagining violent hate speech is a form of cultural gaslighting.[2]

Given the complexity of contemporary anti-fan scenes, we as scholars have enormous scope to decide what discourse should be considered for analysis, what and who should belong to various categories, and how these categories should be named. These decisions are themselves powerful and have political and ethical consequences. If we observe hateful speech and we select anti-fandom as our lens, then we are situating this speech within a paradigm that has historically positioned such discourse as a response associated with audiences. These audiences, in turn, have historically been understood as having an agency that is subtle, idiosyncratic, and possibly even an admirable form of "punching up" to hegemons. It is ironic that a scholarly move intended to recognize the agency of media consumers may ultimately strip them of agency by not fully acknowledging their power to cause harm. As I have argued over the course of this chapter, anti-fan force is a strong force, and it is increasingly being deployed in an oppressive and violent manner. When anti-fans drive a woman such as Quinn from her home with rape and death threats, this is not "punching up." Even figuring it as a form of "lateral violence" (i.e., violence directed at one's peers) is a stretch. Instead, my contention is that this is clearly "punching down," a type of harassment, bullying, and violence that we, as scholars, may inadvertently be supporting if we accept its perpetrators' claims that it is nothing more than a bad review.

Conclusion

Rather than concluding with a shorter and slightly differently worded version of what I have already said, I end this chapter with a thought experiment. Imagine a boxing commentator in a nation where dis-organized violence is not much of a social problem. While the act of organized fighting is necessarily combative and probably controversial, no insurmountable ethical problems arise for the commentator because, as far as she is concerned, she is calling matches that occur in contained spaces according to a set of broadly understood and accepted rules of combat. Now imagine that this nation enters a period of change and unrest and that brutal civil war erupts. This second type of fighting has family resemblances to the first, but the changed context clearly makes it something other than boxing. Consider how puzzling it would be, there-fore, if our commentator remained on the sidelines providing excited, blow-by-blow commentaries of the street violence as if she were still calling a sporting event. It would appear that she is misreading the genre or engaging in ethically questionable behavior herself.

While this analogy is strained and imperfect, it does capture something of my concern about where anti-fan studies could find itself. In a sense, we are also providing commentary on a type of (often combative) activity that used to occur in a tightly delineated way but—because of changed circumstances—has morphed into something that seems palpably differ-ent even though it retains similarities to its previous iterations. Categorizing death threats as an extreme form of anti-fandom does have scholarly precedent (see Gray 2003, 73; 2005, 842). Yet changes in the amount and type of force wielded by anti-fans make this categorization seem increasingly odd. What's more, continuing to make such categorizations could leave us exposed to accusations that we are exculpating those people issuing threats and underplaying the suffering of those who receive them.

One way forward might be for anti-fan scholars to focus only on the equivalent of legitimate, "above-the-belt" fighting: for instance, only anti-fan activity that involves clearly identifiable media texts and audiences and does not include threatening hate speech or people punching each other sideways or downward. It has, however, become increasingly difficult to locate such discourse. The mediasphere is messy, the texts and players are hellishly difficult to taxonomize, the power flows are chaotic and multidirectional, violence is erupting in some quarters, and real people are suffering real hurt as part of agendas that are opaque or deliberately obscured. Choosing to prosecute an anti-fan analysis of a scene involving hate speech but excluding this hate speech because it complicates the analysis does a disservice to the targets of the hate speech. Given the increasing prevalence of this type of anti-fandom, it would also do a disservice to anti-fan studies.

Another option would be to ditch the anti-fan model entirely and to start afresh with something new. Despite the extended critique in this chapter, however, I believe this option would be throwing the proverbial baby out with the bath water. A key benefit of continuing to use some version of the anti-fan model is that it brings critical attention to the fact that much of the vitriol and hateful speech currently proliferating in digital cultures is indissolubly interwoven with popular entertainment and the production and consumption of media texts. A useful way forward, therefore, might involve the use of interdisciplinary hybrids: combinations of anti-fan and other media studies approaches, alongside theoretical lenses drawn from, for example, critical feminist and race theory or discussions of hate speech and free speech in the philosophy of law. At the very least, I hope scholars will consider keeping a closer eye on hate speech in anti-fan discourse and consider foregrounding this in recognition of the unprecedented complexity of digital media cultures and the unprecedented power of those (using, producing, and sometimes hating) artists previously known as "the audience."

NOTES

1 The term "Web 1.0" is generally used to describe those early decades of the Internet when content was mostly static and delivered in a read-only format. "Web
2.0" refers to the shift—most obvious from around 2006—to user-generated
material, interactivity, collaboration, and sharing. "Web 3.0," also known as the
"semantic web" (Naughton 2014), mostly refers to the increased tailoring of
content to suit users' named preferences and previously identifiable habits. Of
particular relevance to this chapter is the legal scholar Danielle Keats Citron's use
of the term "Hate 3.0" to capture the way hate online is also becoming increasingly personalized in that it is being directed at specific people from specific social
groups (Citron 2014, 13).

2 Referring to the 1938 play *Gas Light* by Patrick Hamilton, "gaslighting" refers to
a form of psychological abuse that causes targets to doubt their mental states,
memories, and perceptions.

REFERENCES

@BELIMBLA4. 2015. *Twitter*, May 30. https://twitter.com/belimbla4/sta-
tus/604379648055742464, accessed August 23, 2016.

Andrejevic, M. 2008. Watching *Television Without Pity*: The Productivity of Online
Fans. *Television and New Media* 9, no. 1:24–46.

Bacchiocchi, G. 2016. "'Making a Murderer' Prosecutor Target of Death and Rape
Threats!" *Radar*, February 4. http://radaronline.com, accessed February 6, 2016.

Bad Lip Reading. n.d. YouTube channel. www.youtube.com/user/BadLipReading.

Barker, C., and E. A. Jane. 2016. *Cultural Studies: Theory and Practice*. 5th ed. Los
Angeles: Sage.

Carter, C. 2014. "Twitter Troll Jailed for 'Campaign of Hatred' against Stella Creasy."
Telegraph, March 29. www.telegraph.co.uk.

Click, Melissa A. In this volume. "Introduction: Haters Gonna Hate."

Citron, D. K. 2014. *Hate Crimes in Cyberspace*. Cambridge, MA: Harvard University
Press.

Criado-Perez, C. 2013. "She Called the Police. They Said That There Was Nothing They
Could Do." *Mamamia*, November 14. www.mamamia.com.au.

Dee, J. 2007. "All the News That's Fit to Print Out." *New York Times Magazine*, July 1.
www.nytimes.com.

Encyclopedia Dramatica. n.d.-a. "About." https://encyclopediadramatica.rs.

———. n.d.-b. "List of Sex Moves." https://encyclopediadramatica.rs.

———. n.d.-c. "Zoe Quinn." https://encyclopediadramatica.rs.

Fiske, J. 2011. *Reading the Popular*. 2nd ed. London: Routledge. Originally published
1989.

Foucault, M. 1976. *The History of Sexuality*. Vol. 1: *An Introduction*. Translated by Robert Hurley. New York: Vintage Books.

———. 1980. *Power/Knowledge*. New York: Pantheon Books. Originally published 1972.

———. 1984. "Nietzsche, Genealogy, History." In *The Foucault Reader*, edited by P. Rabinow, 76–100. New York: Pantheon Books.

Gray, J. 2003. "New Audiences, New Textualities: Anti-Fans and Non-Fans." *International Journal of Cultural Studies* 6, no. 1:64–81.

———. 2005. "Antifandom and the Moral Text: *Television Without Pity* and Textual Dislike." *American Behavioral Scientist* 48, no. 7:840–858.

———. In this volume. "How Do I Dislike Thee? Let Me Count the Ways."

Griner, D. 2016. "Reactions to the All-Female Ghostbusters Trailer Prove It'll Be the Most Polarizing Movie of the Year." *Adweek*, March 3. www.adweek.com.

Hall, S. 1981. "Notes on Deconstructing 'the Popular.'" In *People's History and Socialist Theory*, edited by R. Samuel, 227–240. London: Routledge & Kegan Paul.

———. 2005. "Encoding/Decoding." In *Culture, Media, Language*, edited by S. Hall, D. Hobson, A. Lowe, and P. Willis, 117–127. London: Routledge. Originally published 1980.

Helleksen, K. 2009. "Fan Studies 101." *SFRA Review*, no. 287 (Winter). www.sfra.org.

Jane, E. A. 2014a. "'Your a Ugly, Whorish, Slut': Understanding E-Bile." *Feminist Media Studies* 14, no. 4:531–546.

———. 2014b. "'Back to the Kitchen, Cunt': Speaking the Unspeakable about Online Misogyny." *Continuum: Journal of Media and Cultural Studies* 28, no. 4:558–570.

———. 2014c. "Beyond Antifandom: Cheerleading, Textual Hate and New Media Ethics." *International Journal of Cultural Studies* 17, no. 2:175–190.

———. 2015. "Flaming? What Flaming? The Pitfalls and Potentials of Researching Online Hostility." *Ethics and Information Technology* 17, no. 1:65–87.

———. 2017. *Misogyny Online: A Short (and Brutish) History*. London: Sage.

Jason, Z. 2015. "Game of Fear." *Boston Magazine*, May. www.bostonmagazine.com.

———. 2013. *Textual Poachers: Television Fans and Participatory Culture*. Updated 20th anniversary ed. New York: Routledge. Originally published 1992.

Jenkins, H., S. Ford, and J. Green. 2013. *Spreadable Media: Creating Value and Meaning in a Networked Culture*. New York: New York University Press.

LiveLeak. n.d. "Waleed Aly Blames Non Muslims for Paris Attacks," readers' comments in the "below-the-line" section, November 17 [year not specified]. www.liveleak.com.

Martens, T. 2016. "Creators, Fans and Death Threats: Talking to Joss Whedon, Neil Gaiman and More on the Age of Entitlement." *Los Angeles Times*, July 25. www.latimes.com.

McKee, A. 2003. *Textual Analysis: A Beginner's Guide*. London: Sage.

Miller, L. 2011. "Just Write It!" *New Yorker*, April 11. www.newyorker.com.

Naughton, J. 2014. "25 Things You Might Not Know about the Web on Its 25th Birthday." *Guardian*, March 9. www.theguardian.com.

Phillips, W. In this volume. "Like Gnats to a Forklift Foot: TLC's *Here Comes Honey Boo Boo* and the Conservative Undercurrent of Ambivalent Fan Laughter."

Roberts, E. 2016. "Game of Thrones Star Received DEATH THREATS from Viewers after Killing Jon Snow." *Mirror*, April 26. www.mirror.co.uk.

Romano, A. 2016. "Milo Yiannopoulous's Twitter Ban Explained." *Vox*, July 20. www.vox.com.

Ronson, J. 2015. *So You've Been Publicly Shamed*. London: Picador.

Sampson, M. 2016. "Why the 'Ghostbusters' Trailer Is the Most 'Disliked' Movie Trailer in YouTube History." *Screen Crush*, April 29. http://screencrush.com.

Schulze, L., A. B. White, and J. D. Brown. 1993. "'A Sacred Monster in Her Prime': Audience Construction of Madonna as Low-Other." In *The Madonna Connection: Representational Politics, Subcultural Identities, and Cultural Theory*, edited by C. Schwichtenberg, 15–37. Boulder, CO: Westview Press.

Stein, J. 2016. "How Trolls Are Ruining the Internet." *Time*, August 18. http://time.com.

Stuart, K. 2014. "Zoe Quinn: 'All Gamergate Has Done Is Ruin People's Lives.'" *Guardian*, December 4. www.theguardian.com.

Tran, C., and H. McNab. 2015. "'I Never Meant to Hurt a Single Soul': Mother of Twins Who Became an Internet Sensation When She Posted Hilarious Signs about Her Frustrations Hits Back at Angry Critics." *Daily Mail*, July 13. www.dailymail.co.uk.

Willis, C. 2015. "Project Co-host Waleed Aly: 'Why I'm Passionate about Not Being on Social Media.'" *news.com.au*, September 24. www.news.com.au.

3

Hatewatch with Me

Anti-Fandom as Social Performance

ANNE GILBERT

In an effort to gather empirical data to support the notion that television audiences' emotional engagement serves as a predictor for viewing practices, a start-up media analytic company compared Twitter activity that spoke to an emotional response to a show with ratings information for following episodes of that show (Canvs, n.d.). Unsurprisingly, the study concluded that emotional attachment does correlate to viewing patterns—but the emotion with the greatest predictive potential is not "love" or "beautiful" or even "enjoyment"; instead, it's "hate."

In the midst of end-of-year best-of/worst-of roundups, the pop culture website *Vulture* capped off 2012 with a feature on "The Year in Hate-Watching," basking in the "blessed times" that provide an abundance of options for television viewers looking to watch a program they find terrible (Lyons 2012). Willa Paskin of *Salon* considers the "bitchy glee" involved in hatewatching NBC's *Smash* to be "one of life's great pleasures" (2013). In the analytic study noted above, for comedy shows, increases in viewer expressions of "beautiful" while watching comedies resulted in a .3 percent increase in viewership; in contrast, for both reality and drama programming, increases in tweets expressing "hate" corresponded to a .7 percent increase in viewership (Canvs, n.d.). In short, hatewatching—viewing television one deems bad in order to critique, deride, or ridicule it—has, "[in] the past couple years . . . become a thing" (Anders 2014).

I argue that hatewatching has come to operate as a mode of anti-fandom in the everyday. As hatewatching is established in the popular lexicon, anti-fandom is likewise situated as a normalized practice of media consumption. In particular, I consider the role of the social in anti-fandom, as hatewatching is an anti-fan practice that is inherently communal, whereas fandom is not necessarily so. In this chapter, I outline the definition and practices of hatewatching, including the rhetoric of sociality that pervades its discussion. I break down types of hatewatching, and I consider evidence from hatewatchers of two television programs, *Smash* (NBC, 2012–2013) and *Girls* (HBO, 2012–2017), as representative but specific examples of hatewatch practice. The sections that follow investigate the social performance of hatewatching and consider how irony, taste, and social hierarchies function as qualities of anti-fandom. Examination of social and cultural networks that circulate textual dislike enables research on anti-fandom to contribute to a more nuanced perspective of how subgroups organize themselves into hierarchical and discrete publics within the television viewing audience. The performance of hatewatching produces a culturally constructed perspective on television that, through its use of irony and critique, creates an alternative, communal form of media consumption.

Hate It, Can't Wait to Watch It

"Hatewatching," as I use the term, describes viewing a television program or film despite disliking it—or, perhaps, watching as a result of disliking it—usually in order to point out its flaws. It therefore involves specific criteria: judging a text to be of poor quality, continuing to watch, delighting in doing so, and having no reservations about perpetuating these behaviors.

In his classification of anti-fan practices, Jonathan Gray (in this volume) includes the hatewatcher as one way in which the identity of the anti-fan is enacted, and pop culture commentary likewise is brimming with definitions, analyses, and considerations of the habit of hatewatching. That hatewatching demands such self-reflection—and, indeed, often prompts its participants to justify, more than just explain, its appeal—is an illustration of the ways in which we are often uncomfortable with genuine dislike as part of our media consumption behaviors. As Melissa Click (in this volume) points out, the attention paid to the motivations and practices of dislike and disdain do not reflect the significance of these emotions in the engagement of participants. The rhetoric used to rationalize, critique, and organize hatewatching practitioners and their behaviors illustrates the ways in which hatewatching integrates textual dislike into the social pleasures of media participation.

Jonathan Gray and Sarah Murray (2016) argue that media dislike is inherently problematic: As active, engaged viewers, we are not supposed to dislike, and we are meant to treat dislike with suspicion in others because liking has been characterized as a progressive effort to champion the underdog in popular media. Dislike, therefore, becomes a tool of the powerful, a "hegemonic reinforcement" of practices that perpetuate the marginalization of an active viewership (Gray and Murray 2016, 359–360). This discomfort with media dislike is reflected in efforts to pathologize the practice of hatewatching. A *Chicago Tribune* article, for example, defines hatewatching as "an irrational, compulsive act" that involves "luxuriating in the perverse joy of habitually watching something that generates intense feelings of irritation" (Borrelli 2013), and the blog *io9* asks, "Are You Hurting Your Brain by 'Hate-Watching' Bad Television?" (Anders 2014). Although it is not unusual for fan practices to be likened, implicitly or explicitly, with pathological behaviors, what is notable here is that engagement with media is only problematic when it is television that the viewer actively dislikes.

Because, as Gray and Murray note, we have established cultural models of media consumption that are structured around models of love (2016, 359), there is also a pervasive impulse to reframe hatewatching as a practice that is really about an unacknowledged like. For example, the feminist media site *Jezebel* argues that the practice is defined as "watching a show that you *claim* to dislike with the sole purpose of mocking it" (Davies 2013; emphasis added) and goes on to ask, "Is hatewatching even a real thing? Or do we just refuse to admit that we like shitty things?" Emily Nussbaum of the *New Yorker*, who admits to hatewatching *Smash* after her initial good impressions turned sour, wonders, "Why would I go out of my way to watch a show that makes me so mad? On some level, I'm obviously enjoying it. Maybe I secretly love *Smash*" (Nussbaum 2012).

Many are thus quick to assume that hatewatchers lack either self-awareness or self-disclosure and are simply failing to admit that they continue to watch the show because they like it. I argue, however, that hatewatching is neither disingenuous nor deceptive—but it is also not the same as a guilty pleasure. Guilty pleasures are those texts that we relish but that we keep private because to watch and to enjoy these media objects is somehow embarrassing or inconsistent with the interests we advertise openly. Guilty pleasures offer "the associated pleasures of hugging them to [oneself] or of confiding them, under the right circumstances, to a treasured friend" (Spacks 2011, 241). Guilty pleasures are therefore distinct from subjects of hatewatching. While it is perhaps more familiar to frame all active, engaged media consumption in terms of like—whether that like is disclosed or kept carefully concealed—those who defend hatewatching speak of it as a genuine dislike that is reflected only in approaching the practice as one of anti-fandom and a product of media hate.

Hatewatching, according to critic Charlie Jane Anders (2014), is "about something being such a terrible mess, or so repugnant to everything we hold dear, that you can't help but watch the disaster unfold." Willa Paskin of *Salon* considers the "bitchy glee" of hatewatching to be "one of life's great pleasures" (2013). In response to a reader question asking why anyone would waste his time hatewatching, *Vulture* television critic Margaret Lyons (2015) contends that it is fun "watching shows drown in their own hubris. . . . A show that seems like it'll be amazing but turns out to be schlock? That's where the hate-watch lives. Maybe some of those people stayed at the emperor's-new-clothes parade because it's secretly funny to watch someone proudly parade around with his dick out."

Like anti-fandom more broadly, there are different forms of hatewatching, each with their own pleasures and motivations. Reality television, for example, is a popular subject of hatewatching—or what Susan J. Douglas calls "ironic viewing"—because the program content focuses on people we are meant to dislike and behaviors "we are urged to judge and which are designed to make us feel much better about ourselves (Douglas 2013, 149). Jonathan Gray (in this volume) notes that anti-fandom can be motivated by fans who have become disillusioned by the direction of a media property or by fans who remain hopeful a misguided text can right its course. Hatewatching, too, can also manifest in viewers who used to genuinely like a show but find its current episodes to be lacking in the same quality. One critic notes that "it's probably closer to disappointment-watching than hate-watching. That line is really thin, though" (*TV.com* Staff 2016). Hatewatching can also involve what television critic Alan Sepinwall (2015) calls "hope-watching," when viewers tune in to a program they dislike owing to a "belief, founded or not, that there is a good show hiding inside the bad one."

In other words, the choice of what to hatewatch is itself significant and structures a relationship of viewer to television text that speaks to the role that dislike plays in these systems of anti-fandom. As outlined in the analytic study (Canvs, n.d.), hatewatching is most notable in reality and drama programming; for dramas, hatewatchers are most vocal about programs that both fail to meet expectations and lack self-awareness about their own shortcomings. A "how-to" guide for hatewatching even notes this as key: Shows we hatewatch are those that initially draw us in with some promise of entertainment from the premise, the show-runner, the genre, or other early signs of quality (Bahrenburg 2016). While guilty-pleasure television is perhaps marked by programming that is generally considered "bad," this type of hatewatching is particular to television shows that are deemed—by industrial support, critical reception, awards recognition, or cultural parlance—to be good, and hatewatchers share their disdain and critiques in an effort to counter the praise. In this vein, social media backchannels, Internet discussion forums, and review-site comment sections are rife with illustrations of hatewatchers challenging the social validity of particularly disdained programs.

There are a variety of programs that generate productive and vocal hatewatching audiences. For the purposes of this chapter, I focus on two that are both illustrative and representative of the practices and significance of hatewatching. *Smash*, an hour-long musical drama, was hyped heavily before its premiere on NBC in January 2012, but it was canceled at the end of its second season. In contrast, *Girls* is a half-hour comedy on HBO that likewise premiered in 2012 but ran for six seasons and racked up considerable industrial, critical, and popular praise during that time. This chapter does not offer a case study of these two programs; rather, it uses the similarities in the responses to these two high-profile, heavily celebrated, and gleefully disdained programs to discuss the limits and practices of hatewatching. These shows are both are aspirational programs, involving the lives of the wealthy and privileged in New York City, and both were given expensive public advertising campaigns lauding them before they had even premiered.

These shows make illustrative examples of hatewatching as a social phenomenon because hatewatching is designed to deflate the pretensions perceived in the content and counter their claims of quality in a shared experience of taste making.

The Hatewatch Show

The particulars of hatewatching establish it as a mode of anti-fandom, which in turn is oriented against fan and audience practice. It is possible to collapse the boundaries between these categories, but the distinctions can be productive as well. By focusing on the circulation of disdain within communities of hatewatchers and the methods used to critique particular television shows, I argue that hatewatching should be understood as a performance that is necessarily social, one that speaks to reflections on the cultural framing of media consumption and consumers themselves.

For programs deemed to be irrevocably problematic and worthy of ridicule, sharing the details, frustrations, and derision that arise when viewing is a central practice to hatewatching. For *Smash*, the mockery of hatewatching is wrapped up in perceptions that the show failed to live up to its promise. *Smash* was a glitzy, behind-the-scenes melodrama about the making of a new Broadway musical about Marilyn Monroe that featured original songs and high production values. The network pushed the show hard, with a premiere date following the Super Bowl, a heavy advertising blitz, star-studded press tours, and expensive, splashy programs to accompany advance screeners (Ariano 2012). Despite initial excitement, enthusiasm for the show quickly waned, and early cheerleaders became some of its harshest critics; three months after the premiere, Emily Nussbaum declared, "The show has taken a nosedive so deep I'm surprised my ears haven't popped" (2012), and *Huffington Post*'s Maureen Ryan referred to *Smash* as "brain-meltingly awful" by the end of its first season (2012). Despite efforts to retool the failing show for its second season, *Smash* was canceled in May 2013 after two seasons.

In contrast, while HBO's *Girls* also received considerable attention prior to its 2012 premiere, by many metrics this is a program that lived up to the expectations set for it. Advance buzz was largely focused on creator/star Lena Dunham and the promise that the show, a comedy about four twenty-something Brooklyn hipsters attempting to figure out their lives, would constitute a sort of generational touchstone. In the five years since its premiere, *Girls* has also continued to rack up award nominations for Emmys and Golden Globes in acting, writing, and comedy, and the program has retained a high profile as an acclaimed contributor to HBO's quality television programming lineup. Hatewatchers, however, have a different take; disaffected viewers described *Girls* as "examination of an utterly useless and narcissistic generation convinced that their lives are special when, in reality, they're dull and uninspired" (Kubicek 2012). One critic notes, "I spent two and a half seasons hatewatching *Girls* because mainstream media told me that as a millennial female I was supposed to like it. I needed to watch it to be part of the cultural conversation and to not like it somehow made me anti-feminist, but it was torture. . . . The show isn't funny, which is fine, but don't pretend that it is then" (*TV.com* Staff). Unlike *Smash*, where hatewatching is born of a disappointment in the unmet expectations of the show, hatewatching *Girls* is rooted in a need to contradict cultural, critical, and social prestige regularly bestowed upon it.

Sara Ahmed writes that the perception of a shared feeling of hate is what binds individuals into collectives—"Together we hate and this hate is what makes us together" (Ahmed 2004, 26)—and that it is affective attachment that makes the collective be felt as an embodied actuality. Ahmed is writing about strong affective impulses—the hate felt by hate groups—and although hatewatching shares the term, its affect should likely be categorized as an enjoyed dislike. Nevertheless, this theory about affect—that "a gathering is constituted, in part, through the transmission of energetic affects (which may add up to something more than the individual affects of the group's members)" (Brennan 2004, 51)—indicates that the dislike that circulates through the practices of hatewatching are affective bonds that can foster a sense of identity, community, and social belonging.

One blogger, in her "defense of hatewatching" notes that the practice is a family affair: "I watch . . . because it always seems to be on TV and my mom, sister, and yes, my dad, love to hatewatch it as much as I do. Sometimes we actively seek it out just so we can hate on it together" (Cavin 2016). The "how-to" hatewatch guide mentioned previously notes that step 9 involves accepting the hatred, but, more than that, "You say it out loud" (Bahrenburg 2016). Ryan (2012) referred to the "group hate-watch" for *Smash* as an opportunity "share the communal letdown with other witty people who feel just as hacked off by the show's spectacular failure to live up to its potential." One *Entertainment Weekly* reader, adding an assenting voice to the magazine's article on the rise of hatewatching, commented that joining the "hatewatching live viewing/postings [the magazine created] for *Smash* . . . made it oh so much more enjoyable" (cited at Franich 2012). In response to *Vulture*'s call for readers to share their own beloved hatewatching practices, one viewer posted a similar sentiment: "*Smash* was only made bearable with glasses of white wine and *Vulture*'s epic recaps" (cited at Lyons 2012). For *Girls*, multiple sites offer tips on how to host hatewatching parties dedicated to a communal mockery of the show (Sousa 2014; Zimmerman 2013).

Hatewatching is thus necessarily social, as the shared affective experience of dislike is sustained by interpersonal networks. Hatewatching, like irony, requires a likeminded audience to understand, and perhaps share, the speaker's perspective in order to function. Linda Hutcheon argues that the "social nature of the participation in the transaction called 'irony' should not be ignored" (Hutcheon 1995, 17). She indicates that, in fact, irony should not work at all; how can individuals say one thing, mean another, and convey that accurately? Rather than favoring the notion that irony is capable of constructing communities (see Booth 1974), Hutcheon contends that irony is possible because it draws upon already-established "discursive communities." Hutcheon argues that these discursive communities, notable for their "complex configuration of shared knowledge, beliefs, values, and communicative strategies" (Hutcheon 1995, 91) provide contexts in which irony is deployed and interpreted, and it is through these existing social contexts that individuals are able to determine "whether an utterance is ironic (or not), and then what *particular* ironic meaning it might have" (Hutcheon 1995, 11, emphasis in original). Discursive communities explain how irony can work but also why someone might be ironic at all: We make use of irony when we trust it will be understood, and having it understood helps construct or reinforce interpersonal bonds.

Hatewatching functions well in the contemporary era of television because we have established new media backchannels in which the practice of hatewatching—and ironic utterances, sarcasm, and derision—are familiar and well traveled. Hatewatching is, as noted above, a practice that is taken up partly by friends and family in living rooms and over personal communication networks. But it is also a practice easily established on social media—Twitter backchannels are familiar streams on which viewers can follow along with live TV to both praise and deride, and the Internet is home to many specific sites based on pop culture criticism and mockery. Hatewatching, therefore, finds a ready discursive community and established social practice on websites that foster an appreciation for caustic and snarky approaches to television viewing, such as *The Onion*'s *A.V. Club* and the now-defunct *Television Without Pity*. The latter's unofficial continuation site, *Previously.tv*, even devoted a regular feature for a time to hatewatching, cajoling its readers with "You're watching it so that you can get worked up and/or make fun of it. And we probably are too" (*Previously.tv*, n.d.)

Hatewatching online celebrates the camaraderie made possible by a presumed community of like-minded others and should be therefore understood as a social activity. I argue that there is an element of performance as well, one that constructs the continued significance of hatewatching as a practice. Hatewatching is a performance of audience identity that makes use of social bonds for individuals to align themselves with a contrary approach—that of an anti-fan—to popular media.

Matt Hills (2002) theorized fandom as a form of performative consumption, one in which the fan is presupposed to be a consumer of material and media goods, and therefore constrained by the capitalist aims of media production, but also willfully enacts a version of that media that retains a sense of purpose and reflection. Hills notes, "Performative consumption enacts the dialectic at the heart of the fan cult(ure). It is simultaneously a matter of communal and cultural 'exchange-value' and a matter of intensely private or cultic 'use-value'" (Hills 2002, 170).

I argue that hatewatching, as a mode of anti-fandom, enacts this fan culture dialectic in a particular way. Rather than placing an emphasis on material goods, as Hills and others have primarily undertaken in these discussions, hatewatching is focused on immaterial practices of consumption—viewing but also reading, listening, or playing, for other media platforms. In the case of hatewatching, the value of the communal, its performance, takes priority over the meaning construction in consumption itself. Put briefly, hatewatching represents a mode of viewing behavior in which the personal use-value of the television text itself is of secondary importance to the exchange-value of performing a stance—critical and derisive—toward that text for others. In this way, hatewatching is fandom, but it is practiced in such a way that it can be theorized distinctly, as anti-fandom, and is reflective of complex attitudes toward media content and cultural constructs.

The identity of a hatewatcher is one bound to both affect and separation. Hatewatchers hold themselves removed from the television text, communicating implicitly or explicitly an attitude (that of dislike or derision) to accompany an action (watching a particular program). The performance of hatewatching is one that is meant to accrue and display cultural capital: By presenting a critical perspective on popular entertainment, hatewatchers can maintain what Pierre Bourdieu (1984) refers to as a "social distance" from popular entertainment that has received critical, cultural, and industrial support. Susan Douglas likewise views this type of ironic viewing as a shield: "[It] means that you can look like you are absolutely not seduced by the mass media, while then being seduced by the mass media, while wearing a knowing smirk" (Douglas 2013, 150). Bourdieu's approach to the display of knowledge and capital by refined audiences is well analyzed within fan studies, but his concept of removal or distance—establishing a position through rejecting the value of popular tastes—is fruitful ground for anti-fan research. The act of hatewatching requires the sharing of affect while participants simultaneously retain a sense of distance from the textual object, the television show itself.

For hatewatching to function, to be understood as something other than a guilty pleasure or a false consciousness model of viewership, it requires like-minded others to and with whom hatewatching practices can be performed. Without its communal aspect, hatewatching can easily be elided into another form of viewership, fandom, or anti-fandom. As a presentation of practice, however, hatewatching emphasizes the role of the interpersonal and the appeal maintained in the circulation of dislike. What hatewatchers perform—namely, taste and superiority—reflects efforts to distinguish themselves from audiences who are more susceptible to the lure of the popular and who do not have the social or cultural capital to distinguish quality or perform their own disdain.

Bad TV, Good Taste

Hatewatching indicates that there is pleasure to be found in dislike; the "bad object" is enjoyable not because it is secretly good but because of the entertainment it offers through chronicling and categorizing its badness. The more preposterous the content, the further afield from the presumptive notion of "quality" programming, the more fodder the object offers to those who wish to deride it. Because the idea of the bad object is an inherently social construct, the practice of hatewatching is more than a shared perspective among a particular audience subgroup; it is an effort at taste making and a deliberate commentary on the notion of quality.

What is considered "good" or "bad" television programming is determined via negotiations between a host of social and individual factors. Dana Polan has observed that "we often imagine, in our neo-liberal moment, that the exercise of taste happens in a free and spontaneous gravitation of audiences to just those sorts of cultural works that are ready-made for them" (Polan 2007, 261). In other words, Polan asserts that we like to consider taste as purely an aesthetic choice: We as audiences autonomously and independently select the television that we enjoy and consider good, and taste is therefore meritocratic and assigns value to the worthiest cultural objects. Of course, long-standing cultural critique points to the role that taste and consumption play in establishing, reinforcing, and making public class designations and social status: "In the organic complex of habits of thought which make up the substance of an individual's conscious life the economic interest does not lie isolated and distinct from all other interests" (Veblen 1992, 88).

Our tastes, our concept of entertainment and enjoyment, and our notion of what constitutes good and bad cultural objects, are bound up in our perspectives on how they organize and are organized by broader social order (Bourdieu 1984). Critical viewers come to hatewatching, in part, to counter what is perceived to be an inaccurate designation of quality; shows that inspire hatewatching are those that find support and marketing dollars from their network (as did *Smash*, which was aggressively promoted by NBC for months before its midseason premiere; see Carter 2012) or those that receive critical attention that far outpaces their actual ratings (as *Girls* regularly did; see Flint 2013). One gleeful hatewatcher of *Girls*, for instance, defends his practice by essentially blaming HBO for airing it in the first place—"You're expecting the same HBO quality you'd get from their other programs" (Sousa 2014)—and not getting that same quality is grounds to mock the program, its characters, and its very existence. Hatewatching a program, openly designating it as deserving of derision, is as much commentary on the notion of quality in television content as it is a reflection on a particular show.

Anti-fandom critiques what is popular or "good" and situates individual texts among shifting perceptions of what is considered good, desirable, and worth watching. Anti-fandom is thus a process of taste making, and hatewatching is an opportunity for individuals to perform their tastes. In her analysis of Facebook refusers, Laura Portwood-Stacer argues that "we might read conscious rejection as an expression of dissatisfaction that may expose the ideological discord simmering beneath the surface of mainstream consumer culture, as well as the (limited) terrain upon which people feel powered to enact their dissent" (Portwood-Stacer 2013, 7). At times, hatewatching specific programs is specifically articulated to perform a critique of the popular more broadly; hosting a hate-watching party for *Girls* is a productive idea because "with EVERY-BODY on the bandwagon now that the HBO hit has made its way to the common people it's just so . . . well, last year, right?" (Zimmerman 2013). Hatewatching challenges the popular because it situates participants within an explicit conversation of what the popular is and what it does.

As individuals perform structuring choices around their perspective on popular culture, they form what Herbert Gans termed "taste publics." Taste publics are composed of those individuals "with usually but not always similar values making similar choices from the available offerings of culture" (Gans 1999, 94); members of a taste public have a shared perspective and a shared approach to popular culture. Although they are formed differently and for different purposes, the resulting effect is similar to that of the discursive communities that make irony possible. Taste publics allow audiences to shorthand the social process of constructing a shared understanding of what constitutes good television worth enjoying.

Understanding hatewatchers as a taste public renders them an audience subgroup with a purpose: These viewers concentrate their derision on shows like *Smash* and *Girls* in a deliberate effort to argue that these programs should not be considered good television. Both shows have benefited from connections to Hollywood insiders on the production teams, industrial backing in the form of advertising campaigns and network favor, critical appreciation, and popular interest. In the case of *Girls*, this is also compounded by awards attention and its position on HBO, a subscription-based premium cable network. *Smash*, in contrast, was positioned as the last great hope of a flagging broadcast network. Hatewatching is a response to the industrial endorsements and social cues that position these shows as "quality programming." It is a response that takes the position that this assessment is incorrect, that *Girls* is entertaining because it is insufferable and out of touch, not because it gives voice to a particular generational perspective. One disaffected *Girls* viewer likened the show's reception to a case of the emperor's new clothes: "Like others (critics?) were seeing some new duds on the emperor, but no matter how hard I looked, he was naked to me. So I have watched the two seasons, tried to wrap my head around it, and just don't get it" (*Television Without Pity* 2013). Hatewatching itself is not particularly populist; it does, after all, perpetuate the idea of cultural tastemakers, allows viewers to enjoy viewing that is in line with class distinctions without affiliating with them, and upholds the notion of difference between television that is good and popular and television that is bad and popular. However, the performative practices of hatewatching aim to recalibrate the conversation about what constitutes good television.

My TV Is Better than Your TV

If hatewatching is an effort to exert some say-so in establishing which television texts are perceived as "quality," it is also similarly evaluative of audiences. The performance of hatewatching involves commentary on how audience subgroups understand one another. As anti-fans perform their consumption behaviors, they are effectively organizing themselves, other viewers, and fans into a hierarchical construct of the viewing audience.

Discursive communities and taste publics who find entertainment in hatewatching provide commentary upon the practices and preferences of other viewers as much as on the television text itself. In their analysis of *Fifty Shades of Grey* anti-fans, Sarah Harman and Bethan Jones note that "*Fifty Shades* anti-fans position themselves as gatekeepers, thus reinforcing their subcultural capital which in turn enforces taste cultures" (Harman and Jones 2013, 952). This act of "gatekeeping" positions critics—of shows like *Girls* and *Smash* as well as for *Fifty Shades*—as more discerning, knowledgeable audiences who are "performing a service" (Harman and Jones 2013, 959) for a less aware public that might be unaware of the low-value, low-culture assessment ascribed to these particular texts.

The deliberate effort to organize audience subgroups is a practice that is shared by fans as well as anti-fans. As fans articulate preferences, share perspectives, and formulate critiques of program content, they can fragment into subcommunities that negotiate relationships with one another as well as with the text. As a result, fan communities often involve competitiveness and disagreements (Murray 2004) and attempt to attribute positive characteristics to the fan community and portray a beneficial representation to outsiders while excluding the less desirable (Busse 2013). Factions within fandom are therefore often the most severe critics of fellow fans' behaviors. For example, in her analysis of self-perception and divisions within the *Xena: Warrior Princess* fandom Mel Stanfill argues that "fans do not challenge these socially devalued meanings of fandom, but merely apply them to other fans, somewhere out there" (Stanfill 2013, 128). In an effort to normalize their own behavior while acknowledging the potential excesses of fandom, these individuals label other fans and fan groups as less critical, aware, and discerning. Derek Johnson refers to the ruptures that are created as individuals attempt to establish themselves as "genuine fans" as the "ongoing struggles for discursive dominance constitute fandom as a hegemonic struggle over interpretation" (Johnson 2007, 286). However, internal valuation of fan practices, textual interpretation, and community identity are often policed along gender and age lines (Hills 2012), so interpretations of what makes for ideal fan practices are heavily influenced by external markers of cultural capital. Divisions within fan groups establish norms of behavior and create consensus for particular interpretations that valorize certain types of fans and practices differently from others and reveal a tendency for audiences to practice their own modes of consumption by setting them apart from—and, often, above—those of "other" audience subgroups.

Hatewatching's criticism highlights fissures in subgroups or even creates them by pointing to perceived shortcomings in popular media texts and taking issue with their popularity in the first place. Anti-fans segment and organize themselves in order to position the hatewatcher as a counterpoint to a particular mode of consumption. These are viewers cognizant of their goal to "be seen by others as not being duped," to clearly articulate the perspective they hold on television content, and to contextualize the role they play in the broader audience structure (Andrejevic 2008, 38). This indicates, for example, why hatewatchers critique programs by emphasizing their own knowledge and understanding: Detailed criticism, ironic commentary, and cleverly derisive live tweeting point to flaws in the TV show content but also have the potential to portray hatewatchers as articulate, witty, and discerning television viewers. Hatewatchers' criticism, disdain, and alternative perspective on a television program make it clear to those for whom the hatewatching is being performed that they do not watch television the same way as does "everyone else"; as the television critic quoted earlier noted, hatewatchers consider themselves the parade goers who enjoy being the ones who recognize when the emperor is wearing no clothes (Lyons 2015).

Hatewatchers who critique *Girls, Smash,* or other quality programs are performing their role at the top of social hierarchies they are themselves constructing. As hatewatching acts as a presentation of cultural capital, the social status of those who have access to a performance of hatewatching becomes apparent. The practice of hatewatching enacts Bourdieu's concept of distinction, as previously discussed, while also reifying social and economic hierarchies in audiences. Because hatewatching is performed on television programs that benefit from industrial backing or cultural designations of quality, its participants are already members of desirable audience demographic groups: those with high socioeconomic status, high education levels, access to technology for social media backchannel communication, and those with the cultural capital to comment on popular media and expect their commentary to carry weight. As hatewatching becomes an everyday practice, the status of these viewers as desirable, discerning audiences is reinforced, and their own efforts to construct a hierarchy of viewers with hatewatchers at the top, with the mainstream viewers as somewhere below, is validated. Ironic audiences are able to have among them a shared understanding that popularity does not equal quality; perhaps more important, they also present themselves as those who do not watch but who instead hatewatch, and therefore they are in on the joke of popular culture.

Keep Hatewatching On

That hatewatchers celebrate textual dislike subverts expectations for media consumption, prioritizing the social and the circulation of dislike over the pleasures of the text itself. This is, in part, why we study anti-fandom: As consumers behave in challenging ways, they reveal assumptions that shape how popular culture is structured and understood. Anti-fans who practice hatewatching "can turn displeasure into pleasure through the construction of an anti-fan community" (Gray 2005, 854). Hatewatching's ability to successfully deploy and comprehend enjoyment in textual dislike, therefore, means the practice is capable of joining like-minded individuals into a loose cabal of outsiders. Thus hatewatching is not simply about the specific comments meant to critique *Girls* or deride *Smash*; it is an illustration of how anti-fandom works as an organizing principle by individuals seeking to situate themselves as a discrete, and assumedly superior, subgroup of pop culture consumers.

This chapter illustrates the role that social ties and performativity play in anti-fandom, in particular, and in media consumption, more broadly. Hatewatching, as a mode of anti-fandom, is a particularly resonant example: Participants have a shared construction of the mainstream audience and how they watch television and demonstrate to others that they are watching television differently from that construction. This practice, therefore, engages assumptions that audiences make about other viewers, the role of television, and their own role within those structures. I have sought to uncouple the presumption of enjoyment from the practices of media consumption in order to consider the other forms of pleasure and value that can be generated by viewing behaviors—even if it involves viewing something that one genuinely dislikes. Anti-fandom offers pleasures for participants, and analyzing hatewatching offers a way to consider how alternative perspectives on media texts and consumption practices can construct notions of taste, audience hierarchies, and cultural participation that are passed between individuals. Hatewatching is a performance of consumption that takes advantage of discursive practices to form taste publics that challenge accepted examples of quality television, presents an alternative mode of enjoying television content, and provides commentary on appropriate behavior as a discerning audience member and a critical, but not excessive, fan.

This chapter constructs a framework in which hatewatching can be understood, but further research is necessary to expand upon ways in which hatewatching is both interpretive and instructive. In particular, research into how hatewatchers themselves understand the pleasures of their practice, and how the behaviors of hatewatching may relate to modes of participation with audience communities for shows they may enjoy in a more straightforward manner, would add a depth of understanding to the practice. The performative nature of hatewatching illustrates a relationship between an individual and a television text, an alternative perspective that involves disdain and mockery and that situates viewers among constructs of the broader viewing audience and hierarchies of taste. It is the dissent of hatewatching, and of anti-fandom, that provides a means to forge a sense of kinship among its participants and offers an example—one that can certainly extend to other media and other modes of viewing—of the significance of alternative perspectives of consumption.

REFERENCES

Ahmed, S. 2004. *The Cultural Politics of Emotion*. New York: Routledge.

Anders, C. J. 2014. "Are You Hurting Your Brain by 'Hate-Watching' Bad Television?" *io9* (blog), November 3. https://io9.gizmodo.com.

Andrejevic, M. 2008. "Watching *Television Without Pity*: The Productivity of Online Fans." *Television and New Media* 9, no. 1:24–46.

Ariano, T. 2012. "*Smash*tastrophe! A Tribute to NBC's Broadway Drama, the Worst TV Show I've Ever Loved." *Slate*, May 14. www.slate.com.

Bahrenburg, E. 2016. "A 10 Step Guide to Hate Watching a Show." *FSR: Film School Rejects*, July 20. https://filmschoolrejects.com.

Booth, W. 1974. *A Rhetoric of Irony*. Chicago: University of Chicago Press.

Borrelli, C. 2013. "What Does Hate-Watching Mean?" *Chicago Tribune*, February 24. www.chicagotribune.com.

Bourdieu, P. 1984. *Distinction: A Social Critique of the Judgment of Taste*. Translated by R. Nice. Cambridge, MA: Harvard University Press.

Brennan, T. 2004. *The Transmission of affect*. Ithaca, NY: Cornell University Press.

Busse, K. 2013. "Geek Hierarchies, Boundary Policing, and the Gendering of the Good Fan." *Participations: Journal of Audience and Reception Studies* 10, no. 1:73–91.

Canvs. n.d. "Emotions and TV Viewership." New York: Canvs. http://canvs.tv.

Carter, B. 2102. "NBC Spends Millions on the Buildup to *Smash*. *New York Times*, February 5. www.nytimes.com.

Cavin, A. 2016. "In Defense of 'Hate-watching' TV Shows." *Literally, Darling* (blog), May 10. www.literallydarling.com.

Click, M. A. In this volume. "Introduction: Haters Gonna Hate."

Davies, M. 2013. "'Hate Watching' Is Mostly Just Being Embarrassed by Your Own Tastes." *Jezebel*, February 6. http://jezebel.com.

Douglas, S. J. 2013. "*Jersey Shore*: Ironic Viewing." In *How to Watch Television*, edited by E. Thompson and J. Mittel, 148–156. New York: New York University Press.

Flint, J. 2013. "HBO's *Girls*: There's More than One Way to Look at Its Ratings." *Los Angeles Times*, March 18. www. latimes.com.

Franich, D. 2012. "The Rise of Hate-Watching: Which TV Shows Do You Love to Despise?" *Entertainment Weekly*, August 16. www.ew.com.

Gans, H. 1999. *Popular Culture and High Culture: An Analysis and Evaluation of Taste*. New York: Basic Books.

Gray, J. 2005. "Antifandom and the Moral Text: *Television Without Pity* and Textual Dislike." *American Behavioral Scientist* 48:840–858.

———. In this volume. "How Do I Dislike Thee? Let Me Count the Ways."

Gray, J., and S. Murray. 2016. "Hidden: Studying Media Dislike and Its Meaning." *International Journal of Cultural Studies* 19, no. 4:357–372.

Harman, S. and B. Jones. 2013. "Fifty Shades of Ghey: Snark Fandom and the Figure of the Anti-Fan." *Sexualities* 16, no. 8:951–968.

Hills, M. 2002. *Fan Cultures*. New York: Routledge.

———. 2012. "Twilight Fans Represented in Commercial Paratexts and Inter-Fandom: Resisting and Repurposing Negative Fan Stereotypes." In *Genre, Reception, and Adaptation in the "Twilight" Series*, edited by A. Morey, 113–129. Farnham: Ashgate.

Hutcheon, L. 1995. *Irony's Edge: The Theory and Politics of Irony*. London: Routledge.

Johnson, D. 2007. "Fan-tagonism: Factions, Institutions, and Constitutive Hegemonies of Fandom." In *Fandom: Identities and Communities in a Mediated World*, edited by J. Gray, C. Sandvoss, and C. L. Harrington, 285–300. New York: New York University Press.

Kubicek, J. 2012. "The 12 Best Shows to Hate-Watch from 2012." *Buddy TV*. www.buddytv.com.

Lyons, M. 2012. "The Year in Hate-Watching." *Vulture*, December 6. www.vulture.com.

———. 2015. "Why Don't People Stop Watching *True Detective* If They Hate It So Much?" *Vulture*, July 22. www.vulture.com.

Murray, S. 2004. "'Celebrating the Story the Way It Is': Cultural Studies, Corporate Media, and the Contested Utility of Fandom." *Continuum: Journal of Media and Cultural Studies* 18, no. 1:7–25.

Nussbaum, E. 2012. "Hate-Watching *Smash*." *New Yorker*, April 27. www.newyorker.com.

Paskin, W. 2013. "Hate-Watching *Smash* Is One of Life's Great Pleasures." *Salon*, February 5. www.salon.com.

Polan, D. 2007. "Cable Watching: HBO, *The Sopranos*, and Discourses of Distinction." In *Cable Visions: Television beyond Broadcasting*, edited by S. Banet-Weiser, C. Chris, and A. Freitas, 261–283. New York: New York University Press.

Portwood-Stacer, L. 2013. "Media Refusal and Conspicuous Non-consumption: The Performative and Political Dimensions of Facebook Abstention." *New Media and Society* 15, no. 7:1041–1057. doi: 10.1177/1461444812465139. Originally published December 5, 2012.

Previously.tv. n.d. "Hate-Watch Central." http://previously.tv.

Ryan, M. 2012. "*Smash* Finale: Does the Show Learn from Its Mistakes?" *Huffington Post*, May 14. www.huffingtonpost.com.

Sepinwall, A. 2015. "Hope-Watching vs. Hate-Watching in TV's New Golden Age." *Uproxx*, April 16. https://uproxx.com.

Sousa, N. 2014. "A Guide to Hatewatching HBO's *Girls*." *normsousa* (blog), March 5. www.normsousa.com.

Spacks, P. M. 2011. *On Rereading*. Cambridge, MA: Belknap Press of Harvard University Press.

Stanfill, M. 2013. "'They're Losers, but I Know Better': Intra-Fandom Stereotyping and the Normalization of the Fan Subject." *Critical Studies in Media Communication* 30, no. 2:117–134.

Television Without Pity. 2013. Post on forum, "Girls: Voice of Her Generation," March 20. www.televisionwithoutpity.com.

TV.com Staff. 2016. "Pass the Remote: What Shows Do You Love to Hatewatch?" *TV.com*, February 20. www.tv.com.

Veblen, T. 1992. *The Theory of the Leisure Class*. New Brunswick, NJ: Transaction Publishers.

Zimmerman, E. 2013. "How to Make Your *Girls* Hate-Watching Party the Best Ever!" *Whiskey Journal*, February 8. www.thewhiskeyjournal.com.

4

Dissatisfaction and *Glee*

On Emotional Range in Fandom and Feels Culture

LOUISA STEIN

Introduction: Productive Dissatisfaction

"I can't go back to *Glee* after this." "That's it, I'm done with *Glee*." These aren't exact quotes, but they're sentiments that will sound familiar to many a *Glee* fan, and they're sentiments that I myself came close to declaring on more than one occasion. Sometimes quitting a television series sticks, and other times it doesn't. In this essay, I'm interested in the many times in which it doesn't, in the way that negative emotion and frustration, dislike, distaste, disapproval—and sometimes even deep hurt—fit within the ebb and flow of fan engagement, fan communities, and fan production. As Melissa Click describes, "Negative emotions, like hate and disgust, are implicated in fans' expressions of love" (Click, in this volume). Indeed, fan hurt does not preclude fan commitment to a series and its fandom; rather, it is woven into fan commitment and can even reinforce it. Through an exploration of *Glee*'s fan discourse, I argue here that negative fan affect is a key dimension of much of fan culture. I focus on fans of the FOX series *Glee* (2009–2015) who shared their disappointment in GIFs, expressed their critiques through meta analyses, organized their dissatisfaction into politically minded campaigns such as the *Glee* Equality Project, and wove their frustration into their fan fiction and art. These diverse manifestations of fan dissatisfaction turned creative expression serve as models for more mainstream integration of media into everyday emotional expression online.

This essay is one result of my own engagement with *Glee* and *Glee* fandom, which I have also written about in my book, *Millennial Fandom* (Stein 2015, 1–2). As in *Millennial Fandom*, this analysis stems from my own experience of the fandom and fan works. While I have attempted to be comprehensive, the picture I paint here of *Glee* fandom can only be partial, as no study of a particular fandom or even of a given moment within a particular fandom could ever capture the multiplicity of fandom or anyone's experience of it. It is my hope that readers of this chapter will supplement the examples that I have drawn on with examples of their own (including examples relating to other media texts and fandoms). I believe that this expansion will only build upon and enrich a larger vision of fan engagement that is multiplicitous and contradictory and that perhaps more often than not merges positive and negative affect, investment and disenchantment, celebration and critique, and even passion and indifference.

In his contribution to this volume, Jonathan Gray revises his earlier, influential argument about anti-fans to reinvision fans and anti-fans not as opposite poles (or protons) but rather as interrelated positions (Gray, in this volume). He offers an array of possibilities of what this interrelationship might look like, from fans of one sports team being anti-fans of a competing team to fans of a media text objecting to particular dimension of that text, to particular communities of fans positioning themselves in conflict with others.

I appreciate Gray's move to complicate an overly simplistic dichotomy, and I would like to suggest here that we push even further at our assumptions of what constitutes "fan" and "anti-fan" and the relationship between the two. In today's convergence transmedia culture especially, we hold and perform multiple overlapping positions simultaneously. We are rarely if ever singularly a "fan" or "anti-fan" of any given text. "Fandom" amounts to participation in a range of intersecting communities and practices that at any given moment involve a multiplicity of diverse affects and investments, from hurt to hate to disenchantment to interest to amusement to love, from casual perusal to involved personalization.

Truth be told, I don't know if (beyond one's own self-identification) we can productively use "fan" or "anti-fan" as self-enclosed categories, and the same goes for "fandom" and "anti-fandom." To do so suggests divisions and invokes simplistic narratives about both that crumble when we look at the realities of media engagement in a sphere where the term "fan" has been appropriated by industry and mainstreamed in public discourse.

Let me be clear: I don't believe that there ever were simple divides between fan and anti-fan, fandom and anti-fandom, or even fan and casual viewer. But especially in contemporary media culture, we need to investigate not the divides between but the comingling of positive and negative affect in audience culture, including fan culture and anti-fan culture, however we define either. Moreover, by maintaining the fan/anti-fan divide we fuel long-standing, problematic (and gendered) misassumptions about fandom and fans. To move away from an emphasis on categories of communities or types of viewers pushes us to fundamentally let go of underlying assumptions that fans are driven by uncritical love and that any other fans or fan behaviors are exceptions that prove the rule.

Fan love is almost always in constant interplay with a spectrum of negative emotions, from ambivalence to frustration to fear to dissatisfaction to hate. Academic and popular conversations often equate fandom with uncritical celebration and love, but hate, frustration, and negative affect play key roles in fan experience. From its origins, fan studies has posited that fan engagement is born out of the need to change, fix, and add—in Henry Jenkins's words, to "scribble in the margins" (Jenkins 2013, 152). Scribbling in the margins is not just a process of celebratory addition; it is also a way of speaking back, speaking out, critiquing, revising, and even revolting. Much like the anti-fans who tear apart *Twilight* on anti-*Twilight* boards, fans can be deeply critical of a media text's narrative construction and, at times, its attendant ideological work (Pinkowitz 2011).[1] Arguably, it is precisely fans who have the vested interest and thus reason to hate at least dimensions of a television series.

In her introduction to this volume, Melissa Click draws on the work of Sara Ahmed to argue that "individuals' opposition to the hated is simultaneously constitutive of collectivity" (Click, in this volume). On a daily basis within fandom, negative affect informs the collective experience of television (Jones 2016, 53–66). Fans build communities based in part on shared dissatisfaction with the source text that has (assumedly) brought them together in the first place. Think of it this way: Every fan community that is created to focus on a single character or pairing selects that one character or romantic pairing out of the series' multiplicity, thus rejecting the larger series' scope, albeit temporarily, in favor of a more narrow focus. Fans select and prioritize particular characters and storylines for special attention. They may critique the way those characters' storylines are handled by a series, or they may simply celebrate those characters and storylines over others and by celebrating them indirectly critique the rest of the series. Not all character or relationship preferences are born out of dissatisfaction with the text as it is written; fans who, for example, "ship" a text's main narrative romantic pairing may feel confident that said pairing will be united in the end. However, displeasure still mingles with pleasure (albeit perhaps pleasurable displeasure) as fans engage with the building conflict that often accompanies a romantic storyline. In addition, even if a romantic pairing is authorized by the source text, fans may critique how the writers (or even a particular episode) handles their story or depicts their relationship.

By shifting the narrative focus and ideological work of a given source text, fan authorship channels negative fan affect into creativity. Many fan communities channel negative emotion into textual productivity—into fan fiction, art, meta analysis, videos, and the like—deconstructing and reassembling the source text into new, transformative creative works. Even when their overt purpose isn't critical, fans' selections and reassemblages emerge from dissatisfaction with the source text. For *Glee* specifically, fans critique and transform the series' narrative structure or politics, or its featured performers or performances, or both, and in so doing demonstrate their own sense of television's representational responsibility. Dissatisfied fans also model their own media literacy and arguably convey a sense of the audience's interpretative and even productive responsibility.[2] From this perspective, fan critical analyses and transformative productions function as opportunities for fans to right perceived wrongs of the source text, or to educate other fans, or to model cultural citizenship.

The last decade has seen fan modes of engagement transform from niche or cult to more mainstream. Within sites like Tumblr, YouTube, and *DeviantArt*, participants (some self-identified fans, some not) celebrate affect and emotional investment in media in what we might call a "culture of feels." In this culture of feels, participants perform emotional responses to media and to one another and, in so doing, articulate community bonds based on their playful enactment of shared investment in media narratives, characters, and storyworlds (Stein 2015, 154–160). However, this culture of feels is not only about celebration; it is also about (perhaps more about) dissatisfaction, dismay, and pain. "Right

Figure 4.1. "I need a moment" meme from *Glee*.

in the feels" images (from the meme that brought "feels" into the public lexicon) and their various variants ("my emotions!" "I need a moment") try to express what it feels like to be emotionally affected by a media text because of a plot turn or a character's emotive performance or untimely demise.[3]

In its evolving form in the last decade, negative fannish response has served as a tool weaving fan culture into the fabric of popular culture and vice versa. As we see in the work of Lev Manovich and Lawrence Lessig, digital media offer participants the tools to select and combine, to deconstruct and reassemble, and in reassembling to rewrite the raw material of commercial media and to share fan-authored revisions (Lessig 2008; Manovich 2002). As fan creativity has developed and thrived in digital contexts, media fans have developed aesthetics of selection, often driven by dissatisfaction and negative emotion, and these aesthetics of selection as performed by fans have shaped the landscape in popular media culture, modeling a specific way to engage with media. Selection is at the core of cut-and-paste culture—to cut and paste, you must first select, and to select (with intent to cut and paste) means prioritizing some element of a media text over another. In this essay, we look at how *Glee* fans select, cut, and paste in order to critique, rework, and transform unsatisfying media texts into satisfying ones and thus model the possibilities of cultural engagement with popular media in the digital age.

Dissatisfaction Goes Meta

Glee's basic premise brings together a diverse group of outsider teens who together find friendship and community within their high school glee club, including Black, White, Latina, Jewish, Asian, and disabled characters. Much of the press surrounding the show describes it as a progressive series that pushes an agenda of diversity and acceptance, with storylines that address such issues as dis/abilism, sex education, racism, interracial dating, coming out, and bullying. A *Huffington Post* (2011) article describes *Glee* as "the most progressive, boundary-pushing show on network primetime, with particular emphasis on pushing head-on the reality of high school sex, both hetero and homosexual." Popular assessments of the series celebrate its incorporation of diverse characters and its choice to give attention to social issues rarely addressed on television such as LGBTQ identity, race, teen body image, and disability. Showrunner and co-creator Ryan Murphy talked frequently about his intention to make a progressive social impact through *Glee* (see *Huffington Post* 2011). Production discourse surrounding the show continually emphasizes *Glee*'s social agenda, its intent to teach social acceptance and empathy and to provide a positive resource for teens who feel isolated and alienated for any reason.

And yet, no doubt in part because of its public claims to be a progressive text, *Glee* has fallen under attack by fans, popular cultural critics, and academics for its ideological failings. Popular-criticism and/or academically affiliated sites including *Jezebel*, *Racialicious*, *Flow*, and *Antenna* have posted critiques of *Glee*'s ideological politics, citing the series' failure to equally address the various identities invoked in its veneer of diversity. For example, in "When Will *Glee* Stop Ignoring Race?" the website *What Tami Said* argues that, by not offering substantial engagement to the issues faced by Black teen Mercedes, *Glee* simply treats "black female characters in the way they are always treated—as hook singers, as comic relief, as funny sidekicks, as advice givers, as checks on the inclusiveness scorecard, but never as fully-actualized human beings" (Harris 2011). Likewise, in "Meaningful Diversity," Mary Beltran holds *Glee* to task for offering only a veneer of diversity while upholding traditional, hegemonic values (Beltran 2010).[4] Such online commentaries take *Glee* to task for perpetuating the discursive status quo rather than enacting social change. Thus, while much press discourse celebrates *Glee*'s assumed progressiveness, the world of popular-academic criticism leans in the other direction, positing *Glee*'s regressive or ideologically conservative tendencies.[5]

It is not particularly surprising that academic (and some popular critical) discourse would critique network-driven hype about a series' social progressiveness. Academic discourse often critiques the ideological work emanating from the commercial imperatives of the media industry, and some TV critics often attune themselves to similar concerns, with increased blurring between "TV studies" scholarship and television criticism in the last decade.[6] It's perhaps more surprising—at least from someone looking from outside the fan perspective—that self-professed fans of *Glee* would do the same. And yet, why wouldn't fans take to heart the gaps in a series that claims to offer meaningful representation of diverse perspectives? Especially if a series professes to represent the underrepresented and to offer viewers an "authentic" vision of teen experience, and even to serve as an advocate for social change, why wouldn't we expect fans to assess how *Glee* is doing on those fronts and to be frustrated or hurt when the series falls short of living up to its self-stated goals?[7] Fans frequently express dismay, hurt, and betrayal at *Glee*'s representational choices in a wide range of ways, explicitly in written criticism and implicitly in creative work. Fans channel their negative responses to parts or all of *Glee* in what they call "meta" analysis and into fan fiction, art, video, and activism.

Like the popular or popular-academic criticism found on sites such as *Jezebel*, fans write meta critiques that analyze *Glee*'s ideological failings; for example, FicDirectory (2013) suggests that *Glee*'s depiction of wheelchair-wielding Artie falls short because the *Glee* creators fail to present Artie as a full individual beyond his disability.[8] FicDirectory extrapolates to emphasize that her analysis matters because representations matter—they reveal underlying prejudice and shore up that prejudice week after week, and they alienate viewers like herself who hoped that *Glee* would be more successful in capturing the challenges faced by a wider range of teenagers:

> Representation DOES matter. (To quote an approximation of Brittany: "It matters so much I can't believe it.") You know what I think it is? (And this has literally taken me YEARS to be able to articulate . . .) I think it's the fact that, to me, Artie's character and storylines are missing an authentic voice in the writers. Kurt as a character is so very accessible and deep and his experiences—positive and negative—are rooted in a real place. Because so many of them come from Ryan Murphy's heart and soul and experience growing up. With Artie, I feel like I am faced, every week with the writers' interpretation of people in wheelchairs. And whether they know it consciously or not, their prejudice shows through.

Ficdirectory's analysis of Artie contrasts *Glee*'s representation of Artie to the more nuanced representation of Kurt—who himself is perhaps an arguably more successful (as the author puts it, "deep") representation that rises above common stereotypes of gay males and gay male teen experience. Ficdirectory's critique demonstrates how fan criticism often does not take a singular stance but, rather, approaches a television text as necessarily multiplicitous, and the result of a combination of individual and collective authorship. Like much of fan criticism, while stemming from frustration and disappointment, Ficdirectory's analysis does not condemn all of *Glee* outright; rather, it critiques with the vision of what a better *Glee* could look like or, perhaps less optimistically, could have looked like with more diversity on its writing staff.

Fan criticism often explores the various ideological meanings possibly at play, emphasizing their possibility rather than their definitiveness, thus acknowledging moments of potentially resonant representation that coexist alongside (potentially) problematic or limited ones, all dependent on viewer interpretation. Even when a post offers a strong, singular critical perspective, comments often lead to discussions that offer a multiplicity of positions. For example, Racheline Maltese's "*Glee*: Gender, Violence, and Power" considers the way in which a particular storyline/episode in *Glee*'s third season depicts teen peer violence as gendered (Maltese 2012a). Again, the author takes the opportunity to assess the series' approach to the ideological work of representation:

Glee has always been a story about a terrible place in which to be a girl, or gay, or disabled, or different in any way. That makes people angry often, largely because the show doesn't tell us bullying is bad, but merely shows us it is awful and exists largely without correction. But as the adult world encroaches as the stakes get bigger, at least 3.11 reminds us that the powers that be know the only way up is out.

Maltese argues that the dark narrative of the episode in question (which features violent bullying) represents *Glee* creators' larger critique of the bigotism facing teens in school settings and small towns. By arguing that the *Glee* writers at least momentarily convey the idea "that the only way up is out," Maltese reads *Glee*'s ongoing (sometimes seemingly uncritical) representations of bullying as part of the larger critical perspective of "the powers that be"—that is, of the series' creators. She suggests that this underlying critical perspective—usually left latent, for readers to fill in—comes to the fore as direct critique in this episode's troubling depiction of misogynistic and homophobic violence.

In so doing, Maltese's already nuanced critical perspective opens a space for a further multiplicity of critical perspectives and responses. Thus, in a responding post, B. Binaohan (2012) argues that, while bringing visibility to the gendered dimensions of violence, *Glee* uncritically reproduces stereotypical narratives of racial violence and racial submission, narratives with long and lethal media histories:

Of course, many people are already saying how sweet it is that Blaine sacrifices himself for Kurt. Which would be sweet if it were not entirely expected that characters of colour (in TV and movies) always martyr themselves to save white people. It is one of the few acts of heroism allowed PoC [people of color] in the media: we are only noble when saving or upholding institutions of whiteness.[9]

Maltese and Binaohan both offer their interpretations as part of a critique of the larger media landscape and histories of representation of race in film and television. These analyses exemplify the way fans express their personal dissatisfaction with a series in part, without necessarily turning their backs on the series as a whole. They also model how fans perform and share their own frustration as media literacy, including knowledge of ideological tropes in media, and moreover they demonstrate the way these critiques happen as part of an ongoing conversation, a process of iterative meaning making and collective education that extends far beyond the initial reception of the TV series.[10]

Dissatisfaction Spurs Creation

Overt meta discourse is not the only way fans express the ebb and flow of their dissatisfaction with the series' ideological failings. They also channel their dislike into the production of creative fiction, art, and video.[11] In addition, authorial comments to the reader and reader responses to fan creative works also serve as spaces where fans articulate their frustration or disappointment with a series.

In the case of *Glee*, some works of fan fiction take care to explicitly call out *Glee*'s inadequacies, especially as a moral or progressive text, and/or to punish characters for their homophobic bullying, or to educate and rehabilitate characters whose ignorance remains intact in *Glee*. Such stories make explicit latent social critiques that *Glee* makes available but does not quite follow through on. For example, by bringing us inside Kurt's perspective, the multichapter fan fiction work *Come Here Boy* calls out *Glee*'s faculty advisor, Will Shuester, for his passivity and complicity in the face of the homophobic bullying that the teen Kurt Hummel encounters at school and in Glee Club (SugaKane01 2011):

> After he'd effectively missed first period, Kurt walked into Glee . . . and was once again subjected to backhanded insults about his sexuality. . . . Mr. Schue, per his usual modus operandi, did nothing to step in and merely allowed Santana's little barb about gay jokes while Kurt sat in his seat and pretended it didn't bother him that he wasn't even safe when he was supposedly among friends. . . . It was all Kurt could do to simply call the man out on his willingness to ignore the homophobia displayed on a daily basis in his own classroom.

This description presents a scene that viewers will recognize from *Glee*, given that *Come Here Boy* plays with the official storyline rather than throwing it out entirely. Because fan fiction allows us access to characters' inner monologues, we are here privy to Kurt's emotional experience of the scene (as the author imagines/presents it), and from his perspective we hold Mr. Schuester accountable as a teacher for not stepping in to help/protect Kurt and to make his classroom and the educational system a space free from homophobia and bullying. But we also hold *Glee* responsible for not holding Schuester responsible in the same way that *Come Here Boy* does. *Come Here Boy* thus poses the following question: If this fan fiction story can critique Mr. Schuester's leniency with homophobia, why can't *Glee*?

Fan fiction integrates cultural, social, and political literacy in overt ways that *Glee* (perhaps out of concern for being labeled as too didactic) does not. *Come Here Boy* invokes the organization PFLAG (Parents, Families, Friends, Allies United with LGBT) to recuperate a character whose homophobia *Glee* arguably lets slide. In the television series, Kurt's new stepbrother Finn's homophobia surfaces in moments of high emotion to be forgiven in a couple of episodes. In the fan fiction series, Finn and his parents decide to go to PFLAG to, in Finn's words, "get educated." Finn tells Kurt: "I was on the computer earlier and I looked up some stuff . . . the site that I was on said the first step to combating ignorance is education . . . so I'm getting educated" (SugaKane01 2011).

But this story resists even letting Finn's intent to educate himself serve as a happy resolution to a potentially unresolvable problem. Kurt tells Finn, "I don't think there's a short cut here. It's not Glee. We can't sing a song and make it all better. It's just gonna take time and work and a lot of more talking and possibly more yelling" (SugaKane01 2011). Kurt's response critiques Glee's entrenchment in the pacing and ideological narrative structure of Glee as a television series, albeit displaced onto the norms of the (diegetic) Glee Club. But the wink and a nod to the reader comes through quite clearly here: It is *Glee* (the TV series) that offers and sets unrealistic expectations for easy and inevitable closure and forward progress. Such fan performances of knowing critique serve to demonstrate, model, and spread media literacy as a shared cultural stance.

Other works of fan fiction offer their critique in less direct but still quite pervasive ways, as they model alternate representational strategies. Many fans write fan fiction that focuses on one pairing at the expense of others or that rejects major plot developments in a series. For *Glee*, many fan fiction stories focus on Kurt Hummel and his romantic entanglement with season 2 newcomer Blaine Anderson. Season 2 of *Glee* introduces the idyllic Dalton Academy as a sort of queer utopia, a private school haven where Kurt finds acceptance in an all-boys choir and love with crooner Blaine. However, *Glee* limits Dalton to a secondary and temporary story-line and narrative space, a space from which Kurt must eventually return to be reintegrated into the multiplicity of the public McKinley High. In contrast, many works of fan fiction, including the very popular fan fiction series *Dalton* (or what is known among readers as the "Daltonverse"), set Dalton as the main space and narrative focus and do not return Kurt or the plot to McKinley High (CP Coulter 2010). In *Dalton* this significant plot divergence functions as an indirect critique of *Glee*'s representational choices and their ideological implications. The author, CP Coulter, describes *Dalton* as a spin-off show. In her opening authorial notes, she pays deference to the *Glee* authors, even as she announces her intent to take their characters and narrative premise in a different direction:

> The idea of this came from turning over ideas in my head about what Kurt and Blaine's life in Dalton might be like. . . . So in fair warning, I think I can safely say that this "Dalton" will not be following *Glee* continuity. All the better for it, I imagine—the writers are fantastic and they've got one hell of a hit going, and this work is at best, a dilution of that excellence. [CP Coulter 2010]

Despite this dissembling, *Dalton* offers itself as a *Glee* replacement, or at least competition, by mimicking *Glee*'s televisual format, unfolding in "episodes" that are punctuated with musical numbers just like in *Glee* itself. This structuring of *Dalton* as a TV musical series even though it is (fan-)written word rather than musical live action broadcast television pays homage to *Glee*. Yet at the same time, the inclusion of "musical numbers" within "episodes" establishes *Dalton* ontologically/phenomenologically as *Glee*'s equal/competitor/better, since it recreates the TV format but follows the narrative and characterization lines of fans' desires.[12] *Dalton* also features "original" characters and pairings who are given as much time as the characters from the TV series. No surprise then, perhaps, that the Daltonverse developed its own fandom beyond *Glee*, offering some a haven from a show that seemed to continually offer false promise.

In their reviews at *FanFiction* website, fans revel in the mimicry of the Daltonverse, indicating that Dalton is (or at least imagines what would be) a better version of *Glee*. For example:

> Epic. Seriously. Best Klaine story on the site! Wish they would really turn this into a spin off. That would be awesome! :D Can't wait for the next "episode," so please update soon!

> This is honestly one of the best things I have ever ever read. It feeeels like I'm watching a show.

> Oh my gosh! Just read chapters 1–5 and I luv this story to death! They need to have this on TV! It would be favorite show ever. [*FanFiction*, n.d.]

These effusive comments (of which there are many) indirectly and directly function as critiques of *Glee*. Fans of *Dalton* indicate that it should be canon or is "better than canon." "Canon" is the fan term for the officially authored, officially released version of a source text and therefore is the version with narrative authority. For example, one reviewer of CP Coulter's *Dalton* on *FanFiction* wrote "OMG I love this! I've been craving for Dalton boys fanfics for a few days now and I have to say this one's one of my faves. :) All-boys school drama/adventures are exciting, yeah? :D And crazy Dalton boys SHOULD BE CANON DAMMIT. LOL! Looking forward to your next update! :D." It is a short journey from a comment such as this celebrating *Dalton* to comments that in the same move denigrate *Glee* in comparison. This intertwining of celebration and critique is amplified by the fact that *Dalton* and *Glee* were both released serially at the same time, inviting comparison between the two contrasting visions of a somewhat shared narrative space:

> This story is amazing. . . . But I am sad knowing that anything they put on the show won't be as cool as this.

> Can you do us a favor and DO NOT change your original plot, whatever happens to Special Education tonight? Because from the previews, Dalton doesn't look like that much fun.

I. LOVE. THIS. I hate it when fanfic!Glee is better than Reallife!Glee.

I am loving your story, your version of Dalton sounds so much more fun than the one in Glee.

I LOVE these boys! They are so much more awesome than the stuffy ones on the show. Is it okay if i pretend that this is how it actually works, and just ignore the conformist ones from the canon? except Blaine, because i could spend forever looking at Darren Criss' face . . . haha. [*FanFiction*, n.d.]

These comments (and again these are a small sampling of many similar ones) exemplify how fan celebration of *Dalton* as a series comes hand in hand with dissatisfaction and critique of the official TV series version of *Glee*. But these comments also get at how complicated and nonsingular fan engagement is—with *Glee* and with *Dalton*. One comment from above especially encapsulates the complex nature of fan response: "I. LOVE. THIS. I hate it when fanfic!Glee is better than Realife!Glee."[13] This comment suggests that there's a displeasure ("I hate it when . . .") and longing even in the pleasure, in the awareness of the gap between fan fiction/fan desire and the official televisual text.

Indeed, this range of emotion, including dissatisfaction and hurt, plays out in fan response to fan creations as well, especially to serial ones that take on the weight of desired canon. Many of the comments posted in response to *Dalton* encompass a wide range of emotion, especially in the sometimes multiyear gaps between chapters, for example, using anonymity to express frustration, as in a "guest" response to chapter 27 (and the long delay before chapter 28): "FUCKING UPDATE NOW." Fans also fold frustration into their celebration after the fact, as in another reviewer's response to the eventual posting of chapter 28: "The emotional rollarcoaster I went through! This . . . , this was worth the wait!" These comments mirror the play with pleasure and frustration that fans experience that make them turn to fan fiction in the first place.[14]

Dissatisfaction Transforms

As a fan fiction series composed of text rather than sound and moving image, *Dalton* mimics the tropes of the televisual in order to emulate and yet compete with the series. In contrast, fans working with digital video can critique *Glee* in its own medium (or close to it) and can use editing to dismantle the video source text in order to express frustration and critique.

For example, the *Glee* Equality Project (GEP)—a fan-coordinated online network that campaigns for more equitable representation of identity—creates videos that work to simultaneously educate their viewers and lobby for representational change.[15] One GEP video visually categorizes the number of gay-versus-straight kisses on *Glee* to show that the series censors its representation of nonstraight sexuality (*Glee* Equality Project 2012a). This video uses a split screen to depict the cumulative progression and growing tally of straight-versus-nonstraight representations. Another video points out the inequity between the series' depiction of straight and nonstraight intimacy using a combination of images and text to argue that *Glee* limits gay intimacy to public space and makes sure gay characters are "chaperoned" to reduce their implicit threat of depicting gay sexuality (*Glee* Equality Project 2012b).

Both of these videos critique *Glee* and express frustration and disappointment, but they also (*a*) campaign to change *Glee* and (*b*) teach their viewers how to critique representation. Thus their primary purpose appears to be to drive media literacy, with the underlying assumption that media literacy will breed viewer frustration, which will instigate further viewer activism, which will in turn trigger change. These videos convey critique, but critique with the intent to change *Glee*'s flaws into strengths, to help *Glee* to become what it has the promise to be. They use video, the medium of *Glee* (or at least, close to it), to campaign for change, and they situate their desire for change in the goals of the series itself. In so doing they acknowledge the complexity and multiple drives and intent of a television series.

Certainly, in contrast with the GEP's videos, much fan video work at first glance appears to be primarily celebratory, at least of particular storylines or characters. However, as I suggested earlier, singling out a particular storyline arguably results in an indirect dismissal of the rest, a dismissal that may be driven by frustration or displeasure or disinterest. Fans make videos that celebrate particular pairings: in *Glee*'s case, for example, Kurt and Blaine, known by fans as "Klaine," and Brittany and Santana, known by fans as "Brittana." YouTube videos like "Every Klaine

Scene Ever" sew together only the scenes featuring Kurt and Blaine, facilitating fans' selective consumption and releasing these characters and
plotlines from their place within *Glee*'s multiplicitous serial collective.
This is one example of many instances in which *Glee* fans have compiled
footage featuring only Kurt and Blaine to create an alternate text, thus
undermining *Glee*'s larger narrative arcs. With every change in digital
distribution and fan online engagement, new instances have emerged,
from downloadable files to a Tumblr dedicated to embedding these
scenes. Such acts of postproduction and curation demonstrate how
viewer preference can instigate transformative production when combined with access to the necessary tools and modes of distribution.[16]

Fan video work can also direct dissatisfaction beyond the source text.
Remixing multiple sources facilitates larger cultural critiques using fan
authorship traditions. For example, Anoel's fanvid (a remix video of a
visual source text set to a musical soundtrack) "I Love It" speaks back to
those who profess to hate *Glee* for its liberalism and those who dismiss
it as trashy instead of "quality" television (Anoel 2013). The video splices
footage from *Glee* with footage representing other television series, footage of *Glee*'s press coverage, and online representations of fan engagement, synthesizing these varied sources into a carefully orchestrated
flow of moving images against the musical background of Icona Pop's "I
Love It!" Icona Pop's anthem sets a musical tone of playful righteous indignation, directed at those who put down *Glee* and *Glee* fans. This video
criticizes television critics, depicting images from critical darlings *Ar-
rested Development*, *The Wire*, and *Breaking Bad* and declaring them to
be "on another track"; it also attacks conservative critics ("you're in the
seventies"), in contrast celebrating the playful and in-your-face digitally
savvy and liberalism of *Glee* fans ("I'm up in space / a nineties bitch.")
The video ends in a frenetic celebration of *Glee* fandom, depicting visual
images of *Glee* fans intercut with the series itself, all celebrated in opposition to *Glee* haters. Anoel's fanvid celebrates *Glee* wholeheartedly,
defending it from its many detractors, but this video's celebratory flow
also serves as a frustrated critique of popular/critical culture's attempts
to rein in the progressive transgressions of *Glee* and fandom. Anoel's vid
may seem like an unambivalent celebration of *Glee*, but it still stands
as testament to the way in which negative and positive emotions inform fans' engagement with media culture, and moreover it asserts

the multifannishness of media experience and emotional engagement. Fans do not engage with single media texts in a vacuum; rather, they experience them and their surrounding fan cultures as continuous, and continuously transforming, conversations that necessarily contain an ever-fluctuating range of positive and negative emotions. Future study of anti-fandom and the role of negative affect in fandom could greatly benefit from a wider perspective that acknowledges not only the inter-mingling of love, critique, hate, ambivalence, and disaffection but also the interdependence and multiplicity of the mediasphere.

Conclusion

I hope that the cumulative picture I have drawn here conveys the way in which fan critiques do not exist in strict separation from fan love but are rather part and parcel of the fan process of engagement and creative pro-duction and make their home in fan spaces driven by love for characters, plotlines, and even the overarching goals of a series' or of its creators. Fan love and frustration are nuanced and flexible, based on informed media literacy that combines textual close reading and community debate with an awareness of the multifaceted nature of media produc-tion. In their often quite extended performances of critique, including critique channeled into the creation of written fiction and video, fans showcase their media literacy and demonstrate their informed engage-ment with the complex dance of narrative and ideology at work in much of contemporary TV.

Only by moving beyond assumptions that fandom and anti-fandom are separate and mutually exclusive categories can we fully engage with the nuanced processes of audience engagement. Understanding hurt, anger, rejection, bitterness, critique, and disgust as part of fandom opens up a fuller view of fan engagement, of the ebb and flow of individual fan experiences, and of the work of fan communities. It also encourages us to bring a wider set of questions to fan and audience work: How can we understand the role of avatar, meme, GIFset, and comment (not to men-tion fan fiction, art, and video) within a palette of engagement that in-cludes a full range of positive and negative and, most important, mixed response? From this wider perspective, anti-fans as separate commu-nity become not a different animal from fandom entirely but rather another instance of audience engagement, albeit with more negative tone to the palette in play. Negative or even anti-fannish feelings can exist right alongside positive fannish feelings within the same community or within the same fan. This approach also allows us to understand the fascination, if not love, that colors some anti-fan activity. Overcoming the cultural assumptions that underlie simplistic fan/anti-fan dichotomies opens the way for a more nuanced approach to the study of audience communities, be they labeled "fandom," "anti-fandom," or something else entirely.

NOTES

1 For more on anti-fandom, see also Gray (2003, 2005); and Gray and Murray (2016).
2 For more on this, see Booth (2014).
3 For more on this, see Kayley (2013). For discussions of *Glee* fandom online, see Wood and Baughman (2012); and Marwick, Gray, and Ananny (2014).
4 See also Doty (2010).
5 In more conservative venues, press and popular discourse attack rather than celebrate *Glee*'s assumed progressiveness, but in so doing these responses still affirm notions of *Glee* as a progressive text. For example, see Goldberg (2011); and Brown (2011).
6 On the evolving world of TV criticism, see Corner (2006); Ryan (2011); and Seitz (2013).
7 For scholarship that addresses ambivalence within fandom, see the discussion of *The West Wing* fan response in Williams (2015), 81–92. Also see Lothian's (2008) discussion on slash fan fiction and queer female space and race; and Wanzo's (2015) discussion of African American fandom and hip hop.
8 For another discussion of this topic, see Kociemba (2010).
9 Soon after his introduction to the series, fans interpreted Blaine's character as non-White and have debated the significance of his character's intersectional identity, as well as *Glee*'s unwillingness to explicitly address Blaine's experience as a person of color. See Maltese (2012b).
10 These are but a couple of examples of the countless instances of fan "meta" that weave appreciation and dissatisfaction to differing degrees in an ongoing process of analysis and productive critical conversation. Indeed, full websites exist, such as *Deconstructing Glee* (http://deconstructingglee.com) and *Fuck Yeah Glee Meta!* (http://fyeahgleemeta.tumblr.com), where fans congregate to analyze and critique the series by episode and concept.
11 Much literature in fan studies has described the resistive, co-optive, interpretive, or interventionist dimensions of fandom. For an example and overview, see Hellekson and Busse (2014), 8–9. On fan remix as intervention, see Coppa (2008).

12 Because of this ontological parallel, I italicize *Dalton* the way I would a television series, and I do so with any long-form fan fiction that fans engage with as its own entity, complete with its own extensions, etc.

13 Likewise, the comment that critiques *Glee*'s representation of the Dalton boys as "stuffy" and "conformist" also celebrates an individual among them—Darren Criss, the actor who plays love interest Blaine.

14 Indeed, the Daltonverse has inspired its own fan fiction, including a community on *FanFiction* and another on Tumblr. One author on *FanFiction* has even taken up the nomer (user name) "CP Coulter Writes My Canon" and has published fifteen fan fiction stories that build off the Daltonverse specifically, rather than *Glee*.

15 To see the network and videos, visit the *Glee* Equality Project website at http://glee-equality-project.tumblr.com.

16 As fans are quite concerned that this type of reediting might not be considered fair use (although I would argue that these rearticulations are significantly transformative), I will not provide direct links to these sites. For a discussion of issues of citation in fandom and the choice not to provide direct links, see Busse and Hellekson (2012).

REFERENCES

Anoel. 2013. "I Love It." YouTube, August 19. www.youtube.com/watch?v=nZrDYmx2Wdk.

Beltran, M. 2010. "Meaningful Diversity: Exploring Questions of Equitable Representation on Diverse Ensemble Cast Shows." *Flow*, August 27. www.flowjournal.org.

Binaohan, B. 2012. "*Glee* 3 × 11: Gendered Violence? Yes, But Let's Not Forget about Race." *Biyuti Publishing*, February 1. https://publishbiyuti.org.

Booth, P. J. 2014. "Fandom: The Classroom of the Future." In "Transnationalism, Localization, and Translation in European Fandom," special issue, edited by Anne Kustritz. *Transformative Works and Cultures*, no. 19. doi: 10.3983/twc.2015.0650.

Brown, E. R. 2011. "'Glee': Sex, Songs and Sleaze." *NewsBusters*, February 3. www.newsbusters.org.

Busse, K., and K. Hellekson. 2012. "Identity, Ethics, and Fan Privacy." In *Fan Culture: Theory/Practice*, edited by K. Larsen and L. Zubernis, 38–56. Newcastle upon Tyne: Cambridge Scholar Publishing.

Click, M. A. In this volume. "Introduction: Haters Gonna Hate."

Coppa, F. 2008. "Women, *Star Trek*, and the Early Development of Fannish Vidding." *Transformative Works and Cultures*, no. 1. doi: 10.3983/twc.2008.0044.

Corner, J. 2006. "Television and the Practice of 'Criticism.'" *Flow*, September 22. www.flowjournal.org.

CP Coulter. 2010. *Dalton* (series). *FanFiction*, November 29. www.fanfiction.net.

Doty, A. 2010. "*Modern Family*, *Glee*, and the Limits of Television Liberalism." *Flow*, September 24. www.flowjournal.org.

FanFiction. n.d. "Reviews for Dalton." www.fanfiction.net, accessed February 27, 2018.

FicDirectory. 2013. "Tonia Says: *Glee* Meta: On Disability, Accommodations, Representation and Characterization." Tumblr, June 17. http://ficdirectory.tumblr.com/post/53203408220/glee-meta-on-disability-accommodations.

Glee Equality Project. 2012a. "*Glee* Equality Project—Season 3 Kiss Compilation." YouTube, June 18. www.youtube.com/watch?v=iIEhcB8030c.

———. 2012b. "*Glee* Equality Project—Public vs. Private Scenes." YouTube, June 10. www.youtube.com/watch?v=_joNZZhKbaw.

Goldberg, L. 2011. "Parents Television Council Blasts 'Glee's' 'First Time' Episode." *Hollywood Reporter*, November 8. www.hollywoodreporter.com.

Gray, J. 2003. "New Audiences, New Textualities: Anti-Fans and Non-Fans." *International Journal of Cultural Studies* 6:64–81. doi: 10.1177/1367877903006001004.

———. 2005. "Antifandom and the Moral Text: *Television Without Pity* and Textual Dislike." *American Behavioral Scientist* 48:840–858. doi: 10.1177/0002764204273171.

———. In this volume. "How Do I Dislike Thee? Let Me Count the Ways."

Gray, J., and S. Murray. 2016. "Hidden: Studying Media Dislike and Its Meaning." *International Journal of Cultural Studies* 19, no. 4:357–372. doi: 10.1177/1367877915572223.

Harris, T. W. 2011. "When Will *Glee* Stop Ignoring Race?" *What Tami Said*, April 27. www.whattamisaid.com, accessed August, 2016. No longer available online.

Hellekson, K., and K. Busse. 2014. "Introduction: Why a Fan Fiction Studies Reader Now?" In *The Fan Fiction Studies Reader*, edited by K. Hellekson and K. Busse, 1–18. Iowa City: University of Iowa Press.

Huffington Post. 2011. "'Glee' Creator Ryan Murphy Talks Death Threats, Regrets, Controversy," August 5. www.huffingtonpost.com.

Jenkins, H. 2013. *Textual Poachers: Television Fans and Participatory Culture*. Updated 20th anniversary ed. New York: Routledge. Originally published 1992.

Jones, B. 2016. "'I Will Throw You off Your Ship and You Will Drown and Die': Death Threats, Intra-Fandom Hate, and the Performance of Fangirling." In *Seeing Fans: Representations of Fandom in Media and Popular Culture*, edited by L. Bennett and P. Booth, 53–66. New York: Bloomsbury Publishing.

Kayley, T. 2013. "Revisioning the Smiling Villain: Imagetexts and Intertextual Expression in Representations of the Filmic Loki on Tumblr." In "Appropriating, Interpreting, and Transforming Comic Books," special issue, edited by Matthew J. Costello. *Transformative Works and Cultures*, no. 13. doi:10.3983/twc.2013.0474.

Kociemba, D. 2010. "'This Isn't Something I Can Fake': Reactions to *Glee*'s Representations of Disability." *Transformative Works and Cultures*, no. 5. doi: 10.3983/twc.2010.0225.

Lessig, L. 2008. *Remix: Making Art and Commerce Thrive in the Hybrid Economy*. New York: Penguin.

Lothian, A. 2008. "Televisual Transformation and Its Discontents: Slash Fan Fiction, 'Queer Female Space' and Race." *Queer Geek Theory*, April 27. www.queergeektheory.org.

Maltese, R. 2012a. "*Glee*: Gender, Violence, and Power." *Letters from Titan* (blog), February 1. http://lettersfromtitan.com.

———. 2012b. "*Glee*: Passing and the Ongoing Disappearance of Blaine Anderson." *Letters from Titan* (blog), October 11. http://lettersfromtitan.com.

Manovich, L. 2002. *The Language of New Media*. Boston: MIT Press.

Marwick, A., M. Gray, and M. Ananny. 2014. "'Dolphins Are Just Gay Sharks': *Glee* and the Queer Case of Transmedia as Text and Object." *Television and New Media*, vol. 15, no. 7. doi: 10.1177/1527476413478493.

Pinkowitz, J. 2011. "'The Rabid Fans That Take [*Twilight*] Much Too Seriously': The Construction and Rejection of Excess in *Twilight* Antifandom." *Transformative Works and Cultures*, no. 7. doi: 10.3983/twc.2011.0247.

Ryan, M. 2011. "How to Be a TV Critic." *Huffington Post*, December 14. www.huffingtonpost.com.

Seitz, M. Z. 2013. "Seitz: There Has Never Been a Better Time for TV Criticism." *Vulture*, August 20. www.vulture.com.

Stein, L. 2015. *Millennial Fandom*. Iowa City: University of Iowa Press.

SugaKane01. 2011. *Come Here Boy. FanFiction*, December 28. www.fanfiction.net.

Wanzo, R. 2015. "African American Acafandom and Other Strangers: New Genealogies of Fan Studies." *Transformative Works and Cultures*, no. 20. doi: 10.3983/twc.2015.0699.

Williams, R. 2015. *Post Object Fandom: Television, Identity, and Self-Narrative*. New York: Bloomsbury Academic, 81–92.

Wood, M., and L. Baughman. 2012. "*Glee* Fandom and Twitter: Something New, or More of the Same Old Thing?" *Communication Studies* 63, no. 3:328–344.

5

Anti-Fandom Meets Ante-Fandom

Doctor Who *Fans' Textual Dislike and "Idiorrhythmic" Fan Experiences*

MATT HILLS

In this chapter, I want to focus on audiences' self-narratives, particularly considering how fan identity tends to be discursively divided into two phases by people—there is a time "before" participatory community (often in childhood) and a time "after" relevant interpretive communities have affected the self (usually through organized/online fandom). This structuring division means that fan identities are often marked by internalized tensions and/or negotiations between selves and communities, suggesting that to posit "fandom" as a singularly positive or coherent "love" against which anti-fandom can be assessed is necessarily problematic (Duffett 2014). Instead, I argue that we need to address fandom itself as torn between discursive constructs of untutored and tutored phases, or what I am terming "ante-fandom" and socialized/mentored fandom. Following this argument, conceptualizations of anti-fandom are perhaps in danger of becoming overly one-dimensional if they don't acknowledge, and factor in, the related "ante-fandom" through which fans defend their "naïve" tastes—likings that are otherwise devalued or even attacked by sections of socially organized fandom. My purpose in introducing a notion of "ante-fandom" here is not to argue that this should somehow replace a focus on anti-fandom but, rather, that anti-fandom, as a concept, would benefit from taking on a more thoroughly temporal or even longitudinal aspect. I would say that, to date, anti-fandom has frequently been considered in an implicitly synchronic way, taken to indicate a present visceral dislike through which cultural identity is performed in a given moment. By relating work on anti-fandom to what I'm calling "ante-fandom," I am suggesting that specific cultural dislikes can be related to the histories and the different generations of audiences who collide within a particular and long-running fan culture (that surrounding the TV show *Doctor Who*). As Melissa Click argues, we need a far greater sense of exactly "what emotions *do* in fan practices" (Click, in this volume; emphasis in original), and in line with this call, I am suggesting that fan affects can circulate as a way of demarcating different fan generations.

In a sense, difficulties begin with the "atomic" model that's adopted as "a visualizing tool" by Jonathan Gray when he first sets out the notion of anti-fandom (Gray 2003, 68); indeed, the weaknesses of this extended metaphor are accepted, and newly complicated, by Gray himself (see Gray, in this volume). The "atomic" model creates an impression of "positive" fan protons versus "negative" anti-fan electrons, leading to a situation in which Gray's attentive readers are led to ask whether these affects might in fact be more fluid, blended, or processual than the model implies (Click 2007, 313), as well as whether "positive" and "negative" affects can be oscillated between or performed differently in different contexts (Sheffield and Merlo 2010, 220). Equating a "positive" charge with fandom (Goletz 2012, 148) also neglects the complaining, the disappointment, the agitation, and the sheer bloody-mindedness that can be associated with long-term fandoms as they evaluate current media products against "golden ages" in "their" show's past (Tulloch and Jenkins 1995). It is this consensus building, always leaving room for negotiation between varied fan likes and visceral dislikes, that especially interests me here (McKee 2001).

One puzzle of anti-fandom is that, rather like "the fan," it sounds as though it should nominate and capture a single referent. Although fan studies has pretty much demolished that commonsensical idea over time, it returns slightly in the figure of the "anti-fan," meaning that a number of writers have worried away at the concept, stretching—or more precisely, defining it—to cover different empirical cases. As a result, we get the "anti-fan within the fan" (Theodoropoulou 2007, 316), the mocking/critical/negotiating anti-fan (Sheffield and Merlo 2010, 210), the "ironic" anti-fan of so-bad-it's-good pop culture (Gilbert 2012, 175), and a further range of anti-fan possibilities speculatively explored by Gray in this collection (Gray, in this volume; see also Claessens and Van den Bulck 2014). Although Jonathan Gray's seminal (2003) article in the

International Journal of Cultural Studies set out one central idea of the anti-fan—a distant reader who forms his or her image of the disliked text via paratexts (see also Gray 2010)—even then, that account certainly allowed for the possibility that

> fans can become anti-fans of a sort when an episode or part of a text is perceived as harming a text as a whole. . . . Behind dislike, after all, there are always expectations—of what a text should be like, of what is a waste of media time and space. [Gray 2003,73]

Both distant- and close-reading anti-fans are acknowledged here. However, this acknowledgment means that, from its very inception as a term, anti-fandom is somewhat divided into variants. One of these, where "fans can become anti-fans of a sort," highlights that an element of anti-fandom is likely to always-already be present within the frustrations, aggravations and textual critiques demarcating ongoing experiences and discourses of fandom (the positive/negative atomic metaphor obscures this somewhat, as Gray now concedes). Gray's opening salvo on the topic plus the subsequent refinements of other scholars also suggest that anti-fandom really requires a detailed taxonomy: of degrees, of distant or close readers, of qualia (is it earnest/ironic?), of the extent to which a specific anti-fandom might in fact be fan-culturally normative (e.g., it is expected that *Star Trek* fans will dislike series 3 of *The Original Series* or that *Star Wars* fans will dislike *The Phantom Menace*). Any such taxonomy could also consider the extent to which an anti-fandom may be culturally normative, for example reinscribing notions of detested "low" culture or reinforcing valorized "rational" responses versus devalued "emotional" readings of popular culture.

In order to tease out the specific relationship between the "anti-fan within the fan" (Theodoropoulou 2007, 316) and ameliorating, temporal discourses of ante-fandom, I examine how the anti-fandom of close-reading, non-ironic *Doctor Who* fans plays out in relation to different generations of fandom, given that this BBC TV show began in 1963 and celebrated its fiftieth anniversary on November 23, 2013 (despite being off the air between December 6, 1989, and March 26, 2005, bar one 1996 TV movie). Many *Doctor Who* fans have grown up watching the science fiction series, and age can therefore tend to be a predictor of one's favorite Doctor (the role having been played by thirteen different actors to date on TV, barring special cases such as John Hurt's "War Doctor"). Unusually, *Doctor Who*'s lead character, the Doctor, has the capacity to "regenerate" and take on a different physical appearance; diegetically, this is explained as being one of the attributes possessed by Time Lords from the planet Gallifrey (the race the Doctor belongs to). Consequently, although the role was originally played from 1963 by William Hartnell, he was replaced by Patrick Troughton in 1966, who in turn gave way to Jon Pertwee when the program moved into color in 1970. Tom Baker then became the fourth Doctor in 1974, before bowing out in 1981, with Peter Davison taking over. Other 1980s Doctors included the sixth and seventh incarnations played by Colin Baker and Sylvester McCoy, respectively, before Paul McGann took on the mantle in a 1996 TV movie. And when the show was reimagined for a 2005 audience by BBC Wales, Christopher Eccleston assumed the lead role for one series before David Tennant and then Matt Smith were cast. At the time of writing, Peter Capaldi has completed his tenure as the twelfth Doctor, after appearing briefly in "The Day of the Doctor" and then taking on the title role properly at the conclusion of "The Time of the Doctor."

Doctor Who fanlore holds that "your Doctor"—the era to which one feels the greatest attachment—will be the one watched at a certain age: "I think it's fair to say that the 'classic era' of the show is generally the one you watched when you were twelve" (Gray 1995, 34). Fan-cultural socialization means that fans become distinctly aware of relatively normative fan-favorite Doctors (and stories)—along with generally detested phases of the show—but as I demonstrate, this discourse of learnt fandom tends to layer over, and not wholly displace, what is proclaimed and performed as the lived fandom belonging to earlier passions and engagements with the series. Consequently, rather than anti-fandom operating as an external force outside *Doctor Who* fan culture, visceral dislike is directed at certain eras of the show and particular stories by fan consensus, with this then being deflected and reflexively disavowed by fans for whom the version of *Doctor Who* typically hated within fandom is in fact their beloved favorite. As such, "ante-fandom" offers one way to manage affective tensions between different generations of fans coming to *Doctor Who* at different times, therefore somewhat defusing or qualifying the pointed anti-fandom that otherwise circulates within the community. Ante-fandom also explicitly draws on a notion of temporality: It is the age of the particular fan, and the period when the fan first became fascinated by *Doctor Who*, that qualifies her or his love for this particular era of the show.

The type of anti-fandom located within fan cultures can pose a risk to group identity, threatening to fracture the community into warring factions. However, fan cultures usually draw on a value system of inclusivity and emotional togetherness (Jenkins 2013; Van den Bulck et al. 2016, 521), and so culturally managing both visceral and learnt dislike becomes a significant part of any long-running fandom such as *Doctor Who*, where, for example, the Official *Doctor Who* Fan Club was formed after Keith Miller's contact with the production office in 1971 (Miller 2012), while the *Doctor Who* Appreciation Society, still running today, first emerged in 1976 (O'Day 2013). The discursive move of appraising a lead actor (and by implication, era of the program) as personally liked has even been incorporated metatextually into the special 2007 minisode, "Time Crash" (Basu 2010). Philosopher Kevin S. Decker suggests that this fan discourse had potentially entered the show's production far earlier:

> The deepening contrasts between appearances and personalities of the various Doctors in the 1980s may have been an effort by [then producer John] Nathan-Turner to recapture the 1960s and 70s phenomenon of audience identification with a particular actor, now called "my first Doctor." [Decker 2013, 12]

Although he's right to note this powerful identification between (usually) child viewers and a particular Doctor, Decker conflates "my" and "first," whereas fan discourse doesn't rigorously insist on these being one and the same:

> Tom Baker was my Doctor. I forgot about Jon Pertwee within the first ten minutes of Tom's debut. With his wild staring eyes and insane toothy grin, he was some way from the suave dandy played by . . . Pertwee, but by the time the Fourth Doctor had donned his . . . inordinately long multicoloured scarf, I was hooked. Mum thought he was "much too silly", but she was wrong. [Perryman 2013, 23–24]

Instead, the key attributes of *Doctor Who* ante-fandom are both that it is looked back on from the adult fan's knowing perspective—highly aware of how anti-fandom is currently performed normatively within the community—and that it is simultaneously expressed as an *authentic* (i.e., unlearnt or somehow socially untainted) emotional reaction. Opposable to models and theories of emotion as socially circulating (Ahmed 2004), this *narrative of individualized affect* markedly denies the role of others in shaping one's fan emotions (something that is otherwise present in the communal performances and affects of anti-fandom) and performs its authenticity precisely as a kind of asocial affect that emerges purely within the fan self. At the same time, the actor/character who is embraced doesn't need to be the very first who was watched (although see Booth [2013] on first viewings of *Doctor Who*). Specific stories can also be (re)valued by fans in this manner, as in the following examples:

> The eighties . . . was—for me—the high point of *Doctor Who*. . . . The eighties also represented the last decade in which I enjoyed the show by myself. I wasn't viewing the show through the prism of collective fandom, coming to each episode loaded down with . . . judgements. . . . It is a testament to these fandom-free viewings that I actually thought *Time-Flight* was quite good. And I still do, damn you all. [Twist 2010, 264]

> I bloody love *The Trial of a Time Lord*. Yes, really. . . . I've put my cards on the table, and I can safely assume you disagree. . . . I've always been happy to have controversial opinions and I'm always pleased to discover many of them aren't that controversial any more. . . . I'm not an apologist. I'm not a lone defender. Maybe I'm not a defender at all. I just genuinely loved this piece of television. [Monaghan 2010, 297, 301]

Such "fandom-free" viewings, cut adrift from the shifting fashions and harsh criticisms of the affective community, are hence equated with "genuinely" loving a particular part of the program before fan-cultural capital and its emotional norms have been developed and before one has been mentored in the "subtle demands placed upon . . . members of fandom—expectations about what . . . interpretations are "legitimate", and so forth" (Jenkins 2013, 88).

Ante-fandom amounts to what I've called elsewhere a kind of "two-step fandom," effectively sidestepping implications of collective fan conformity/affect via a discourse of "pre-discursive encounters" (Hills 2013b, 188; see also Hills 2005). But despite Emily Monaghan's protest above that she's perhaps "not a defender," her awareness that the serial *Trial of a Time Lord* is highly likely to be disliked by fellow fans means that such fan writing remains in self-reflexive opposition to fandom's current and dominant consensus. Similar to the *Doctor Who* canon, versions of *Who* that are detested by the community remain "discursively managed, and it is this, finally, that enables [us] . . . to account for the difference in status of various texts. . . . It is always open to challenge . . . and can . . . change over time" (McKee 2004, 183). For example, Jon Pertwee's Doctor fell greatly out of favor in the early nineties—partly as a consequence of the newfound availability of his era on video—but the pendulum of fan fashion has swung back since then, as a result of shifting fan discourses (Hills 2013a, 231; McKee 2001, 13). Writing in 1993 Dave Owen warned at the time: "Try walking into a gathering of British *Doctor Who* fans . . . and saying that your favourite part of *Doctor Who* history is the Jon Pertwee stories and you are likely to be laughed out of court [by] . . . all the Pertweehaters" (Owen 2010, 104).

Although *Who* fandom is stratified along all sorts of lines (specialisms in fan activity, e.g., reviewing or writing fanfic; U.S. versus UK fandom; classic versus "new *Who*" fandom; gendered differences, etc.), age remains a significant factor owing to the program's longevity (Hadas 2009) allied with fluctuating norms of fan interpretation. Paul Booth and Peter Kelly interviewed 110 attendees (of the 1,100 present) at the Chicago TARDIS Convention and found older fans musing on the influx of young newbies:

> Those of us who are the old guard . . . were going to conventions in the nineties and noughties when there was no series [on TV]. . . . And so, we're the hardcore fans. . . . With the new series, now there's thousands of people coming to the conventions. You feel sort of crotchety, who are these kids? They don't even know who Jon Pertwee [the actor portraying the third Doctor] is. . . . It's all good because a lot of them are coming to you. ["]Well you were into the old series, which DVD should I buy[?"] . . .

It's coming full circle so you feel like you're the mentor figures. ["Chris,"
quoted in Booth and Kelly 2013, 62]

Here, an older fan partly criticizes the relatively low fan-cultural capital of more recent devotees (Hills 2002) and partly notes that his own
fan-cultural capital is now recognized and affirmed by these same
"kids." A singular hierarchy is posited, with the "hardcore" mentoring
the newbies. This "mentor" role reinforces the notion that introducing
any new fan to the "particular program . . . requires a rehearsal of the
basic interpretive strategies and institutionalized meanings common to
the group" (Jenkins 2013, 72), and hence that fandom's protocols need
to be properly learned. However, the concept of a monolithic "hardcore" fandom is difficult to sustain, as some fans will have watched the
show from 1963 onward, others will have been attending conventions
from the 1970s onward (well ahead of the "wilderness" years of the
nineties and noughties when *Who* wasn't on TV), and still others will
have become fans during the non-TV years (C. O. Jones 2013) or as a
result of the revived BBC Wales's incarnation (Giblin 2011). For what
might be dubbed "first wave" fandom, William Hartnell and Patrick
Troughton are likely to be "their" Doctors; for children of the 1970s,
Pertwee and Tom Baker are far more probable, since at that point (pre-
video) the older stories were inaccessible and could only be consumed
via novelizations. For the "hardcore" fan quoted by Booth and Kelly,
fan-cultural authority "comes full circle" precisely because he would
once have been the subordinated, "inauthentic" fan interloper need-
ing to be mentored and socialized into fandom by more experienced,
knowledgeable fans. Rather like other fan groups I've studied, "subcultural distinctions seem to become primarily temporal rather than
spatial" in this instance (Hills 2005, 166); being in the know means
being there at the right time (Wood 2009, 305) and in the right generation of viewers (Wood 2007, 61, 63).

Discourses of ante-fandom are not simply used to position fans "authentically" outside of prevailing fan-cultural norms of affect, though.
The discursive work performed by "my Doctor" is also puzzled over
by some fans, aware that they cannot slot their lived experience into
this template:

They say your first is important, will stay with you forever and set the standard for all future comparisons. Well, what's interesting for me is that while I do fondly remember many third Doctor stories . . . Jon Pertwee . . . is definitely not my favourite Doctor. . . . He should be my Doctor and I wonder why he isn't. [Lyttle 2012, 35]

Or,

I adore ol' Sixie to bits. . . . By rights, he should have been My Doctor, since I only caught the tail end of Peter [Davison]'s incarnation and Colin [Baker] was the first actor in the role who I saw right from the start. But if *The Twin Dilemma* hadn't gone out at the end of Peter Davison's last season, I might easily have missed seeing him at all. [Philips 2012, 20]

Each of these published fan accounts sets up an enigma. Why wasn't Pertwee embraced in the way that might be fan-culturally expected? And why wasn't Colin Baker when he, too, "should have been" for the younger fan here? Both writers offer an explanation: Jonathon Lyttle argues that, rather than having "my Doctor," he instead has "my companion" because "Jo Grant is still my favourite . . . I love [actress] Katy Manning in a way that I can't fully comprehend or explain" (Lyttle 2012, 35). Andrew Philips blames a change in scheduling, since *Doctor Who* was moved back to its traditional UK Saturday night time slot in 1985, having been broadcast during the week in preceding seasons. Philips playfully reverses older fans' (and dominant fan-cultural) belief that the show belonged on a Saturday: "What sort of foolishness was this, putting the show out on Saturdays? Didn't they realize that us kids were out playing? *Doctor Who* was an after-school teatime event, not an easily missable weekend show!" (Philips 2012, 20).

What these memoirs demonstrate is that, as the discourse of "my Doctor" has become central to managing anti-fandom within the community, then it has become just as much of a convention as the dominant anti-fandoms it supposedly evades. A discourse aimed at securing personal idiosyncrasy and individualized affect in the face of communal fan evaluations hence self-deconstructs, shading into its own opposed term—even descriptions of "my Doctor" become insufficient here to ground a sense of "fandom-free" self-authenticity. As Alan McKee has astutely observed,

> The consensus learned by "critical rote" is particularly criticised in this community in terms of a key tenet which is also—unsurprisingly—a key tenet of *Doctor Who* itself. This tenet is the assertion that individualism and the right to dissent must be defended. . . . On television, the Doctor regularly overthrows tyrannical regimes which stop their citizens from expressing themselves by inciting the citizens to a revolutionary aware-ness of their own individuality. In the fan community, . . . writers . . . take on just such a subject position for themselves. [McKee 2001, 11–12]

This subject position extends not merely to deploying ante-fandom against consensus anti-fandom, but also into forms of dissent that are individualistically directed against the very category of "my Doctor." This indicates the priority given to performances of individualized affect within *Doctor Who* fandom, even while fans amass, share, and circu-late collective knowledge, interpretation, and emotion (Booy 2012, 115; Jenkins 2013, 88). As such, divisions in fan studies between "those . . . who write within and about fandom (as a larger network of affiliations and practices) and those who write about individual fans and their per-sonal meaning-making" rather miss the fact that "tensions within fan studies between individualized and social accounts" (Jenkins, in Jenkins and Scott 2013, xiv) are analogued, I would say, by the exact same ten-sions played out *within* fan communities. Likewise, to theorize affect *only* as social and circulatory (Ahmed 2004) misses the dimension, however fantasized or problematic it may be, of individualized and asocial affect. In the case of *Doctor Who*, versions of nonironic and close-reading anti-fandom within the fan culture are positioned as (communally powerful) "social accounts" that have to be negotiated via "individualized accounts" of ante-fandom. The latter are either assumed to be "fandom-free" or are themselves subjected to neoindividualization when they start to be per-ceived as a new mode of (discursive) social account.

Unlike the sports "anti-fan within the fan," there is less sense of a pre-programed, rival anti-fandom that *Doctor Who* fans are supposed or required to indulge in. Although *Star Trek* has sometimes been cast in such a role, this dislike is by no means automatic or widely shared by

"Whovians," unlike the case of sports fandom and its fierce rivals. Instead, "anti-fandoms within fandom" have emerged somewhat contingently as a matter of the program's history: As its ratings fell and it was no longer deemed to be a "popular" mainstream show, it was put on "hiatus" (i.e., canceled for a year) in the era of Colin Baker's sixth Doctor, before being canceled in 1989 when seventh Doctor Sylvester McCoy was in the role. Partly as a result of this waning cultural presence, and partly owing to fans' aesthetic evaluations, the Colin Baker and McCoy eras are often cited as a low point for the series and as a time of creative decline or exhaustion (see Booy 2012; Chapman 2006). Indeed, the *Doctor Who Magazine* poll, "The Mighty 200" (surveying the show's first two hundred stories, from 1963 up to the "Planet of the Dead" episode in 2009) was based on more than 6,700 fan responses, and the bottom three stories were Colin Baker and Sylvester McCoy ones, with these two Doctors also scoring the lowest average marks. Fan respondents aged over thirty-six years old also placed more McCoy and Baker stories at the bottom of the poll (P. Griffiths 2009, 18–42). In an earlier *Doctor Who Magazine* survey of fan preferences, carried out in 1998, the Baker and McCoy eras also proved to be unpopular (Gillatt 1998), and stories such as *The Twin Dilemma*, *Timelash*, and *Time and the Rani* have continued to sit near the bottom of fan polls. Indeed, when *Doctor Who Magazine* published special editions focused on each Doctor, carrying an article per story, Baker's debut in *The Twin Dilemma* was described as having a "fearsomely rotten reputation" (Gatiss 2003, 14). *Timelash*, meanwhile, was said to be

> a story whose title has become a byword for the extreme and upsetting rubbishness that occurs when *Doctor Who* goes totally pear-shaped. . . . *Timelash* . . . happens to be unfortunate in punching every single one of the obvious fan-embarrassment buttons in one fell swoop. [Macdonald 2003, 32–33]

The writer of a piece about *Time and the Rani* doesn't focus on the story itself but instead writes about witnessing studio filming:

> May bank holiday and I was in the vast T[elevision] C[entre] 1, observing the afternoon session: the rehearse-record of scenes in the Rani's laboratory. . . . So, although for many fans this Pip and Jane Baker tale remains

a bitter pill to swallow, I'll always have fond memories of its making. [Mulkern 2005, 20]

These sentiments, where some *Who* becomes a "byword for . . . rubbish-ness" or a "bitter pill," articulate a specifically historicized anti-fandom of "bad" *Doctor Who* (which is not dependent on one character, like Jar Jar Binks and *Star Wars* anti-fandom, or focused on one auteur figure since producer John Nathan-Turner worked on the program across the eighties).

Consequently, UK fans who were around ten years old in 1989, such as the author of the blog *The Art of Arfon*, display an awareness that "their" Doctor, Sylvester McCoy, is often disliked:

> There is one slight problem with complaining about new fans . . . it does make me somewhat a hypocrite, because *Doctor Who* was into its second decade by the time I discovered it. . . . In fact . . . the era of the show that I held dear was very often sneered upon by other fans. . . . Whenever I am asked "who's your favourite / who was your Doctor?" my answer is always "Colin Baker was my first Doctor. However, Sylvester McCoy is MY Doctor." [A. Jones 2013]

If McCoy is the victim of a significant (but contested) anti-fandom—to the extent that his admirers are often defensive within fan circles—then the 1996 TV movie has also claimed its fair share of fan opponents, largely owing to the accusation that *Doctor Who* had been "Americanized" and the character represented as half-human (see Wright 2011). Robert Kozinets has traced a similarly historicized unfolding of anti-fandoms among *Star Trek* fans:

> Should *Star Trek* be used to critique *Star Trek*? Fans' already well-developed creative proclivity has now been married to abhorrence for manifestations of *Star Trek*. The fans hated . . . recent TV series (particularly *Enterprise*). Their animosity creates considerable fan activity aimed at . . . dissociat-ing . . . it from the official lore of *Star Trek*. [Kozinets 2007, 202]

Likewise, *Doctor Who* is frequently used by its fans to critique *Doctor Who*. But neither this, nor *Who* fandom, are purely about "the fans'" dislike, as if fandom is wholly united: There is a reasonably dominant fan-cultural narrative (regarding peaks and troughs in program quality), but individual fans' self-narratives can and do diverge from this, often as a matter of when they were born and when they first became passionately interested in the show. There is thus a kind of fannish "idiorrhythm" displayed here (Barthes 2013, 6–10), whereby fans navigate between the individual and the collective and do so within relatively small groups (enclaves of fans within the wider fan culture).

"Idiorrhythm" is a term used by Roland Barthes in *How to Live Together*, in a very different context from fan studies, to be sure. But for Barthes, this word captures and elevates into research a certain "fantasy" motivating his work, one in which "each subject lives according to his own rhythm" (2013, 6). Idiorrhythm concerns "the interstices, the *fugitivity* . . . of the manner in which the individual inserts himself into the social code" (Barthes 2013, 7–8; emphasis in original). It is therefore set against "macro-groupings . . . because their structure is based on an architecture of power . . . openly hostile to idiorrhythmy" (8). In Barthes's work, "idiorrhythmic clusters" raise the issue of not falling into line with a dominant cultural or physical power, and he gives an anecdotal example:

> From my window (December 1, 1976), I see a mother pushing an empty stroller, holding her child by the hand. She walks at her own pace, imperturbably; the child, meanwhile, is being pulled, dragged along, is forced to keep running. . . . She walks at her own pace, unaware of the fact that her son's rhythm is different. And she's his mother! Power . . . is effected through disrhythmy, heterorhythmy. [Barthes 2013, 9]

The "hurts of history" (Alters 2007) that idiorrhythmic *Doctor Who* fans have to compensate for, then, are not changes in ideology (past media content being more obviously homophobic or sexist) but, rather, changes in the TV show itself. Loving the sixth or seventh Doctors means frequently having to justify your affects and tastes: It means confronting a hostile "macro-grouping" of dominant fandom that follows a heterorhythmy of favored texts and eras. Age and the self-narrative of "becoming-a-fan" form key strategies of defense against the social code of anti-fandom-within-fandom; individuals deploy discourses of lived ante-fandom (contrasted against later learned fandom) to explain their personal *Doctor Who* likings. As one keen fan of Colin Baker recounts in a fanzine article: "Heartfelt thanks to Colin Baker and long live the sixth Doctor. My Doctor. Whether you like it or not" (Pollitt 2010, 103, quoting Baker's dialogue from *The Twin Dilemma*). For, as Mark Duffett has noted: "First fans can actually become *anti-fans* of new members of the fan community [meaning that] old and new fans can be antagonistic towards each other" (Duffett 2013, 50; emphasis in original), with the tastes of younger fans who initially got into *Who* during the tenures of Colin Baker or Sylvester McCoy being devalued by longer-term fans who had already grown up with Hartnell or Troughton.

C. Lee Harrington and Denise Bielby have called for more work on self-narrative, ageing, and the life course in fan studies:

> The narrative turn taking place . . . focuses on the construction of self-narratives . . . and their evolution across time. [This] points to the potential fruitfulness of exploring unfolding media narratives and unfolding self-narratives in tandem and across time—and in the context of age, aging, and life course progression. This is an important next step within fan studies. [Harrington and Bielby 2010b; see also 2010a]

Although a range of work has focused on "enduring" and lifelong fandom (Kuhn 2002; Stevenson 2006), as well as recently tackling ageing and subcultural identity (Bennett 2013; Hodkinson and Bennett 2012), I would suggest that this important longitudinal development—and emphasis on temporality—has not yet convincingly caught up with work on anti-fandom (although Jonathan Gray touches on the temporal issue of fleeting/enduring anti-fandom; see Gray, in this volume). In relation to long-running film and TV franchises with multigenerational audiences, and fans who have followed texts across their life course from childhood onward, a longitudinal focus would enable theorists to address how "anti-fandom within the fan" emerges historically and contingently in relation to shifting media narratives, as well as how fans' "unfolding self-narratives" can intersect with forms of anti-fandom, either expressing it or being "sneered upon" by dominant sections of the fan culture for their idiorrhythmic fandom. Types of anti-fandom are thus embedded in *Who* fandom, leaving fans of different generations to navigate the idiorrhythms of their particular becoming-a-fan-stories, whether this means loving Sylvester McCoy's Doctor or purely being a fan of new *Who*. In the latter case, open anti-fandom is partly suppressed and modified, owing to the recognition that new lifeblood and "vitality" can be brought into the fan culture (Booth and Kelly 2013, 61), even if this fan energy lacks hardcore "authenticity" for longer-term devotees who aim to take on a "tutoring" role. But fans who have been fully socialized into fandom across the life course while retaining their affective investment in the "wrong" Doctors have to defend their tastes and emotions against devaluation both from more "senior," older fans and from those aligned with dominant fan-cultural narratives of the show's past.

One possible development emerging from this perspective is that, although some anti-fandoms may be fan-culturally normative (e.g., an anti-fandom of Colin Baker and Sylvester McCoy among *Doctor Who* fans)—arrayed against idiorrhythmic generational fandoms—other *anti-fandoms may themselves be idiorrhythmic* (e.g., what of anti-fans of normatively and fan-culturally popular actors such as Tom Baker or David Tennant?). Analyzing the defenses and justifications of idiorrhythmic anti-fans (expressing anti-fandoms that are themselves marginal and secluded within the wider fan culture) remains a separate topic that may further regenerate theories and empirical case studies of anti-fandom's affective complexity. Ultimately, though, displays of idiorrhythmic generational fandom (or anti-fandom) and expressions of fan-culturally normative anti-fandom tend to work in concert as "part of a collective cultural performance" of *Doctor Who* fan culture and its varied subcommunities (Hill 2015, 176).

The Doctor's many incarnations are not only embraced by different generations of fans in terms of variously being "their" Doctors, mind you. In terms of unfolding self-narrative, there is also the matter of what happens *after* one's favored Doctor has departed from the role. Lance Parkin suggests that, when regeneration is linked to a raft of other changes in the show's format, then the cumulative impact of this widespread textual change can be highly alienating for a devoted viewer:

> I've always had a nagging sensation that the [Peter Davison] era wasn't right. Now, it's not uncommon in fandom—for many fanboys my age,

> *Doctor Who* was Tom [Baker], K9, Romana and jokes, and they were all gone in the space of a year. . . . For a British fan in 1981 it was a big deal. Reading a couple of entries in the *DWM Fifth Doctor Special* . . . it really seems like . . . my fellow fanboys retain deep scars from what they call, perfectly straight-faced, a "trauma." [Parkin 2009,139]

Using the language of emotional upset in a slightly different, more romantic register, Angela Giblin offers an extended metaphor for her own response to the departure of David Tennant in 2010:

> Poor Matt Smith. . . . I was still in mourning for the loss of *my Doctor*, my first love. . . . Smith didn't do anything wrong. But he didn't do anything right, either. It was like the first date with a new man who unwittingly takes you to the restaurant you used to go to with that still much loved ex. . . . Eleven [is] the perfect rebound Doctor. . . . He's the one my friends set me up with and said was just perfect for me but was actually a bit *too* nice, *too* interesting, *too* funny and too *soon* for me to ever really love. [Giblin 2011, 35–36]

Mark Duffett has suggested that significant changes in a musician's image and style of performance might constitute "an element of *invited anti-fandom*" (2013, 49, emphasis in original), that is, attempting to find new audiences while knowingly shocking or challenging established fans. This idea could certainly be retooled and related to *Doctor Who*'s periodic reimaginings, which far from being limited to its 2005 revival (Hills 2010) have consistently marked the show's history. Yet neither Parkin nor Giblin, post–"their" Doctor, are completely driven away from the series. Instead, these fans' self-narratives encounter periods of "post-object" adjustment (Williams 2011): nagging doubts, and a sense of not quite being able to move on emotionally, that are neatly captured in Giblin's concept of a "rebound Doctor." Rather than outright anti-fandom being invited here—or rather, incited as an unwitting side effect of textual regeneration—it seems more appropriate to consider these ambivalences as a state in which fandom and colorations of "anti-fandom within the fan" (Theodoropoulou 2007, 316) collide in more nuanced and mixed ways. These are not haters. But nor are they merely disgruntled, critical fans seeking to rewrite the source text. More specifically, there is another powerful discursive construction of "before" and "after" conveyed in these self-narratives and a mode of ante-fandom that is less about evading collective anti-fan norms and more about positing an almost prelapsarian or valorized prior phase of intense fan affect. This mode of ante-fandom again works to secure self-authenticity (and posit textual authenticity), implying that a fuller fan "love" has been subsequently displaced or degraded by the unfolding text:

> Pertwee's Time Lord had, in my eyes, died. Replaced by an impostor who looked nothing like him. . . . I didn't enjoy [Robot] . . . very much. . . . Mum thought him silly, and so did I initially. Him prancing around in a series of daft costumes . . . was played for comedy. Pertwee's stories had humour, but it wasn't overt. This was like letting a big kid loose with the dressing-up box. [Griffiths 2007, 57]

And yet these self-narratives of emotional engagement are also provisional and potentially open to revision. Nick Griffiths's fan autobiography, *Dalek I Loved You*, goes on to recount how, "after that dodgy debut . . . [Tom Baker] had come up trumps. Everyone in the know remembers The Ark in Space with reverence. . . . Within weeks, he had made the role his own" (Griffiths 2007, 73). Similarly, Giblin's metaphor of being on the "rebound" doesn't wholly foreclose the possibility of finding a new *Doctor Who* to love, and Parkin's fandom evidently survived the TV transitions of 1981.

As I've argued across this chapter, the overarching ante-fandom of "my Doctor" typically acts discursively as an anchoring self-narrative of authenticating, individualizing fan experience and affect that are opposed to fan-cultural norms of emotive anti-fandom (for more on this subcultural individualization, see Kahn-Harris 2007, 127). In a sense, ante-fandom allows fans to situate their fan identity in relation to an "experience of marginalization" (Gray and Murray 2016, 364) within wider fan-communal consensus and circulation of affect, just as Jonathan Gray and Sarah Murray (2016) have argued that media *dis*likes can be meaningfully articulated with marginalized voices outside the domain of fandom.

Other versions of ante-fandom such as a "rebound Doctor" are more readily subject to amendment and reevaluation over time. And, in a similar way, dominant anti-fandoms within the community can also "vacillate ... [over a longer time scale;] although there is a (contested) agreement at any given time about which are the best [and worst] stories, ... fans know that this will change in five or ten years" (McKee 2001, 14). What I have sought to do here, via my case study of *Doctor Who*, is flag up the need for work on anti-fandom to engage more centrally with diachronic, or even generational, issues of (fan-)cultural identity and affect, as well as considering more carefully how specific modes of anti-fandom can emerge within fan cultures. Like Jonathan Gray (in this volume), I, too, am arguing for a more nuanced take on anti-fandom's different varieties. Given that *Doctor Who* is such a long-running TV show, considering the temporality and history of fan (dis)likes becomes especially important in this case. Where both idiorrhythmic ante-fandom and communal anti-fandom are concerned, it seems that time waits for no fan.

REFERENCES

Ahmed, S. 2004. *The Cultural Politics of Emotion*. New York: Routledge.

Alters, D. 2007. "The Other Side of Fandom: Anti-Fans, Non-Fans, and the Hurts of History." In *Fandom: Identities and Communities in a Mediated World*, edited by Jonathan Gray, Cornel Sandvoss, and C. Lee Harrington, 344–356. New York: New York University Press.

Barthes, R. 2013. *How to Live Together: Novelistic Simulations of Some Everyday Spaces*. New York: Columbia University Press.

Basu, B. 2010. "When Worlds Continue: The Doctor's Adventures in Fandom and Metatextuality." In *Ruminations, Peregrinations and Regenerations: A Critical Approach to Doctor Who*, edited by Chris Hansen, 164–176. Newcastle upon Tyne: Cambridge Scholars Publishing.

Bennett, A. 2013. *Music, Style and Aging: Growing Old Disgracefully?* Philadelphia: Temple University Press.

Booth, P. 2013. "The First Time." In *Fan Phenomena: Doctor Who*, edited by Paul Booth, 72–83. Bristol: Intellect.

Booth, P., and P. Kelly. 2013. "The Changing Faces of *Doctor Who* Fandom: New Fans, New Technologies, Old Practices?" *Participations: Journal of Audience and Reception Studies* 10, no. 1:56–72. www.participations.org.

Booy, M. 2012. *Love and Monsters*. London: I. B. Tauris.

Chapman, J. 2006. *Inside the TARDIS*. London: I. B. Tauris.

Claessens, N., and H. Van den Bulck. 2014. "A Severe Case of Disliking Bimbo Heidi, Scumbag Jesse and Bastard Tiger: Analysing Celebrities' Online Anti-Fans." In *The Ashgate Research Companion to Fan Cultures*, edited by Linda Duits, Koos Zwaan, and Stijn Reijinders, 63–75. Farnham: Ashgate.

Click, M. 2007. "Untidy: Fan Response to the Soiling of Martha Stewart's Spotless Image." In *Fandom: Identities and Communities in a Mediated World*, edited by Jonathan Gray, Cornel Sandvoss, and C. Lee Harrington, 301–315. New York: New York University Press.

Decker, K. S. 2013. *Who Is Who? The Philosophy of Doctor Who*. London: I. B. Tauris.

Duffett, M. 2013. *Understanding Fandom: An Introduction to the Study of Media Fan Culture*. London: Bloomsbury.

———. 2014. "Fan Words" In *Popular Music Fandom*, edited by Mark Duffett, 146–164. London: Routledge.

Gatiss, M. 2003. "The Twin Dilemma: I Am What I Am." *Doctor Who Magazine*, special ed. no. 3: *The Complete Sixth Doctor*, 14–15.

Giblin, A. 2011. "Do You Ever Get over Your First Doctor?" In *Shooty Dog Thing: 2th and Claw*, edited by Paul Castle and Jon Arnold, 34–36. Andover: Hirst Books.

Gilbert, A. 2012. "Between Twi-Hards and Twi-Haters: The Complicated Terrain of Online 'Twilight' Audience Communities." In *Genre, Reception and Adaptation in the "Twilight" Series*, edited by Anne Morey, 163–179. Farnham: Ashgate.

Gillatt, G. 1998. "The *DWM* Awards." *Doctor Who Magazine* 265:4–29.

Goletz, S. W. 2012. "The Giddyshame Paradox: Why "Twilight"'s Anti-Fans Cannot Stop Reading a Series They (Love to) Hate." In *Genre, Reception and Adaptation in the "Twilight" Series*, edited by Anne Morey, 147–161. Farnham: Ashgate.

Gray, J. 2003. "New Audiences, New Textualities: Anti-Fans and Non-Fans." *International Journal of Cultural Studies* 6, no. 1:64–81.

———. 2010. *Show Sold Separately*. New York: New York University Press.

———. In this volume. "How Do I Dislike Thee? Let Me Count the Ways."

Gray, J., and S. Murray. 2016. "Hidden: Studying Media Dislike and Its Meaning." *International Journal of Cultural Studies* 19, no. 4:357–372.

Gray, S. 1995. "Hits and Misses." *Doctor Who Magazine* 232:34.

Griffiths, N. 2007. *Dalek I Loved You: A Memoir*. London: Gollancz.

Griffiths, P. 2009. "The Mighty 200!" *Doctor Who Magazine* 413:18–42.

Hadas, L. 2009. "The Web Planet: How The Changing Internet Divided *Doctor Who* Fan Fiction Writers." *Journal of Transformative Works and Cultures*, no. 3. doi: 10.3983/twc.2009.0129.

Harrington, C. L. and D. Bielby. 2010a. "A Life Course Perspective on Fandom." *International Journal of Cultural Studies* 13, no. 5:429–450.

———. 2010b. "Autobiographical Reasoning in Long-Term Fandom." *Journal of Transformative Works and Cultures*, no. 5. doi: 10.3983/twc.2010.0209.

Hill, A. 2015. "Spectacle of Excess: The Passion Work of Professional Wrestlers, Fans and Anti-Fans." *European Journal of Cultural Studies* 18, no. 2:174–189.

Hills, M. 2002. *Fan Cultures*. London: Routledge.

———. 2005. "Ringing the Changes: Cult Distinctions and Cultural Differences in US Fans' Readings of Japanese Horror Cinema." In *Japanese Horror Cinema*, edited by Jay McRoy, 161–174. Edinburgh: Edinburgh University Press.

———. 2010. *Triumph of a Time Lord: Regenerating Doctor Who in the 21st Century.*
London: I. B. Tauris.

———. 2013a. "Anniversary Adventures in Space and Time: The Changing Faces of
Doctor Who's Commemoration." In *New Dimensions of Doctor Who*, edited by Matt
Hills, 216–234. London: I. B. Tauris.

———. 2013b. "'Tim Is Very Personal': Sketching a Portrait of Tim Burton's Auteur-
ist Fandom and Its Origins." In *The Works of Tim Burton: Margins to Mainstream*,
edited by Jeffrey Weinstock, 179–193. New York: Palgrave Macmillan.

Hodkinson, P., and A. Bennett. 2012. *Ageing and Youth Cultures.* Oxford: Berg.

Jenkins, H. 2013. *Textual Poachers: Television Fans and Participatory Culture.* Updated
20th anniversary ed. New York: Routledge. Originally published 1992.

Jenkins, H., and S. Scott. 2013. "*Textual Poachers*, Twenty Years Later." In *Textual
Poachers: Television Fans and Participatory Culture*, by H. Jenkins, updated 20th
anniversary ed., vii–l. New York: Routledge.

Jones, A. 2013. "Reflections of a *Doctor Who* Fan: The Grumpy One . . . ." *The Art of
Arfon* (blog), May 31. http://arfonjones.blogspot.co.uk.

Jones, C. O. 2013. "Life in the Hiatus: New *Doctor Who* Fans, 1989–2005." In *Fan Phenomena: Doctor Who*, edited by Paul Booth, 38–49. Bristol: Intellect.

Kahn-Harris, K. 2007. *Extreme Metal: Music and Culture on the Edge.* Oxford: Berg.

Kozinets, R. V. 2007. "Inno-tribes: *Star Trek* as Wikimedia." In *Consumer Tribes*,
edited by Bernard Cova, Robert V. Kozinets and Avi Shankar, 194–211. Oxford:
Butterworth-Heinemann.

Kuhn, A. 2002. *An Everyday Magic: Cinema and Cultural Memory.* London: I. B. Tauris.

Lyttle, J. 2012. "The Complete History of Doctor Who (1963–1989)." In *You and Who: A
Doctor Who Fan Anthology*, edited by J. R. Southall, 32–39. Tadworth: Miwk.

Macdonald, P. 2003. "Timelash: Money's Too Tight to Mention." *Doctor Who Magazine*, special ed. no. 3: *The Complete Sixth Doctor*, 32–33.

McKee, A. 2001. "Which Is the Best *Doctor Who* Story? A Case Study in Value Judge-
ments outside the Academy." *Intensities: The Journal of Cult Media*, no. 1 (2001).
https://intensitiescultmedia.com.

———. 2004. "How to Tell the Difference between Production and Consumption: A
Case Study in *Doctor Who* Fandom." In *Cult Television*, edited by Sara Gwenllian-
Jones and Roberta E. Pearson, 167–185. Minneapolis: University of Minnesota Press.

Miller, K. 2012. *The Official Doctor Who Fan Club.* Vol. 1: *The Jon Pertwee Years.* Edinburgh: Pegimount Press.

Monaghan, E. 2010. "Greater than the Sum of Its Parts." In *Time Unincorporated:
The Doctor Who Fanzine Archives.* Vol 2: *Writings on the Classic Series*, edited by
Graeme Burk and Robert Smith? 297–301. Des Moines, IA: Mad Norwegian Press.

Mulkern, P. 2005. "Time and the Rani: The Great Pretender." *Doctor Who Magazine*,
special ed. no. 10: *The Complete Seventh Doctor*, 20.

O'Day, A. 2013. "Social Spaces: British Fandom to the Present." In *Doctor Who in Time
and Space: Essays on Themes, Characters, History and Fandom, 1963–2012*, edited by
Gillian I. Leitch, 25–43. Jefferson, NC: McFarland.

Owen, D. 2010. "Jonny Come Home" (1993). In *Time Unincorporated: The Doctor Who Fanzine Archives*. Vol. 2: *Writings on the Classic Series*, edited by Graeme Burk and Robert Smith? 104–106. Des Moines, IA: Mad Norwegian Press.

Parkin, L. 2009. *Time Unincorporated: The Doctor Who Fanzine Archives*. Vol. 1: *Lance Parkin*. Des Moines, IA: Mad Norwegian Press.

Perryman, N. 2013. *Adventures with the Wife in Space*. London: Faber & Faber.

Philips, A. 2012. "The Taking of Planet Wilf (Part One)." In *You and Who: A Doctor Who Fan Anthology*, edited by J. R. Southall, 19–21. Tadworth: Miwk.

Pollitt, E. 2010. "We've Got Love for You If You Were Who in the Eighties!" In *Shooty Dog Thing*, edited by Paul Castle, 101–103. Andover: Hirst Books.

Sheffield, J., and E. Merlo. 2010. "Biting Back: Twilight Anti-Fandom and the Rhetoric of Superiority." In *Bitten by Twilight: Youth Culture, Media and the Vampire Franchise*, edited by Melissa A. Click, Jennifer Stevens Aubrey, and Elizabeth Behm-Morawitz, 207–222. New York: Peter Lang.

Stevenson, N. 2006. *David Bowie: Fame, Sound and Vision*. Cambridge: Polity.

Theodoropoulou, V. 2007. "The Anti-Fan within the Fan: Awe and Envy in Sport Fandom." In *Fandom: Identities and Communities in a Mediated World*, edited by Jonathan Gray, Cornel Sandvoss, and C. Lee Harrington, 316–327. New York: New York University Press.

Tulloch, J., and H. Jenkins. 1995. *Science Fiction Audiences: Watching Doctor Who and Star Trek*. London: Routledge.

Twist, S. 2010. "Don't You (Forget about Me)." In *Time Unincorporated: The Doctor Who Fanzine Archives*. Vol 2: *Writings on the Classic Series*, edited by Graeme Burk and Robert Smith? 264–267. Des Moines: Mad Norwegian Press.

Van den Bulck, H., N. Claessens, J. Mast, and A. Kuppens. 2016. "Representation of Fandom in Mainstream Media: Analysis of Production and Content of Flemish Television's *Superfans*." *European Journal of Cultural Studies* 19, no. 6:513–528.

Williams, R. 2011. "'This Is the Night TV Died': Television Post-Object Fandom and the Demise of *The West Wing*." *Popular Communication* 9, no. 4:266–279.

Wood, T. 2007. *About Time*, vol. 6: *The Unauthorized Guide to Doctor Who, 1985–1989: Seasons 22–26, the TV Movie*. Des Moines, IA: Mad Norwegian Press.

———. 2009. *About Time*, vol. 3: *The Unauthorized Guide to Doctor Who, 1970–1974: Seasons 7–11*, expanded 2nd ed. Des Moines, IA: Mad Norwegian Press.

Wright, P. 2011. "Expatriate! Expatriate! *Doctor Who: The Movie* and Commercial Negotiation of a Multiple Text." In *British Science Fiction Film and Television*, edited by Tobias Hochscherf and James Leggott, 128–142. Jefferson, NC: McFarland.

PART II

Anti-Fandom and Identities

6

The Politics of Against

Political Participation, Anti-Fandom, and Populism

CORNEL SANDVOSS

From Participatory Culture to the Tea Party

In exploring political participation as a form of (political) fandom, this chapter assesses how the process that Jonathan Gray, Lee Harrington, and I (2017) have described as "fanization" affects political engagement, activism, and movements and thus aims to explore the premises and consequences of the fanization of democracy by building on two themes of recent scholarship, the first being the growing body of that work documenting the eroding boundaries between realms of political and popular communication by highlighting the degree to which popular entertainment and culture become significant spaces of political discourse and action (see Brough and Shresthova 2012; Gray, Jones, and Thompson 2009; Hartley 1999; Hill, Canniford, and Millward 2016; Jenkins 2014; J. Jones, G. Byam, and A. Day 2012; Ruddock 2005; Sandvoss 2007; Street 2004, 2012; van Zoonen 2005; and Wood, Corbett, and Flinders 2016), and the second being the degree to which political communication adopts tropes, narrative techniques, and styles from popular entertainment and celebrity discourses (Marsh, 't Hart, and Tindall 2010; Scammell 1995, 2007; Street 2012; and Wheeler 2013). Research analyzing the coverage of political campaigns, for instance, has repeatedly highlighted the tendency of political journalists to privilege a "game frame" or "horse race frame" that reshapes elections as a partisan competition mirroring the emotional engagement with sport (Aalberg, Strömbäck, and de Vreese 2012; Cushion and Thoms 2018; Lewis and Wahl-Jorgensen 2005; Sandvoss 2013; and Semetko and Boomgaarden 2007). The textuality of contemporary political coverage thus actively invites the reading position of the fan based on a partisan identification framed in a sportslike competition (see also Dean 2017; and Jungherr 2012).

Stephen Coleman (2003) highlighted similar parallels between political enthusiasts and (reality) television fans as far back as the height of reality TV programming after the turn of the century, a particularly prescient analysis in light of Donald Trump's later successful convergence of his reality television persona into political celebrity and an accompanying fan culture. Jonathan Gray (2017) has in reference to both Silverstone (1994) and Morley (2000) emphasized the sense of belonging, security, and identity many regular news consumers derive from their regular and emotionally engaged following of news media. Laurie Ouellette (2012) explored the formation of a fan culture around the emergent Sarah Palin brand, a significant precursor and trailblazer of Trump fandom.

Beyond the textual convergence of popular political communication, the unprecedented dissemination of means of media production and dissemination in digital convergence culture quickly informed progressive political movements, such as Howard Dean's initially highly successful 2004 presidential bid—which was driven by digital communication technologies yet undone by television (Jenkins 2006)—as well as Barack Obama's successful presidential bid in 2008, informing the optimism of Jenkins's vision of a convergence culture that is not only more participatory but also more democratic. While he concedes in light of the latter critique by Hay (2011) and others (Couldry 2011; and Turner 2011) that "there is nothing about participatory culture that would inevitably lead to progressive outcomes," the fundamental assumption in Jenkins's (2014, 285) assessment remains that access and participation will advance progressive goals through the sociotechnological space of convergence media: "Even if we do succeed in broadening cultural and political participation, this will not make all other ideological conflicts go away. Rather, for me, the fight for a more participatory culture has to do with ensuring as many people as possible have access to the platforms and practices through which future struggles over equality and justice will take place." Implicit in this line of argument is the assumption that *modes* of participation and engagement in convergence culture are ideologically neutral and that greater participation translates to greater equality over time.

However intuitive such assumptions may seem, they fail to account for the consequences of an affective and emotional fanlike participation. In contrast, I wish to argue here that being a fan or an anti-fan means more than being participatory by exploring the premises and consequences of the fanization of politics in reference to the particular case identified in James Hay's (2011) critique: the rise of the Tea Party in the United States since 2008.

Fan cultures are commonly situated between spaces of mass and niche communication, between top-down and bottom-up content creation, and between large-scale marketing campaigns and fan enthusiasm. Initial fan objects around which such cultures form are often those at the heart of entertainment industry strategies: From *Star Wars* or *Lord of the Rings*, to elite sports and music, fan objects are frequently hot-ticket, high-production-value texts. In their detailed and insightful study of the Tea Party movement, Theda Skocpol and Vanessa Williamson (2013) document a similar interplay between a top-down campaign and grassroots activism. Much as Donald Trump's presidential campaign was initially launched to the applause and cheers of paid actors (Mathis-Lilley 2017), the Tea Party movement was initiated by political operators, large donors, and (mass) media platforms. With the initial spark to the movement, and its brand, provided by a coincidental television moment—CNBC's reporter Rick Santelli's on-air outburst over the Obama administration's bailout initiatives in response to the collapse in the U.S. housing market in the 2008 credit crunch—that proved a highly spreadable message across media platforms, the moment was quickly utilized by existing political actors:

> One of the most important consequences of the widespread Tea Party agitations unleashed from the start of Obama's presidency was the populist boost given to professionally run and opulent refunded right-wing advocacy organizations devoted to pushing ultrafree-market policies. Along with Republican Party operatives, who had long relied for popular outreach on independent-minded and separately organized Christian conservatives, national free-market advocacy operations would, via the Tea Party, enjoy new ties to grassroots activists willing to prioritize fiscal anti-government themes. One political action committee pulled the old wine of GOP consultants and big-money funders into a new bottle

labeled Tea Party Express (TPE), which allowed them to seem closely aligned with grassroots citizens. Other existing national organizations, such as FreedomWorks and Americans for Prosperity, suddenly saw fresh opportunities to push long-standing ideas about reducing taxes on business and the rich, gutting government regulations, and privatizing Social Security and Medicare. [Skocpol and Williamson 2013, 9]

In seizing on this opportunity, such organisations and interests could rely upon a number of media personalities and outlets—from celebrity, far-right radio hosts Rush Limbaugh and Glenn Beck to cable network Fox News—whose business model hinges on offering ultraconservative and far-right content and who quickly "amplified the public attention grassroots Tea Partiers were receiving" (Skocpol and Williamson 2013, 8). Yet, however much the Tea Party movement was initiated and driven by the interests of those commanding considerable wealth, levers of power, and control of media platforms—such as the case of the ultra-conservative and, indeed, far-right billionaire Koch brothers—there is little doubt that the Tea Party, and the subsequent Trump support, have been a participatory movement in the mold of convergence culture: "From spring to fall 2009 and onto in 2010, local activists operating without central direction created legions of local tea parties meeting regularly, usually once a month, but in some cases weekly" (Skocpol and Williamson 2013, 8). In addition to attending meetings and protest activities, most local branches had created web presences, and many members reported actively discussing Tea Party policies online or with friends, families, and acquaintances. In their practices, the Tea Party members in Skocpol and Williamson's study echo the media use and degree of social organization frequently associated with fans in participatory culture, and they reflect Abercrombie and Longhurst's (1998) mapping of different fan practices: the narrower their fan object, the more selective and specialized their media consumption, and the tighter their social networks. Tea Party members operate like fans toward the enthusiasts' end of spectrum of most fandoms. Fans with a general interest in baseball, for example, will follow the coverage in newspapers and watch occasional games on ESPN, whereas fans of a particular team like the Yankees will subscribe to the YES cable network dedicated to the team and occasional attend games. Yankee enthusiasts are more likely to listen to specialist podcasts, read fanzines, and be season-ticket holders. In the same way, those with a broad interest in politics or even conservative politics will lean toward national, center-right media, while Republican Party activists gravitate toward specialist broadcast offerings such as Fox News, while also being more enunciatively active online and offline, becoming embedded in the loose social networks of fellow fans. Tea Party activists often follow a yet more specialist diet of niche content providers such as Glenn Beck—as Skocpol and Williamson (2013, 134) report, "Either deliberately or unconsciously, the people we interviewed often used phrases and arguments from the Beck show"—while being part of close, in situ social networks. Much like the enthusiasts in Abercrombie and Longhurst's (1998) typology, to these committed activists or 'fans', their own activity often becomes the actual focal point and fan object: "The people who are most engaged in Tea Party undertakings at the local level—arranging a meeting or carpool, running precinct committee, quizzing officeholders, attending school board meetings— are not the type of people who shout [the loudest at protests]" (Skocpol and Williamson 2013, 20). In turn, Skocpol and Williamson describe how Tea Party meetings present a space enriched through debate and discussion, where conflicting ideological positions—in particular, those of social conservatism, Christian fundamentalism, and libertarianism— are mediated, highlighting the ways in which such activists groups serve as meaningful interpretative communities.

Political Fandom and the Politics of Against

For all these parallels there is, of course, a notable difference in the ideological position of the enunciative and textual productivity of fans through which these interpretive communities are formed in fan cultures surrounding popular entertainment and the case of the Tea Party movement. Far from challenging or subverting existing inequalities in power through transformative work, content created by Tea Partiers reinforced and reiterated historical inequalities regarding gender, ethnicity, class, sexuality, and age, aiming to eradicate much of the social and cultural change of the postwar era. To Jenkins (2014, 285) the Tea Party hence constitutes the exception to the rule: "Alongside the rise of the Tea Party, we have seen some dramatic developments in recent years, as, for example, undocumented youths are using the circulation of grassroots videos to call out the Obama administration's record of deporting more people than in the previous Bush administration and, through this process, pushing him to pass the DREAM act by executive decree." With the benefit of hindsight, Jenkins's optimism seems misplaced: The DREAM act has since become one of the casualties of the Tea Party–propelled presidency of Donald Trump (Shear and Davis 2017). More significantly, however, a closer analysis of the ideological substance of Tea Party support reveals that, in its structures, practices, and motivations, fan participation is not a neutral medium that equally facilitates all possible political discourses equally (see Ruddock 2005; and Sandvoss 2007). For the purposes of this analysis we thus need to shift our focus from the structural parallels between fan cultures and political fandom, in the case of Tea Party support, to the affective foundations of the bond between political fans and their fan objects that is in the discourses of Tea Partiers.

The Premises of Political Fandom and Anti-Fandom

The overwhelming theme that sparked the momentum of the Tea Party movement and subsequently served as the central narrative to maintain activism and enthusiasm was one of opposition. The Tea Party from its inception was formulated and positioned *against*, rather than *for* a given cause. Despite the often glaring and wide ideological gulf between, for instance, social conservatives and libertarians who joined the ranks of the Tea Party, activists were united by their dislike and antipathy— even hatred—of their perceived common enemy: Democratic president Barack Obama:

> Nowhere are Tea Party fears more potently symbolized than in the presidency of Barack Hussein Obama. The policies and person of the forty-fourth President were the subject of immense suspicion at every Tea Party event or interview we attended. It is no coincidence that Tea Party activism began within weeks of President Obama's inauguration. Several interviewees dated their concerns about the country and national politics to Obama's election or the 2008 campaign. . . . Various articles have quoted Tea Party members saying that Obama is a secret Muslim, a foreigner, a

Socialist, a Communist, a Nazi—or maybe all of the above! Obama the un-American is an overarching theme. Stoked by demagogues like Donald Trump, the claim about President Obama's otherness and illegitimacy reached its apogee in "Birtherist" claims that Obama was not really born in the United States. [Skocpol and Williamson 2013, 77–79]

The political activism of Tea Partiers was thus derived less from an initial positive identification with a given fan object than from a form of anti-fandom underpinned by a "politics of against." Obama and, more broadly, Democrats served as the textual space through which an anti-fan object was constructed. The centrality of an Other against which the own political cause is imagined by Tea Partiers is shared with populist movements that have emerged across the Western world and beyond since the inception of the Tea Party a decade ago. The bewilderment of many European politicians confronted with negotiation partners from the United Kingdom who have failed to formulate what aims they seek to achieve through the United Kingdom's withdrawal from the European Union (Kahn 2018) lucidly illustrates the essence of a political movement primarily formulated against a symbolic Other, devoid of any material objectives, or at least objectives that could be achieved by the course of action chosen. The Brexit movement in Britain, both its official campaign and grassroots response, was singularly sustained through an act of dislike, rejection, and anti-fandom. Similarly, Trump's successful 2016 presidential bid utilized many of the discourses, emotions, and, indeed, activists of the Tea Party movement. Far-right, populist movements across Western Europe—such as the Sweden Democrats; Lega Nord and the Five Star Movement in Italy; Austria's FPÖ (Freedom Party); and Germany's Alternative für Deutschland—are defined through their rejection of an imagined Other—the Euro currency, other regions, the European Union, and immigrants—themes that across many Eastern European countries are central to the ideologies of parties in government (such as Fidesz in Hungary and Poland's PiS[Law and Order Party]).

On a superficial level, this interplay between fanlike activism in politics and the significance of an imagined Other, or what we can describe as an *anti-fan object*—a text or textual field (such as a politician, political party, or political cause) with which users regularly and emotively engage, yet through strongly negative emotions—is reflective of the partisanship arising out of community memberships. A strong identification with a given political party or course, much like fan affiliations in different forms of popular culture, becomes part of fans' identity positions, which in turn are reinforced through fan practices and performances (Duffett 2012; Hills 2002; and Sandvoss 2005a), including the articulation of differences and distinctions to other (fan) groups. "Politics," as Skocpol and Williamson (2013, 47) observe, "is about who we are—often in contradiction to 'them,' to the types of people that are not fully part of our imagined community."

Notably, there has been a strong tradition in the study of fans and audiences in the context of convergence culture that separates questions of identity and community. Much of Jenkins's failure to recognize the more-than-coincidental interplay between fan cultures and the Tea Party lies, I think, in his focus on collective agency without exploring of the intrapersonal premises shaping identity and, by extension, community membership. In Jenkins's (2014, 283) eyes, "There has always been a sharp divide between those who study individual fans and those who study fandom as an imagined and imaginative community." While Jenkins is correct that the strand of fan research his own work has shaped has examined fan communities and cultures solely as communities and their practices, the analysis of individual fans—or, more precisely, the bond between fan and fan object—has rarely been undertaken in isolation but in a growing body of work that examines the interplay between individual fans and community and between agency and structure, thereby offering an understanding of the premises and consequences of fanization in politics as well as elsewhere in contemporary culture.

In other words, such work has sought to examine not only the practices and technologies arising in fan cultures but the fundamental intrapersonal needs and desires reflected in a given fan's (or anti-fan's) investment in the first place. The obvious conceptual starting point for work that seeks to understand the interplay between self and its environment and how fan practices and communities are shaped by the intrapersonal bond between fan and fan object is object relations theory. The work of object relations theorists such as D. W. Winnicott, Melanie Klein, and, less frequently, Wilfred Bion has been widely drawn upon in studies of audiences over the last two decades (see Bainbridge and

Yates 2014; Harrington and Bielby 1995, 2010; and Hills 2002, 2007) for its capacity to conceptualize the fundamental interplay between self and object world at the heart of fan emotions and practices as both highly personal yet inherently embedded in wider social and cultural systems through fan texts and interactions with fellow fans and fan communities. In contrast to Winnicott's more conventional model of human development (Craib 2001), Klein's work is of particular interest in the study of negative emotions and processes of othering in fan-type media engagements. In developing the Freudian tripart concept of self, Klein (2000) proposes that the young ego during its paranoid-schizoid phase seeks to negotiate the inner conflict between the id's polarities of the libidinal forces of the Eros and its death drive, Thanatos, through acts of projective identification and object splitting that allow for the preservation of the "good" as much as for the containment of "bad" aspects of self (such as persecutory fear) that are displaced from the self onto the external object. Klein's work has been discussed in detail elsewhere (Elliott 1999; Hinshelwood and Fortuna 2018), as has its application and uses in the study of the relationship between fans and texts (Hills 2002; Sandvoss 2005a; and Stacey 1994). For our purposes, Anthony Elliott (1999) highlights the possible negative emotions in the relation between fan and object of fandom or anti-fandom: Klein's work reminds us that the relationship between the self and the world is maintained through series of fantasies that are shaped by our inner condition. In such fantasies the object of fandom, as much as its opposite—the object of anti-fandom—is controlled through projective fantasies. The fan object is integrated into the fan's sense of self and thus becomes an important identity resource, one that is reflected in the centrality of the cultural symbols and texts with which we build an affective relationship, including politics, as highlighted above by Skocpol and Williamson (2013). Importantly, for the purposes of the analysis of political anti-fandom, however, the processes by which the emotive bond between the fan and fan object is formed inherently follow the dichotomous structure of the id; they are informed by the binary distinction between "good" and "bad" that, originating in the id, is transposed onto the external object. Much of Elliott's (1999, 2014) work on fan culture and celebrity focuses the projective control over the fan object unleashed by fans and the potential of the failed fan object, not an unusual outcome for political fan objects (Sandvoss 2012).

Yet in politics, as elsewhere in contemporary media culture, objects of anti-fandom, which as spaces for the projection and externalization of persecutory fears are controlled in their external symbolic form, are common spaces for projective fantasies. Fandom, much like language, thus effectively operates through a matrix of binary distinctions in which the self and its projective imagination are articulated as much as through what is disliked, rejected, or even hated—through the anti-fan object—as through the fan object. In sports, support for a given team is often closely associated with the anti-fandom of another team in rivalries that are widely and intersubjectively recognized (see McCulloch, in this volume; and Theodoropoulou 2007). Fans of different genres and fields of popular culture frequently resent associations of the fan object with a different cultural text adopted with their projective identification (see Hills 2012), and fans of quality television are keen on distinguishing their fan object from televisual forms they consider of lesser value, particularly reality TV (Jones 2015). While all such forms of anti-fandom of course articulate the role of taste as a structuring and structured structure that approaches to the study of fans, drawing on Bourdieu (1984), have acknowledged, we need to map the emotional fabric of such distinctions through the functions they fulfill intrapersonally, not just interpersonally. The emotional significance of objects of fandom and anti-fandom, on which fan practices are based, derives from their function as spaces of projection and introjection that impose the polarities of the id onto the object world. The forms of, and projective identification on which, the relationship between the fan and the fan object rest and through which the fan object becomes affectively meaningful as an imagined space of the idealized "good" object, and distinguished from the projectively imagined Other, is therefore the *premise*, not the consequence, of the emotions through which (political) fandom operates. In other words, forms of fanlike political enthusiasm are not a neutral medium of participation that serves as an expression of otherwise unrelated ideologies and worldviews. Instead, the fanization of political participation and activism privileges the dichotomous perception of the world that necessitates a symbolic Other against which the "good" fan object as projection of self is constructed. In his wider discussion of Klein's work, Elliott (1996) points to the potential implications for the propensity of binary political discourses that arise from processes of projection and introjection. These tendencies appear to be amplified in political fandom, driven by a projective imagination that necessitates and drives symbolic Othering. The anti-fan object thus often supersedes a coherent ideological goal in contemporary fanlike political enthusiasm. In policy discussions among Tea Partiers, ideological positions are frequently incoherent and reflect less general universal moral or ideological principles than the relative impact of policies on Tea Partiers' themselves:

> Rank-and-file Tea Party participants evaluate regulations and spending very differently, depending on who or what is regulated, and depending on the kinds of people who benefit from various kinds of public spending. . . . At the grassroots, Tea Partiers want government to get out of the way of business. Yet at the same time, virtually all want government to police immigrants. And the numerous social conservatives in the Tea Party ranks want authorities to enforce the conception of traditional moral norms. More tellingly still, almost all Tea Partiers favor generous social benefits for Americans who "earn" them; yet in an era of rising federal deficits, they are very concerned about being stuck with the tax tabs to pay for "unearned" entitlements handed out to unworthy categories of people. [Skocpol and Williamson 2013, 56]

What unifies Tea Partiers is thus, not a coherent ideological vision, but their antagonism toward a projected Other that is imagined in both directions of a linear social hierarchy, both in the form of a supposed elite (here President Obama and the Democratic Party) and the "undeserving," those who in Tea Partiers' imagination ought to be less privileged than themselves but who are wrongfully rewarded by "the elite." Their activism and emotive involvement in politics is thus as much a form of anti-fandom as fandom, or, in Kleinian terms, the projection of bad elements of self onto the external Other in order to both externalize and control them is at least as powerful a driver of participatory political fan cultures than the affective identification with the fan object.

These discourses among Tea Party enthusiasts mirror political engagement in other contemporary emotively fueled political movements. The ire of Brexiters is also directed against the Other of the supposed elite (the United Kingdom's political establishment, then-prime minister David

Cameron, the institutions and officials of the European Union, and so on) as well as the "undeserving," in this case, as so often in populist discourses, migrants. However, beyond acknowledging projects that are closely related to the Tea Party—such as Trump support, the Brexit campaign, and further European anti-immigration parties—it is important to acknowledge that such othering arising out the projective identification with the fan object and against the anti-fan object may lend itself more easily to right-wing and far-right ideologies based on essentialist assumptions and classifications but that fanlike movements on the political left are also reshaped by the intrapersonal premises upon which their fans' engagement rest. Enthusiastic supporters of Jeremy Corbyn's leadership of the Labour Party in the United Kingdom, for example, equally construct their affective engagement in politics in primary reference to anti-fan objects. Like Tea Partiers and Brexiters, Corbyn fans define themselves in opposition to a symbolic Other that also includes the elites (in particular, those perceived as Blairites and part of the New Labour project, as well as the Conservative Party) and the "undeserving" privileged by the elites (here the "superrich," bankers, landlords, etc.). While antagonism is of course identified as the fundamental historical force for economic and social change in Marxist political thought, the construction of Corbyn support and fandom as an anti-neoliberal movement has complicated its relationship with principles of cosmopolitanism and globalism and constitutes a sharp departure from principles of equality, inclusion, and universalism at the heart of postwar social democratic and socialist political thought. This ambiguity is reflected in Corbyn's repeated legislative support for withdrawal from the European Union with no recognition of the loss of rights of UK residents from other EU countries and his rhetoric in which EU migrants are constructed as a symbolic Other (as in Corbyn's infamous remarks alleging pressure on wages for UK-born workers as a result of the "wholesale importation" of Labour from Eastern Europe [Wearing 2017] and Labour's validation of a rhetoric of "we" and "them" between British and non-British EU citizens and UK residents with a critique of global capitalism readily transforming into the xenophobe Othering of those transgressing the frame of the national). With the word "solidarity" missing from the Labour manifesto for the 2017 general election entirely and the word "freedom" only featuring a single time (in the context of affirming that freedom of movement will be restricted), Labour's general election slogan encapsulates the extent to which their own political course focuses in on the self and pivots it against a symbolic Other: "For the many, not the few."

The Consequences of Political Fandom and Anti-Fandom

In outlining the consequences of the fanization of politics, including the rise of anti-fandom, Corbyn supporters thus provide a particularly lucid illustration of the extent to which fandom shapes not only the form or intensity of political participation but the substance of politics itself.

The strong currents of anti-fandom in Corbyn support result in a divergence of form and substance in political fandom similar to that I observed in the positive relationship between Obama fans and fan objects (Sandvoss 2013). While Kleinian approaches to fan audiences reveal the dichotomous nature through which the affective bond between fan object and anti-fan object operates, in the fan practices that integrate this initial projective identification into everyday-life articulations of identity, a self-reflective bond between fan and fan object is formed that underscores the affective bond to the fan object as an important marker of self-identity. As such, fans are concerned with preserving this self-reflective bond even when the fan object is subject to transformations in ways that conflict with fans' initial projective reading, thus coming to serve as partial servomechanism of the fan object (see Sandvoss 2003, 2005a). Obama fans thus proactively sought to negotiate particular challenges to their fandom, such as Obama's failure to advance changes to firearms legislation following the Sandy Hook Elementary School massacre in 2012, by critically reflecting on and adjusting their own values, adopting strategic and technical considerations over their substantive beliefs (Sandvoss 2013). In the case of fans and supporters of Jeremy Corbyn, an initially largely unknown candidate for the Labour leadership whose main distinction was not being associated with previous Labour governments and New Labour, it is the anti-fan objects of former prime minister Tony Blair, the Conservative Party, and notions of neoliberalism that are central in sustaining projective identification with Corbyn. In response to Corbyn's support of government legislation advancing Brexit, consistent with this long record of voting against European integration, Corbyn fans who supported remaining in the European Union took up interpretive strategies justifying the cause of political action they morally disagreed with. Like Obama fans, they privileged technical over substantive considerations: Frequently, Corbyn supporters argued that it wasn't "electorally wise" to oppose Brexit at this point, thus relegating substantive beliefs, such as their actual opposition to revoking fellow UK residents' rights, to strategic considerations—thereby prioritizing considerations of political spin, the persistent use of which alienated many Corbyn supporters from the former Tony Blair government and whose support for continued European Union membership is seen to legitimize Corbyn's more hostile stance toward the European Union.

At the other end of the political spectrum, Tea Partiers and Trump supporters of socially (ultra)conservative and evangelical Christian beliefs have been driven to extraordinary strategies in their reading and appropriation of personal misconduct—including serial adultery and boasting about a history of sexual and misconduct by Donald Trump (and even statutory rape, as in the case of Republican Alabama Senate candidate Roy Moore)—profoundly at odds with traditional Christian morality, commonly pointing to forgiveness and second chances as integral parts of Christianity (though they are less inclined to do so for political opponents). The degree to which the fan object here is sustained primarily through the anti-fan object is illustrated in the words of *The Federalist* website contributor Denise C. McAllister (2017) who, likening the current political confrontation in the United States to a war, reminds her readership that "god uses all kinds of 'immoral' men and women to bring about his purposes." In this ultimate triumph of form over substance, any past and perceivable future actions of Trump, as the perceived polar opposite to these activists' anti-fan object, are likely to be inconsequential to their continued fanlike support. While reflective of their participatory engagements, the internalization of the cynicism of political spin by political fans from Trump to Corbyn restricts the transformative potential of fans' political participation to facilitate a more democratic political process, much as Mark Andrejevic (2008, 44) observed in relation to the "snarky" television fans' participation on message boards such as *Television Without Pity*: "A savvy identification with producers and insiders facilitated by interactive media fosters an acceptance of the rules of the game."

The fanization of politics thus serves as a reminder that the rise of participatory culture does not in and of itself translate to—and, in current sociopolitical conditions, even mitigates against—democratization, as on closer analysis the fanlike engagements in politics explored in this chapter appear to advance populist, rather than democratic, participation. Much discussion has centered in political science on the question of whether populism can be meaningfully described as an ideology, albeit borrowing Michael Freeden's (1996) notion of a "thin-centered" one (see, e.g., Fieschi 2004; and Mudde 2004). Some—for example, Paris Aslanidis (2016)—suggest that populism constitutes a particular type of discourse, rather than ideology, a view not dissimilar to Freeden's (2017, 3) own assessment of populism in relation to the implosion of the far right, populist UK Independence Party following the EU referendum: "A thin-centred ideology implies that there is potentially more than the centre, but the populist core is all there is; it is not a potential centre for something broader or more inclusive. It is emaciatedly thin rather than thin-centred." Whether conceptualized as an ideology or discourse, however, this populist core, according to Ben Stanley (2008), finds its root in political antagonism, and hence the binary interplay between fan and anti-fan object that I've documented here: "To the vague intuition that 'populism' says something about the relationship between 'the elite' and 'the people' this approach replies that populism is a product of this relationship. Populism is predicated upon an antagonistic relationship between the two entities, and is latent wherever the possibility occurs for the emergence of such a dichotomy." In this sense the binary engagement with politics as a result of its fanization creates a causal relationship between fanlike engagements with politics and populism. Populism, in contrast to Laclau's (2005) initial proposition, is thus not confined to material, class-motivated conflict but fueled by symbolic antagonism. Exploring the emotive qualities and premises of contemporary participatory engagements in politics hence suggests a need to conceptualize populism, not just as an ideology or discourse, but as a particular mode of reception and engagement—one that has commonly been described as "being a fan."

Concluding Remarks

In this chapter I have documented a number of instances of the emergence of participatory, fanlike political movements over the last decade. As one of its earliest exponents, the Tea Party movement, in particular, illuminates the technological and social context as much as its inter- and intrapersonal premises: Maintaining the emotional bond between fan and fan object through processes of projection and introjection, such fandom privileges forms of reading and political engagement that reinforce binary-opposed fan and anti-fan objects. Fanlike engagements in politics, I suggest, are therefore more than a coincidental expressions of new participatory opportunities through convergent media; fandom, and with it, anti-fandom constitute a form of political participation that affects its substance, facilitating a mode of reception and engagement that privileges the antagonisms at the heart of populist, rather than democratic, mobilization. Based on this initial examination of the interplay between political fandom and anti-fandom, participation and populism, three considerations follow:

First, much of the focus on studies of media users in the context of participatory culture has remained with users, prosumers, fans, and their productivity themselves, even when inviting a more critical exploration of user practices as in recent studies of "trolls" (Phillips 2015) and anti-fans. While a more nuanced analysis of the diffuse fields of power and a more complex interplay between structure and agency in participatory culture has distinguished the second and the third wave of fan studies from its precursors' political advocacy for and celebration of fans (Gray, Sandvoss, and Harrington 2007), even the introductory analysis of forms of political anti-fandom highlights the moral imperative to extend the study of fans and users to outsiders who suffer the consequences of policies that reflect polarizing discourses (such as the tens of millions of refugees and migrants who are often the first casualty of Othering in self-centered, populist sentiment), as well as those who become part of the textual formations that to others serve as (political) objects of anti-fandom. While for analytical purposes we treat mediated representations of individuals that are part of fan texts and anti-fan texts as textual formations alone, the individuals becoming subjects to such texts are profoundly affected by being semiotically utilized in projective readings of anti-fans. As much as there is a "violence of expectation" directed at the fan object to fulfill fans' projective fantasies, the individuals who are read as part of the anti-fan object find themselves confronted with the same "violence of expectation" to fulfill the anti-fans' negative projective fantasies, thus being subjected to crass, highly threatening, and abusive interactions, with frequently dramatic personal and professional consequences. As much as it is important to recognise "anger" as a force of potential political transformation and change (Wahl-Jorgensen, forthcoming), we must acknowledge, analyze, and formulate responses to the dramatic risks and consequences of fanlike participation in politics that affect diverse groups from those exposed through their public office—such as Labour MP and Remain campaigner Jo Cox, who was killed by a supporter of the extreme right Britain First in the days before the EU referendum in June 2016—to those who inadvertently end up in social media storms and are thrust onto a national media stage.

Second, the proliferation of political anti-fandom presents a challenge not only to individuals but to collective forms of political organization and the media ecologies upon which they are based. Concerns over the increasing fragmentation of the public sphere (Sunstein 2007), polarization (Baum and Groeling 2008; and Davis 2005), and the emergence of echo chambers (Leccese 2009) have more recently been supplemented with concerns regarding the textual form of political debate and, particularly, information in terms such as "fake news" (Jankowski 2018). In his seminal text developing the concept of the anti-fan, Jonathan Gray (2003, 71) observed that "anti-fans construct an image of the text—and, what is more, an image they feel is accurate—sufficiently enough that they can react to and against it," highlighting the importance of paratexts, "those semi-textual fragments that surround and position the work" in doing so. In political fandom and anti-fandom, formerly distinct texts, such as news, are intersected with paratexts, including user-created content, and integrated into wider textual fields, in which boundaries around textual formations such as fan objects are drawn by users rather than textual producers. By conceptualizing emotive, partisan, and regular engagement in political discourses as fandom and anti-fandom we can thus begin to explore how transformations of political discourse are shaped by practices of fans' reading practices through which the emotive focal points of their engagement with politics are maintained. Or, put simply, studying fans and anti-fans in politics shifts the question from which news and information we believe to which news and information we *choose* to believe.

Last, we need to stress the methodological limitations and challenges. If there is, as I suggest here, no linear causality between participation and democratization, analyzing and finding responses to the interplay between fans and anti-fans and democracy becomes primarily an empirical challenge. Beyond the small set of secondary data used here, political enthusiasts' motivations, emotions, and fan practices in their regular engagements with mediated politics are rarely captured. To formulate meaningful responses to the challenges to political debate and democratic processes arising out of political anti-fandom, further research that examines different forms of political fandom and anti-fandom across media and electoral systems is needed. In developing strategies to overcome the dichotomous engagement with politics through fan and anti-fan objects, it seems, we have to overcome our own disciplinary binaries between fan studies and political communication research.

REFERENCES

Aalberg, Toril, Jesper Strömbäck, and Claes H. de Vreese. 2012. "The Framing of Politics as Strategy and Game: A Review of Concepts, Operationalizations and Key Findings." *Journalism* 13, no. 2:162–178.

Abercrombie, Nicholas, and Brian Longhurst. 1998. *Audiences: A Sociological Theory of Performance and Imagination.* London: Sage.

Andrejevic, M. 2008. "Watching *Television Without Pity*: The Productivity of Online Fans." *Television and New Media* 9, no. 1:24–46.

Aslanidis, P. 2016. "Is Populism an Ideology? A Refutation and a New Perspective." *Political Studies* 64, no. 1:88–104.

Bainbridge, C., and C. Yates, eds. 2014. *Media and the Inner World: Psycho-cultural Approaches to Emotion, Media and Popular Culture.* Houndmills: Palgrave.

Baum, M. A., and T. Groeling. 2008. "New Media and the Polarization of American Political Discourse." *Political Communication* 25, no. 4:345–365.

Bourdieu, P. 1984. *Distinction: A Social Critique of the Judgement of Taste.* London: Routledge & Kegan Paul.

Brough, M. M., and S. Shresthova. 2012. "Fandom Meets Activism: Rethinking Civic and Political Participation." *Transformative Works and Cultures*, no. 10. doi: 10.3983/twc.2012.0303.

Coleman, S. 2003. "A Tale of Two Houses: The House of Commons, the Big Brother House and the People at Home." *Parliamentary Affairs* 56:733–758.

Couldry, N. 2011. "More Sociology, More Culture, More Politics." *Cultural Studies* 25, nos. 4–5:487–501.

Craib, Ian. 2001. *Psychoanalysis.* Cambridge: Polity Press.

Cushion, S., and R. Thoms. 2018. *Reporting Elections: Rethinking the Logic of Campaign Coverage*. Cambridge: Polity Press.

Davis, R. 2005. *Politics Online: Blogs, Chatrooms, and Discussion Groups in American Democracy*. New York: Routledge.

Dean, J. 2017. "Politicising Fandom." *British Journal of Politics and International Relations* 19, no. 2:408–424.

Duffett, M. 2012. *Understanding Fandom*. New York: Continuum.

Elliott, A. 1996. "Contradictions of the Imagination: Freud in the Stream of Modernity." In *Subject to Ourselves: Social Theory, Psychoanalysis and Postmodernity*, by A. Elliott, 39–64. Cambridge, MA: Polity Press.

———. 1999. *The Mourning of John Lennon*. Berkeley: University of California Press.

———. 2014. "'I Want to Look Like That!' Cosmetic Surgery and Celebrity Culture." *Cultural Sociology* 5, no. 4:463–477.

Fieschi, C. 2004. "'Introduction." Special issue on populism. *Journal of Political Ideologies* 9, no. 3:235–240.

Freeden, M. 1996. *Ideologies and Political Theory: A Conceptual Approach*. Oxford: Clarendon Press.

———. 2017. "After the Brexit Referendum: Revisiting Populism as an Ideology." *Journal of Political Ideologies* 22, no. 1:1–11.

Gray, J. 2003. "New Audiences, New Textualities: Anti-Fans and Non-Fans." *International Journal of Cultural Studies* 6, no. 1:64–81.

———. 2017. "The News: You Gotta Love It." In *Fandom: Identities and Communities in a Mediated World*, 2nd ed., edited by J. Gray, C. Sandvoss, and C. L. Harrington, 75–87. New York: New York University Press.

Gray, J. A., J. Jones, and E. Thompson, eds. 2009. *Satire TV: Politics and Comedy in the Post-network Era*. New York: New York University Press.

Gray, J., C. Sandvoss, and C. L. Harrington. 2007. "Introduction: Why Study Fans?" In *Fandom: Identities and Communities in a Mediated World*, edited by J. Gray, C. Sandvoss, and C. L. Harrington, 1–18. New York: New York University Press.

———. 2017. "Introduction: Why Still Study Fans?" In *Fandom: Identities and Communities in a Mediated World*, 2nd ed., edited by J. Gray, C. Sandvoss, and C. L. Harrington, 1–18. New York: New York University Press.

Harrington, C. L., and Bielby, D. 1995. *Soap Fans: Pursuing Pleasure and Making Meaning in Everyday Life*. Philadelphia: Temple University Press.

———. 2010. "Autobiographical Reasoning in Long-Term Fandom." *Transformative Works and Cultures*, no. 5. doi:10.3983/twc.2010.0209.

Hartley, J. 1999. *The Uses of Television*. London: Routledge.

Hay, J. 2011. "'Popular Culture' in a Critique of the New Political Reason." *Cultural Studies* 25, nos. 4–5:659–84.

Hill, T., R. Canniford, and P. Millward. 2016. "Against Modern Football: Mobilising Protest Movements in Social Media." *Sociology*. doi: 10.1177/0038038516660040.

Hills, M. 2002. *Fan Cultures*. London: Routledge.

———. 2007. "Essential Tensions: Winnicottian Object-Relations in the Media Sociology of Roger Silverstone." *International Journal of Communication* 1, no. 1:37–48.

———. 2012. "'Twilight' Fans Represented in Commercial Paratexts and Inter-Fandoms: Resisting and Repurposing Negative Fan Stereotypes." In *Genre, Reception, and Adaptation in the "Twilight" Series*, edited by Anne Morey, 113–129. Farnham: Ashgate.

Hinshelwood, R. D., and T. Fortuna. 2018. *Melanie Klein: The Basics*. Abingdon: Routledge.

Jankowski, N. W. 2018. "Researching Fake News: A Selective Examination of Empirical Studies." *Javnost—The Public: Journal of the European Institute for Communication and Culture* 25:248–255. doi: 10.1080/13183222.2018.1418964.

Jenkins, H. 2006. *Convergence Culture: When New and Old Media Collide*. New York: New York University Press.

———. 2014. "Rethinking 'Rethinking Convergence/Culture." *Cultural Studies* 28, no. 2:267–297.

Jones, B. 2015. "Antifan Activism as a Response to MTV's 'The Valleys.'" *Transformative Works and Cultures*, no. 19. doi: 10.3983/twc.2015.0585.

Jones, J., G. Byam, and A. Day. 2012. "Mr. Stewart and Mr. Colbert Go to Washington: Television Satirists outside the Box." *Social Research* 79, no. 1:33–60.

Jungherr, A. 2012. "The German Federal Election of 2009: The Challenge of Participatory Cultures in Political Campaigns." *Transformative Works and Cultures*, no. 10. doi: 10.3983/twc.2012.0310.

Kahn, S. 2018. "UK Brexit Negotiating Has Been 'a Shambles' Demonstrating 'Unpreparedness' and 'a Lack of Professionalism.'" *Independent*, February 21. www.independent.co.uk.

Klein, M. 2000. "Notes on Some Schizoid Mechanisms." In *Identity: A Reader*, edited by P. Du Gay, J. Evans, and P. Redman, 130–143. London: Sage.

Laclau, E. 2005. *On Populist Reason*. London: Verso Books.

Leccese, Mark. 2009. "Online Information Sources of Political Blogs." *Journalism and Mass Communication Quarterly* 86, no. 3:578–593.

Lewis, J., S. Inthorn, and K. Wahl-Jorgensen. 2005. *Citizens or Consumers: The Media and the Decline of Political Participation*. Maidenhead: Open University Press.

Marsh, D., P. 't Hart, and K. Tindall. 2010. "Celebrity Politics: The Politics of Late Modernity?" *Political Studies Review* 8, no. 3:322–340.

Mathis-Lilley, B. 2017. "FEC Document Concludes Trump Paid Actors to Attend Event at Which He Launched 2016 Campaign." *Slate*, January 20. www.slate.com.

McAllister, D. C. 2017. "Why It's Justified to Vote for a Morally Questionable Politician." *The Federalist*, November 28. http://thefederalist.com.

McCulloch, R. In this volume. "A Game of Moans: Fantipathy and Criticism in Football Fandom."

Morley, D. 2000. *Home Territories: Media, Mobility and Modernity*. London: Routledge.

Mudde, C. 2004. "The Populist Zeitgeist." *Government and Opposition* 39:542–563.

Ouellette, L. 2012. "Branding the Right: The Affective Economy of Sarah Palin." *Cinema Journal* 51, no. 4:185–191.

Phillips, W. 2015. *This Is Why We Can't Have Nice Things*. Cambridge, MA: MIT Press.

Ruddock, A. 2005. "Let's Kick Racism out of Football—and the Lefties Too!" *Journal of Sport and Social Issues* 29, no. 4:369–385.

Sandvoss, C. 2003. *A Game of Two Halves: Football, Television and Globalization*. London: Routledge.

———. 2005a. *Fans: The Mirror of Consumption*. Cambridge: Polity Press.

———. 2005b. "One Dimensional Fan: Toward an Aesthetic of Fan Texts." *American Behavioural Scientist* 49, no. 3:822–839.

———. 2007. "Public and Publicness: Media Sport in the Public Sphere." In *Media and Public Spheres*, edited by R. Butsch, 58–70. Houndmills: Palgrave.

———. 2012. "Enthusiasm, Trust, and Its Erosion in Mediated Politics: On Fans of Obama and the Liberal Democrats." *European Journal of Communication* 27, no. 1:68–81.

———. 2013. "Toward an Understanding of Political Enthusiasm as Media Fandom: Blogging, Fan Productivity and Affect in American Politics." *Participations: Journal of Audience and Reception Studies* 10, no. 1:252–296.

Scammell, M. 1995. *On Message: Communicating the Campaign*. London: Sage.

———. 2007. "Political Brands and Consumer Citizens: The Rebranding of Tony Blair." *Annals of the American Academy of Political and Social Science* 611:176–192.

Semetko, Holli A., and Hajo G. Boomgaarden. 2007. "Reporting Germany's 2005 Bundestag Election Campaign: Was Gender an Issue?" *Harvard International Journal of Press/Politics* 12, no. 4:154–171.

Shear, M. D., and J. H. Davis. 2017. "Trump Moves to end S+DACA and Calls on Congress to Act." *New York Times*, September 5. www.nytimes.com.

Silverstone, Roger. 1994. *Television and Everyday Life*. London: Routledge.

Skocpol, T., and V. Williamson. 2013. *The Tea Party and the Remaking of American Conservatism*. New York: Oxford University Press.

Stacey, J. 1994. *Stargazing: Hollywood Cinema and Female Spectatorship*. London: Routledge.

Stanley, B. 2008. "The Thin Ideology of Populism." *Journal of Political Ideologies* 13, no. 1:95–110.

Street, John. 2004. "Celebrity Politicians: Popular Culture and Political Representation." *British Journal of Politics and International Relations* 6, no. 4:435–452.

———. 2011. *Music and Politics*. Cambridge: Polity.

———. 2012. "Do Celebrity Politics and Celebrity Politicians Matter?" *British Journal of Politics and International Relations* 14, no. 3:346–356.

Sunstein, C. R. 2007. *Republic.com 2.0*. Princeton, NJ: Princeton University Press.

Theodoropoulou, V. 2007. "The Anti-Fan within the Fan: Awe and Envy in Sport Fandom." In *Fandom: Identities and Communities in a Mediated World*, edited by J. Gray, C. Sandvoss, and C. L. Harrington, 316–327. New York: New York University Press.

Turner, G. 2011. "Surrendering the Space." *Cultural Studies* 25, nos. 4–5:685–699.

van Zoonen, L. 2005. *Entertaining the Citizen*. Lanham, MD: Rowman & Littlefield.

Wahl-Jorgensen, K. Forthcoming. *Emotions, Media and Politics*. Cambridge: Polity Press.

Wearing, D. 2017. "Labour Has Slipped Rightwards on Immigration. That Needs to Change." *Guardian*, July 25. www.theguardian.com.

Wheeler, M. 2013. *Celebrity Politics: Image and Identity in Contemporary Political Communications*. Cambridge: Polity Press.

Wood, M., J. Corbett, and M. Flinders. 2016. "Just like Us: Everyday Celebrity Politicians and the Pursuit of Popularity in an Age of Anti-politics." *British Journal of Politics and International Relations* 18, no. 3:581–598.

7

Hating Skyler White

Gender and Anti-Fandom in AMC's Breaking Bad

HOLLY WILLSON HOLLADAY AND MELISSA A. CLICK

On August 23, 2013, the *New York Times* published an opinion piece by actress Anna Gunn, claiming, "I Have a Character Issue." Gunn, who played Skyler White on the AMC drama *Breaking Bad*, noted that her character is the natural antagonist to the show's protagonist, her methamphetamine manufacturing kingpin husband Walter, insofar as Skyler is "the one character who consistently opposes Walter and calls him on his lies" (Gunn 2013, para. 5). While Gunn admitted that she "was aware that [Skyler] might not be the show's most popular character" (para. 5), she argued that the fan response to Skyler and to Gunn had been particularly vitriolic; comments on Facebook groups such as "I Hate Skyler White" had extended past calling Skyler a "shrieking, hypocritical harpy" and "annoying bitch wife" to include threats on Anna Gunn's life. Ultimately, Gunn concluded that the hatred of her character was rooted in societal perceptions about women, pointing out that, "because Skyler didn't conform to a comfortable ideal of the archetypical female, she had become a kind of Rorschach test for society, a measure of our attitudes toward gender" (para. 13).

Breaking Bad, which premiered on January 20, 2008, centers on Walter White, a mild-mannered high school chemistry teacher who is diagnosed with inoperable lung cancer in the pilot episode. Unbeknownst to Skyler, Walter begins manufacturing methamphetamine with his former high school student Jesse Pinkman, ostensibly to leave money for his family upon his death. Like many of the characters on *Breaking Bad*, Skyler White is complicated and morally complex, and her motivations change over the course of the series. In the first season, she is the mother of a teenage son with cerebral palsy who is pregnant with a second child, writing short stories and selling personal items on eBay to help provide for her financially strained family. Walt becomes increasingly secretive until he finally reveals to a suspicious Skyler in season 3 that he has been cooking and selling meth. Although Skyler initially demands a divorce from Walt in exchange for her silence about his involvement in the drug trade, she never files the divorce papers and slowly begins aiding Walt in laundering drug money through the car wash they eventually purchase together. By the end of the series, Skyler has become fearful of Walt and finally demands he leave their house after Skyler's brother-in-law Hank, a Drug Enforcement Administration agent, is murdered by rival drug dealers as he attempts to arrest Walt.

Fan blogs and sites dedicated to the series reveal little sympathy for Skyler's position. Facebook groups that cropped up during the run of the series include "Kill Skyler White," "Anti Skyler White Team," and "The Official I HATE Skyler White Group." Tumblr users have penned posts titled "I Hate Skyler White and You Should Too" and "Skyler White Is a Horrible Person." Numerous conversations on Reddit debate viewers' feelings about Skyler. Hashtags like #IHateSkyler allow Twitter users to organize their dislike for the character, and numerous fake user accounts, such as @YaGirlSkyler, exist on Twitter to imitate and scrutinize Skyler's character and actions. The aforementioned "I Hate Skyler White" Facebook page, perhaps the most active with over thirty thousand followers, is a collection of fan-created memes and curated articles denigrating the character. Comments on photos of Skyler range from those critical of her character's actions (a meme of Skyler with the caption "Morally opposed to Walt making meth, willingly commits fraud, had an affair and launders money") to the violently misogynistic ("Someone stick a dick in that damn mouth! Fuck you Skyler!"). After Gunn published her *New York Times* editorial, members of the Facebook group who had previously sought to focus their hatred on Skyler began to view Gunn herself as fair game:

> But after Gunn called us out by name with her ridiculous editorial in the *New York Times*, the gloves were off, and we were no longer Gunn-shy. . . . It became apparent to us that Gunn is not acting when she plays Skyler. She is actually a shrieking harpy in real life too. . . . We still want to keep

the focus on hating the character of Skyler White, but we don't mind jabs against Gunn anymore. Fuckin' histrionic bitch.

Indeed, other *Breaking Bad* fans shifted their criticism from Skyler to Gunn; in a post asking why they hate Skyler White, user comments include "She is beyond ugly and can't act for shit" and "The idiot actress that plays her thinks people hate her because she's a 'strong woman.' Oh please, Anna Gunn, kill yourself."

Critical analysis of the series offers ample justification for the hatred surrounding Skyler's character and of Gunn herself. Megan Cox, for example, argues that Skyler hatred is developed from both the two-dimensionality of the character and the series' narrative conventions. She suggests, "It's hard to build empathy with a character whose internal conflicts are never fully explored—instead, she often seems to just be getting in the way of the story, as another obstacle for her husband" (Cox 2013, para. 4). Echoing this point, Andy Greenwald attributes the distaste for Skyler to series creator Vince Gilligan's failure to properly develop her character: "Due to his female characters' distance from the story he set out to tell, [series creator Vince] Gilligan . . . simply never found out a way to make them as compelling as the males" (Greenwald 2013, para. 5). Further, as Gunn maintains in her opinion piece, some of the negative fan reactions to Skyler's character are predicated on the moral decisions she made as she joined Walt's life of crime. Jen Chaney contends that, in addition to Skyler no longer serving as the moral compass of the show, "What bothers [fans] is a certain hypocrisy they detect in her, stemming from the fact that she objects to Walt's meth business—an objection that finally convinced him to quit cooking—yet continues to potentially benefit from all that dirty money" (Chaney 2013, para. 9).

Other critics, though, echo Gunn's suggestion that the vitriolic responses to Skyler are rooted in the nagging-wife trope she embodied in the early seasons, indicating that fan criticism is deeply influenced by gendered expectations of female characters and of women broadly. While Chaney (2013) maintains that the early representation of Skyler as a shrewish wife might have justified angry sentiments from fans, these feelings did not shift as the narrative progressed. Reflecting on a scene in the first season in which Walt, frustrated about Skyler's constant questioning of his whereabouts, demanded that she "climb down out of [his]

ass," Chaney argues, "But [Skyler] was being *sooooo* naggy and Walt's irritation was so relatable in that moment that a lot of viewers immediately
set their Bunsen burners of Skyler hate to the highest possible flame and
never cranked them down" (Chaney 2013, para. 6; emphasis in original).
Erin Gloria Ryan suggests that hatred of Skyler is symptomatic of a larger-
scale hatred of women on television who stand in the way of antihero
protagonists and who serve as "the proxy for unfulfilled manchildren and
their unresolved hatred for their own mothers or sisters or ex-girlfriends"
(Ryan 2013, para. 3). Indeed, Vince Gilligan maintained that Skyler's gender identity was wholly responsible for the backlash to her character; in
an interview preceding the final season, he dismissed Skyler's detractors
as "misogynists, plain and simple" (Brown 2013, para. 21).

In this chapter, we analyze *Breaking Bad* fans' hatred of Skyler White
and Anna Gunn to explore the connections between fans' investments
in contemporary American television's depictions of antiheroes and
fans' active dislike of a media text or character, a phenomenon Jonathan
Gray (2003) describes as "anti-fandom." We demonstrate that the hatred
Breaking Bad fans we interviewed expressed toward Skyler is articulated
in terms of both the protagonist/antagonist relationship and anti-fans'
perceptions that Skyler contributed to Walt's emasculation. Specifically,
Skyler anti-fandom is rooted primarily in two contradictions articulated
by viewers: first, her role as the series' "moral compass" juxtaposed with
her character's moral failings, and, second, the perception that Skyler's
character was weak while simultaneously being understood as the "annoying bitch wife" who impeded Walter's path to success. Moreover, we
conclude that the hatred that extended extratexually from Skyler White
to Anna Gunn offers another troubling illustration of the misogynistic frustrations increasingly expressed in a social media environment
where anti-fans' discussions of their hatred of female characters and actual women are regularly displayed in memes, hashtags, and chat rooms
(e.g., #GamerGate, or the reaction to the 2016 reboot of the film *Ghostbusters*). In this case, we suggest that viewers' sympathy with Walter
White, who is often cited as an illustration of "masculinity in crisis" (Albrecht 2015; Lotz 2014), translated to disdain for Skyler. As Anna Gunn
suggests about the treatment of both her character and herself, we argue
that sympathy for Walt and hatred of Skyler became a vehicle for the
expression of support for traditional masculinity in a broader context,

rather than a reflection on the gender dynamics in the diegetic world of *Breaking Bad*. We believe that the gendered anger directed toward Gunn offers an opportunity to explore the questions about the increasingly powerful online anti-fan activity that concerns Emma A. Jane, who asserts that calling violent, explicit, and threatening online commentary "anti-fandom" conceals misogynistic and racist cyberhate and leaves fan scholars "exposed to accusations that we are exculpating those people issuing threats and underplaying the suffering of those who receive them" (Jane, in this volume). Exploring the interactions between televisual representation, fandom, and gendered hate, we encourage future anti-fan studies to consider the preexisting hate that often becomes embedded with anti-fandom and also the impact of anti-fandom on its targets who are typically members of marginalized groups.

Male-Centered Serials, Complex Television, and a Deeply Invested Audience

Understanding *Breaking Bad* fans' negative reactions to Skyler White and Anna Gunn involves recognizing the changes that have increasingly shaped U.S. televisual storytelling and audience reception since the 1990s. In *Cable Guys*, Amanda Lotz (2014) suggests that changing conditions produced a trend in programming developed by a range of niche cable networks including HBO, FX, and AMC, which produced and aired series that portray male characters struggling with their identities in a world changed by the impact and outcomes of second-wave feminism. Lotz calls these programs "male-centered serials." For much of U.S. television's history, she notes, male characters' roles and gender identities warranted little scholarly interest in part because of their consistency and conformity (Lotz 2014, 9). Lotz attributes the break in continuity of television's portrayals of male characters partly to the industry's "multi-channel transition," a period from the mid-1980s to the mid-2000s in which expanding choices and technologies, in addition to a resultant loss of the networks' control over viewers, created an opportunity for cable networks to produce and market original narrative serials to target newly fragmented audiences and build network identity. Coupled with changing cultural norms in the United States around gender, this new competitive television environment generated an interest in portrayals of men who grapple with prevailing patriarchal masculinities while embracing aspects of a more "feminist masculinity" (35) or a masculinity restructured, for example, to reduce male privilege and foster romantic and familial relationships that are more egalitarian.

In *Complex TV*, Jason Mittell examines the impact on American television of shifts in industry, technology, and viewing practices over the same time period (Mittell 2015, 41) and similarly suggests that the shifts spawned a group of programs unified by their use of the characteristic he calls "narrative complexity." Television programs that are narratively complex, Mittell describes, have "redefin[ed] the boundary between episodic and serial forms, with a heightened degree of self-consciousness in storytelling mechanics, and demand[ed] intensified viewer engagement focused on both diegetic pleasures and formal awareness" (53). The economic viability of narratively complex programming, Mittell maintains, is rooted partly in the fervent, impassioned, and dedicated responses of audiences, reactions that outshine responses to conventional programming. Audiences' commitment to and engagement with narratively complex programming also creates "robust online fan cultures and active feedback to the television industry" (35).

In line with Lotz's focus on the "flawed protagonists" (2014, 63) in male-centered serials, Mittell also notes that many complex television serials focus on a male antihero, a character who is a repugnant, corrupt, and "morally questionable" figure (2015, 142). These protagonists typically lead middle-class lives working in frustrating and unfulfilling jobs and find themselves in morally complex situations trying to provide for family needs and reconcile their failures as husbands and fathers. While such characters seem unlikely driving forces of passionate audience engagement, Lotz (2014) argues that male-centered serials offer unprecedented character depth, which enables viewers to know more about the male characters at the center of complex serials. Feeling as though they know the characters deeply, audiences enjoy thinking about complex characters' actions, a point Mittell emphasizes: "One of the pleasures of watching complex television is engaging with a sense of ludic play and puzzle-solving analysis, and attempting to read the minds of nuanced, multifaceted characters is fertile ground for such playful viewing practices" (2015, 132).

Although neither Lotz's nor Mittell's projects involve direct engagement with the fans of the shows they discuss, both speculate about how they believe viewers are likely to respond to the male protagonists of male-centered serials. Lotz, for instance, posits that viewers' depth of knowledge about the protagonists' motivations would make viewers more forgiving of their flaws and failures, enabling "audiences to root for them even though they clearly do bad things and also very well may be bad men" (2014, 80). Mittell likewise suggests that feelings of closeness and intimacy with morally ambiguous characters would develop from viewers' fascination, sustained over many seasons of programming, with the antiheroes in complex television serials (2015, 149).

While both scholars recognize the complex relationships viewers forge with male-centered serials' flawed protagonists, they differ in their characterizations of fans' ultimate feelings about antiheroes. Lotz, for instance, resists the idea that viewers would feel pleasure in identifying with flawed protagonists and argues that, while viewers empathize with the motivations of male characters' actions, their repugnant actions would keep viewers from seeing antiheroes as role models worthy of emulation. Instead, she asserts that viewers would use antiheroes' stories to process cultural anxieties around masculinity and interpret their stories as "cautionary tales, each posing the conundrum of finding the balance among aspects of patriarchal and feminist masculinities" (2014, 186). Mittell, however, holds a somewhat different perspective, particularly because he sees Walter White as an "exceptional and atypical" antihero (2015, 151). He argues this because, in Walt's original state (before he "broke bad"), he is a sympathetic and decent but boring character with whom it is difficult to identify. As the merciless meth-making and meth-dealing Heisenberg, however, Walt is powerful and engaging. This difference likely has an important impact on viewers' responses to Walt, as Mittell articulates: "The series pushes Walt further and further across the moral line, making us root for him to do hideous things for our entertainment" (159). Given that Walt's original impetus for becoming a meth maker was to support and protect his family, viewers drawn into Walt's world find themselves at odds with his original goals, knowing that his accumulation of power is consequentially destroying his family and likely will destroy him as well. Mittell agrees with Lotz about the audiences' ultimate response to *Breaking Bad* when he hypothesizes that Walt's amoral, villainous acts ultimately reconfigure him as an object of "narrative contempt" (254) and result in a loss of sympathy from the audience, a result Mittell posits will vary among viewers. This variance in viewers' responses to Walt may help explain the hatred some fans have for Walt's wife Skyler.

Given that the antiheroes at the center of narratively complex serials are men, the serials' messages about gender, combined with audiences' perspectives on gender, are certain influences on viewers' reactions to antiheroes. Lotz argues that narratively complex televisual serials like *Breaking Bad* offer viewers an unprecedented and unflinching look at the complexities of men's lives in contemporary U.S. culture, especially "their most dark and damaged places" (2014, 54). Yet while the protagonists in male-centered series flail and ultimately fail in their quests to rebuild and repair their families, Lotz praises the programs for "avoid[ing] the once-common trope of blaming women and feminism for unmooring men from the gender scripts and cultural privileges of the past" (58). While this may be true for the other serials Lotz examines in *Cable Guys*, Mittell points out that in *Breaking Bad* viewers mostly see Skyler from Walt's perspective, which frames her as bothersome, annoying, and "an obstacle to his self-realization" (2015, 254). Emphasizing the frequency and seriousness of Walt's repeated threats to, and manipulations of, Skyler, Mittell suggests that, if the series was told from Skyler's perspective, it would function "in part as a 'women's film' told in reverse, told through the rationalizing perspective of the abusive spouse whom we only slowly grow to recognize as the villain" (257). Those viewers who maintain Walt's perspective and continue to root for him to become even more violent, dominant, and powerful would be rooting, contrary to Lotz's premise that women and feminism are not targets of the flawed protagonists of male-centered serials, for the triumph of patriarchal masculinity and thus against Skyler White. The way to make sense of *Breaking Bad* fans' hatred of Skyler, a text both Lotz and Mittell argue from a textual perspective functions as a critique of hegemonic masculinity, is therefore to understand the depth of some fans' identification with Walt despite his misdeeds and eventual confession that his actions were motivated by a narcissistic self-interest, not his family's protection. *Breaking Bad* is thus, as Mittell asserts, "a text that has prompted misogyny, both by attracting such people to its audience and by triggering hateful reactions among a significant subset of viewers, and such cultural practices cannot simply be overridden or invalidated by a nuanced textual analysis" (2015, 348).

Online forums and social media feeds are fertile grounds for sharing the hateful reactions of this subset of fans because networked, participatory spaces facilitated by convergence culture allow the like-minded to find each other, emboldening the expression of viewpoints that may be less palatable or permissible when expressed offline. Henry Jenkins, Joshua Green, and Sam Ford (2013) argue that this environment, an outcome of Web 2.0, has made fan practices that were once cult or marginal more normal or mainstream. In such an environment, "a media text becomes material that drives active community discussion and debate at the intersection between popular culture and civic discourse" (Jenkins, Green, and Ford 2013, 168).

While Jenkins, Green, and Ford (2013) imagine that such engagement can lead to activism and social change, it also has built a breeding ground for hateful discourse incorporating misogynistic, racist, and homophobic attitudes, among others. Emma A. Jane notes the increasing prevalence of the hostile online messages she calls "e-bile." She asserts that such texts utilize "profanity, ad hominem invective, and hyperbolic imagery of graphic—often sexualized—violence" that "sometimes manifests as a direct threat, but most commonly appears in the form of hostile wishful thinking" (2012, 3). Jane highlights the fact that men are more likely to be the producers of e-bile and that women are more likely to be targeted by it. Like harassment women receive offline, Jane notes that e-bile's "textual sadism" has become increasingly normalized while its targets are criticized for being too sensitive or taking it too seriously (12).

Thus Jane cautions that some activity seen as anti-fandom may be more than audience response to a media text deemed provocative. She urges anti-fan scholars to incorporate discussions of ethics into their examinations of anti-fandom, particularly because anti-fan discourse is becoming more threatening and also because networked culture allows anti-fans to more easily contact celebrities directly and target ordinary people (Jane 2014, 185). Reminding scholars that such hatred expressed offline would be called "sexism" or "racism" (177), Jane underscores the real-life consequences e-bile can have on its targets, including anxiety and distress as well as disengagement from social media.

Taking these crucial concerns into account with the intention of illuminating the complexity of the forces at play, we interviewed thirty fans of *Breaking Bad* in September and October 2013, just after the airing of the fan-favorite and critically acclaimed episode "Ozymandias" and through the weeks immediately following the series' conclusion. As part of a larger project (Click and Holladay 2018), we recruited self-identified fans through online forums, such as Reddit and fan sites specific to *Breaking Bad* fandom, and conducted one-on-one interviews via Skype. Participants ranged in age from twenty to seventy (mean age 41.7) and were equally male and female. The majority of those with whom we spoke were White (twenty-seven), heterosexual (twenty-seven), and from the United States (twenty-two), although our interview participants hailed from four continents. All participants' names have been changed to preserve their confidentiality.

The interviews ranged in length from twelve to fifty-two minutes. We asked participants their general thoughts and feelings about the ending of the series, how they would describe each major character and the major characters' relationships with each other, and how they hoped the series would end. Hoping to better understand viewers' perceptions of Skyler anti-fandom, we also asked fans to share their feelings about Skyler and referenced Gunn's (2013) *New York Times* article as a way to invite participants to consider why a significant segment of the viewership held such a negative perception of the character. From these transcripts, we identified salient themes in how these fans spoke about hatred of Skyler White. We discuss these themes below.

Antihero Identification and Moral Failure

In line with Lotz's (2014) and Mittell's (2015) speculations, most interview participants indicated that *Breaking Bad*'s narrative was structured in such a way that they were encouraged to root for Walt, the series' protagonist. Some participants pointed out that identification with Walt and his struggles as the central character made them more likely to perceive Skyler as obstructing Walt's ambitions, no matter how unethical Walt's means for achieving success. Ashley (thirty-two, American) shared that, "if you identify with Walt and you think he is standing in for you in some way, it could be easy to see how Skyler is messing up your life, and maybe that's why you would be angry with her." Similarly, Elijah (twenty-nine, American) maintained that Skyler was "killing every one of Walt's dreams" and reinforced the importance of Walt's role as a protagonist:

> It's a show that's about Walt living his dream of being the boss and killing people and cooking meth, but that's a dream after a life of like nothing. That's the part that you can identify with. More than just the being in debt, Walt is just a guy who wants to live his dream even if it's a really messed up dream. . . . So, Skyler is just standing in the way of that.

Walt, then, provided a lens through which these participants could see themselves, and that identification contributed to their dislike of Skyler.

Several participants attributed Skyler's reluctance to support her husband's illegal activities to her role as the moral center of the show. Jacob (nineteen, Canadian), for instance, called Skyler the "moral compass" of the series and explained that she wanted "to do what's right, that's why during the whole show [she is] always unhappy and feels terrible about everything . . . she is not as able to wash away the guilt like Walt can do." Observing that "Skyler did some things the right way, and yet we didn't agree with her," Giovanna (twenty-six, Brazilian) suggested that the audience justified Walt's actions because they felt for him: "We saw him suffering with his cancer and the money issues and that company . . . we saw Walter suffer so much." Santiago (twenty-three, Argentinian) indicated that Skyler's moral decision making was faulty, which led her to be unsympathetic to Walt. She shared, "I don't like Skyler's character because she is such a moralist . . . for her it is like if Walt was cooking meth or doing something illegal, that's all it takes for her to stop loving him. She didn't want to understand why and what was happening inside of Walt's head." Giovanna's and Santiago's comments support Mittell's assertion that watching Walt's transformation and sharing knowledge that he keeps from the other characters would build strong feelings of identification in viewers who would find themselves "aligned to an immoral criminal whom we remember as having once been decent and sympathetic" (2015, 163). Thus Giovanna and Santiago use their knowledge of Walt's motivations for illegal activities and violence to justify their dismissal of Skyler's moral judgment.

Yet others expressed that their anti-fandom was rooted in their feelings that Skyler compromised her own morals. Daniel (twenty, American) explained that, when Skyler decided to participate in Walt's drug empire, a move that ultimately corrupted her, fans found her to be more likeable: "I think people started to let up a bit when she finally started to go along with it, but at that point, that's when she finally compromised her morals." But many interview participants criticized Skyler for her inability to resist becoming involved with Walt's drug empire. Brian (forty-four, American), for example, observed that "she gets somewhat seduced by the money," while Ashley compared her to Carmela Soprano, the wife of crime boss Tony Soprano in *The Sopranos*: "At first she wants nothing to do with [a life of crime], but then after awhile she gets into it and gets corrupted." Thus, although Skyler eventually began to support Walt's life of crime, her initial role as the series' "moral compass" made this decision seem hypocritical and further contributed to fans' dislike of her.

Skyler's relationship with her former boss, Ted Beneke, drew the most ire from participants. Ben (twenty-seven, American) called her extramarital affair with Beneke a "questionable decision," while Dawn (forty-seven, American) compared Skyler's transgression directly to Walt's fidelity to the marriage, claiming that fans did not like Skyler "because she cheated on him with Ted . . . and Walter didn't cheat on her one bit." Greg (fifty-nine, New Zealander) read Skyler's relationship with Ted as particularly malicious, suggesting it enabled Skyler to manipulate Walt:

> At least part of when she starting having the affair [with Ted] was an attempt to control Walt, even if she didn't really realize it herself. That's something I guess women are hesitant to do because obviously if it comes down to physical confrontation between them and their partner or whoever, they can't hold their own that way, so they get better at being aggressive in other ways, you know?

Although he suggested that she was not necessarily cognizant of the reasons behind her affair, Greg viewed Skyler's relationship with Ted as a tool of emotional, feminized "aggression" against Walt, which she wielded in lieu of the masculine, physical aggression Walt exerted in much of the series.

Many saw Skyler as the "moral compass" of the series, and when her actions were of questionable morality, she was judged harshly, even though Walt's poor moral decision making often had much more disastrous implications. Like Walt, and many of the other characters on *Breaking Bad*, participants recognized Skyler as a morally complex individual; she received criticism for being both too moral and not moral enough. Viewers' displeasure when Skyler exerted her own agency resonates with Lotz's (2014) suggestion that viewers are uncomfortable with flawed female characters and Mittell's assertion that complex, strong female characters "can yield a backlash against an aggressive, morally questionable female character, who is often viewed as more of an unsympathetic 'ball-busting bitch' than the charismatic rogue that typifies most male antiheroes" (2015, 150). As evidenced by Greg's comment above, viewer perception of Skyler is deeply grounded in the gendered expectations of her character, and a significant amount of anti-fandom stems from her perceived failures as a woman and wife to Walt. Similar to the Facebook groups and other online comments Gunn (2013) mentioned in her *New York Times* editorial, these participants articulated feelings about Skyler that were negatively evaluative of how her moral complexity interacted with her femininity and the impacts that Skyler's complexity had on Walt's success.

Skyler's Weakness, Walt's Emasculation, and Misogyny

Many participants acknowledged that Walt held a disproportionate amount of power in his relationship with Skyler and, for some, that led them to read her as a "weak" person. A number of participants indicated that Skyler's circumstances—the family's financial strain and her commitment to her infant daughter and son with special needs—limited her choices, trapping her in an unhealthy relationship. As Greg pointed out, "Someone like Skyler, she's in a dreadful situation. She is the equivalent of battered women's syndrome, really . . . what she's been going through. Even though Walter hasn't bashed her he has mentally absolutely tortured her. She hasn't had anywhere to go." Brenda (fifty-one, American) was also sympathetic to Skyler's situation, sharing that "she was stuck. She had a baby that she didn't necessarily [plan] . . . it was kind of late in life and things weren't quite going her way, either . . . she kind of got sucked into this, really." However, despite viewing Skyler as "a victim of circumstance," Brenda still criticized her for not exhibiting the strength to "make better choices."

Others concluded that specific elements of Skyler's relationships with Walt contributed to their evaluation of Skyler as less than Walt. For Juan (forty-eight, American), the relational imbalance between Walter and Skyler began long before the pilot episode and Walt's cancer diagnosis. He questioned whether Skyler was ever Walt's "intellectual equal" and went on to observe that

> I think she's superior to him in social terms . . . but it also seems like one of those situations in your life where you are like, "Oh, he didn't get Jane and he went with Mary," like Mary is just the consolation prize. I want to say he sort of settled. Just because, in the same way, why is he teaching high school, you know? He could be working for Pfizer, hundreds of pharmaceutical companies. It's not so much that he settled for her, but it's sort of like, you know, "I'm lonely. I need a girlfriend." It's not that he just settled for her, he'd already begun settling for other things.

Viewers who perceived this relational inequality argued that it exacerbated the power imbalance that emerged as Walt began a life of crime. For example, Susan (sixty-one, American) mentioned that Skyler was unable to stand up to Walt, suggesting that, while Walt and Skyler were "in love early on," the depiction of their relationship from the series' beginning rendered Skyler "powerless . . . she didn't know what the fuck to do, and she just tried to fight but she knew she was not going to win." Echoing this sentiment, Pam (fifty, American) referenced a scene in the third-season episode "I.F.T.," in which Skyler calls the police to have Walt removed from their home, remembering that "there was an episode where she called the police because Walter had moved back in the house and the police were like, 'Well there's nothing we can do. There's no recourse.' They couldn't make him leave and she was totally helpless." Thus some participants decided that Skyler had relatively little power in her relationship with Walt from the beginning of their relationship, and that imbalance only became greater as Walt grew more influential in the drug business and, in turn, more self-assured. Some hatred of Skyler was rooted in her perceived weakness and also in a lack of respect for her character.

Yet a significant segment of the *Breaking Bad* fans we interviewed adopted the opposite perspective, using an array of gendered pejoratives to describe Skyler's character. Even those who liked Skyler or were indifferent to her were quick to list the terms others evoked in the hatred of her: "annoying," "pushy," "bossy," "overemotional," and "like a mosquito" were all terms used to describe the character. Those who sided with Walt throughout the run of the series, despite his violent, often ruthless means to success, were especially critical of Skyler, and "bitch" was the term primarily used to express that dislike. Pam, who sympathized with Skyler's characterization, commented on her perception of anti-fan reactions to Skyler, noting that

> all the [Skyler] hater polls and comment sections say, "She's such a bitch! She needs to let him do what he wants to!" And I'm like, "Really? Oh my god! You can't be that much on the side of Walter White!" I think people more are rooting for him and I am just incredulous. I cannot believe this is happening!

Ben offered a similar observation of anti-fans who saw "[Skyler] not, sort of putting up with Walt's shit, and they see that as her being a bitch." Giovanna, who acknowledged many of Walt's wrongdoings, still had little sympathy for Skyler's interference with Walt's business. She shared: "Walt, he was doing something wrong. He was dealing drugs and that put the family in danger. I liked Walt so much. I forgave him for doing [bad things]. But Skyler, she was a bitch so many times."

In addition to the negative terms applied to Skyler generally, some participants rationalized the hatred toward her character by condemning what they saw as her failure to let Walt "be a man." Patrick (twenty-six, American) lamented that Skyler was "so anti-Walter. Even from the get-go, she kind of makes him seem emasculated, like he's this boring guy." Although a number of aspects of Walt's characterization in the pilot episode were stereotypically emasculating (e.g., his typically feminized teaching profession, his deferential personality), participants held Skyler directly responsible for contributing to his emasculation as well. For instance, Jada (forty-seven, American) pointed out that "I never felt any romantic or sexual chemistry between Anna Gunn and Bryan Cranston. I didn't believe them as a couple throughout the entire series. She's bigger than he is, I never found her to be sexually appealing." Deeming Anna Gunn and, in turn, Skyler, "bigger than him" and not feminine enough to be sexually attractive reinforces femininity as diminutive and masculinity as physically imposing and thus implies that Skyler emasculates Walt. Further, although Eric (forty-four, American) indicated that, he "never really hated Skyler," he does say he can

> see where people think that she's holding him back. She's not understanding his primal need to be master of the family, and he asserted more confidence and control [as his drug empire grew] and she kinda resented that. . . . I can see where people would think that Skyler was sabotaging Walt emotionally on the home front. There wasn't anything she could sabotage when Walt was outside of the home, but he knew that she can sabotage him emotionally inside the home, or keep him out of the home from seeing his kids.

In this instance, Eric argued that Skyler contributed to Walt's emasculation through "emotional manipulation" and by denying him his natural right to be "master of the family" as a man.

When asked why Skyler was the subject of so much hatred in the *Breaking Bad* fan community, several participants took the opportunity to speculate on the broader cultural climate undergirding anti-fandom of Skyler. Wielding arguments similar to both Anna Gunn (2013) and Vince Gilligan (Brown 2013), participants often rooted Skyler hatred in cultural misogyny. Skyler was, for some, a proxy for the dysfunctional relationships anti-fans had with specific women in their own lives. Barbara (sixty-nine, American) suggested that anti-fans "had the shallow vicarious pleasure of seeing Walt get away with things, and they probably have resentments and hatred towards women in their lives who they feel are boxing them in." Juan asserted that "people hate her because they hate their moms and they hate their wives. It's like, 'Ugh. I don't want another woman telling me what to do!'" Others, though, suggested that the problem reflected in Skyler hate was much larger than Skyler, or any specific woman; as Jessica (thirty-three, Canadian) observed, "I don't think it's anything about her. It's because we live in a misogynistic, patriarchal society. . . . I don't think anybody likes to see power taken away from rich, White men, or powerful White men, in our society." Similarly, Jacob pointed out how culturally wide-reaching this misogyny is:

> I think that people talk about the progress we have made in America, like you ask men what they think about progress in sexism and you ask White people about progress in racism, and I mean, you get drastic, different responses if you ask a woman or if you ask a Black person. So, I think that this show is kind of beautiful. They showed the dark side of the husband . . . but I still think there is a long way to go in terms of having respect for a wife that stays at home. I think it's that's what basically makes them hate Skyler.

Importantly, each of these participants assumed that Skyler anti-fans are men, but there are certainly female Skyler anti-fans in the *Breaking Bad* fan community. In this study, the participants' observations point to the cultural expectations of women, particularly in their relationships with men. More important, their observations, alongside the comments of anti-fans who used gendered pejoratives to describe Skyler and suggested she was holding Walt back from his "primal needs," also underscore that fans' perspectives about gender roles deeply affect the judgments they make about Walt and Skyler and their relationship.

Conclusions

In July 2016, Milo Yiannopoulos, *Breitbart* senior editor at the time, was banned from Twitter in response to his incitement of numerous racist and sexist tweets directed at Leslie Jones, who was one of four women cast in the remake of the film *Ghostbusters*. This move by Twitter, an attempt to condemn harassing and abusive comments on its site, came only after Jones fought off attacks for weeks and ultimately announced she would be leaving Twitter. Unsurprisingly, banning Yiannopoulos did not end the attacks on Jones, and her website was hacked and vandalized the following month, with many of her private photos being made public. Twitter's ban on one user to deal with its abusive climate was both too overdue and too trivial to make much of an impact on a social media environment that for many years has been hostile to women (Hess 2014), particularly young and non-White women (Goodfellow 2017; Marwick

2016) and women with public visibility (Gardiner et al. 2016; Zuppello 2016). A 2014 study by the Pew Research Center found that 40 percent of social media users had experienced harassment and that 73 percent had observed harassment in social media (Duggan 2014). Legal scholar Danielle Keats Citron underscores the disruption and distress that the targets of cyber harassment and cyber stalking endure, arguing that such behavior "has a devastating and lasting impact on victims" (Citron 2014, 19).

Scholarship on anti-fandom often focuses on anti-fans' resistance to media texts and celebrities they find boring, banal, or excessive, heralding their snark, cleverness, and opposition to the powers that be. But alongside these instances of anti-fandom run darker, more ominous instances of dislike and hate. While many of the *Breaking Bad* fans we interviewed were not perpetrators of this darker form of anti-fandom, their feelings about Skyler White reveal that some instances of anti-fandom are driven by identification with a character's struggle (a crisis of masculinity with which they may identify) and/or by deep-seated biases (in this case, about gender and sex roles). Whether tied to character, to identification, or to biases, anti-fans' hateful responses to Skyler reveal the ways emotion can circulate to express support of a particular position or as a response to a perceived threat. Scholarship on the cultural impact of emotion, like Sarah Ahmed's (2004) work on hate, can be useful for developing a clearer understanding of why marginalized groups are often targets of such hate and how these expressions of hate affect fan communities. As scholars invested in understanding, supporting, and participating in fan communities and the digital environments they inhabit online, we must be willing to examine the hateful perspectives anti-fans take, and we also must explore the impact of their hate on their targets. As a celebrity on a highly popular television serial, Anna Gunn had a platform from which she could speak about her "character issue," but many other targets of anti-fandom, including other fans, do not have such opportunities. To truly understand the ways dislike and hate circulate in fan communities, fan scholars must be willing to examine and interrogate biases, viewpoints, and actions that we find distasteful.

REFERENCES

Ahmed, S. 2004. *The Cultural Politics of Emotion*. New York: Routledge.
Albrecht, M. M. 2015. *Masculinity in Contemporary Quality Television*. New York: Routledge.

Brown, L. 2013. "In Conversation: Vince Gilligan on the end of *Breaking Bad*." *Vulture*, May 12. www.vulture.com.

Chaney, J. 2013. "Why You Hate Skyler White." *Esquire*, September 5. www.esquire.com.

Citron, D. K. 2014. *Hate Crimes in Cyberspace*. Cambridge, MA: Harvard University Press.

Click, M. A., and H. W. Holladay. 2018, in press. "Breaking Up with *Breaking Bad*: Viewers' Perspectives on Morality and Finality in the Critically Acclaimed AMC Series." In *Everybody Hurts: Transitions, Endings, and Resurrections in Fandom*, edited by R. Williams. Iowa City: University of Iowa Press.

Cox, M. 2013. "Why Do Many *Breaking Bad* Fans Love Walter White but Hate Skyler?" *bitchmedia*, September 25. www.bitchmedia.org.

Duggan, M. 2014. "Online Harassment." Washington, DC: Pew Research Center, October 22. www.pewinternet.org.

Gardiner, B., M. Mansfield, I. Anderson, J. Holder, D. Louter, and M. Ulmanu. 2016. "The Dark Side of Guardian Comments." *Guardian*, April 12. www.theguardian.com.

Goodfellow, M. 2017. "Misogynoir: How Social Media Abuse Exposes Longstanding Prejudices against Black Women." *New Statesman*, February 27. www.newstatesman.com.

Gray, J. 2003. "New Audiences, New Textualities: Anti-Fans and Non-Fans." *International Journal of Cultural Studies* 6, no. 1:64–81.

Greenwald, A. 2013. "Three Thoughts on Anna Gunn's Editorial about Rabid Fan Hate of Skyler White." *Grantland*, August 26. Retrieved from http://grantland.com.

Gunn, A. 2013. "I Have a Character Issue." *New York Times*, August 23. www.nytimes.com.

Hess, A. 2014. "Why Women Aren't Welcome on the Internet." *Pacific Standard*, January 6. Retrieved from https://psmag.com.

Jane, E. A. 2012. "'You're a Ugly, Whorish, Slut': Understanding E-bile." *Feminist Media Studies* 14:531–546.

———. 2014. "Beyond Antifandom: Cheerleading, Textual Hate and New Media Ethics." *International Journal of Cultural Studies* 17:175–190.

———. In this volume. "Hating 3.0: Should Anti-Fan Studies Be Renewed for Another Season?"

Jenkins, H., J. Green, and S. Ford. 2013. *Spreadable Media: Creating Value and Meaning in a Networked Culture*. New York: New York University Press.

Lotz, A. D. 2014. *Cable Guys: Television and Masculinities in the 21st Century*. New York: NYU Press.

Marwick, A. 2016. "A New Study Suggests Online Harassment Is Pressuring Women and Minorities to Self-Censor." *Quartz*, November 24. https://qz.com.

Mittell, J. 2015. *Complex TV: The Poetics of Contemporary Television Storytelling*. New York: NYU Press.

Ryan, E. G. 2013. "Goodbye and Good Riddance, Angry Little Men Who Hate Skyler White." *Jezebel*, September 30. Retrieved from https://jezebel.com.

Zuppello, S. 2016. "Why We Let Famous Women Get Bullied Online." *Rolling Stone*, July 21. www.rollingstone.com.

8

Why All the Hate?

Four Black Women's Anti-Fandom and Tyler Perry

ALFRED L. MARTIN, JR.

On February 25, 2005, Tyler Perry's first feature film, *Diary of a Mad Black Woman*, debuted in movie theaters. Distributed by Lionsgate, the film was largely panned in mainstream press. The Associated Press's Christy Lemire suggested that, "in short, [the movie is] the diary of a mess" (Lemire 2005). While the Gannett newswire's Jack Garner did not find anything redeeming about the film, he conceded that perhaps white people "just don't get [Tyler Perry]"(Garner 2005). Despite its critical evisceration, *Diary* stunned the industry when it opened in the top spot on its opening weekend, grossing nearly $22 million at the box office. *Backstage* writer Brian Fuson positioned the film's box office as "a huge industry upset" because it bested Will Smith's romantic comedy *Hitch*, which opened the same weekend and was expected to easily win the weekend (Fuson 2005). After the incongruity between the critical response to *Diary* and its box-office receipts, Perry and Lionsgate decided to forego advanced screenings for Tyler Perry's next film, *Madea's Family Reunion* (2006). In an interview with the *New York Post*, Lionsgate president Tom Ortenberg said, "We are not going to spend $50,000 for the privilege of negative reviews for a film that isn't going to be affected by them" (Lumerick 2006). Ortenberg's quote gestures toward the ways the film's core audience seems to be unconcerned with the ways mainstream (*read*: white) press reviews Tyler Perry's films. Instead of a reliance on aesthetics (the trait upon which many mainstream reviewers often base their critiques), Perry's films seemed to tap into an affective response, one that white reviewers and viewers perhaps "didn't get." Demonstrating that Perry's audience does not rely on reviews per se, *Madea's Family Reunion* was the top-grossing film in its opening weekend, collecting $30 million in box-office receipts. However, in 2008 Lionsgate's distribution president Steve Rothenberg said, "Playing to a predominantly African-American audience" is the primary way that Tyler Perry has achieved success (DiOrio 2008). This essay is concerned with the intersection of this predominantly black audience that consumes Tyler Perry's films but do so while disliking—and even hating—them.

This essay argues that black audiences cannot be accurately conceptualized as a monolithic group of "fans" vis-à-vis Perry's oeuvre. Instead, this essay investigates the contours of displeasure that the black female viewers I interviewed experience with respect to his work—a still relatively unexamined axis of identities within fandom/anti-fandom scholarship. In 1992, John Fiske regretted "being unable to devote the attention to race which it deserves, but I have not found studies of non-white fandom. Most of the studies so far undertaken highlight class, gender and age as the key axes of discrimination" (Fiske 1992, 32). More than twenty years later, Henry Jenkins indicted fan studies because it "has been 'colour blind' in all of the worst senses of the term" (Jenkins 2014, 97). Four years after Jenkins' further indictment of fan studies, scant attention has been paid to black fandom or anti-fandom. Rebecca Wanzo forwards that the reticence to investigate the intersections of race and fan/anti-fan studies is rooted in the ways race "troubles some of the claims—and desires—at the heart of fan studies scholars and their scholarship" (Wanzo 2015). In an attempt to grapple with the ways race might complicate anti-fandom studies, this essay engages with black women anti-fans.

I am interested in interrogating consumers who Jonathan Gray theorizes as "those who strongly dislike a given text . . . considering it inane, stupid, morally bankrupt and/or aesthetic drivel" (Gray 2003, 70). But more than that, I investigate the ways these black female viewers not only articulate their dislike of Perry's media output but also rationalize a continued engagement with media from which they derive little or no enjoyment. While these black viewers certainly critique Perry's media output, I am not interested in those viewers who reject Perry by, as bell hooks argues, refusing to look at such images as "a gesture of resistance, turning away [as] one way to protest" (hooks 1992, 121). Nor am I interested in studying what black viewers think Perry's films get "right," as

Kennaria Brown, Shannon Baldon and Amber Stanton do in their 2013 study of black Tyler Perry audiences (Brown, Baldon, and Stanton 2013). Rather, I am interested in exploring those viewers who critique Perry but continue to engage with his films.

The present study intervenes in the fandom/anti-fandom literature by studying the contours of black anti-fandom with respect to black-cast media texts, which are often maligned and/or neglected in fan and media studies research. However, as Kristen J. Warner suggests, studying the ways black women's fandom operates around media texts is fruitful because of how it illuminates the ways, in the absence of media images of blackness, black women fans "make do" by latching onto *any* black representation to make their identities recognizable (Warner 2015, 37). Additionally, black anti-fans help to illuminate the ways black fans work as what Jacqueline Bobo calls "cultural readers," those who interweave the cultural with other aspects of their lives (Bobo 1995, 22). I suggest that Gray's taxonomy of anti-fandom (Gray, in this volume) may not be entirely applicable to black women's anti-fandom. While Gray offers that his taxonomy is not exhaustive and certainly positions anti-fandom as a complex phenomenon, this essay suggests that black women's anti-fandom may be even more complex with respect to why and how they continue to engage with Perry's films.

This essay is implicitly informed by auteur theory/authorship studies, in the ways that the *Cahiers du Cinema* (as discussed by Gray) positioned the author as the "singular artistic [genius] with coherent visions behind true film" (Gray 2013, 90). As the anti-fans interviewed in this essay articulate, they are keenly aware of Perry's involvement in the direction, writing, and production of his work. As such, the women in this study understand Perry as an auteur and hold him singularly responsible for the images they see on-screen.

Using in-depth interviews with four black, female, self-professed Tyler Perry haters, this essay investigates the frameworks these black female anti-fans use to situate their continued consumption of Tyler Perry media products even as they reproduce their miserable experiences of watching his films. Methodologically, this project employs one-on-one interviews with four self-identified anti-fans in Detroit. Each initial interview lasted between sixty and ninety minutes, and I supplemented those interviews with shorter follow-up interviews for clarification. By using semistruc-

tured, open-ended questions, interviewing respondents for longer periods of time, and conducting follow-up interviews, I collected data that
are richer than those I would have collected by conducting shorter interviews with a larger set of respondents because I allowed the black women
in this study to engage in an open discussion about Tyler Perry and his
films and let our conversation develop organically. Rather than seeking a
set of data that could be extrapolated across all black female anti-fans, I
engage more fully with a smaller pool of respondents. The women, whose
real first names are used in this essay, range in age from thirty-nine to
forty years old, have at least a bachelor's degree, and represent several
family formations—Channon, forty, and Tiffani, forty, are married with
children; Marquita, thirty-nine, is a divorced mother of two; and Danielle, thirty-nine, is single without children.

These four black women were recruited via my own personal network.
With each of the women in this study, I have a close embodied/"real
world" relationship. While this methodology can best be described as
selective sampling, studying these four black women is illustrative as
a springboard for further research on black women and anti-fandom.
Studying middle-class, educated black women helps to illuminate the
ruptures in the alleged monolithic notion that black people embrace
Tyler Perry and the films he produces. It is not "just" that these middle-
class, educated black women hate Tyler Perry's films; rather, their responses to Perry's films highlight the complex ways taste cultures, social
ties, and the culture industries converge to structure their anti-fandom.

"It's Just Not Positive, It's Not Uplifting": The Politics of Respectability and Tyler Perry's Images

A preoccupation with black media images remains a prescient concern
for the black women in this study. Largely, these women prefer images
that fit into certain categories. The images fit into what Evelyn Brooks
Higginbotham calls a "politics of respectability," a set of beliefs taken up
by black women in the early part of the twentieth century that endorsed
hegemonic idea(l)s about behavior in an effort not only to uplift but
also to reform the black race with the ultimate goal of achieving equal
rights (Higginbotham 1994, 187). For the women in this study, media
images deemed "positive" should have some degree of uplift, described

by Christine Acham as "a struggle between the elitist groups and more popular forces evident in the push for education, economic rights, and social advancement" (Acham 2004, 5). Danielle specifically invokes uplift language when she says, "I don't see where there is anything I see in his movies, where I'd say I would want to emulate that or that reflects my life. It's just not positive, it's not uplifting . . . it's not any of that" (Danielle 2015). Danielle and the other women in this study are cognizant of the ways media images can help to reinforce ideals about blackness. Marquita describes the images Tyler Perry writes for his films as "coonery," suggesting that the images are closely associated with the coon stereotype, in which black characters are presented as objects of amusement and as black buffoons (Bogel 1973, 7). "I think that when I watch a Tyler Perry film, I always get the laughable, the silly . . . it's just way too much of the extra silly, the extra demeaning, the extra cartoon-ish . . . ya know?" (Marquita 2015). Marquita's imagining of the "coonery" she associates with Tyler Perry is rooted in her preference for films most closely defined as "dramas" or 'biopics": "Just because they . . . they leave a better feeling. Ya know I mean . . . what with the other . . . historical movies and biopics, you kind of feel some kind of way when it's done because it's not always pleasant" (Marquita 2015). In other words, part of Marquita's hesitance to embrace Tyler Perry's films is rooted in genre. Perry's films do not, at least for Marquita, resonate within the realm of "serious" topics; instead, they trade on a comedic and affective response in lieu of dealing with "serious" issues. Danielle posits that part of her dislike for the images Tyler Perry produces is rooted in his, not her, problematic adherence to a politics of respectability. She says:

> The fact that you take every physical stereotype about black people, and then say go to church, get a black man and that will fix it. And you will have to do no work on your own and that you have no self worth unless you have a man. You know, it's very offensive to me. Because I feel like I do have worth, and I'm not married, and I don't have children, and I'm getting ready to turn forty. . . . So now the fact that I have accomplished all these other things in my life, I negate it because I chose not to get married and have kids. I don't appreciate that. And it is a slap in the face to all the women who, for whatever reason, happen to be single raising children. [Danielle 2015]

While Danielle prefers images that reflect a "positive" image of black people that will uplift the race, she concomitantly recognizes the problematic of constructing a "positive" image in only one fashion. Perry's politic constructs "positive" imagery in a monolithic way: educated black people, who enter into intraracial, heterosexual marriage and produce children. To be granted membership within this group of "positive" black media images, then, one has to, without deviance, subscribe to such a fashioning. As Danielle illuminates, her failure (because she is unmarried) to subscribe wholly to the "positive" representation triad seeks to negate her membership. In this way, part of Danielle's anti-fandom is rooted in her affective distance from Perry's work because it positions her personal brand of respectability as not "good enough" to fit within the narrow confines of a cinematic politics of respectability.

Channon believes that Tyler Perry has created a new stereotype that draws on uplifting images but saddles them with problems. Channon says, "I would say that Tyler Perry helped create the stereotype of this super-hyper educated black individual that has an incredible amount of problems. . . . Is he trying to expose the fact that you can be really educated and be a mess at home?" (Channon 2015). While Channon acknowledges that the upper-class, educated black person is among the more respectable representations of blackness, she nevertheless is concerned about the ways this image, in Perry's hands, is muddied with a host of problems, including marital discord and childlessness. With the construction of these problems central to the characterizations, the images are more difficult for Channon to connect with and contribute to the ways she distances herself from Perry's films.

Tiffani also distances herself from Perry's films. She believes his films reach for the "low-hanging fruit." She theorizes Perry's films as "remedial. There's no depth to them. . . . He just reaches for the basic audience that are looking for that . . . they can understand his films. . . . He is just reaching for a specific group of people that don't have many movies to identify with. [They] don't have many characters to identify with and have a lot of time and movie money on their hands." She goes on to suggest that part of the lack of depth in Perry's writing is rooted in the ways he understands and imagines his audience: "He will have his characters say, 'Oh look at us, we are so successful,' I mean like verbatim, 'I am a doctor with one hundred patients a day, and you, you are an attorney at the top of your field . . ' It's like he has to exploit those things because most of his audience is not going to get that" (Tiffani 2015). Tiffani's understanding of the ways Tyler Perry writes dialogue structures the ways she understands his media output as "remedial." It is conceived of as remedial because it fails to understand the black audience as being semiotically sophisticated and unable to connect the narrative dots without dialogue making explicit the ways the story should be decoded. Channon underscores Tiffani's disidentification with Perry's films and the ways they do not appeal to her by saying, "I don't really have anything against slapstick or silly humor, but I prefer more thoughtful humor. . . . I wouldn't laugh at a movie, like *Booty Call*, ever. Or anything in that genre, although I recognize that people would find it funny, it does not appeal to me" (Channon 2015). Tiffani and Channon begin to get at the ways a politics of respectability undergird their anti-fan responses to Tyler Perry's films in their interviews. Ultimately, Tyler Perry films are imagined as "not for" the black middle-class anti-fans I interviewed because of the ways they eschew story and character development in lieu of appealing to black religious affect. Connected to this notion that Perry's films are not for black middle-class viewers, the women I interviewed understand his films and the stories they tell as uninteresting. For example, Marquita suggests that Hollywood could "do better" by greenlighting more films "about jazz, more about science, more about medicine. Ya know? How come we haven't heard the Charles Drew story?[1] And Hollywood has a way of making uninteresting stuff interesting, so I don't buy that they can't make it interesting. They can" (Marquita 2015). Marquita explicitly believes the narrative ground Perry tills is problematic in that it does not appeal to her sense of "good stories." Ultimately, Tiffani, Marquita, and Channon's responses implicitly gesture toward Bourdieu's conceptualization of distinction, in which Tyler Perry's work is positioned as more "remedial" than that of other black filmmakers. Perry's work, then, is dismissed as "lower, coarse, vulgar, venal, [and] servile" (Bourdieu 1984, 7). Filmmakers Spike Lee and Antoine Fuqua are, in contrast, thought to produce and write "quality" work vis-á-vis Perry, even if their box-office returns do not tend to best Perry's.

However, as with Gray's conceptualization of *The Simpsons*'s anti-fans, these Tyler Perry anti-fans had an exceptional degree of engagement with, and knowledge of, Tyler Perry's work that was not rooted in a passing recognition of Perry and his cinematic output but reflected a deeper engagement with the films that actually held "considerable meaning for them" (Gray 2003, 65). Channon had seen many of Perry's films, including his 2010 film *For Colored Girls*, his adaptation of Ntozake Shange's *For Colored Girls Who Have Considered Suicide When the Rainbow Is Enuf*. But even that engagement with the film is structured by a politic that suggests that Perry's films are not for her (and by extension, women and people like her): "I really related to *For Colored Girls*. Having read the book, and seen the play, I related to it. But I felt like it wasn't from my generation, it was like from my mom's generation, and so, I was hoping he was going to do something with it that I could say, 'Now this is for my generation.' That's kind of what I was hoping for. And then I realized, 'Man, this is not going to come off good in a movie.' Having [the movie] handed to Tyler Perry [as director], I was so afraid of what it might turn out to be" (Channon 2015).

Channon's conceptualization of Perry's *For Colored Girls* suggests that she came to the film with a set of intertextual knowledges and expectations about the source material as well as about Perry's ability to handle such material. Put another way, Channon forwards a privileging of both the literary text and the "legitimate" theatrical space as "high art"—higher art than Perry's talents, in her conceptualization, allow him to achieve.

Perry's alter ego, Madea, and the films he makes that include the character are particularly problematic for the women in this study. This ire and dislike of the character is rooted in two broad structures. First, the respondents suggest that the character, because Perry uses her so frequently, should have some sense of character development. In other words, the women in this study recognize Madea, but they expect the character to be a fully fleshed out character with dimensions. As Tiffani succinctly forwards, Madea, as written by Perry, is not exactly a one-dimensional character but is "maybe two[-dimensional]. . . . No, she is 1.5 dimensional" (Tiffani 2015). Second, and somewhat related, because the character Madea is perceived as one that is not fully developed, she is disavowed as not appealing to particular taste cultures that call for fully realized characterizations. Tiffani crystalizes the ways taste and distinction undergird her feeling about Madea by arguing that the character has appeal, just not for her:

[Madea] appeals to people [who] are looking for . . . they don't want to think too hard about their laughs and can identify with the one matriarch figure in their family who was protective or still is protective and full of wisdom and a "take no prisoners" type. Like I said, that is how my grandmother is but not as . . . but not like . . . right down to toting a gun. But she has also evolved as a woman, as a person. She might not appreciate everything, but she is definitely more open as a person than she probably was thirty or forty years ago, in baby steps. She is the same person, but she has mildly evolved with the world. Whereas a character like a Madea has not. [Tiffani 2015]

For Tiffani, then, her dislike of Tyler Perry suggests that his films hold appeal for those who "don't want to think hard" about the media they consume. Tiffani constructs those who like Tyler Perry's films as those who possess lower socioeconomic status and lower levels of formal education. As such, Tiffani posits that Perry's films, and the characters within them, are not for those who possess cultural capital, even as they carry with them a degree of self-recognition.

Tiffani also alludes to the inability of characters within Perry's films to seem like fully developed characters, that they are drawn in broad strokes with little to no evolution or depth. In this way, particularly because Madea is reminiscent of her own grandmother, Tiffani wants the character to embody some semblance of verisimilitude. Tiffani is not seeking *just* a truth but also an accuracy that resembles the ways she constructs truth. However, Tiffani is not alone in this construction. Marquita concurs:

Ya know, we all have a big mama, a nana, a mimi, a . . . ya know, whatever we call our great-grandmother . . . matriarch of the family, but she doesn't always look like that, like mine certainly doesn't. She's a strong black woman, but she's by no means a larger-than-life, loud-talking, neck-rollin', grit-ball-bearin' kind of black woman. So, when you're dealing with people that maybe never have experienced what it is to have a . . . never have seen or experienced a black matriarch, if they walk away from a Tyler Perry film thinking, 'Oh, all big mamas act like Madea.' . . . Ugh. . . . He's kind of done us a disservice. [Marquita 2015]

Marquita's hatred for Tyler Perry's films is twofold. First, she believes that, by writing Madea in a way that conforms to some beliefs about black women generally, and black grandmothers specifically, the character functions as stereotypes do—to flatten out and essentialize representational tropes. Connected to Marquita's understanding of the function of stereotypes are parasocial relationships, which suggest that media consumers can develop beliefs about people, whether real people or fictional characters, through their mass-mediated relationship with their on-screen personas (Schiappa, Gregg, and Hewes 2006). Given that those outside of black and brown communities have been increasingly consuming Tyler Perry's films (particularly after his distribution deal with Lionsgate), Marquita argues that this particular image of black womanhood, as created by a black man, does "a disservice" to black image making.

The anti-fandom the black women in this study illuminate for Tyler Perry's films is rooted in the ways he crafts images that fail to conform their imagining of "positive" black images, which are always already bound within a politics of respectability and taste cultures. Put more explicitly, Danielle suggests that Perry actually makes exploitation films, similar to some black-cast films of the 1970s: "In his films you get D-class actors, you get a D-class everything. You get sub-par everything . . . sub-par location, sub-par crew, sub-par budget, and then you say, Here you go" (Danielle 2015). However, the question remains: If these women hate the stories and cinematography of Perry's films, why do they continue to consume them? The next section of this essay explores this question.

"I Mean . . . for Us It Was More Family Bonding Time": Strong Ties and Anti-Fandom

For the women in this study, hatred for Tyler Perry's films largely clusters around the ways he crafts images of blackness, which is related to a disidentification with his films and the kind of humor in which they traffic. If these anti-fans hate the media Tyler Perry produces, then why do they watch? These women cannot be described as "hatewatching," an act defined as watching a media text "you claim to dislike with the sole purpose of mocking it" (Davies 2013). They often do not discuss the films with others or their dislike for them. Rather, consuming Perry's films is rooted in social ties. As Mark Granovetter details, strong ties are characterized by a "combination of the amount of time, the emotional intensity, the intimacy . . . and the reciprocal services which characterize the tie" (Granovetter 1973, 1361). This section explores the ways Tyler Perry anti-fandom is produced by a desire to maintain social ties. In other words, these black women's anti-fandom is specifically tied to Perry's films—without his films and the social ties they engender, these women may have otherwise ignored Perry's work.

The black women in this study report a hesitation to express their dislike for Perry's films. This hesitance is mostly rooted in a desire to be inoffensive to those black viewers who enjoy Perry's films. As Tiffani details, "If I am talking to a friend that has an appreciation for his films, typically the conversation is going to end really, very quickly. Because I know I'm likely to offend, because what they find endearing, and I don't want to do that. . . . I couldn't talk to my grandma about my dislike for Tyler Perry movies because she would say, 'Oh that's a good movie,' and I was like 'Grandma, that movie is terrible,' but she would just not understand. She would not get my reason and then she would think that I was being snotty" (Tiffani 2015). Tiffani illuminates the ways the women in this study are not simply hatewatching.

Rather, what emerges is a connection to Tyler Perry rooted in the maintenance of familial and friend networks, or what is called "strong ties" in social network theory. A tie is simply a relationship between two people (or a group of people), and the thing (or things) that bind them together. However, the strength of a tie is determined by examining a number of factors including "frequency of contact, duration of the association, intimacy of the tie, provision of reciprocal services, and kinship" (Haythornthwaite 2002, 386). For the women in this study, the desire to be with family members and friend networks structures a reengagement with Perry, even as the experience of watching is not pleasurable. Tiffani sees the films with her parents, three siblings and son. "The first Tyler Perry movie we saw together was because my dad wanted to see it. . . . We did family movie dates. I mean . . . for us it was more family bonding time. . . . So, now that we don't do family movie dates anymore, I don't go see those movies anymore." Even as Tiffani's family, except for her father, generally felt the same way, they continued to go because the patriarch wanted to see the films: "I think we all felt the same way pretty much. It was a couple laughs, maybe, but in the end . . . my dad probably got the most out of it because he had convinced himself already that the Madea character was like his mother." Tiffani's consumption of the films is limited to the theatrical/familial experience, and she does not watch the films on cable or DVD and says she would "be more inclined to watch *Family Feud*" than a Tyler Perry film on television (Tiffani 2015). Tiffani, then, underscores the ways watching Perry's films is always and only about the experience of seeing the films in a theater with family.

Danielle consumes Perry's films because of her relationship with her cousin: "I went kicking and screaming to my first Tyler Perry film. But, I had gone out of state to visit her, and that was the point of the visit—to spend time with her. And the second one I saw was when I visited her in Baltimore. She is married with three kids, so those movies are not appropriate for kids. Her husband does not enjoy them, will not see them. . . . So I wasn't going to not give her her time off as a mom and a wife and then tell her she couldn't enjoy herself. She enjoys them" (Danielle 2015). Danielle structures her consumption of Perry's films in two ways. First, she, like the other women in this study, is concerned with maintaining her strong tie with her cousin. But second, and related, Danielle's consumption is rooted in caring for her cousin. Her mention of giving her cousin "time off" from her family suggests a stronger tie that clearly outweighs the experience of actually seeing a Tyler Perry film. The exchange for her displeasure is the pleasure her cousin receives from both having "time off" and spending time with her cousin.

Channon recalls, "I started seeing Tyler Perry movies with a mix of cousins and friends, and it was the majority ruling on the movie choice, so I think it was more of a bonding decision." Like Tiffani and Danielle, Channon did not necessarily opt into seeing a Tyler Perry film; rather, her desire to stay connected to family and friend networks superseded her desire to have a pleasurable viewing experience. Channon also gestures toward her desire to maintain harmony. By suggesting that the "majority rules" with respect to the movie chosen, Channon underscores the import of the strong ties she has with her networks. More important, Channon learned the consequences of submitting to an unpleasureable experience in exchange for the pleasurable experience of being among friend and family networks: "Some of my cousins really like all things

Tyler Perry—the movies and TV series . . . good, average, or bad. Over time, in casual conversation during holidays or a get together, I may have turned my nose up to the mention of one of his TV shows or the latest movie, and so I think they've stopped asking me to go with them" (Channon 2015). In this way, then, the engagement with/enjoyment of Tyler Perry's films, coupled with a silence if one finds the experience problematic, is the price of admission to maintain strong social ties. As Caroline Haythornthwaite argues, "There is also an ongoing ebb and flow in ties: they grow in strength as people get to know each other better, and decline as the reason for the strong association reaches its conclusion" (Haythornthwaite 2002, 387). Channon discovered that by talking about her displeasure with Perry's films she was excluded from the strong Tyler Perry filmgoer's tie. This is particularly important when considering that the maintenance, and perhaps strengthening, of the tie was the main reason Channon chose to engage with Tyler Perry's films in the first place.

The women in this study articulate the uneasy interplay among friendships/familial bonds, anti-fandom, and Tyler Perry. In some ways, transforming a popular proverb helps to articulate these women's anti-fandom: blood is thicker than Perry. They are willing to endure his cinematic output because they love their family and friends. But more than that, they forward that the anti-fandom they embody must be a quiet anti-fandom—at least in the presence of familial networks. In order to maintain relationships, not only must they consume his films, they must do so without expressing their displeasure. In this way, these black women cannot be described as hatewatchers, because they are denied the pleasure of hating.

"I Kind of Feel Obligated . . .": Tyler Perry, Anti-Fandom and the Culture Industries

A keen awareness of the ways blackness, representation, and Hollywood intersect complicates and informs the anti-fandom of the black women in this study. This section explores the ways these black women's anti-fandom is situated within an awareness of the interconnectivity of Hollywood, black cultural production, and the politics of film funding. As Sheril Antonio argues with respect to Hollywood's production of black media, "Proof of profit, and not race exclusively, was more the motive for deciding which films would be made" (Antonio 2002, 3). Following this logic, Marquita tends to see Tyler Perry's films on "opening weekend so they get box-office credit." This is a way for her to support a black artist in Hollywood. "To my understanding, part of the reason projects aren't greenlit is because Hollywood is determined that we don't support our films. So if I just show up with my dollars, I fly in the face of that, ya know what I mean? I'm saying 'Ha-ha, yes we do!' Good, bad or ugly, we're there for each other. We'll work it out later on, ya know?" (Marquita 2015). Marquita illuminates the tensions between anti-fandom and the culture industries. While she actively dislikes Perry's films, she also understands the often-racist logics that structure Hollywood's engagement with black-cast films and black audiences. Channon also underscores the ways her hatred of Tyler Perry's films is complicated by a desire to support black film: "I kind of feel obligated to [see his films], you gotta go see the Tyler Perry movie, the brother is doing his thing. You gotta go do that, you gotta support him" (Channon 2015).

However, Danielle does not necessarily see the utility in supporting black films. She says, "I don't go see a film just because it was produced by a black person. Most of the Tyler Perry films, I didn't see until they hit TV because I'm like 'I'm not paying for that trash.' To me, my money has value, and those films don't warrant paying for them" (Danielle 2015). As such, Danielle only sees Tyler Perry's films to maintain her strong tie to her cousin, not out of some sense of support for black film, generally, or Tyler Perry's films specifically. Danielle implicitly suggests a break between the support of black-cast films she dislikes and black-cast films she likes. In other words, Danielle is unwilling to support Tyler Perry because she believes it will send the message that his films represent the kinds of films black audiences want to see. Rather, when not nurturing her tie with her cousin, she reserves her money for other black-cast films that are more in line with her tastes, like *Best Man Holiday* (2013), which she suggests

> had a black cast but, to me, that was very much just a movie. Because there was nothing in that movie that was just "this applies only to black people." You have people of all races struggling with their faith, and how it affects their life. . . . And so, because you could have taken that black

cast, replaced them with a white cast, and it would have no impact on the movie in my mind except for you would have gotten a different demographic audience. [Danielle 2015]

Danielle gestures toward the ways that postracial ideologies underscore her engagement with "good" black-cast films. There is little requirement that the story be specific to an imagined "black experience," but it should have a semblance of universality. Channon looks for a similar kind of universality and cites *Set It Off* (1996) as a film that "just happened" to have a black cast: "It just has a good story, but I can see that story play out in pretty much any culture in the United States that is having economic depravity. So it could be in a Latino neighborhood, or it could be in a poor neighborhood in Boston, it could be, you know, it could anywhere. The fact that they are black just made it better, but it didn't take away from the story" (Channon 2015). Channon complicates the universality by arguing that *Set It Off*'s blackness has a multiplying effect—it doesn't detract, but makes the experience better. When Tiffani's family stopped going out on "family dates," her engagement with Perry's films stopped. When Channon expressed her dislike for Perry's films, she was boxed out of that social network, and when Danielle is not visiting her cousin, these films cease to hold any import or cultural capital. In this way, consumption and strong ties are inextricably linked to the (dis) pleasures derived from Tyler Perry's cinematic output for these black women.

Highlighting the complex relationship between hatred and black cultural production, the black women in this study articulate the ways an engagement (or disengagement) with Perry's films is closely tied to black-cast film production. Whether it is Channon and Marquita's continued engagement with Perry's films to ensure additional black films are greenlit or Danielle's insistence that she only consumes black-cast films that fit within her construction of "good" black-cast films in the absence of personal social ties, these black women make decisions based on the ways they think Hollywood films are produced, funded, and disseminated.

Conclusion: Four Black Women, Tyler Perry and Anti-Fandom

This study explores the ways the anti-fandom of four black, middle-class women is complicated by a trifecta of concerns: black image production, the culture industries, and social ties. Unlike bell hooks's study of black women and media reception, these black women are not picking out a character in Perry's films to identify with their particular woes and frustrations (hooks 1992, 120). Rather, other than appreciating the fact that Perry has navigated a Hollywood system that so often seems closed to black filmmakers, the women in the present study see little to celebrate with respect to Perry's work.

However, this study also suggests that the import of social and familial networks can structure a continued engagement with a hated media object. In other words, watching Perry's films is not about "hatewatching" for these women, nor is it about the acquisition of cultural capital from knowing about (or publicly hating) Tyler Perry's media output. Rather, these women watch because the ones they love watch. They spend their money and two hours of their time to connect with their family members and friends—even if it is in the dark. In this way, for the four black women in this study, seeing Tyler Perry films is driven by a desire to maintain social networks, not necessarily the content of the films. More than anything, this essay sheds light on the ways these four black women balance their dislike of Perry's films with their desire for close relationships and support of black Hollywood production. For these women, hate is a tricky thing that exists outside of their personal taste but within a complex network that includes black image production, the culture industries, and social ties. Because of the ways representational politics functions in a mediated world, anti-fandom for these black women does not fit into the taxonomy of anti-fandoms Gray discusses (in this volume) but, rather, expands it. Ultimately, the answer to the question "Why all the hate?" is complex. While the black women in this study hate Tyler Perry's films, they feel obligated to consume them in order to demonstrate that a black audience exists for Hollywood-produced films and because of a desire to remain connected with family and friends who like Perry's output. Future work should continue to consider the ways anti-fandom and race intersect to investigate the complex ways familial ties, a politics of respectability, and ideas about

Hollywood production complicate anti-fandom. For the women in this study, anti-fandom has little to do with the celebration of a "bad object" or wanting to impress others with their knowledge of a text they claim to hate; rather, while they hate Perry's films, they continue to consume them in order to maintain close social ties and to demonstrate that black audiences exist for black-cast media.

NOTE

1 Charles Drew was an African American scientist and researcher whose pioneering work advanced knowledge about blood transfusions.

REFERENCES

Acham, C. 2004. *Revolution Televised: Prime Time and the Struggle for Black Power.* Minneapolis: University of Minnesota Press.

Antonio, S. D. 2002. *Contemporary African American Cinema.* New York: Peter Lang.

Bobo, J. 1995. *Black Women as Cultural Readers.* New York: Columbia University Press.

Bogel, D. 1973. *Toms, Coons, Mulattoes, Mammies and Bucks: An Interpretive History of Blacks in American Films.* New York: Viking Press.

Bourdieu, P. 1984. *Distinction: A Social Critique of the Judgment of Taste.* Translated by Richard Nice. Cambridge, MA: Harvard University Press.

Brown, K., S. Baldon, and A. Stanton. 2013. "Getting It 'Right?': African American Women Reading Tyler Perry." In *Interpreting Tyler Perry: Perspectives on Race, Class, Gender, and Sexuality,* edited by Ronald L. Jackson II and Jamel Santa Cruze Bell, 240–254. New York: Routledge.

Channon. 2015. Interview by author, March 19. Tape recording. Austin, TX.

Danielle. 2015. Interview by author, March 13. Tape recording. Austin, TX.

Davies, M. 2013. "'Hate Watching' Is Mostly Just Being Embarrassed by Your Own Tastes." *Jezebel,* February 13. www.jezebel.com.

DiOrio, C. 2008. "Tyler Perry Struggles to Draw White Moviegoers. *Today,* April 1. www.today.com.

Fiske, J. 1992. "The Cultural Economy of Fandom." In *The Adoring Audience: Fan Culture and Popular Media,* edited by Lisa A. Lewis, 30–49. New York: Routledge.

Fuson, B. 2005. "Audiences Fall for 'Woman.'" *Backstage,* February 28. www.backstage.com.

Garner, J. 2005. "Diary of a Mad Black Woman." *Rochester (NY) Democrat and Chronicle,* February 25. www.democratandchronicle.com.

Granovetter, M. S. 1973. "The Strength of Weak Ties." *American Journal of Sociology* 78, no. 6:1360–1380.

Gray, J. 2003. "New Audiences, New Textualities: Anti-Fans and Non-Fans." *International Journal of Cultural Studies* 6, no. 1:64–81.

———. 2013. "When Is the Author?" In *A Companion to Media Authorship,* edited by Jonathan Gray and Derek Johnson, 88–111. New York: Wiley.

———. In this volume. "How Do I Dislike Thee? Let Me Count the Ways."

Haythornthwaite, C. 2002. "Strong, Weak, and Latent Ties and the Impact of New Media." *Information Society* 18, no. 5:385–401.

Higginbotham, E. B. 1994. *Righteous Discontent: The Women's Movement in the Black Baptist Church, 1880–1920*. Cambridge, MA: Harvard University Press.

hooks, b. 1992. *Black Looks: Race and Representation*. Boston: South End Press.

Jenkins, H. 2014. "Fandom Studies as I See It." *Journal of Fandom Studies* 2, no. 2:89–109.

Lemire, C. 2005. "'Diary of a Mad Black Woman' Reveals Chaos of Plot Devices." *Athens (GA) Banner-Herald*, February 24. www.onlineathens.com.

Lumerick, L. 2006. "Advance Film Reviews in Critical Condition." *New York Post*, February 23.

Marquita. 2015. Interview by author, April 20. Tape recording. Austin, TX.

Schiappa, E., P. B. Gregg, and D. E. Hewes. 2006. "Can One TV Show Make a Difference? *Will & Grace* and the Parasocial Contact Hypothesis." *Journal of Homosexuality* 51, no. 4:15–37.

Tiffani. 2015. Interview by author, March 5. Tape recording. Austin, TX.

Wanzo, R. 2015. "African American Acafandom and Other Strangers: New Genealogies of Fan Studies." *Transformative Works and Cultures*, no. 20. doi: 10.3983/twc.2015.0699.

Warner, K. J. 2015. "ABC's *Scandal* and Black Women's Fandom." In *Cupcakes, Pinterest, and Ladyporn: Feminized Popular Culture in the Twenty-first Century*, edited by Elana Levine, 32–50. Urbana: University of Illinois Press.

9

Just Sexual Games and Twenty-Four-Hour Parties?

Anti-Fans Contest the Global Crossover of Reggaetón Music Online

MICHELLE M. RIVERA

Introduction

Over decades, the music industry constructed the Latin music market and expanded it globally by subsuming Latin American, Hispanic, and Latin(a/o) audiences under convenient pan-ethnic labels. Seeking to sustain the interest of the Latin youth market that was peaked during the "Latin pop" boom of the 1990s and early 2000s, the Latin music industry repackaged and rebranded reggaetón music as pan-Latin and as a "new" Latin urban youth-driven genre—out of which a burgeoning Latin urban niche market also emerged. Latin urban brand identity works to expand reggaetón's reach under the pan-Latin umbrella by linking together audiences and fans across geographies, and by targeting a younger demographic presumably based on shared language (bilingual/Spanish/English dominant). And yet, this chapter demonstrates how these pan-Latin branding strategies that seek to provide catchalls for multiple racial and ethnic identities, dually alienate interpellated anti-fans. I examine how these catchall categorizations are met with cultural resistance, particularly among anti-fans of reggaetón, who reveal a complex relationship with reggaetón—expressing *frustration* and ardently resisting interpellation as the target audience for this Latin urban branded and ethnically and racially commodified form. Jonathan Gray defined anti-fandom as "the realm not necessarily of those who are against fandom per se, but of those who strongly dislike a given text or genre, considering it inane, stupid, morally bankrupt and/or aesthetic drivel" (Gray 2003, 70). Extending from this definition, I underscore the importance of widening the lens of anti-fan studies to critically engage how cultural resistance functions as an organizing principle for those who are ethnically and racially marked and marketed to on that basis. I hypothesize that anti-fandom, dislike, and/or hate for a text or genre can also serve as a means to reject the ways fans/anti-fans are constructed and interpellated as audiences or target markets—particularly for those constructed in ethnically and racially marked, coded, classed, and gendered ways. Deploying a methodology of Internet discourse analysis, I interrogate how anti-fans of reggaetón use online spaces to affirm their complex, hybrid identities and taste cultures in relation to the conflated representations of Latinidad they encounter globally through reggaetón's crossover. Engaging participatory online music anti-fandom, this chapter interrogates a cross section of anti-fans' multilayered responses to reggaetón's global crossover and investigates the interpersonal dynamics of reggaetón's anti-fans/fans in an anti-reggaetón forum maintained online between 2006 and 2009.[1] This chapter and other relevant work (M. Rivera 2011, 2017) offer a critical framework to examine how vectors of difference and hierarchies of taste intersect through anti-fandom.

The Global Crossover of Reggaetón

Reggaetón is a controversial and provocative Afrodiasporic musical phenomenon derived from 1990s Puerto Rican Underground rap—later repackaged as a pan-Latin and Latin urban genre during its commercial crossover in 2004. It has been used as a marketing tool to promote everything from toothpaste to politicians' campaigns in the United States, the Caribbean, and across Latin America. Reggaetón experienced mainstream crossover into the global music market in 2004, which led to widespread diffusion on radio airwaves (Rossman 2012); in film; on television, award shows, and magazines; and across multiple entertainment platforms. Its popularity translated into reggaetón/urban-themed clothing lines, merchandising and advertising deals, an ancillary mobile-driven market, and various Internet sites devoted to newsfeeds, music, and video streaming. During this marketing blitz around reggaetón, radio broadcast and satellite stations reformatted programming around the United States and abroad to provide a then-burgeoning Latin urban or hurban (Hispanic + urban) format with content—some venues and music streaming playlists rotating reggaetón songs around the

clock (Hinckley 2005; Navarro 2005; Resto-Montero 2016). Mass exposure gave the genre a newfound commercial viability, which aside from
lining the pockets of industry executives and merchandisers spawned a
backlash against reggaetón that carries on forcefully among anti-fans.

Debatably, the backlash against reggaetón emerged out of a reaction
against commercialized conceptions of Latinidad that were ascribed to
the genre and its "Latin Urban" audiences through commercial crossover.
There are integral linkages between the Latin urban aesthetics of reggaetón
and the discourses of authenticity—vital to the marketing of reggaetón on
a global scale. Reggaetón is a musical form that is largely symbolically
linked to the urban centers of Puerto Rico—"de la disco al caserío" (from
the discotheque to the housing projects; Dinzey-Flores 2008, 35). Zaire
Dinzey-Flores argues that the "urban socio-spatial community actual-
ized between the disco, the barrio, the caserios, and the street" through
reggaetón's lyrics "underscores poverty, violence, masculinity, and race as
vital constructs of an authentically urban experience" (ibid.). On the one
hand, resistance to the genre derives from a level of disidentification with
Latin urban ascriptions. On the other hand, rejection of the genre derives
from "deviant" associations previously attached to Underground music,
which is considered a precursor to reggaetón (Marshall 2009; R. Rivera
2009). Scholars trace how reception to Underground music was fraught
with tension, as state interventions imposed censorship and bans of Underground music, videos, and (el perreo) dance during the mid-1990s in
Puerto Rico and again in the early 2000s (Negrón-Muntaner and Rivera
2007; R. Rivera 2009; Santos 1996). Following reggaetón's crossover, news
media and scholarly sources tracked similar forms of censorship imposed
against reggaetón songs, videos, and performances in the Dominican Re-
public as well as in Cuba (Ahorre.com 2006; G. Baker 2011). Previous bans
against Underground music were premised on alleged obscenity violations from sexist and misogynist treatment of women in the music videos,
explicitly sexual lyrics, and allusions to drugs, sex, and violence in songs
and performances (Báez 2006; E. Baker 2005; Negrón-Muntaner and Rivera 2007; Santos 1996). Resistance to reggaetón from anti-fans also manifests in the form of taste distinctions and hierarchies, whereby reggaetón
is relegated to low culture, and several "obscenity" violations previously
railed against Underground music recirculate through anti-fans' contemporary interpretations about reggaetón.

Theoretical Framework: Broadening the Scope of Music Anti-Fandom and Fandom

Contemporary work in fan studies has remained attuned to how fans "are embedded in the existing economic, social, and cultural status quo"—whereby "taste hierarchies and structures among fans themselves are described as the continuation of wider social inequalities" (Gray, Sandvoss, and Harrington 2007, 6). Henry Jenkins underscores the continued importance of engaging how taste and cultural hierarchies operate within fandom (Jenkins 2014, 92, 98). Specifically citing Pierre Bourdieu's theorizations of taste in *Distinction* (1984), Jenkins draws attention to "the entrenched power expressed through efforts to police cultural hierarchies" in the formation of taste (92). Entrenched power is evident not only in efforts to police cultural hierarchies or in the establishment of taste distinctions themselves; rather, hierarchies of power are also revealed through the interpersonal dynamics of fans/anti-fans, particularly in digital and online spaces. I would add that racialized and ethnically marginalized fans/anti-fans also use digital and online spaces to assert their taste cultures as a means to reclaim their representational authority from the culture and advertising industries as well as from the mainstream media, where they are continually marginalized. On disentangling these structures of power, Jenkins offers that

> Bourdieu's primary focus was on the ways in which taste was shaped by class divisions, but we might extend his ideas to talk about how taste is racialized, shaped by who has access to particular cultural experiences and discursive resources, structured by who is encouraged or discouraged from displaying particular kinds of cultural preferences and enflamed by our collective tendency to defend our tastes primarily through the expression of distaste and disgust towards others' tastes. [Jenkins 2014, 98]

Accordingly, interrogating the creation and policing of taste distinctions requires intersectional analyses, as these distinctions are shaped by hegemonic power relations and divisions along axes of class, race, ethnicity, sex, gender, and nation, among others. My approach in this study is to turn a critical eye toward the structural hierarchies that both enable and constrain reggaetón anti-fans/fans—emphasizing the importance of understanding how anti-fans carve out their own spaces online to negotiate their complex, hybrid, and intersectional identities as they also mediate texts they hate and love. I recognize that this is not an either/or discussion. There is a tendency in scholarship on online music fandom to frame music fans/anti-fans in an either/or context. Either they are controlled by corporations/advertisers who use digital delivery systems to data mine, impinge on fans' privacy, and atomize, monitor, and "automate" them (McCourt and Burkart 2007, 261–268), or they are empowered via their tech-savvy functionality as "amateur experts" in music/artist/band promotion (Baym and Burnett 2009). Within the context of this study, I see anti-fans of reggaetón forcefully disrupting this binary by virtue of the ways they bring their cultural, ethnic, gender, racial, class, sexual, religious, and political identities to bear on their negotiations of the musical taste cultures they privilege and hate. These findings map onto what audience reception studies work on ethnic media has been attuned to for several past decades, which is the importance of conducting analyses that acknowledges and "accounts for the impacts of ethno-racial identity, sexuality, class, and (trans)national identity on the performance and *reception*" (Cepeda and Rosales 2017, 386; emphasis added). This is particularly relevant given a subject of analysis such as reggaetón music, which "operates in such a myriad of geographies and cultural dynamics" (Rivera-Servera 2009). It is counterproductive to ignore the impact of these intersections on the music or in relation to the genre's consumption, reception, fandom, and anti-fandom. Thus, it is imperative that work on anti-fandom move toward interrogating how these multilayered intersections potentially inform one another and how they might influence the investment that anti-fans have in expressing their dislike and/or hatred through various anti-fan practices—including disengagement (Gray and Murray 2016).

Recognizing work on anti-fandom that does not hesitate to call out fan/anti-fan practices that explicitly seek to subvert discussions of race and power, Dominique Johnson's (2015) excellent reading of the African American female character Michonne in the *Walking Dead* television and book series, carefully elucidates how *antiblack racial antagonisms* are pervasive in the dominant construction of Michonne as well as in the fan communities' reception that rejects race, sex, and gender critiques of the show. This reading also serves as an important call to anti-fan studies to "interrogate constructions of race, gender, class, sexuality, and other social formations that form the core of social differentiation in current civil society" as a means to address "how power must be concerned with power's presence in everyday circumstances across a broad social spectrum" (Johnson 2015, 272–273). In many ways, this approach shares common threads with Jacqueline Bobo's (1995) seminal work on *counterreception* among African American women, Frances Aparicio's (1998) study on *selective listening* practices among Latina audiences of salsa music, and Angharad Valdivia's (2000) negotiated reading of *frustration* across Latina reception analysis. These formative studies emphasized the complex interpretive strategies that female audiences of color have enacted as a means to negotiate and confront hegemonic cultural representations across media. The findings of these studies lend themselves to a rethinking of "frustration" within anti-fan studies as compelling racial, sex, and gender critiques against media producers, advertisers, and larger systems of representation, versus sheer disdain of a particular text in isolation from these other salient variables.

In the realm of pop music, this opens up the opportunity to shift analyses on music fandom from the empowerment/control binary to a broader understanding of what belies the frustration of reggaetón's anti-fans and why they go against the grain. Here, Mark Duffett's research on "adversarial" music fans is informative in that it seeks to understand "hecklers" who go out of their way to disrupt live music performers/performances and are often willing to violate social norms to do so (Duffett 2009, 40, 44). Duffett observes that "fandom thus becomes a responsive action: a counterperformance about a performance" (45). While Duffett acknowledges that the performer still holds the microphone and wields the power of *amplification* to drown out the heckler's disruption, nonetheless, the heckler's act of resistance demonstrates that "an illegitimate speaker can have something more valuable to say than the artist" (54). Duffett foregrounds this power struggle as evidence of a *symbolic economy* that "exposes the expectations, power mechanisms, and unequal social relations that facilitate live popular music" (ibid.). Annette Hill's study on anti-fandom describes live wresting events as a "public performance of power relations" (per Stephen Coleman 2010) between promoters, wrestlers, fans, and anti-fans (Hill 2015, 176). Hill suggests that, "if we consider power in performative terms, then we can look at modalities of power and how it is experienced in mediated and lived realities" (187). This is an important theoretical consideration given the diversity of experiences that anti-fans bring to the arena and the ways their participation shapes and is shaped by their own lived realities.

As this relates to music fandom, Duffett's study directs us to the ways music fandom/anti-fandom goes beyond music. It suggests that, by ignoring the more adversarial and provocative aspects of music fandom, one remains wedded to an ossified "illusion of unanimity" (per sociologists McPhail and Wohlstein 1983), thereby assuming audiences are "self-selected groups of satisfied consumers who share common interests" (Duffett 2009, 39). Liz Giuffre's study highlights the importance of looking beyond the pleasure of music, claiming that "the other side of popular music's appeal, popular music anti-fandom, is fundamental to how popular music fandom works" (Giuffre 2014, 54). The reality is that hecklers, trolls, and anti-fans abound within the scope of music fandom, and their interests and investments in assuming these identities could not be more diverse. My aim in the following analysis is to extend beyond a contained scope of what is considered music anti-fandom and interrogate a digital site of participatory music anti-fandom that reveals complex underlying and intersecting layers of negotiation mediated by fervent anti-fans/fans of reggaetón from across the globe.[2]

Findings

The Politics of Representation: Negotiating Ethnic, Racial, and National Identity through Reggaetón

Reggaetón, like hip hop, is a musical and cultural form that is racialized and ascribed markers of deviancy—associations with violence, drug use, the "underclass," gang culture, and prison life—embedded within the culture of poverty theory (Lewis 1965). Even as reggaetón has crossed over into the mainstream music market and been sanitized in terms of lyrical content, image, and performances, those original markers of deviancy persist in reggaetón's anti-fan rejection, and these attachments serve as fodder and fuel to the add to the anti-fan campaign. Here, for example, anti-fan *yago* sparks a debate about reggaetón artists being drug addicts:

Re: [bezantil2005] anti-reggaetón arguments

Yago

WELCOME TO THE ANTI-REGGAETÓN BROTHERHOOD, READY
TO PUT THIS GARBAGE ON BLAST. MY WIFE USED TO LIKE THE
CRAPATON BUT I AM CONVINCING HER AND NOW SHE HARDLY
LISTENS TO IT (IT WON'T TAKE MUCH MORE [CONVINCING]
THOUGH). ANOTHER THING, REGGAETÓN IS FULL OF GANG-
BANGERS SINCE DADDY YANKEE WAS A GANGBANGER BEFORE
THEY SHOT HIM AND HE HAD TO LEAVE THE GANG TO DEDI-
CATE HIMSELF TO SINGING THIS GARBAGE. TO DAISY AND
ALIANNA PLEASE DO NOT COME WITH YOUR VULGARITIES.
THIS FORUM IS CALLED ANTI REGGAETÓN ARGUMENTS, DO
NOT RUIN THE FORUM, SHOUT OUT TO BEZANTIL, AND ALSO
TO GORNOTEN AND RENZO.
THE AUTHOR, YAGO

Re: [yago] anti-reggaetón arguments

Daisy8756

First of all it is not full of gangbangers because from what I know
whitney houston is a drug addict and she is a crazy woman and she does
not sing reggaetón and britney spears also has a bunch of tattoos and is
another drug addict and from what I know does not sing reggaetón . . .
and daddy yankee is famous for his music not for his scandals . . . even
shakira had to put out a reggaetón song . . . and I don't know what you
are talking about when you say vulgar when the first vulgar ones are you
guys and my goodness you really know the history of daddy yankee and
that with you not liking him . . . o.k.

Re: [daisy8756] anti-reggaetón arguments

Yago

THE HISTORY OF DADDY YANKEE I READ PRECISELY ON THIS
FORUM OF ANTI-REGGAETÓN ARGUMENTS THAT SOME REG-
GAETÓN ARTIST INTRUDER DARED TO POST.
LOGIC DICTATES: NOT ALL DRUG ADDICTS AND GANGBANGERS

ARE REGGAETÓN ARTISTS, BUT ALL REGGAETÓN ARTISTS ARE
DRUG ADDICTS AND GANGBANGERS
DAISY, I WOULD NOT WANT TO OFFEND YOU, THAT IS NOT
MY CUSTOM IN THIS FORUM, AND HERE GOES THE QUESTION:
GIVEN YOUR NICKNAME, ARE YOU PERHAPS 14 YEARS OLD.
SHOUT OUTS TO ALL OF MY ANTI-REGGAETÓN BROTHERS
YAGO

A tactic used against defenders of reggaetón, who are predominantly self-reporting female participants in the forum and fans, is to marginalize them through vulgar sexist and racist discourse, as in the following post where *renzo* responded to a comment by *daisy8756*:

Re: [daisy8756] anti-reggaetón arguments

Renzo

Hold on disturbed little girl . . . to move your ass for a bunch of ugly black crapatoneros . . . 😒
I got that letter from an anti-crapaton forum . . . dedicated to Alan Garcia and all those crapatoneros who only listen [to] garbage 😊

Most forum comments from *yago* and *daisy8756* speak to issues of representation. Some participants, like *darsenn*, speak directly to the ways reggaetóneros are represented in the media:

Re: [yago] anti-reggaetón arguments

darsenn

TO BEGIN WITH . . . I DON'T KNOW BUT I THINK THAT THE
MAJORITY OF REGGAETÓN'S SUPERFANS ARE PROBABLY UNDER
25 YEARS OLD . . . RIGHT?
FROM THERE WE CAN DEDUCE THEIR QUICK, EASY, AND NAÏVE
DISPLAYS OF UNCONDITIONAL DEVOTION TOWARD THIS TYPE
OF MUSIC. . . . I DON'T THINK THAT A FACTOR LIKE 'ITS IN
STYLE' IS A DECISIVE ONE HERE.

WE SHOULDN'T BE SO RADICAL HERE, NOT SAY: "THAT MUSIC
IS GARBAGE UGGGGG" OR "IT IS THE BEST THING THAT COULD
EVER HAVE BEEN INVENTED" BECAUSE SUCH EXTREMES ON
BOTH SIDES LACK SOUNDNESS TO SUSTAIN A DEBATE.
IN REALITY IT IS A LESSER GENRE OF MUSIC, IT IS NOT AT THE
HEIGHT OF ROCK, SALSA, JAZZ, BLUES OR OTHER APPROPRI-
ATE RHYTHMS FROM EACH OF OUR COUNTRIES, I DON'T THINK
IT IS BAD FOR PEOPLE TO ENJOY THEMSELVES DANCING WITH
SIMPLE REFRAINS, IF THEY WANT TO DO IT LET THEM, BUT WE
CANT TALK ABOUT A "PHILOSOPHY OF REGGAETÓN," IT CAN'T
BE BECOME THE CENTER OF ONE'S LIFE, TO TRY TO TALK, TO
DRESS AND TO BEHAVE LIKE THOSE IDIOTS IN THOSE VIDEOS
IS PATHETIC.

**DO YOU GUYS REALIZE THAT REGGAETÓN CONTRIBUTES
TO THE FORMATION OF THE STEREOTYPE OF THE STU-
PID LATINO? HAVEN'T YOU GUYS THOUGHT ABOUT THAT?
ARE OUR COUNTRIES JUST SEXUAL GAMES AND A 24 HOUR
PARTY?**[3]

WE SHOULD ALSO CONSIDER THAT RHYTHMS LIKE THIS ONE
ARE IMPOSED ON US BECAUSE THE MEDIA BOMBARDS PEOPLE
ALL DAY LONG AND THEY WIN BY VIRTUE OF IMPOSITION AND
THEN THEY ARGUE THAT THEY PUT THESE MUSIC OUT "BE-
CAUSE IT IS WHAT THESE PEOPLE ARE ASKING FOR" DO YOU
GUYS AT LEAST REALIZE THIS? OR DO ALL THE REGGAETÓN
FOLKS THINK WITH THEIR LOWER HEAD?

Here, there is a strong reaction against the flattening of difference
and conflation that occurs via representation of Latin Americans and
Latinos/as in the media, and anti-fans want to make it clear that they
do not want to be lumped in with reggaetón and what it represents. To
create distance from reggaetón and make it even more evident in the
forum space, many participants exert their racial, ethnic, and national
identities as a means to distance themselves from Puerto Rico—one
of the often-claimed birthplaces of reggaetón—and another target of
anti-reggaetón disdain. For instance, *renzo* and *dios349* express their
views:

Re: [alianna98] anti-reggaetón arguments

Renzo

Ok. . . . we await your photo then . . . to see if you have to right to offend my country like you did before. Additionally, I will respond to you with the following:

NOT EVEN IF I WAS CRAZY WOULD I BE FROM A COUNTRY THAT DOESN'T EVEN HAVE A FLAG, THAT SELLS THEIR COUNTRY FOR A FEW DOLLARS FROM THE ANGLOS, AND WHO CREATE OFFENSIVE MUSIC LIKE REGGAETÓN.
BE MORE ORIGINAL AND BELIEVE SOMETHING THAT IS YOUR OWN, STOP IMMITATING RAP OR HIP HOP AND OTHER GENRES CREATED BY THE USA.
AND YOUR GANGBANGERS CAN KICK ROCKS AND STAY IN PUERTO RICO.

😒

Re: [alianna98] anti-reggaetón arguments

Renzo

Ohhh and what happened? . . . did the dress fit? 😊 . . . and take into ac-count that I have been kind and not posted the other photos . . .
At least I have a Country, we are not a colony of anybody, not slaves of some Anglos. . . . You people are, you have been slaves all of your lives, of the Spanish and later of the USA. . . .
Better that you don't make me talk, like I told you. . . . we can talk about music, and I don't have anything against your country, this forum is about Anti-Reggaetón and we should talk about that, if you'd like to persist.
And if you want to know the wonders of Peru, it is very simple, just look for forums like "Viva Peru gentleman," or other similar ones that are easy to find.
I don't want to fight with you, if you were a man I would not have a problem, but I don't like fighting with women . . . so we shall end this discussion in peace 😌

Re: [lisa1010] anti-reggaetón arguments

Dios349

To lisa1010 and all of those tolerant of this crap that is widespread all over, I have had it up to my balls with the toleration for this b%$#ass invention and that we are all the same and c&%$sucking things like those, I respect a person who is fair, honorable, hard working and decent, things that reggaetón imbeciles are not, and who have the balls to do nothing other [than] dishonor and bring the culture of South American down to the ground, because it is a music of delinquents, drug traffickers, gangbangers, bitches, and a million other things, and I am from Asturias, and here there are many decent immigrants that are against this b%$#ass garbage and all that it entails, they work, they make a dignified living and they respect my language, my traditions and everything related to my culture, but coincidently those who do not even respect my LANGUAGE saying that they refuse to learn Asturiano because they are a b%$#ass piece of crap those who listen to that garbage walk around like delinquents and extort from their fellow countrymen who just for working to be honorable and not wanting to join their street gang and be a lazy bum and a piece of crap criminal without going further into this example this is a Colombian guy who works as a pizza delivery man, and whom these reggaetón sons of bitches attacked and among several of them beat up just because of his COLOMBIAN nationality and for working instead of joining them to make delinquent crap, another example are Africans who come to live as best they can, who do not demand anything they only ask to be left in peace, well those gangbanger sons of bitches call them shitty NEGROS and they throw merchandise on the floor and they rob them, that music and those people what they do is put honorable south americans who come here to find a better future in a bad spot, and on top of that those bastards if they see two or 3 people they won't even look they way, the day I have a problem with one he'd better run, because I'll stick that reggaetón right between his ass and his latin boss's, cuz THIS IS NOT THE UNITED STATES, this is ASTURIAS.

ALL TOGETHER SOUTH AMERICANS AND ASTURIANS UNITED AGAINST REGGAETÓN, BECAUSE SKIN COLORS DO NOT SEPARATE US RATHER THE STUPIDITIES OF A SELECT FEW DO.

Health and good luck with the destruction of regeton on the lands of south america.

This debate illustrates how negotiations of reggaetón also correspond to mediations of national, racial, and ethnic identities, which play a significant role for participants in fan/anti-fan communities of ethnically and racially marked cultural forms, and in this case, a Latin-branded global commodity. The participants embroiled in this debate (*renzo, alianna98,* and *dios349)* negotiate multiple sites of identity, including national identity, through their negotiations of reggaetón anti-fandom. Within their complex negotiation of this racially and ethnically marked genre known as reggaetón, these participants simultaneously attempt to carve out a space where they can assert and negotiate their hybrid and intersectional identities through their participatory fandom. In doing so, these fans/anti-fans also assert themselves as interactive subjects online who are speaking back to their marginal representation online and offline. Whether they like reggaetón or take the anti-reggaetón position, they are all strongly concerned with the message that reggaetón sends to society about them—even if they feel reggaetón doesn't represent them in the first place. This underscores the marginal spaces that still exist for Latin(o/a) representation, even or especially in the context of a Latin-branded cultural form like reggaetón that attempts to represent Latin(o/a) populations globally. There is a sense among forum participants that they are being *spoken for* in the mainstream media and by the culture and advertising industries, as they are interpellated as the audience for reggaetón solely by virtue of their shared language and/or ethnic identity.

"Indecent" and "Disturbed Little Girl(s)": Policing Female Sexuality in Reggaetón and El Perreo

The "argumentos anti-reggaetón" forum is a male-dominated site, and only a few participants (*rosa99, alianna98, daisy8756*) who reveal themselves as women frequently post comments. Female forum participants often defend reggaetón, while male participants attack reggaetón and fiercely attack the women who defend the genre. There is a strong undercurrent of postfeminist discourse waged within the anti-reggaetón debates in the forum, whereby male anti-fans appropriate and turn phrases drawn from popular feminism to challenge female forum participants who disagree with their points of view on the genre. They enact what Yvonne Tasker and Diane Negra refer to as "othering of feminism" and construct it as "extreme, difficult, and unpleasurable" (Tasker and Negra 2007, 4). Feminist perspectives are largely silenced in this space, unrecognized, or harshly disparaged. This ensures that normative sex/gender roles remain status quo in the forum, as several anti-fans work to recuperate them time and time again.

Throughout the forum, *renzo* and *yago* often come to one another's defense, mostly against the female participants. *renzo* posted the second response after *yago* initiated a chat stating, "YAGO FRIEND, YOU KILLED IT WITH THAT ARTICLE, IT IS VERY GOOD, I CONGRATULATE YOU ☺." Then *yago* replied to *renzo* using *renzo*'s real name, saying, "[xxxxx], my friend, check it, it's been a while since anyone has seen you anywhere. We have new participants in the forum, some are in favor of reggaetón, others are in our alliance. !!!DIE REGGAETÓN!!! YAGO." The relationship between *yago* and *renzo* lends itself to camaraderie and an alliance that manifests in power plays of symbolic aggression against others in the forum—particularly against participants who indirectly or directly identify themselves as female. For example, *renzo* responded to *yago*'s previously mentioned post, "I took some vacation time, but here I am again . . . just tell me how many there are chief ☺ . . . !!! We will finish with all the crapatoneros!!! . . . ☺" With *yago* and *renzo* positioning and posturing in the forum as the "chiefs," they tend to dominate the conversation, spark new debates about why others should join their alliance of hate against reggaetón, and double-team those in favor of reggaetón. This form of posturing mimics what Melissa Click describes in the introduction to this collection, asserting that "hate differentiates among subjects (creating a "them" against which groups are positioned), and positions the other ("them") as a threat whose proximity endangers something that is loved (e.g., a media text, celebrity, or convention)" (Click, in this volume). This aggression among alliance members demonstrates strong affective response dually waged against reggaetón and fans considered interlopers in the forum that are subject to the boundaries set and policed by this anti-fan alliance.

Arguments waged here also call out uneven representations of pop music artists in mainstream media. *daisy8756* points out the hypocrisy of associating drug addiction and gang activity with reggaetón artists when the media has not given equal visibility to the deviancy of celebrities outside of the realm of the reggaetón genre (Whitney Houston, Britney Spears, and Shakira). *yago* remains committed to reinscribing common representational tropes that seek to keep particular groups, like reggaetóneros, marginalized for their "deviance." *darsenn* makes a connection between the way reggaetón or reggaetóneros are represented in the media and how that contributes to the formation of stereotypes about Latin Americans, Hispanics, and/or Latinos/as. The sentiments of *darsenn* imply that reggaetón is the problem, as *darsenn* appears to have internalized the associations of deviancy and indecency about reggaetóneros. In other words, it isn't the media's construct of reggaetón or how reggaetón artists engage in forms of strategic essentialism or "self-tropicalization" in order to gain access to mass media representation (Aparicio and Chávez-Silverman 1997); rather, it is the essence of reggaetón and its markers of deviance that produce stereotypes. In this analysis, there is no mention of the market forces investing time and money in promoting these commodified images to increase global visibility and accumulate global capital. And yet, *darsenn* challenges these media representations and finds that they provide a narrow or symbolically annihilating frame for Latinidad and for Latinas/os by portraying them as stupid. In addition, *darsenn* observes that other Spanish-language dominant countries are often represented within tropes of exoticism, eroticism, and libidinous pleasures—pointing to sexual and party imagery. These are representations that *darsenn* doesn't identify with and challenges others in the forum to consider and challenge as well. There is a sense of cohesion with other forum participants that *darsenn* tries to establish. *darsenn* uses the online fan/anti-fan space to raise collective awareness about other crucial factors missing within the anti-reggaetón debates at large. Discursive terms such as "we should" and "do you all realize?" address not only those posting in the forum but also potential lurkers or trolls who might visit the forum but not necessarily post to it.

Through this post *darsenn* appears to weigh other arguments posed in the anti-reggaetón forum, while at the same time working through and negotiating personal valuations. At first *darsenn* attributes stereotypes of Latinos/as in the media to reggaetón, and later *darsenn* calls the media into question again. Is it the media or the genre (or a global capitalist system) that contributes to problematic representations, or all of the above? *darsenn* encourages others to question how the media imposes cultural products, like certain forms of "selected" pop music, on audiences under the guise that they (the audience) clamor for its production and that the culture industry is simply supplying that demand. Anti-reggaetón forums are full of anti-fans who react against the increased visibility that reggaetón has received since its crossover. These reactions predominantly come in the form of what *darsenn* has expressed in the forum—for example, arguing that reggaetón does not represent Latinos/as, or that the representations of reggaetón imposed by the media represent nothing more than stereotypes of Latin Americans, Hispanics, and Latinos/as.

Concluding Discussion

Originally, this study sought to interrogate the frustrations of reggaetón anti-fans. And yet, this investigation revealed that anti-fans are classed, gendered, and racialized in particular ways by the culture industries and mainstream media, which affects their relationship to the images, discourses, and popular culture constructed and disseminated by these representational regimes of power. It is against these structures of power that anti-fans mitigate their own representational authority and/or loss of it by asserting taste hierarchies that are also highly gendered, racialized, ethnically coded, and classed in complex and contradictory ways. It is imperative that scholars adopt a frame of analysis that does not dismiss these intersecting layers of mediation. Jenkins acknowledges the persistent gap within fan studies on "non-white" fandom and specifically calls for "more research into the specific fan geographies and politics that emerge within fandoms with a high degree of participation from people of colour. . . . Such work would have to confront the reality that fandom mirrors larger forms of segregation within culture at large" (Jenkins 2014, 97). Rebecca Wanzo locates rich scholarship on African American audiences and fans (Bobo 1995; Brown 2001; Early 1988, 1989; hooks 1992; Means Coleman 1998; Perry 2004; and Rose 1994) that typically falls outside the purview of fan/anti-fan studies. She calls for a new genealogy of fan/anti-fan studies that is inclusive of black cultural and acafan (academic fan) criticism across fields of study, which she insists "requires breaking down the line between criticism and the study of the fan" (Wanzo 2015).

Fans/anti-fans who are not fluent in English—the lingua franca of the Internet—are also invisible for the most part. This study examined a Spanish-language-dominant online forum. Recognizing the politics of translation, it was still important to highlight Spanish-dominant anti-fans as interactive subjects online—actively engaged in anti-fan practices and participatory culture. The anti-fan studies canon must include work that is conversant in other languages and explores anti-fans across geographies. As a means to more comprehensively engage anti-fandom as an alternative site of identity formation and negotiation, anti-fan studies should account for what this means for historically marginalized groups of anti-fans who are largely lacking representational parity in mainstream media. In this collection, Gray proposes "a theory of *cultural exhaustion* to explain the frustration, anger, alienation, and hence anti-fandom that arise when an individual or community is constantly being misrepresented, not represented, insulted, and/or left out by media" (Gray, in this volume). This theory is worth further exploration as an entry point. Acknowledging the tax on those who approach anti-fandom from a position of marginalization from mainstream media is a critical first step. As a point of departure, how can anti-fandom be understood from a position of *cultural exhaustion* versus from the position of anti-fans who are already recognized within the dominant frame of media? What are the observable effects of cultural exhaustion? Are these effects observable through anti-fan practices, through affective engagement in anti-fandom, or through negotiations of anti-fans' individually hybrid and dynamic identities? Is anti-fandom a site where these culturally frustrated anti-fans can negotiate the many complex layers of their identity—whereby comparison, the source of their frustration, rests with mainstream media/specific texts/the culture industries for not allowing this to be the case through dominant systems of representation? It is my hope that these questions and the findings of this study help guide future work and broaden the ways we examine race, ethnicity, and resistance to culturally dominant systems of representation through anti-fandom.

NOTES

1   The anti-reggaetón music forum under examination is part of *Foros Nueva* (New forums) on the pseudonymously named website *Nueva* (www.nueva.com). Internet users from around the globe participate in chat forums on this website, but the anti-reggaetón forum under investigation predominantly consists of users from parts of Spain, Latin America, and the Caribbean. This anti-reggaetón forum is one of many participatory anti-fan sites available under the broader category of *música foros* (music forums) on the *Nueva* website. I monitored the anti-reggaetón forum from its initial posts in January 2006 through December 2009. This forum has attracted at least 87,697 *visitas* (visitors) to the site and generated over 1,200 responses. Some participants identified themselves by gender explicitly or implicitly. Few participants self-identified by race, but a majority did reveal some form of national identity or country of origin. Based on a grounded theory approach, I excerpted posts that centered on issues of representation and ethnic, racial, sexual, gender, and national identity, as these were all recurring themes that emerged through the process of open coding the anti-reggaetón debates at large. I selected posts from participants who were very active on the *Foros Nueva*—some posting over six hundred times (in various forums on the *Nueva* website)—and from participants who posted only a handful of times. I excerpted several posts together to provide more contextual background for a particular debate.

2   In this study, I include excerpts from the pseudonymously named *Nueva* website (www.nueva.com) anti-reggaetón chat forum. Existing research on Internet inquiry ethics as outlined by the Association of Internet Researchers (2002, 2012), Given (2008), Markham and Baym (2009), and Sveningsson-Elm (2009) finds that "*chat exchanges in publicly accessible chatrooms*" are under "fewer obligations to protect autonomy, privacy, confidentiality" (Association of Internet Researchers 2002; emphasis added). Measures were taken to protect autonomy, privacy, and confidentiality in the chat forums under investigation, including pseudonyms for all forum participants as well as for the forums. Excerpts in Spanish are also translated into English to add an additional layer of identity protection for the forum participants.

3   Emphasis added.

REFERENCES

Ahorre.com. 2006. "No Reggaetón en D.R.," April 9. www.ahorre.com.

Aparicio, Frances. 1998. *Listening to Salsa: Gender, Latin Popular Music, and Puerto Rican Cultures*. Hanover, NH: Wesleyan University Press.

Aparicio, Frances, and Susana Chávez-Silverman, eds. 1997. *Tropicalizations: Transcultural Representations of Latinidad*. Hanover, NH: University Press of New England.

Association of Internet Researchers. 2002. "Ethical Decision-Making and Internet Research: Recommendations from the AoIR Ethics Working Committee." Chicago: Association of Internet Researchers. https://aoir.org.

———. 2012. "Ethical Decision-Making and Internet Research: Recommendations from the AoIR Ethics Working Committee (Version 2.0)." Chicago: Association of Internet Researchers. https://aoir.org.

Báez, Jillian M. 2006. "'En Mi Imperio': Competing Discourse of Agency in Ivy Queen's Reggaetón." CENTRO: Journal of the Center for Puerto Rican Studies 18, no. 11: 63–81.

Baker, Ejima. 2005. "A Preliminary Step in Exploring Reggaetón." In Critical Minded: New Approaches to Hip Hop Studies, edited by Ellie M. Hisama and Evan Rapport, 107–123. Brooklyn: Institute for Studies in American Music.

Baker, Geoffrey. 2011. Buena Vista in the Club: Rap, Reggaetón, and Revolution in Havana. Durham, NC: Duke University Press.

Baym, Nancy K., and Robert Burnett. 2009. "Amateur Experts: International Fan Labour in Swedish Independent Music." International Journal of Cultural Studies 12, no. 5: 433–449.

Bobo, Jacqueline. 1995. Black Women as Cultural Readers. New York: Colombia University Press.

Bourdieu, Pierre. 1984. Distinction: A Social Critique of the Judgement of Taste. Translated by Richard Nice. Cambridge, MA: Harvard University Press. Originally published 1979.

Brown, Jeffrey A. 2001. Black Superheroes, Milestone Comics, and Their Fans. Jackson: University Press of Mississippi.

Cepeda, María Elena, and Alejandra Rosales. 2017. "An Indecent Proposal: Latino Masculinity and the Audience in Latina/o Music Video." In The Routledge Companion to Latina/o Media, edited by María Elena Cepeda and Dolores Inés Casillas, 385–401. New York: Routledge.

Click, Melissa A. In this volume. "Introduction: Haters Gonna Hate."

Coleman, Stephen. 2010. "Acting Powerfully: Performances of Power in Big Brother." International Journal of Cultural Studies 13, no. 2:127–146.

Dinzey-Flores, Zaire. 2008. "De la Disco al Caserío: Urban Spatial Aesthetics and Policy to the Beat of Reggaetón." CENTRO: Journal of the Center for Puerto Rican Studies 20, no. 2:34–69.

Duffett, Mark. 2009. "'We are Interrupted by Your Noise': Heckling and the Symbolic Economy of Popular Music Fandom." Popular Music and Society 32, no. 1:37–57.

Early, Gerald. 1988. "The Black Intellectual and the Sport of Prizefighting." Kenyon Review 10, no. 3: 102–117.

———. 2012. "Ringworld." In At the Fights: American Writers on Boxing, edited by George Kimball and John Schulian, 357–369. New York: Library of America. Originally published 1989.

Giuffre, Liz. 2014. "Music for (Something Other than) Pleasure: Anti-Fans and the Other Side of Popular Music Appeal." In The Ashgate Research Companion to Fan Cultures, edited by Linda Duits, Koos Zwaan, and Stijn Reijnders, 49–62. London: Ashgate.

Given, Lisa M. 2008. "Ethics and New Media." In *The Sage Encyclopedia of Qualitative Research Methods*, edited by Lisa M. Given, 277–279. Los Angeles: Sage, 2008.

Gray, Jonathan. 2003. "New Audiences, New Textualities: Anti-Fans and Non-Fans." *International Journal of Cultural Studies* 6, no. 1:64–81.

———. In this volume. "How Do I Dislike Thee? Let Me Count the Ways."

Gray, Jonathan, and Sarah Murray. 2016. "Hidden: Studying Media Dislike and Its Meaning." *International Journal of Cultural Studies* 19, no. 4:357–372.

Gray, Jonathan, Cornel Sandvoss, and C. Lee Harrington. 2007. "Introduction: Why Still Study Fans?" In *Fandom: Identities and Communities in a Mediated World*, edited by Jonathan Gray, Cornel Sandvoss, and C. Lee Harrington, 1–18. New York: New York University Press.

Hill, Annette. 2015. "Spectacle of Excess: The Passion Work of Professional Wrestlers, Fans, and Anti-Fans." *European Journal of Cultural Studies* 18, no. 2:174–189.

Hinckley, David. 2005. "Reggaetón Gets Solo Tryout on Station Formats." *New York Daily News*, July 27. www.nydailynews.com.

hooks, bell. 1992. *Black Looks: Race and Representation*. New York: South End Press.

Jenkins, Henry. 2014. "Fandom Studies as I See It." *Journal of Fandom Studies* 2, no. 2:89–109.

Johnson, Dominique Deirdre. 2015. "Misogynoir and Antiblack Racism: What the Walking Dead Teaches Us about the Limits of Speculative Fiction Fandom." *Journal of Fandom Studies* 3, no. 3:259–275.

Lewis, Oscar. 1965. *La Vida: A Puerto Rican Family in the Culture of Poverty—San Juan and New York*. New York: Random House.

Markham, Annette N., and Nancy K. Baym, eds. 2009. *Internet Inquiry: Conversations about Method*. Los Angeles: Sage, 2009.

Marshall, Wayne. 2009. "From Música Negra to Reggaetón Latino: The Cultural Politics of Nation, Migration, and Commercialization." In *Reggaetón*, edited by Raquel Z. Rivera, Wayne Marshall, and Deborah Pacini-Hernández, 19–76. Durham, NC: Duke University Press.

McCourt, Tom, and Patrick Burkart. 2007. "Customer Relationship Management: Automating Fandom in Music Communities." In *Fandom: Identities and Communities in a Mediated World*, edited by Jonathan Gray, Cornel Sandvoss, and C. Lee Harrington, 261–281. New York: New York University Press.

McPhail, Clark, and Ronald Wohlstein. 1983. "Individual and Collective Behaviours within Gatherings, Demonstrations and Riots." *Annual Review of Sociology* 9:579–600.

Means Coleman, Robin R. 1998. *African American Viewers and the Black Situation Comedy: Situating Racial Humor*. New York: Routledge.

Navarro, Mireya. 2005. "Mad Hot Reggaetón." *New York Times*, July 17. www.nytimes.com.

Negrón-Muntaner, Francis, and Raquel Z. Rivera. 2007. "Reggaetón Nation." *NACLA Report on the Americas* 40, no. 6:35–39.

Perry, Imani. 2004. *Profits of the Hood: Politics and Poetics in Hip Hop*. Durham, NC: Duke University Press.

Resto-Montero, Gabriela. 2016. "The Unstoppable Rise of Reggaetón." *Splinter*, January 25. https://splinternews.com.

Rivera, Michelle M. 2011. "The Online Anti-Reggaetón Movement: A Visual Exploration." In *Seeing in Spanish: From Don Quixote to Daddy Yankee—22 Essays on Hispanic Visual Cultures*, edited by Ryan Prout and Tilmann Altenberg, 281–299. Newcastle upon Tyne: Cambridge Scholars Publishing.

———. 2017. "Crossover Fail: "'Nigga'/Flex's 'Romantic Style in Da World." In *The Routledge Companion to Latina/o Media*, edited by María Elena Cepeda and Dolores Inés Casillas, 402–418. New York: Routledge.

Rivera, Raquel Z. 2009. "Policing Morality, Mano Dura Stylee: The Case of Underground Rap and Reggae in Puerto Rico in the Mid-1990s." In *Reggaetón*, edited by Raquel Z. Rivera, Wayne Marshall, and Deborah Pacini-Hernández, 111–134. Durham, NC: Duke University Press.

Rivera-Servera, Ramón H. 2009. "Musical Trans(actions): Intersections in Reggaetón." *TRANS: Revista Transcultural de Música*, no. 13. www.sibetrans.com.

Rose, Tricia. 1994. *Black Noise: Rap Music and Black Culture in Contemporary America*. Hanover, NH: Wesleyan University Press.

Rossman, Gabriel. 2012. *Climbing the Charts: What Radio Airplay Tells Us about the Diffusion of Innovation*. Princeton, NJ: Princeton University Press.

Santos, Mayra. 1996. "Puerto Rican Underground." *CENTRO: Journal of the Center for Puerto Rican Studies* 8, nos. 1 and 2:219–231.

Sveningsson Elm, Malin. 2009. "How Do Various Notions of Privacy Influence Decisions in Qualitative Internet Research?" In *Internet Inquiry: Conversations About Method*, edited by Annette N. Markham and Nancy K. Baym, 69–98. Thousand Oaks, CA: Sage.

Tasker, Yvonne, and Diane Negra, eds. 2007. *Interrogating Postfeminism: Gender and the Politics of Popular Culture*. Durham, NC: Duke University Press.

Valdivia, Angharad N. 2000. *A Latina in the Land of Hollywood and Other Essays on Media Culture*. Tucson: University of Arizona Press.

Wanzo, Rebecca. 2015. "African American Acafandom and Other Strangers: New Genealogies of Fan Studies." *Transformative Works and Cultures*, no. 20. doi: 10.3983/twc.2015.0699.

10

"I Just Hate It Now"

The Supracultural Anti-Fans of BBC Radio 3

ROBERTA PEARSON

I don't have a love/hate relationship with R3 any more. I just
hate it now. slits throat. [WibbleAgain 2012]

The pseudonoymous WibbleAgain posted the above comment to an
online discussion about BBC Radio 3, the UK public service broadcasting radio channel that programs classical music. Over the last few years,
Radio 3 has sought to broaden its audience and compete with its commercial challenger, Classic FM, by becoming more accessible—that is,
by appealing to mainstream listeners lacking much prior knowledge of
classical music (see Furness 2013). Radio 3's accessibility policy responds
to the neoliberal market's pressures upon public service broadcasting
and aligns the channel with that market's erasure of distinctions between
the formerly culturally separate fields of classical and popular music. But
it has alienated many of the channel's once loyal listeners, giving rise to
expressions of discontent like WibbleAgain's that merit serious consideration. As Jonathan Gray tells us,

> Behind dislike . . . there are always expectations—of what a text should
> be like, of what is a waste of media time and space. . . . Studying anti-
> fan disapproval and/or dislike . . . would offer media and cultural studies
> meaningful re-entry points to discussing quality, values and expectations,
> allowing us to focus on the range of everyday viewers' values, and on how
> they interact with media consumption, use and meaning. (Gray 2003, 73)

Radio 3's moving closer to the mainstream violates the expectations
and challenges the values of many who had composed the core audi-

ence; for them, greater accessibility equals lesser quality. The disaffected listeners' concerns reveal a particular audience's response to the cultural and media realignments of the last several decades that have altered interactions with media consumption, use, and meaning. This chapter first specifies the meanings of "supracultural," "fan," and "anti-fan" with regard to classical music and classical music radio. It next examines classical music's incorporation into the mainstream in order to establish the broader cultural and economic context that accounts for the current configuration of British classical music radio and for the disaffected listeners' anger. It then discusses the competition between Radio 3 and Classic FM and concludes with an analysis of the negative reactions to the former's perceived "dumbing down."

Defining "Supracultural," "Fan," and "Anti-Fan" in the Field of Classical Music

In some respects, Sarah Thornton's description of youth subcultures applies to the unhappy members of Radio 3's core audience: "This contrast between 'us' and the 'mainstream' is . . . directly related to the process of envisioning social worlds and discriminating between social groups. Its veiled elitism and separatism enlist and reaffirm binary oppositions such as . . . the distinguished and the common" (Thornton 1995, 5). These listeners believe that Radio 3's new policy results in the erosion of the distinction between classical and popular music and between Radio 3 and more "common" broadcasters, especially Classic FM. The channel's new programming threatens their envisioning of the social world by blurring the boundaries between social groups in a manner that devalues their long-standing loyalty. However, it would be wrong to call these listeners "subcultural," a term usually equated with the subordinate. Mike Savage says that music "is an unusually polarized cultural field" that "plays a key role in defining elite cultural forms, but is also central to many kinds of popular sub-cultures, especially for the relatively disadvantaged, youth groups and ethnic minorities" (Savage 2006, 161).[1] Radio 3 listeners are relatively advantaged (almost 90 percent own their homes or have a mortgage, and 78 percent fall into the highest socioeconomic category), relatively older (with a mean age of fifty-seven with 46 percent retired), and overwhelmingly white (95 percent; see Bowie 2004). Most crucially, as I demonstrate below, they believe that their knowledge of, and love for, a musical form that until a half-century ago was a central element of a hegemonic high culture endows them with a cultural capital that distinguishes them from others. Therefore I have dubbed them "supracultural," a term that captures their opposition to the mainstream, their economic capital, and their self-perceived cultural capital.

But if these listeners are supracultural, are they also fans? Does classical music have fans in the sense that the term is understood by fan studies scholars? In a previous chapter on high-cultural fandom that discussed fans of Bach and Shakespeare, I wrote that the "label of 'fan' [would] extend popular culture practices to the rarefied realms of baroque music and Elizabethan drama, a leveling that those with allegiances to the supposedly higher realms of 'serious' music and literature might resent" (Pearson 2007, 98). As opposed to "fans," high-culture adherents are frequently accorded the neutral terms "buffs"/"enthusiasts"/"devotees" and sometimes the positively valued terms "aficionados"/"cognoscenti"/"connoisseurs," which have "implications of specialized, and more importantly, worthwhile knowledge" (98–99). While these high-culture adherents might resist the "fan" appellation, as I demonstrated later in the chapter Bach fans engage in fannish behavior: "the total immersion in the text, the merging of fantasy with reality, the delusional behavior that the elitist critics of popular culture have so often deplored" (Pearson 2007, 108). Psychologist Christopher Spencer and musicologist Stephanie Pitts have also discussed the implications of nomenclature in the classical music field: "Writing on 'fan' behaviour comes closest to analysing the sense of belonging and community that arises from pursuing shared interests with like-minded people, but it has tended to focus on popular music only, with strong interest in classical music being viewed instead as 'the obsession of the aficionado [who] is rational (high class, educated) and therefore benign, even worthy.'" But like me, they argue that classical music lovers behave like fans, having "the same desire to connect more closely" with those "for whom they have a high regard" (Pitts and Spencer 2007, 229). The sociologist Claudio E. Benzecry's ethnography of Argentine opera devotees reveals many behavioral affiliations with popular culture fandoms, thus providing further justification for labeling classical music consumers as fans similar to those investigated by fan studies scholars (Benzecry 2011).

If it's appropriate to characterize the disaffected listeners as classical music "fans," is it also appropriate to characterize them as Radio 3 "anti-fans"? Vivi Theodoropoudou says that "anti-fans emerge whenever binary oppositions are established between two fan objects"; in this case, "dislike of object A results from liking object B; where the hatred for something is dictated by the love for something else and the need to protect the 'loved one'" (Theodoropoudou 2007, 316, 318). The supracultural cohort constructs a binary opposition not between two different objects but between the current and past incarnations of Radio 3; they hate the former, love the latter, and constantly urge the BBC to reinstate the "loved one." In this sense, the supraculturals resemble the anti-fans of television programs thought to have "jumped the shark"; hell hath no fury like a fan scorned. But one cannot understand the supracultural fans' fury at Radio 3's mainstreaming without understanding, first, the emergence and constitution of the classical music mainstream and, second, Classic FM's successful exploitation of that mainstream.

Roll over Beethoven: From High Culture to the Mainstream

> Well, early in the mornin' I'm a-givin' you a warnin'
> Don't you step on my blue suede shoes. . . .
> Roll over Beethoven and tell Tschaikowsky the news.

Chuck Berry's 1956 hit (covered by the Beatles in 1963) gave warning that the long-standing customary deference accorded by all segments of society to Beethoven and Tschaikowsky was coming to an end. For many decades prior to the 1950s, Western culture valorized the classical over all other musical forms, but the later years of the twentieth century saw this cultural hierarchy collapse. By the end of the century musicologist Robert Fink declared that "the cultural authority of the classical music canon is gone." Fink explained that, "from the late nineteenth century to about 1965, canonical European concert music occupied a secure . . . position at the top of a generally accepted hierarchy of musical culture"; this led to the dominant consensus "that Beethoven was Music the way the Mona Lisa was (and still is) ART" (Fink 1998, 141, emphasis in original). Savage tells us that Pierre Bourdieu identified "the tension between classical and elite musical forms and popular music as central to the more general opposition between high and popular culture," but, as postmodern theorists writing in the 1980s argued, this opposition began to break down in the 1960s (Savage 2006, 161). According to Andreas Huyssen, "The boundaries between high art and mass culture have become increasingly blurred" (1986, viii), while Jim Collins said that "cultural production is no longer a carefully coordinated 'system,' but provides a range of simultaneous options that have destabilized traditional distinctions between High Art and mere 'mass culture'" (Collins 1989, 2). By the beginning of the twenty-first century, classical music, stripped of its high-culture authority, had become just one more offering in that range of simultaneous options. As musicologist Julian Johnson put it, "The specific claims of . . . classical music are simply not heard in contemporary culture and indeed are hardly voiced anymore. Classical music is not consciously rejected; it is simply one cultural option among many" (Johnson 2002, 20).

Beethoven has rolled off the pinnacle of the cultural hierarchy and over into the mainstream. According to Savage, data from the United Kingdom's Cultural Capital and Social Exclusion survey reveal that classical music attracts more listeners than some forms of popular music: "Taste communities do not map entirely easily onto familiar ideas about 'high' and 'popular' music: . . . classical music emerges as relatively popular, whilst forms of popular music . . . remain . . . distinctly unpopular to mainstream taste" (Savage 2006, 161). Savage concludes that "classical music . . . emerges as a mainstream, established musical field" (169). Thornton speculates that classical music's "abundant use in television commercials to advertise products of all kinds, from butter and baked beans to BMWs" results from its being "the least disliked of all types of music by most sectors of the population" (Thornton 1995, 13). A 2002 market study commissioned by fifteen U.S. orchestras concludes that "classical music . . . has been so thoroughly appropriated by mass culture that it has all but disappeared for its ubiquity" (Audience Insight LLC 2002, 18).

Whether classical music's ubiquity stems from its being least disliked, or whether its being least disliked leads to its ubiquity, there is no question that it is indeed ubiquitous. We are exposed to it when shopping, riding elevators, holding on customer service phonelines, overhearing mobile ringtones, walking through airports, boarding airplanes, eating

in restaurants, going to the cinema, and watching television. For example, very aware of chance encounters with classical music while writing
this chapter, I noted the use of Allegri's *Miserere* in *The Leftovers* (HBO,
2014–2017), Handel's aria "Lascia ch'io pianga" in *Dominion* (SyFy, 2014–
2015), Mozart's *Ave Verum Corpus* in *The Intruders* (BBC America/BBC
2, 2014) and both Mozart's *Requiem* and Chopin's Waltz no. 10 in B
Minor in *Forever* (ABC, 2014–2015). Only in the last example was the
music's cultural authority a plot point; in a flashback to the 1950s, a time
when Chopin, Beethoven, and Tschaikowsky still perched securely on
the pinnacle of the cultural hierarchy, father and son debated the merits
of Chopin versus jazz. By episode's end the Chopin fan and the jazz fan
were happily playing each other's music, testifying to the leveling of cultural hierarchies between the 1950s and the present.

But what kind of classical music has mass culture appropriated to
appeal to mainstream tastes? Musicologists designate the music of the
late eighteenth and early nineteenth centuries as classical (Mozart),
distinguishing it from the seventeenth- and eighteenth-centuries baroque (Handel) or the nineteenth-century romantic (Chopin). In general usage, the term broadly encompasses sacred and secular Western
art music from the medieval period to the twenty-first century. Mainstream classical music, however, constitutes a mere fraction of this vast
repertoire, only that most suited to commodification. As early as 1932
Theodor Adorno said, "The role of music in the social process is exclusively that of a commodity; its value is that determined by the market"
(Adorno 2002, 391). The neoliberal market has vastly accelerated that
commodification to the extent that, as Johnson says, classical music
now functions "more or less successfully as another kind of commercial
music. The kind of classical music that flourishes in this environment is
that which is adaptable to the dominant functions of commercial music;
other kinds of classical music . . . are often far less adaptable and tend to
be excluded" (Johnson 2002, 27). The market adapts certain composers
and forms to the dominant functions of commercial music by eradicat-
ing the signs of distinction between popular and classical music, most
notably in the crossover market that emerged in the early 1990s.

Album covers used to signal classical music's cultural authority with
pictures of dignified men (and they were almost always men) dressed
in formal attire, conducting their orchestras or playing their instru-

ments. Now, as Fink tells us, "Onto the covers of classical CDs and record magazines troop phalanxes of sexpot violinists in revealing poses, diminutive virtuosi, floating monks—and at the head of the parade, the infamous Three Tenors" (Fink 1998, 142). In their resemblance to equivalently sexpot pop singers, sexpot violinists (unlike their authoritative predecessors, exclusively female) align classical music with the popular, but Plácido Domingo, José Carreras, and Luciano Pavarotti, known collectively as the Three Tenors, have perhaps done most to popularize the genre with mainstream listeners. Their album *The Three Tenors in Concert* exceeded ten million in sales, making it the best selling classical album of all time and leading, as Julie Lee says, "to a string of highly popular crossover albums that topped pop charts" (Lee 2003, 20). For many, it is these albums and performers that define classical music; according to the market survey mentioned above, the crossover market has "effectively and lucratively tapped into an expanded definition of classical music that resonates with a larger public" (Audience Insight LLC 2002, 17). This expanded definition of classical music includes that most readily accessible to mainstream listeners: operatic arias, Pachelbel's Canon and Vivaldi's *Four Seasons*, orchestral "pops," and so forth. The crossover market is composed primarily of what Savage characterizes as "'light classical' music, defined as a form of 'mainstream', rather than avant-garde classical music: Mozart or Vivaldi rather than Schoenberg or Stravinsky" (Savage 2006, 162). Excluded from the mainstream are the more obscure parts of the historical repertoire that appeal to supracultural fans—for example, the avant-garde (Stravinsky) and atonal (Schoenberg), chamber music (even Mozart's), and the majority of pre-eighteenth-century music (with occasional exceptions such as the Allegri *Miserere* and a sprinkling of Purcell).

Functionality also determines inclusion/exclusion from the mainstream. The "shopping mall and restaurant compilations" that contribute to classical music's ubiquity, says Johnson, privilege "music that tends to create one mood or emotion by doing one main thing" (Johnson 2002, 35). Functionality goes far beyond creating suitable mono-mood backgrounds for shopping or eating; the market now provides classical music for every human need, desire or activity. Johnson speaks of "CD compilations of classical music with titles like Classic Moods or Classic Relaxation" (Johnson 2002, 35), while Fink refers to "pallid collections of classical 'greatest hits' . . . thematized according to time of day (Bach at Bedtime); hawked by spurious scientific claims (Mozart Makes You Smarter) . . . even sorted by sexual preference (Sensual Classics, Out Classics)" (Fink 1998, 142). A quick check of Spotify turns up countless classical music compilations to relax by, study by, chill by, romance by, and so forth. These compilations commodify by extracting movements suiting their declared function from longer compositions originally intended to be heard in their entirety. Says Johnson, "The first movement of Beethoven's Moonlight Sonata works well in [doing one main thing], but the final movement of the same sonata does not. By the same token, the Adagietto of Mahler's Fifth Symphony is popular in a way that the Scherzo from the same symphony is not" (Johnson 2002, 35). The market selects movements on the principle of "no unwanted passages," the promise made in a 1990s television commercial for a compilation of "the greatest classical music"—the mainstream consists of the "wanted passages" or, rather, the passages that the market has taught mainstream listeners to want. It is this mainstream that Classic FM has so profitably exploited.

A Warm Bath versus a Power Shower: Classic FM and Radio 3

Johnson says that classical music has "achieved some startling successes" by adapting to the "new . . . commercial world." He cites Classic FM's rapid "dwarfing" of Radio 3's audience as an example (Johnson 2002, 35). Launched in 1992, by 1999 the channel had become "the nation's number one national commercial radio station . . . with more than six million adults . . . tuning into the station every week." Commenting on these listener figures, Classic FM Managing Director and Program Controller Roger Lewis said, "As this century comes to a close, access for a broad based mass audience to classical music has at last been created" (PR Newswire 1999). Classic FM created this audience by complying with the diktats of the mainstream market: erasing distinctions between the popular and the classical and emphasizing the latter's functionality. The channel says that its mission is "to make classical music accessible and relevant to a modern audience through its engaging style" (Global, n.d.). This engaging style, as Andrew Crissell points out, involves shaping "classical music to the format of a pop station" (Crissell 2002, 248), a familiar and reassuring one to listeners accustomed to popular music radio's conventions. Viewers interact with the channel through phone-ins, emails, tweets, requests, and dedications and by voting for the "greatest pieces of classical music" for the daily "Hall of Fame Hour." The programming matches the rhythms of everyday life: "More Music Breakfast" offers music to eat by; "Classic FM Drive" provides "great get-you-home music"; "Smooth Classics" delivers "the smoothest sounds" to relax by at bedtime; and at 1 A.M. DJ Nick Bailey "eases you into the day with music to recharge your batteries" (Classic FM, n.d.).

The playlist is restricted, drawn from the limited mainstream repertoire, and repetitive, with certain compositions regularly featured. The channel, says John Welford, "tends to play an unending sequence of 'standards'. . . . Composers whose works get a lot of airtime include Beethoven, Schubert, Brahms, Tchaikovsky and Rachmaninov [but] only their best known compositions will get heard very often, so it will not be long before Schubert's Trout Quintet, Tchaikovsky's 1812 Overture or Rachmaninov's 2nd Piano Concerto comes along" (Welford 2013). As Robert Weedon notes, the requisite commercials also influence the playlist; playing a lengthy composition in its entirety means less advertising time, which means "losing capital." "You will often only hear the familiar opening movement of a symphony or a concerto's slow central movement. . . . This regrettably leads to pieces not being fully understood as a musical sequence by the audience, just as a nice piece of aural relaxation" (Weedon 2013).

In 2013, Roger Wright, then controller of Radio 3, indirectly criticized the competition. "Classical music is not about relaxing—I . . . get exasperated by some colleagues in our world who seek to reduce it to nothing more than a warm bath—I was glad when Radio 3 was referred to, by contrast, as a power shower." A musical power shower should "stimulate, energise, console . . . challenge and confuse us" and make "our lives immeasurably more rich" (Wright 2013). As articulated in its mission statement to "inform, educate and entertain," enriching listeners' lives has been one of the BBC's fundamental principles since its 1922 founding (BBC 2011). Its public service remit required it to cater for the tastes of all segments of the population while simultaneously offering a wide range of cultural forms, from the popular to the high. This remit was made manifest in the 1946 establishment of three channels that mirrored the period's dominant cultural hierarchy: the populist

Light Programme, the middlebrow Home Programme and the high-brow Third Programme, which played classical music. In 1967, when the BBC launched its first pop music station, Radio 1, the Light Programme became Radio 2, the Home Programme Radio 4, and the Third Programme Radio 3. Neither the Third Programme nor Radio 3 were intended to create a "broad based mass audience" for classical music; both were perceived as being unabashedly elitist. Said the *Daily Mail's* Brian Sewell, "With its reputation for intellectual and aesthetic severity, The Third Programme endowed to Radio 3 a solid audience to whom its uncluttered and hard-edged severity appealed, while others grew into it when they wearied of shallow popular music" (Sewell 2011). More succinctly, Welford says that Radio 3 had "a reputation for being stuck up and cerebral." (Welford 2013). But the channel's position at the top of the cultural hierarchy, combined with its insulation from market forces by virtue of its public funding, meant not having to worry about audience numbers or, for many years, commercial competition.

The dissolution of cultural hierarchies and the triumph of neoliberal market logics that threaten the public service ethos have made it harder for Radio 3 to defend appealing solely to a relatively small number of supracultural fans. As Johnson says of classical music more generally, "The burden of proof falls on those who want to assert the aesthetic value of music that does not seem to have sufficient commercial value to survive without some intervention in market economics." It's no longer possible to assert "that some music is greater than other music . . . in the face of a completely opposite commercial valuation" (Johnson 2002, 17). The fact that Radio 3's audience hovered around the two million mark, roughly one-third of Classic FM's, became a matter of concern; Welford says "the boffins at the BBC" made a conscious decision to "popularise the channel, but without going as far in this direction as Classic FM" (Welford 2013). But Classic FM now claims that Radio 3 has become as populist as its commercial competitor. The channel's written submission to a parliamentary review of the BBC complained that Radio 3 has been making "major programming changes" to "gradually erode the gap" between the two channels. These changes include "greater interaction from listeners, including phone-ins, requests and dedications," "broadcasting short works or extracts during peak period, rather than playing multi-movement pieces in full," and introducing a "lighter repertoire."

In conclusion, Classic FM warned that Radio 3's emulation of its pop music format "erodes the choice available to listeners" (Furness 2014). The Friends of Radio 3, an independent listeners' organization established in 2010, agree:

> Classic FM is Classic FM. It aims to present classical music in an accessible way to a broad audience. It should be left to do that without Radio 3 trying to muscle in. In the face of considerable evidence to the contrary, the BBC denies that Radio 3 has been copying its rival at all. It should not be allowed to get away with claiming that broadcasting a live concert every evening is enough to satisfy some "niche" audience, so that an extensive part of the remaining classical schedule can happily concentrate on serving "normal members of the public" who will appreciate a service which is a marginal cut above a Classic FM-without-the-adverts, and won't frighten horses. [Friends of Radio 3 2014]

Radio 3's mainstreaming has failed to increase audience numbers. Radio Joint Audience Research reported in July 2014 that "the classical music station saw its audience shrink by 120,000 year-on-year to 1.88 million" (*BBC News* 2014), below the two million mark established as the channel's benchmark since Radio Joint Audience Research began counting audiences in 1999. New listeners are not jumping into Radio 3's new warm bath—indeed, it seems that many former listeners are jumping out of it and yearning for the old power shower.

The Alienation of Fans

Gray says that "it is unsurprising that anti-fannish moments and practices have often been those that fan scholars find most fascinating, since it is at these sites . . . that the analyst can find out what it is that the fan truly likes or liked, what the text's best self should be according to the fan(s), and hence what has gone wrong" (Gray, in this volume). The supracultural anti-fans' opinions attest both to their perceptions of Radio 3's "best self" and to "what has gone wrong." Their opinions also align quite neatly with theories of culture offered by Bourdieu and Adorno; although sometimes seen as incompatible, these theorists offer different perspectives that both help to illuminate the anti-fans' position.

Bourdieu's theories of taste and distinction partially account for the anti-fans' negative reaction to Radio 3's new programming; they believe that their self-perceived cultural capital differentiates them from those "normal members of the public" content with a service only a cut above Classic FM. But, says Thornton, "Distinctions are never just assertions of equal difference; they usually entail some claim to authority and presume the inferiority of others" (Thornton 1995, 10). Frequently used by both journalists and anti-fans, the phrase "dumbing down" encapsulates this presumption of intellectual inferiority; self-evidently, it also attests to a belief in the continued relevance of cultural hierarchies. The *Daily Mail's* Brian Sewell listed his objections to the current Radio 3, the first of which was "the BBC diktats which insist every programme be dumbed-down in the endless quest for mass-market appeal." He gave as an example a request by "Margaret from Bedfordshire" for Shubert's *Trout Quintet*. Margaret told listeners "how she had heard it on the Isle of Mull and was then granted a few bars of it on Radio 3—but only after she'd read out what was virtually an essay on the glorious experience. . . . Does anyone really tune into Radio 3 to hear such witterings?" (Sewell 2011). Poor Margaret's "witterings," together with her choice of that mainstream mainstay, the *Trout Quintet*, reinforced the assumption that the "normal members of the public" lack the requisite cultural capital to appreciate a service superior to Classic FM. A Friends of Radio 3 member quoted in a *Telegraph* article also complained about listener requests. Radio 3 "encourages people to ring in with a suggestion and then we have to hear them burbling on about why that piece reminds them of their holiday while those who are very, very knowledgeable about classical music are sidelined" (Ward 2011).

The "knowledgeable" anti-fans resent the fact that Radio 3's quest for new listeners entails catering to the less knowledgeable listeners' mainstream tastes rather than to their own supracultural tastes. Sarah Spilsbury, a spokesperson for the Friends of Radio 3, asserted that Wright, the Radio 3 controller, had "imported all the tricks of popular, downmarket broadcasting to help win over a new audience" (Spilsbury 2011). These "tricks"—the requests, the wittering and burbling, the extracts, the constant repetition of overly familiar works—elicit the anti-fans' fury. As Bourdieu says, "The most intolerable thing for those who regard themselves as the possessors of legitimate culture is the sacrilegious reuniting of tastes which taste dictates shall be separated" (Bourdieu 1984, 56–57). The anti-fans believe that classical music should still occupy a privileged position at the top of a cultural hierarchy and object to Radio 3's conformance to the mainstream's functionalism and erasure of distinction. Ralph Spurrier, in a letter responding to *Classical Music Magazine*'s article about the current state of the channel, said that it should "be proud of the intellectual demands that classical music demands as a high culture" (Classical Music Staff 2014). An anti-fan commented in the *Telegraph*, "For gawds sake don't apologise for the great culture" (comment, in White 2011). Listener Neil Sheldon believes that "music does not exist to wake up the proles and their 'kids' and send them off happily to school or work with lollipop excerpts (not forgetting that said 'proles' are potentially far more discerning than given credit for)" (Classical Music Staff 2014). In a similar vein, the *Telegraph*'s Michael White complained that Radio 3 is now "selling art as relaxation—as if Bach, Brahms, and the other towering giants of music churned out all those notes for tired executives to sleep through" (White 2011). Listener Arthur Bayley pointed to the equivalences made between classical music mainstream favorites and formerly revered composers: "The first thing I disliked was the 'chart' which was dominated to start with by Andre Rieu; 'nuff said, I think!! To have a 'chart' where, say, Bach can be supplanted by some comparative nonentity just devalues the whole currency" (Classical Music Staff 2014).

A Bourdieu-esque analysis accounts for the anti-fans' opposition to the mainstream but does not fully explain their discontent. A more complete understanding of their position requires turning to Adorno: "Through the total absorption of both musical production and consumption by the capitalist process, the alienation of man has become complete" (Adorno 2002, 391). The alienation of fans stems not only from their self-perceived cultural capital but also from their recognition of the neoliberal market forces that have compelled Radio 3's conformance to the mainstream. Christine Pryce's letter to *Classical Music Magazine* said, "It feels so unfair that even Radio 3 has to succumb to 'market forces' when it isn't subject to a market as such!" (Classical Music Staff 2014). White advised Controller Wright that "there's no disgrace in being a minority station if the reason for your modest pull is that you aim high. Serious art will never compete with *EastEnders* for the national interest—but its value can't be measured in those terms" (White 2011). Lachlan Burn wrote to *Classical*

Music Magazine, "Surely the whole point of public funding is to remove the need to be popular, so that the station can pursue that which is good, though not necessarily popular—be aspirational, rather than seeking to satisfy the greatest number by delivering what most people like?" (Classical Music Staff 2014).

Some anti-fans call for a return to public service broadcasting's fundamental principles as articulated by the BBC's first director general, John Reith. As the BBC itself has said, the term "'Reithian values' has become a byword for public service broadcasting" (*BBC News* 1999). Central to those values was giving the audience what it needed rather than what it wanted—educating and uplifting rather than appealing to popular tastes. One anti-fan protesting Radio 3's mainstreaming recounted a telling, if perhaps apocryphal, anecdote that summarizes this policy: "Asked if he would give the listeners what they wanted, Reith famously replied, 'Oh no! Something much better than that'" (Classical Music Staff 2014). The article in *Classical Music Magazine* that engendered a plethora of anti-fan responses is headlined "If Radio 3 Is to Keep a Safe Distance from Classic FM, It Needs to Embrace Reithian Values." Its author, Richard Steinetz, asked, "Where are the Reithian values which [Director General] Tony Hall has promised to re-embrace, and which Reith himself defined as to educate and inform as well as entertain? Hall is quoted as committing to 'quality over populism', remarking that 'the good does not always have to be popular'. Please Radio 3: may we have less repetition, more breadth, more intellectual . . . adventure!" (Steinitz 2014). His readers agreed. "It's not a task of rocket-science complexity to set matters right and back squarely honoring those Reithian principles—Inform, Educate. . . . and Entertain—and with that undoubted relative emphasis" (Classical Music Staff 2014). A commenter on a *Telegraph* article wrote, "I thought that under the terms of its Charter the BBC was mandated to educate? If that's the case, how does the current approach, which encourages mindless enjoyment, meet the terms of the Charter?" (comment, at Ward 2011).

The anti-fans protest that Radio 3's surrender to market forces prioritizes entertainment over information and education and advocate returning to public service values. We might term this a "rational anti-fandom," based as it is on a reasonable analysis of the economic forces at play reinforced with knowledge of the BBC's history. By contrast, we might term their resentment at Radio 3's catering for "normal members of the public" rather than for them an "affective anti-fandom," based as it is on the anti-fans' own deeply held feelings about their supposedly superior cultural capital. To return to Thornton's formulation, the channel's new programming threatens the anti-fans' envisioning of the social world by blurring the boundaries between social groups in a manner that devalues both their cultural capital and their long-standing loyalty. Their enduring faithfulness animates another affective element of their anti-fandom; they mourn the loss of Radio 3's central role in their everyday lives and the sense of "belonging and community"—which Spencer and Pitts identify as central to fandom—that it engendered. Simon Frith says that radio forms a personal bond with its listeners and connects them to an imagined community of those with similar tastes. "On 'our' station we expect to hear our kind of music. . . . And radio is also a way of suggesting a broader taste community. Our personal musical likes and dislikes are publicly confirmed, and deejays and presenters have a particularly important role in treating music as a form of social communication" (Frith 2002, 42). A commenter on a *Telegraph* article wrote, "I used to have what [I] call (my music) on all day," but that person has now stopped listening. "Please can we have our old Radio 3 back [?]" (White 2011). Radio 3's mainstreaming has severed the anti-fans' personal bond with the channel and ceased the public confirmation of their supracultural tastes.

Many of those who wrote to *Classical Music Magazine* declared their prior devotion to Radio 3: "I have been an ardent listener to Radio 3 and the Third Programme before that since about 1950"; "Woke up to radio 3 and 3rd programme for forty years"; "Radio 3 was the mainstay of my life for several decades"; "I am a lifelong listener to Radio 3"; and "I have been a regular listener for close on 50 years." They testify to the channel's importance in educating and informing them: "All my life R3 has informed my music taste and built and extended it"; "It has been an education to me, introducing me to music that has enriched my life"; "It was a source of knowledge as well as the medium for hearing classical music"; "I have been educated and inspired by radio 3 since the 70s"; and "I acquired my whole musical education from the Third Programme and its successors." They say that the channel's transformation has had a profound impact upon them: "I sometimes have to turn off before I throw a brick through the window. This is awful, since I love classical music"; "Radio 3 has become dumbed down to the point where it is no longer the uplifting experience it once was"; "Morning is my ideal time for listening to good music and I have felt bereft for the last few years since retirement as it's just irritating and not worth listening to"; and "I think that my life is not as rich as it used to be." They have stopped listening to Radio 3 and have sought alternative sources of classical music more aligned with their supracultural tastes: "I have almost ceased to listen because of my disappointment with style of presentation and content"; "I tend to rely on CDs in my car as I can rely on listening to good music in full"; and "I evacuated to Swiss Classique and have stayed with them ever since" (Classical Music Staff 2014).

Whether affectively or rationally motivated, the anti-fans' anger was frequently directed at Radio 3's former controller Roger Wright, perceived as responsible for the station's "dumbing down" in the pursuit of new listeners. Alan Davey, who took over the job in January 2015, promised that he will not be "dumbing down" but "wising up." The phrase "dumbing down," so frequently employed by the anti-fans, has clearly become toxic; Davey's wordplay implied that Radio 3 will honor the public service ethos of educating and informing. He promised that "he would make sure Radio 3 continued 'doing what Radio 3 does best—offering complex culture, arts and ideas within the reach of lots of people.'" But the phrase "lots of people" acknowledges the neoliberal market forces that drive public service broadcasting to compete with its commercial rivals for audiences. Referring to Radio 3's uncompromisingly elitist predecessor, he said, "What the original Third Programme didn't do was offer people context . . . a way of approaching the complex culture that's offered." He implicitly said that his version of Radio 3 would address the tension between the public service ethos and the neoliberal market. "If you do complex culture properly, it makes sense to people" (*BBC News* 2014). Does Davey's statement offer hope to the anti-fans, or it mere rhetorical spin? Deeds, not words, must answer this question.

Nonetheless, Davey's words speak directly to Radio 3's dilemma, as do the anti-fans' sentiments, which, as I said above, reveal a particular audience's response to the media and cultural realignments of the last several decades that have altered interactions with media consumption, use, and meaning. With regard to cultural realignments, the anti-fans resist the toppling of cultural hierarchies that has birthed the classical music mainstream. With regard to media realignments, they object to neoliberal market logics that compel public service broadcasting to pursue larger audiences by giving equal, if not greater, weight to entertaining as that given to educating and informing. With regard to media consumption, the anti-fans have abandoned radio and sought alternative sources for classical music. And with regard to uses and meaning, they positively valued the Radio 3 that aligned with their tastes and enriched their lives; the new Radio 3 has primarily negative meanings for them.

This case study of Radio 3's supracultural anti-fans demonstrates that the study of anti-fandom can contribute significantly to media and cultural studies' understanding of audiences' positions within broad cultural and economic contexts. It also implicitly demonstrates a current failing of anti-fan and, indeed, fan studies. As I have argued elsewhere, while "fan studies has extensively engaged with the popular and even occasionally with the middle-brow . . . it has almost entirely refused to engage with the high," which usually "figures only as a repressive other against which to celebrate the virtues of the popular" (Pearson 2007, 99). This repressive high culture's adherents have been assumed to be happily complicit with the hegemonic, while popular culture adherents have been valorized as resistant. But I have shown that the supracultural anti-fans resist the hegemony of the neoliberal market both affectively and rationally. The supracultural may be just as oppositional as the subcultural, yet the alignment among the former's class, tastes, race, and, to some extent, gender causes them to be consistently overlooked by scholars attracted to the popular and the subcultural; to paraphrase Orwell, "subcultures good, supracultures bad." But further examination of the tastes and practices of supracultural fans and anti-fans may reveal much. For example, are the supracultural anti-fans a phenomenon unique to classical music radio, or do they have parallels among the audiences of other cultural forms usually considered to be high culture—art, the theater, the opera? Are they a phenomenon unique to the United Kingdom, or do they have parallels in other countries such as the United States? If we're looking for resistance to current hegemonic configurations, we may need to reexamine our assumptions about worthy objects of study.

NOTE

1 For further discussions of cultural studies' association of musical subcultures with the young, the disadvantaged, and minorities, see Frith and Goodwin (1990); and Thornton (1995).

REFERENCES

Adorno, T. W. 2002. *Essays on Music*. Berkeley: University of California Press.

Audience Insight LLC. 2002. "Classical Music Consumer Segmentation Study: How Americans Relate to Classical Music and Their Local Orchestras." John S. and James L. Knight Foundation. Princeton, NJ: Cultural Policy and the Arts National Data Archive. www.cpanda.org.

BBC. 2011. "Mission and Values," December 21. www.bbc.co.uk.

BBC News. 1999. "UK Let That Be a Lesson to You All," November 18. www.bbc.com.

———. 2014. "New BBC Radio 3 Controller 'Will Not Dumb Down,'" October 22. www.bbc.com.

Benzecry, C. E. 2011. *The Opera Fanatic: Ethnography of an Obsession*. Chicago: University of Chicago Press.

Bourdieu, P. 1984. *Distinction: A Social Critique of the Judgement of Taste*. Translated by Richard Nice. Cambridge, MA: Harvard University Press.

Bowie, A. 2004. "Radio 3 Audience Research." *AdamBowie.com* (blog), November. www.adambowie.com.

Classical Music Staff. 2014. "Letters Regarding Radio 3." *Classical Music Magazine*, March 21. www.classicalmusicmagazine.org.

Classic FM. n.d. Digital radio station, 100–102 FM. www.classicfm.com.

Collins, Jim. 1989. *Uncommon Cultures: Popular Culture and Post-modernism*. New York: Routledge.

Crissell, A. 2002. *An Introductory History of British Broadcasting*. 2nd ed. London: Routledge.

Fink, R. 1998. "Elvis Everywhere: Musicology and Popular Music Studies at the Twilight of the Canon." *American Music* 16, no. 2 (Summer): 135–179.

Friends of Radio 3. 2014. "Time for a Change," July 16. News archive. www.for3.org.

Frith, S. 2002. "Music and Everyday Life." *Critical Quarterly* 44, no. 1:35–48.

Frith, S., and A. Goodwin, eds. 1990. *On Record: Rock, Pop, and the Written Word*. London: Routledge.

Furness, H. 2013. "Radio 3 Boss Defends Playing of Film Scores and TV Themes." *Telegraph*, December 29. www.telegraph.co.uk.

———. 2014. "Classic FM Claims BBC Radio 3 'Apes' Its Output for More Listeners." *Telegraph*, January 25. www.telegraph.co.uk.

Global. n.d. "Classic FM: The UK's Favourite Classical Music Station." London: Global Media Company. www. global.com.

Gray, J. 2003. "New Audiences, New Textualities: Anti-Fans and Non-Fans." *International Journal of Cultural Studies* 6, no. 1:64–81.

———. In this volume. "How Do I Dislike Thee? Let Me Count the Ways."

Herald Scotland. 2014. "Radio 3 Boss in Quality Vow," October 22. www.heraldscotland.com.

Huyssen, Andreas. 1986. *After the Great Divide: Modernism, Mass Culture and Post-modernism*. Basingstoke: MacMillan.

Johnson, J. 2002. *Who Needs Classical Music? Cultural Choice and Musical Value*. Oxford: Oxford University Press.

Lee, J. 2003. "A Requiem for Classical Music?" *Regional Review—Federal Reserve Bank of Boston* 13(Quarter 2): 14–23. www.bostonfed.org.

McCulloch, R. In this volume. "A Game of Moans: Fantipathy and Criticism in Football Fandom."

Pearson, R. 2007. "Bachies, Bardies, Trekkies, and Sherlockians." In *Fandom: Identities and Communities in a Mediated World*, edited by Jonathan Gray, Cornel Sandvoss, and C. Lee Harrington, 98–109. New York: New York University Press.

Pitts, S. E., and C. P. Spencer. 2007. "Loyalty and Longevity in Audience Listening: Investigating Experiences of Attendance at a Chamber Music Festival." *Music and Letters* 89, no. 2:227–238.

PR Newswire. 1999. "Classic FM Creates Mass Audience for Classical Music with Record Listening Figures," June 10. www.prnewswire.co.uk.

Savage, M. 2006. "The Musical Field." *Cultural Trends* 15, nos. 2–3 (June/September): 159–174.

Sewell, B. 2011. "Why Radio 3 Is No Longer Music to My Ears." *Daily Mail*, September 25. www.dailymail.co.uk.

Spilsbury, S. 2011. "Radio 3 Is Letting Its Listeners Down." *Guardian*, October 5. www.theguardian.com.

Steinitz, R. 2014. "If Radio 3 Is To Keep a Safe Distance from Classic FM, It Needs to Embrace Reithian Values." *Classical Music Magazine*, March 14. www.classicalmusicmagazine.org.

Theodoropoudou, V. 2007. "The Anti-Fan within the Fan: Awe and Envy in Sport Fandom." In *Fandom: Identities and Communities in a Mediated World*, edited by Jonathan Gray, Cornel Sandvoss, and C. Lee Harrington, 316–327. New York: New York University Press.

Thornton, Sarah. 1995. *Club Cultures: Music, Media and Subcultural Capital*. Middletown, CT: Wesleyan University Press.

Ward, V. 2011. "Radio 3 Fans Complain Station Is 'Dumbing Down.'" *Telegraph*, September 1. www.telegraph.co.uk.

Weedon, R. 2013. "Classic FM and Market Research." *Image Dissectors*, June 22. www.imagedissectors.com.

Welford, J. 2013. "Which Is Best for Music: BBC Radio 3 and Classic FM." *Entertainment360*, January. www.entertainmentscene360.com.

White, M. 2011. "Radio 3 Is Getting out of Tune with Its Audience." *Telegraph*, September 3. www.telegraph.co.uk.

WibbleAgain. 2012. "Classical What Are You Listening To?" *Just the Talk*, March 26. https://justthetalk.com.

Wright, R. 2013. "Royal Philharmonic Society Annual Lecture, 2013." *RPS: Royal Philharmonic Society*. http://royalphilharmonicsociety.org.uk.

PART III

Anti-Fandom in Real Life

11

A Game of Moans

Fantipathy and Criticism in Football Fandom

RICHARD MCCULLOCH

YES YES YES YES FUCKING YES. 4 wins on the bounce,
first time we've done that in 2 years! [#T21]

Anyone who says we're not on the ascent can go suck a frig-
ging lemon. [#T25]

I now struggle to think of any [player] on the first team that
I'd consider "dead weight". That's an incredible difference
from last season. The future is bright. [#T1014]

The above statements, all taken from a popular online forum, are fairly
typical examples of football (soccer) fan discourse in times of victory.[1]
Enthusiastic exclamations of delight sit alongside optimism and relief,
while other comments playfully mock those who had previously criticized or underestimated the team.

It was March 10, 2013, in England, and fans of Liverpool Football
Club (hereafter Liverpool) were celebrating a 3-2 victory against a strong
opponent, Tottenham Hotspur. Six days later, however, following Liverpool's 3-1 defeat to Southampton, the same forum took on a very different complexion:

Wages should be stopped, starting with [the] manager. Shocking, disgusting and embarrassing. [#S12]

Absolute shite. Tactically inept. Again. [#S61]

This team lacks desire, conviction, will to win . . . whatever you want to call it. . . . Massive changes are needed in the summer to make this club competitive. [#S148]

While undoubtedly a drastic turnaround in mood, these comments are not indicative of erratic, fickle, or unusual fan behavior. This case study of Liverpool fans is not an anomalous one, nor am I drawing attention to a moment of schism within a particular online community. In fact, what this juxtaposition (and the title of this chapter) should emphasize is precisely how *fundamental* criticisms and complaints are to (football) fan discourse. As a gauge of the level or nature of someone's investment in a text, an emphasis on pleasure is, at best, incomplete and, at worst, demonstrably misrepresentative. Moaning matters, especially when it is directed toward something or someone we claim to love.

Prior to the publication of this anthology, several academic studies of anti-fandom and divided fan communities had been productive in reminding us that media texts are not consumed solely for "positive" reasons (Alters 2007; Gray 2003, 2005). *Star Wars* fans famously bonded over their shared hatred of *Episode I: The Phantom Menace* (Brooker 2002); *Buffy the Vampire Slayer* fans argued over the shortcomings of season 6 (Johnson 2007); and films such as *The Room* (McCulloch 2011) and *Twilight* (Click, Aubrey, and Behm-Morawitz 2010; Pinkowitz 2011) have amassed large, passionate audiences that, in different ways, revel in textual "badness." Nevertheless, the term "anti-fandom" implies an inherent separation between those who "like" and "dislike" a particular fan object. Dislike, hatred, and negative affect have long been associated with the "other side of fandom" (Alters 2007), yet in this chapter, I call for a reevaluation of negative affect and its importance to fandom. What I term "fantipathy" regularly functions as an important, routinized mode of discourse for fans within fan communities, especially (but not exclusively) in relation to team sports, where criticism of one's own team is not merely tolerated but often actively encouraged. Fantipathy may appear to be a symptom of individual detachment or collective disagreement, but I argue that it serves a number of deceptively "positive" rhetorical functions—negotiating moments of crisis, facilitating social bonds with other fans, and performing (sub)cultural capital. Quite simply, if we really want to understand the role that anger, frustration, hatred, and dislike play in the consumption of popular culture, then to concentrate solely on anti-fandom is to ignore negative emotions where they are most prevalent.

Method

This research is based on postings from the popular Liverpool forum, *Red and White Kop* (www.redandwhitekop.com; hereafter *RAWK*), chosen because of the high volume and variety of postmatch conversations that appear there. Content differs wildly, from overjoyed to vitriolic, impassioned to apathetic, and from cursory statements of opinion to thoughtful analysis.[2] The data sample consists of 2,481 postings collected from the forum's "post match discussion" threads, with comments pertaining to one of three consecutive Liverpool fixtures between March and April 2013: Southampton 3-1 Liverpool (March 16, 2013; 1,230 posts), Aston Villa 1-2 Liverpool (March 31, 2013; 457 posts), and Liverpool 0-0 West Ham (April 7, 2013; 794 posts; see *Red and White Kop* 2013a, 2013c, 2013d). Focusing on consecutive games provided an element of consistency to the study, ensuring that any positivity or negativity on display was unlikely to be linked to significant changes in the team's league position. In order to demonstrate fantipathy's pervasiveness, it was also vital that the study considered fan responses in relation to victories, defeats, and draws (ties), hence why this particular period of inconsistent results was selected for investigation.

All comments were read, manually coded, and interpreted in line with Robert Kozinets's approach to "netnographic" data analysis (Kozinets 2009, 118–135), and I include numerous quotes to illustrate broader discursive patterns and rhetorical strategies. Data were procured from a deliberately narrow range of postmatch discussions to provide a focused and practicable case study. While the narrow sample range inevitably imposes certain limitations on the findings, my aim is to emphasize the conceptual aspects of football fan negativity that potentially *can* be extrapolated to other fandoms and other consumption contexts, as well as to the questions and implications that such discourse raises for fan studies and audience research more generally. It is this theoretical context with which I begin my discussion.

The Adoring Audience? Fandom, Anti-Fandom, and Fantipathy

Early fan studies research adopted what has been described as a "strategically positive" approach to its subject—deliberately countering the popular perception of fans as excessive, deviant, and immature, and instead emphasizing their ability to resist and rework texts in complex ways (Hellekson and Busse 2002, 132; Johnson 2007, 285). As the title of one seminal anthology suggests, the discipline has partly developed from the assumption that fans constitute "the *adoring* audience" (Lewis 1992; emphasis added). Importantly, fan studies have acknowledged from the beginning that there is more to fandom than celebration. In *Textual Poachers*, for example, Henry Jenkins rightly observes that fan responses to popular media "typically [involve] not simply fascination or adoration but also frustration and antagonism, and it is the combination of the two responses which motivates their active engagement with the media" (Jenkins 1992, 24). In this chapter, however, I demonstrate that existing research on fans and negative emotions has failed to adequately explain how these seemingly conflicting responses can work together. Frustration and antagonism are all too frequently downplayed, and the "combination" of positivity and negativity to which Jenkins refers tends not to be explored in much depth—instead, they are seen as separate emotional registers that operate for different reasons, at different moments, and for different groups of audiences.[3]

In 2003, Jonathan Gray maintained that research into television audiences was inadvertently skewed toward fans, whereas anti-fans and non-fans were invariably ignored or forgotten. He described these neglected audiences as viewers who "watch distractedly, in bits and/or casually; many, too, hate or dislike certain texts. When one's relationship to the text is *no longer one of close affect*, though, the very nature and structure of that text changes" (Gray 2003, 65; emphasis added). By this definition, fans remain "positive" and in close proximity to the "nucleus" of a text, while anti-fans are generally "negative" and lack textual familiarity. Non-fans, in contrast, may have detailed textual knowledge but tend not to share fans' emotional involvement in the text (73–74). As evidenced by the quotes that opened this chapter, Liverpool fans on *RAWK* represent something of a challenge to this definition, consistently showing themselves to be capable of fluctuating between intense positivity and intense negativity.

Their position along a spectrum of pleasure/satisfaction is thus constantly in flux. They may resemble Gray's anti-fans in many ways, but their relationship to the club appears to remain one of "close affect," and textual familiarity is uniformly high. My point here is not that Gray's categories do not exist but that, as he contends in his chapter in this collection, the distinction between fan, anti-fan, and non-fan can be far subtler than scholarship has hitherto acknowledged (Gray, in this volume).

Derek Johnson goes some way toward addressing this complexity when he describes fan communities as sites of "hegemonic struggle over interpretation and evaluation through which relationships among fan, text, and producer are continually articulated, disarticulated and rearticulated" (Johnson 2007, 286). However, this suggests that moments of "fan-tagonism" occur between *different* sets of fans or between fans and producers. It does not describe the unequivocal denigration of the text/object that is so typical of Liverpool fans on *RAWK*, nor does it allow for the possibility that the same fan might be capable of multiple or fluctuating responses to the same issue, event, or object. Crucially, the negativity to which I refer is also distinct from the "anti-fan within the fan" described by Vivi Theodoropoulou (2007), in which fandom for one object is expressed through anti-fandom (in the form of hatred, bitterness, and criticism) of a rival object. In those cases, fandom is a precondition of anti-fandom, and therefore both positions exist within the same fan. Yet such negativity is always directed *away* from the fan object and toward something external/Other that is perceived as a threat. Although this form of anti-fandom is certainly evident on *RAWK* (Liverpool fans often express strong negativity toward local and/or competitive rivals, such as Everton and Manchester United), the criticism I am describing here is something different.

This chapter is concerned with what I term *fantipathy*—a specific mode of critical fan discourse taking place within a fan community and characterized by professed dissonance between fan and fan object/text. Resembling anti-fandom, but performed by an otherwise unwavering fan, it may take the form of expressions of personal dissatisfaction ("[I'm] really pissed off with some of the gutless performances this season"; #S329) or evaluative utterances that pronounce the object to be defective or lacking in "quality" ("Utterly woeful by all parties concerned": #S343). Ien Ang points out in her study of *Dallas* audiences that "no single experience, certainly no experience of something as complex as a long-running television serial, is unambiguous: it is always ambivalent and contradictory. The 'totalizing' labels of love and hate conceal this" (Ang 1985, 13). The same can be said of Liverpool fans, since the negativity they express is more of a temporary subject position than a bounded, defining identity label. Just as Ang observes that "not a single [one of her participants] is indifferent to *Dallas*" (14), *RAWK* users never cease to be *fans* of Liverpool. Criticism is often severe, but as the following section demonstrates, fantipathy ultimately appears to stem from a desire for results and performances to improve.

The Men Who Swear at Scapegoats: Fantipathy and Textuality

Of all the differences between the three postmatch threads under consideration in this chapter, one of the most instantly noticeable is the variation in number of responses:

Southampton 3-1 Liverpool: 1,230 posts
Aston Villa 1-2 Liverpool: 457 posts
Liverpool 0-0 West Ham: 794 posts

Although this is a meager sample of just three games, the inverse correlation between positive results and volume of responses is striking; defeat against Southampton is met with roughly 2.7 times the number of posts as the victory against Aston Villa. Intrigued by this disparity, I decided to test whether this trend was consistent across the rest of the 2012–2013 season (see table 11.1).

TABLE 11.1: Postmatch discussion threads on the *Red and White Kop* website (Barclays Premier League matches only, 2012–2013)

	No. of games	Total comments (season)	Average comments per thread	Most comments in single thread	Fewest comments in single thread
Wins	16	10,416	651	1,156	261
Draws	12	12,660	1,055	1,424	438
Losses	9	15,141	1,682	2,224	1,190

Note: Average (mean) figures are rounded to the nearest whole number. One outlying result was excluded after being deemed unrepresentative—Liverpool's 2-2 home draw with Chelsea, April 21, 2013. After Liverpool's Luis Suárez controversially appeared to bite Chelsea's Branislav Ivanovic on the arm, the postmatch debate on the *Red and White Kop* (*RAWK*) forum involved a vastly disproportionate number of posts, as fans speculated about Suárez's likely punishment. The *RAWK* website is at www.redandwhitekop.com.

Of course, quantities alone tell us nothing of the content or tone of the responses, yet the broad trend is very clear: The worse the result is for Liverpool, the greater the number of posts will likely appear on *RAWK* following the match. Even the *least* talked-about league defeat of the season received more postmatch comments than the *most* talked-about victory. Defeats and draws thus consistently provoked more fan discussion than victories, which in turn suggests that fan discourse thrives on disappointment, underachievement, and deficiency. As "quality" declines, fans seemingly have more to say. In order to explain why this might be, we must first consider the specificities of the complaints and the extent to which content and/or tone differs depending on the outcome of the game.

Liverpool's defeat to Southampton provides a rich demonstration of just how critical football fans can be toward their own team. Not a single one of the 1,230 *RAWK* postings suggested that the result was undeserved or that the referee had made any significant errors. Instead, scapegoats were sought *within* the club, both as individuals and as collectives:

[Manager/head coach, Brendan] Rodgers fucked this game up big style. At times too clever for his own good. [#S126]

[Midfield player, Joe] Allen sure was horrific. . . . It looks like such a struggle for him to accomplish absolutely anything at the moment. [#S349]

Some of the senior players need to have a good fucking hard look at themselves. [I] seriously can't pick a good performance out of that lot today, fucking awful. [#S731]

Cornel Sandvoss has noted that football fans regularly use the first person plural—"we"—to talk about the club they support. He argues that this is a linguistic manifestation of the relationship between fan and club, with the club not being considered the object of fandom so much as a unit formed within the fan (Sandvoss 2003, 35). To criticize one's team is therefore, in a sense, to criticize oneself and the fandom writ large. Unlike the celebratory postvictory remarks that opened this chapter, however, notice that the comments above are not aimed at the "we" or "us" of Liverpool FC but at specific, distinct elements of the club/

team. Through fantipathetic discourse, fans continuously reassess what is (and is not) included in the club-fan unit, creating a relatively fluid text with inconsistent boundaries. However angry or upset football fans become, the search for (and identification of) scapegoats ensures that there will always be another aspect of the text that remains immune from criticism.

This spatial vindication—assuaging "badness" by locating it in isolated parts of the text—is also enacted on a temporal level. Running through fans' disapproval here is a subtle yet ongoing tone of impermanence, suggesting that even the more severe problems are not beyond repair: Brendan Rodgers' cleverness cost Liverpool *this* game; Joe Allen is playing badly *at the moment*; and it is difficult to pick out a good performance *today*. Even the most critical fan comments are underpinned by allusions to the text's essential worthiness, so the dissonance hinted at by Liverpool fans on *RAWK* is less about rejecting the fan object than it is about acknowledging and coming to terms with expectations that have not been met.

Fantipathy and scapegoating allow fans to reconfigure their sense of the text's boundaries, as well as distancing the problematic elements from what they perceive to be the "true" text. As Jonathan Gray puts it, "Behind dislike . . . there are always expectations [of] what a text should be like" (Gray 2003, 72). This is true of anti-fandom as well as fantipathy, in that both involve the highlighting of imperfections; however, where anti-fandom pronounces the text to be *intrinsically* flawed, fantipathy sees flaws as *isolated* blemishes that only *temporarily* inhibit one's ability to experience the text as it "truly" is. Expressing these anxieties might therefore be compared to what Jenkins describes as fan fiction writers "scribbling in the margins" of their favorite television shows and "molding" characters to suit their own interests (Jenkins 1992, 155–161). The presence of so many angry and expletive-laden postings on *RAWK* could easily mask the textual play involved in fantipathy, but it is clear that Liverpool fans are engaged in a complex process of negotiated interpretation.

But what happens to fantipathy in moments when perceptions of textual "quality" or "badness" are more ambiguous—when fan displeasure is present, but not all-consuming? Responses to the 0-0 draw with West Ham were more measured than the Southampton defeat, with one representative response declaring, "Disappointed we didn't win today. Thought we were in control, but somehow they had the best chances"

(#WH625). Again, scapegoats were many and varied, but fantipathy's targets noticeably moved *beyond* those within the club: "Fat Sam [Allardyce, West Ham's manager] used shit house tactics and the referee was woeful" (#WH568). Criticism of underperforming Liverpool players was balanced out by a significant increase in discussions of external agents, suggesting that improved results may lead to less introspection. Where fan expectations are being met, there appears to be less need for fans to "remold" the text and overcome their own feelings of dissonance.

Crucially, though, fantipathy never seems to disappear. If the final score were the only matter of importance to fans, we would expect little to no fantipathy after victories. Yet, in the wake of the game against Aston Villa, in which Liverpool overturned a 1-0 deficit to eventually win 2-1, fans on *RAWK* were still keen to point out the flaws in their team's performance:

The concerns I have are the defense conceded a soft goal (again) and Lucas [Leiva] not displaying the control of midfield that was typical of him pre-injury.... We definitely need reinforcements in his position and sharpish. [#AV89]

Good win but my God.... I am shitting it every time the opposition gets the ball and [attacks]. Well done to the lads but we have work to do at the back. [#AV27]

We were poor 1st half, turned it round 2nd half and got the 3 points. Still lots of problems and if you cant see that then you're deluded. [#AV166]

So weak through the middle of defence. We need two new centrebacks. Nothing great about coming back against a team that poor, it shows how far we've fallen that we see it as a great result. [#AV181]

In the context of the positive outcome of the game, the inclination toward negativity here is fascinating. More/different players are needed, the opposition looks likely to score every time it attacks, and a win can only really be celebrated if it is against a strong team. Again, these comments reveal a broad consensus that the team has numerous defensive problems but little agreement about precisely how to fix them. A particular midfielder, both central defenders, the manager, and the team as a whole are variously blamed, but for what exactly? Why is it that some fans feel so compelled to identify shortcomings even when the team has won? The increased use of "we" and "us" here is worth noting, since it suggests that victories provide fans with a greater sense of stability and togetherness. It is surely significant, however, that, despite some differences in frequency, tone, and intensity, the *content* of postvictory complaints closely mirrors those made postdefeat. Therefore, despite the diagnostic imperative that often drives it, *RAWK* users' fantipathy appears to be more concerned with the *quest* for answers and improvements than anything that might conceivably happen as a result of fan discussions; its instrumental value far outstrips its intrinsic value.

Along with the figures noted in table 11.1, what this trend suggests is that there is an important social dimension to fantipathy whereby forum discussion is fueled more by critical comments than exclamations of delight. One oft-quoted episode of the British sitcom *The IT Crowd* neatly encapsulates this social angle, when the show's nerdy computer technicians feign an interest in football to help them make conversation with their male colleagues. Using a website called *Bluffball*, Maurice Moss (Richard Ayoade) memorizes a variety of stock phrases that he can use to pass himself off as a football fan, including "Did you see that ludicrous display last night?" and "The problem with Arsenal is, they always try to walk it in" (*The IT Crowd* 2008). Of course, this is a fictional situation written for comic purposes, but it is significant that football fandom here is characterized as a predominantly negative (i.e., critical) cultural practice—one in which the ability to *complain* about a team and highlight its flaws becomes a valuable social skill.[4] But as much as fantipathy can play a social function, it is also a discursive mechanism through which fans can position themselves as "experts"—knowledgeable enough to explain how and why the team might not be playing to its potential. As the following section makes clear, however, precisely how much value individual fans place on such criticism is very much open to debate.

Are You Not Entertained? Justifying and Rejecting Fantipathy

As we have seen, despite its apparent "negativity," fantipathy contributes to fan discourse in a number of "positive" ways. For the individual fan, criticizing the fan object appears to help to reconcile contradictory feelings of devotion and frustration. For fan communities as a whole, the collective pursuit of problems and solutions seems to play an important social role, fostering inter-fan connections in support of a shared goal (i.e., improvements to the team). Nevertheless, the ubiquity of fantipathy on a forum such as *RAWK* should not be mistaken for universal acceptance. To some fans, criticizing one's own team remains a paradoxical, even heretical act—an expression of dissatisfaction or disillusionment toward an ostensibly beloved entity. Accordingly, not all expressions of negativity are deemed equally acceptable. How, then, do fans negotiate these boundaries of acceptability?

This question is a familiar one among *RAWK* users, who routinely enter into debates about whether or not they should be criticizing their own team. While many fans are quick to criticize, fantipathy remains a source of intense consternation for others. Fandom, lest we forget, is as much about making judgments about *other fans* as it is about a particular fan object. As one user wrote in the wake of the defeat to Southampton, "What a load of c*nts you lot are. We win together, we lose together, stop pointing fingers, stop being c*nts and accept we got it wrong, we were beaten, that's it" (#S39). Here, the fan agrees with others' negative assessment of the game—that Liverpool "got it wrong"—but simultaneously rejects fantipathy as an acceptable mode of discourse. The emphasis on "winning together" and "losing together" implies that externalizing one's negativity risks dividing the fan community or undermining confidence in the team. I argued above that fantipathy can be read as a response to anxieties about textual instability, but here, the fan's concern is that fantipathy may itself be *causing* instability. Because so many *RAWK* users resort to criticism regardless of the outcome of a particular game, confrontation between fans is extremely commonplace. When these comments appear in postmatch threads, they often lead to a subdebate about whether or not criticism is warranted, appropriate, or acceptable. Following the Southampton game, for example, several fans made their thoughts on this matter abundantly clear:

> We shouldn't accept mediocrity tho, completely embarrasing display not acceptable for Liverpool Football Club. [#S135]

C*nts for not being happy about a loss to a [team near the bottom of the league]? aha, yeah. [#S144]

This whole message board might as well go away if we aren't allowed to vent and talk about why we got it wrong and who we feel was at fault. I suppose you'd rather us drink the kool aid and look the other way though. [#S161]

Fantipathy is thus justified in a number of intriguing ways. One revealing post explicitly states that the very reason for the message board's existence is to provide a space for diagnosing problems, apportioning blame, and the shared expulsion of anger or frustration. This implies that fantipathy is such a fundamental part of fandom that, without it, fans would have little need to talk to each other. Fans who eschew fantipathy are accused of "looking the other way," which speaks volumes about the potential for critical comments to foster inclusivity and, perhaps surprisingly, bring the community *closer* to the fan object and/or to each other. As noted above, there are numerous social benefits that come with sharing one's frustration with like-minded fans, so refusing to criticize the team may actually be interpreted as a rejection of the fan community more broadly.

This is also a question of competing perceptions of the "authentic text" (Cubbison 2005). Just as one fan claimed after the Aston Villa victory that, "if you cant see [Liverpool's defensive problems] you're deluded," here we see references to "drinking kool aid" and "accepting mediocrity." Whether in defeat or in victory, refusing to criticize one's own team is equated with the refusal (or inability) to see events as they "truly" are, recalling the shifting textual boundaries discussed in the previous section. Moreover, noncritical fans are positioned as less ambitious and, by extension, happy for the team to accept "mediocrity." By this logic, the more critical a fan is toward his or her fan object, the more she or he cares about its "quality," effectively rendering fantipathy as a vehicle for fan-cultural capital (Fiske 1992; Thornton 1995). As Matt Hills has argued, however, fandom often finds itself caught between notions of community and of competitive hierarchy (Hills 2002, 46–64), and this tension is routinely laid bare when clusters of fans criticize the negativity of others. As one riled *RAWK* user wrote, for instance,

So many snide fuckers in here and a few who are probably glad we lost so they can stand up and shout "I was right, the manager was wrong", sad fuckers. [#S186]

Fiske observes that "fan cultural knowledge differs from official cultural knowledge in that it is used to enhance the fan's power over, and participation in, the original, industrial text" (Fiske 1992, 43). In football, however, where fandom and fan object form one single unit, elevating oneself above the text is, to some fans, to simultaneously elevate oneself above other fans. The posting above is thus responding to what she or he perceives to be a prioritization of hierarchy over the fan object itself.

As a community, *RAWK* returns to this debate with such regularity that, as with the scapegoating discussed above, the *process* of deliberation seems more important than any answers that are arrived at (see Busker 2008, para. 3.2). On *RAWK*, questions of whether criticism is "appropriate" or not are asked repeatedly, but fans invariably fall on both sides of the debate, and rarely will anyone withdraw their argument or change their mind. One comment in particular spoke very strongly to this notion of curiously predictable uncertainty:

Not actually about the match, more in response to the negativity from a few. Fuck me, you remind me of the bit in Gladiator where Russell Crowe runs out, stabs everyone and screams "Are you not entertained?" because they boo him. . . . Week after week I see comments such as "The real trick is winning when we're not playing well." [Well] that's exactly what we did today, [but] are you happy with that? Are you fuck . . . So I ask you, what the fuck exactly do you want? [#AV278]

Fan expectations when playing a strong side like Tottenham will likely differ from a match against the usually lower ranked West Ham, but whoever the opponent, there will always be some aspect of a performance that is potentially open to criticism. The fan above, speaking after the victory over Aston Villa, is evidently frustrated because he or she interprets negativity as unnecessary, particularly given the result that day. Indeed, if no result can eradicate fantipathy, one might legitimately question why such fans keep coming back to *RAWK*. But there is more going on here than a dispute over how one should (or should not) support their team, as the comment specifically links enjoyment/fulfillment ("Are you happy . . . ?") to temporal context ("[with] what we did today"). One commonly recurring source of consternation, for instance, is discursive inconsistency, with swift fluctuations between collective positivity and collective negativity sometimes being treated with skepticism or contempt:

> We beat Spurs last week to win three on the bounce and everyone was talking about [qualifying for] Europe and one albeit shite performance later Rodgers has been awful all season? Zip it for fucks sake. Its embarrassing. [#S212]

> We were all praise when 4 man attack worked out against Spurs and when it doesnt today it is [the manager's] fault?? Give me a break!! [#S197]

> Get a grip! You were probably the same person waxing lyrical about the team last week and the way we play! [#S145]

In some ways, these are peculiar complaints, especially given the frequency with which fans switch from praise to criticism of their team. Indeed, Liverpool had just followed victory against a strong opponent with defeat against a far weaker team, so the community's fluctuating mood could simply be said to be a reflection of the team's (very tangible) results. What such quotes seem to be attesting to, then, is not fans' inconsistency per se but the relative importance that *narrative* plays in their relationship to the team. In short, all fans seek to contextualize results and position them in relation to longer-term narratives, but some are getting the narrative "wrong." These examples are closer to the "hegemonic struggle" to which Johnson refers (2007, 286), with fans disagreeing over how best to make sense of particular games and performances. *Red and White Kop* users' response to the ludicrousness, contradictions, hypocrisies, and perceived misinterpretations of other fans is often to highlight and disparage them through sarcasm:

> Forget all the positivty of recent weeks and call for the end of the world. WE ARE DOOMED!!! [#S114]

> We should get rid of everything associated with Liverpool Football Club ever after that game. . . . Lets 'av it boys. Who's got the pitchforks? [#S189]

Here, fantipathy is positioned as something to be dismissed and/or laughed at, with flippant comments and sarcastic language clearly suggesting that it should not be taken seriously. What is particularly interesting about these examples, however, is that they reimagine the line between the "inside" and "outside" of the Liverpool fandom and therefore the line between fantipathy and anti-fandom. The evocation of end-of-the-world prophecies ("WE ARE DOOMED!") and angry vigilante mobs ("Who's got the pitchforks?") implies a section of the community that is overly (or even dangerously) committed to its principles, unwilling to embrace change, and who should be ostracized. We can see this even more clearly when we consider which instances of fantipathy received more responses than others. One such controversial comment declared,

> I have to laugh when people talk about Rodgers being some sort of decent manager. He has been woeful all season. Today's debacle simply adds to the catalogue of errors. He has zero tactical ability at this level and thinks that the odd good performance is justification for his "system", which doesn't work anyway. This guy is simply playing at being a Liverpool manger. [#S170]

Postmatch conversations on *RAWK* typically unfold as a collective outpouring of opinion and emotion, with very few people addressing each others' specific arguments. In this case, however, at least five users responded directly to post #S170, some of which captured the intriguing insider/outsider distinction in a particularly blunt fashion: "What a load of shit. I take it you're a [Manchester United fan]?" (#S188). There were plenty of other comments in the thread that had made similar criticisms about the manager, so why should this one generate such indignation? While there are a number of possible explanations for this, the only recognizable difference between these criticisms is that, here, the fan's damnation is total: Brendan Rodgers has been "woeful all season," has "zero tactical ability," and is fundamentally out of his depth as Liverpool manager. Unlike the scapegoating discussed above, the negativity here refers to permanent, unsolvable, and unmitigated problems, and it is interesting that the community should then respond with a resounding cry of, "You are not one of us!" The fan's criticism is not only rejected but also Othered. This is significant because it draws attention to the subtle distinction between fantipathy and anti-fandom. Fantipathy tends to be tolerated or encouraged by other fans because it is targeted (isolated) and/or temporary, meaning that the fan object retains its essential value; anti-fandom, however, is rejected because it refuses to acknowledge that value, even implicitly. The poster and his or her opinions are deemed to be incompatible with the rest of the forum, but the barely perceptible line between acceptability and unacceptability suggests that the distinction between fantipathy and anti-fandom, and the inside and outside of the community, are constantly being (re)negotiated.[5]

Conclusion: Making Fan Objects Great Again

In the process of introducing and unpacking the concept of fantipathy, this chapter has sought to challenge some of the key assumptions that underpin existing definitions of fandom and anti-fandom. Namely, I have argued that dislike, criticism and negativity should not be seen as indicators of low emotional investment,[6] nor should our study of these emotions be restricted to anti-fans. As one *Economist* blogger neatly described it,

> Football . . . works on a principle of deferred (sometimes endlessly deferred) gratification, promising but withholding a heaven of success reached by most [fans] only very rarely. The scarifying waiting, with all its failures and disappointments, is not incidental to the attraction: it is, I think, much of the point. [Bagehot 2009]

Fan studies thus needs to reposition negativity as a fundamental component of *fandom* and to develop more nuanced methods of capturing the ever-fluctuating affective relationship between fan and fan object.

As vitriolic as it can become, fantipathy is not the paradoxical act it may appear to be, especially given the specific ways in which fans frame and justify their criticism, reducing its denunciatory potential. Processes of scapegoating and references to impermanent (and therefore solvable) problems, for example, allow for the possibility of heavy criticism without tarnishing the ultimate sanctity of the text. By indirectly invoking positive but attainable expectations of the text that are not presently being fulfilled, fantipathy might even be thought of as helpful for negotiating perceived threats and contradictions—a way of *strengthening* some fans' devotion to their fan object. Their comments may be extremely critical in some cases, yet they are almost universally underpinned by a desire for the text/object to improve. Seen in this way, fans emerge as "sharp critics who speak from a stakeholder's perspective" (Jenkins 2014, 95).

Clearly, there are some fundamental characteristics of team sports fandom that would not apply to, say, fans of a music artist or television show. Sports are, for instance, inherently competitive in a way that differs from other forms of popular culture, and final scores can provide far more tangible measures of "success" or "quality." Despite the rise of transnational audiences in the 1990s, football fandom also tends to be more closely tied to notions of "home" than other fandoms, to the extent that switching allegiances to another team is still very much seen as taboo behavior (Hawksley 2014; Sandvoss 2003, 72–100, and 2005, 64–65).

These points aside, there are far more similarities between sports and other forms of fandom than media studies scholarship tends to acknowledge. For instance, football fans contextualize games in relation to broader, overarching narratives about clubs and players. In conjunction with (and/or in response to) the media, they create, maintain, and develop attachments to a rotating cast of heroes, villains, cult icons, and rivalries. They devour gossip and rumors, buy merchandise, design and produce their own fan art (banners, flags, vids, Internet memes, tattoos, etc.), share knowledge relentlessly, engage in ritualistic behavior (see Hills 2002, 125–129), and develop pieces of writing that, in a different online community, would certainly be labeled "fan fiction" (Waysdorf 2015). The similarities are there, and to my mind, there are three key ways in which future research might probe those connections and expand on these initial arguments in useful ways.

First, we can be confident that fantipathy exists across a multitude of fandoms, but does its importance vary depending on the *kind of text* to which it refers? If an episode of *Game of Thrones* is perceived by fans to be subpar, does fantipathy play a different role for them than it would for fans of a reality series like *Keeping Up with the Kardashians* or a primetime comedy show such as *Saturday Night Live*? Would it make a difference if the text was highbrow or lowbrow, widely praised or widely hated? What if the "text" is not a film, television series, or novel but a person, brand, or even a place?

Second, we need to ask *who* engages in fantipathy, and why. Which audiences are most likely to participate in, be entertained by, or otherwise be inclined toward criticizing something they love? Does this mode of discourse map coherently onto their life course (Harrington and Bielby 2010) or habitus (Bourdieu 1984)? If so, under what social, cultural, or personal circumstances does fantipathy tend to become important, enjoyable, or productive? And if, as argued above, fantipathy is to some extent tied to subcultural capital, is it also linked to performances of masculinity (Hollows 2003), or can we locate it just as readily in predominantly female fandoms, too?

Finally, we need to take seriously the *uses and implications* of fantipathy. And this goes far beyond fandom as it is usually envisaged. After all, Cornel Sandvoss (2013, 285) has convincingly argued that political enthusiasm can be meaningfully understood as a form of fandom. It involves repeated emotional commitment, the use of digital media for sourcing stories from a wide variety of publications, participation in interpretive communities/fairs (Sandvoss and Kearns 2015), and textual productivity. This argument feels all the more germane as I write this conclusion in November 2016—barely five months after the United Kingdom's Brexit referendum saw the country vote to leave the European Union and within days of Donald Trump's surprise "antiestablishment" victory in the U.S. presidential election. Both successful campaigns succeeded amid rhetorical whirlwinds of heavily critical, emotionally charged, but also ostensibly optimistic discourse about the two nations: "Taking our country back" and "Making America Great Again," respectively. Political analysts will, of course, be picking apart the root causes of these results for years. For now, though, we can at least say that both votes were preceded by scapegoating, dislike, hatred, and frustration that were directed toward perceived *internal* threats just as much as more traditional external boogeymen like immigrants or foreign aggressors. Trump targeted much of his ire toward the alleged "nastiness" and "crookedness" of his Democratic opponent, Hillary Clinton, and the "horrible" federal government he claimed she represented, while pro-Brexit campaigners appealed to affective dimensions of British identity and community, explicitly rejecting the tangible economic arguments of "experts" (Sandvoss 2016). If we have indeed entered a "posttruth" age, the need to study and understand the role that negative emotions play in our mediated consumption of popular culture is surely of paramount importance.

NOTES

1   All fan comments quoted in this article have been transcribed verbatim, with spelling, punctuation, grammar, typographical errors and expletives (whether self-censored or written in full) all left untouched. Each quotation is identified by a letter corresponding to the game to which it refers (AV = Aston Villa; S = Southampton; T = Tottenham Hotspur; WH = West Ham United) and a number indicating its chronological position in the postmatch discussion thread. For quotes pertaining to the Tottenham Hotspur match, see *Red and White Kop* (2013b).

2   *Red and White Kop* users have a reputation for being "unrealistically" positive and/or defensive about their team, as illustrated by the existence of the Twitter account @RAWK_Meltdown (www.twitter.com/RAWK_Meltdown). Far from skewing my findings, however, my choice of forum demonstrates that negativity is such an intrinsic part of football fandom that it flourishes even in spaces renowned for their positive bias. In any case, equivalent online spaces, filled with negativity, exist for virtually every European football team.

3   Scholars have long debated the various definitions and functions of "affect," "emotion," and "feeling" (see Click, in this volume). The fact that I use these terms relatively interchangeably throughout the chapter is not, however, to dismiss those previous debates. Rather, I am following the lead of William Proctor, whose useful discussion of the topic questions the practical applicability of such theory and concludes by proposing that we might be better off approaching affect as a "site of struggle between all of these forces and factors . . . a conflation of emotional, physiological, psychological, cognitive and more" (Proctor 2013, 208).

4   There are definite parallels here with the work of Mark Andrejevic, who identifies similar discourse in his study of the forum *Television Without Pity* (www.televisionwithoutpity.com), which was shut down in 2014. He describes users' "snarkastic" comments and recaps as a form of "added value," creating entertainment out of otherwise dull or contrived shows, and doing so primarily for the benefit of other users (Andrejevic 2008, 32–37).

5   Again, this resonates with Andrejevic's study of *Television Without Pity*, in which he observes "two, *not entirely distinct*, types of forums: those populated by serious fans who admire the show and those devoted to viewers who love to mock the

shows being discussed. . . . The boundary between these two groups is far from clear" (Andrejevic 2008, 31; emphasis added).

6 Beyond fan studies, this idea is mirrored by Barker and Brooks's mapping of distinctions between *Judge Dredd* audiences. Those with high levels of investment tended to experience it far more "intensely" than "low investors" (whether positively or negatively), consistently had far more to say in interviews and focus groups, and maintained clearer evaluative criteria (Barker and Brooks 1998, 232).

REFERENCES

Alters, Diane F. 2007. "The Other Side of Fandom: Anti-Fans, Non-Fans, and the Hurts of History." In *Fandom: Identities and Communities in a Mediated World*, edited by Jonathan Gray, Cornel Sandvoss, and C. Lee Harrington, 344–356. New York: New York University Press.

Andrejevic, Mark. 2008. "Watching *Television Without Pity*: The Productivity of Online Fans." *Television and New Media* 9, no. 1:24–46.

Ang, Ien. 1985. *Watching Dallas: Soap Opera and the Melodramatic Imagination*. London: Methuen.

Bagehot. 2009. "Of Masochism and Football." *Economist*, August 27. www.economist.com.

Barker, Martin, and Kate Brooks. 1998. *Knowing Audiences: Judge Dredd—Its Friends, Fans and Foes*. Luton: University of Luton Press.

Bourdieu, Pierre. 1984. *Distinction: A Social Critique of the Judgement of Taste*. Translated by Richard Nice. London: Routledge.

Brooker, Will. 2002. *Using the Force: Creativity, Community and Star Wars Fans*. London: Continuum.

Busker, Rebecca Lucy. 2008. "On Symposia: Livejournal and the Shape of Fannish Discourse." *Transformative Works and Cultures*, no. 1. doi: 10.3983/twc.2008.049.

Click, Melissa A. In this volume. "Introduction: Haters Gonna Hate."

Click, Melissa A., Jennifer Stevens Aubrey, and Elizabeth Behm-Morawitz. 2010. *Bitten by Twilight: Youth Culture, Media, and the Vampire Franchise*. New York: Peter Lang.

Cubbison, Laurie. 2005. "Anime Fans, DVD, and the Authentic Text." *Velvet Light Trap* 56 (Fall): 45–57.

Fiske, John. 1992. "The Cultural Economy of Fandom." In *The Adoring Audience: Fan Culture and Popular Media*, edited by Lisa A. Lewis, 30–49. London: Routledge.

Gray, Jonathan. 2003. "New Textualities, New Audiences: Anti-Fans and Non-Fans." *International Journal of Cultural Studies* 6, no. 1:64–81.

———.2005. "Antifandom and the Moral Text: *Television Without Pity* and Textual Dislike." *American Behavioral Scientist* 48:840–858.

———. In this volume. "How Do I Dislike Thee? Let Me Count the Ways."

Harrington, C. Lee, and Denise Bielby. 2010. "A Life Course Perspective on Fandom." *International Journal of Cultural Studies* 13, no. 5:429–450.

Hawksley, Rupert. 2014. "Why Aren't Football Fans Allowed to Swap Teams?" *Telegraph*, February 26. www.telegraph.co.uk.

Hellekson, Karen, and Kristina Busse, eds. 2002. *The Fan Fiction Studies Reader*. Iowa City: University of Iowa Press.

Hills, Matt. 2002. *Fan Cultures*. London: Routledge.

Hollows, Joanne. 2003. "The Masculinity of Cult." In *Defining Cult Movies: The Cultural Politics of Oppositional Taste*, edited by Mark Jancovich, Antonio Lázaro-Reboll, Julian Stringer, and Andy Willis, 35–53. Manchester: Manchester University Press.

The IT Crowd. 2008. "Are We Not Men?" Season 3, episode 2. London: Channel 4 Television.

Jenkins, Henry. 1992. *Textual Poachers: Television Fans and Participatory Culture*. London: Routledge.

———. 2014. "Fandom Studies as I See It." *Journal of Fandom Studies* 2, no. 2:89–109.

Johnson, Derek. 2007. "Fan-tagonism: Factions, Institutions, and Constitutive Hegemonies of Fandom." In *Fandom: Identities and Communities in a Mediated World*, edited by Jonathan Gray, Cornel Sandvoss, and C. Lee Harrington, 285–300. New York: New York University Press.

Kozinets, Robert V. 2009. *Netnography: Doing Ethnographic Research Online*. London: Sage.

Lewis, Lisa A., ed. 1992. *The Adoring Audience: Fan Culture and Popular Media*. London: Routledge.

McCulloch, Richard. 2011. "'Most People Bring Their Own Spoons': *The Room*'s Participatory Audiences as Comedy Mediators." *Participations* 8, no. 2:189–218.

Pinkowitz, Jacqueline M. 2011. "'The Rabid Fans That Take [*Twilight*] Much Too Seriously': The Construction and Rejection of Excess in *Twilight* Antifandom." *Transformative Works and Cultures*, no. 7. doi: 10.3983/twc.2011.0247.

Proctor, William. 2013. "'Holy Crap, More *Star Wars*! *More Star Wars*? What If They're Crap?': Disney, Lucasfilm and *Star Wars* Online Fandom in the 21st Century." *Participations* 10, no. 1:198–224.

Red and White Kop. 2013a. "Liverpool 0-0 West Ham Post Match Discussion," April 7. www.redandwhitekop.com.

———. 2013b. "Liverpool 3-2 Spurs: Full Time," March 10. www.redandwhitekop.com.

———. 2013c. "Post Match Discussion: Villa 1 (Benteke) Liverpool 2 (Henderson, Gerrard Pen)," March 31. www.redandwhitekop.com.

———. 2013d. "Southampton 3-1 Liverpool: Full Time," March 16. www.redandwhitekop.com.

Sandvoss, Cornel. 2003. *A Game of Two Halves: Football, Television and Globalization*. London: Routledge.

———. 2005. *Fans: The Mirror of Consumption*. Cambridge: Polity Press.

———. 2013. "Towards an Understanding of Poltical Enthusiasm as Media Fandom: Blogging, Fan Productivity and Affect in American Politics." *Participations* 10, no. 1:252–296.

———.2016. "Welcome to UKoslavia? Liquid Identities and Liquid Politics in the Age of Brexit." *Medium*, June 28. https://medium.com.

Sandvoss, Cornel, and Laura Kearns. 2015. "From Interpretive Communities to Interpretive Fairs: Ordinary Fandom, Textual Selection and Digital Media." In *The Ashgate Companion to Fan Cultures*, edited by Linda Duits, Koos Zwaan, and Stijn Reijnders, 91–106. Farnham: Ashgate.

Theodoropoulou, Vivi. 2007. "The Anti-Fan within the Fan: Awe and Envy in Sport Fandom." In *Fandom: Identities and Communities in a Mediated World*, edited by Jonathan Gray, Cornel Sandvoss, and C. Lee Harrington, 316–327. London: New York University Press.

Thornton, Sarah. 1995. *Club Cultures: Music, Media and Subcultural Capital*. Cambridge: Polity Press.

Waysdorf, Abby. 2015. "The Creation of Football Fandom Slash Fiction." *Transformative Works and Cultures*, no. 19. doi: 10.3983/twc.2015.0588.

12

Like Gnats to a Forklift Foot

TLC's Here Comes Honey Boo Boo *and the Conservative Undercurrent of Ambivalent Fan Laughter*

WHITNEY PHILLIPS

On January 5, 2012, American television station TLC aired the season 5 premiere of its hit reality show *Toddlers & Tiaras*, a program devoted to the wild and wooly world of child beauty pageants. This particular episode profiled six-year-old Alana Thompson, an aspiring pageant princess from McIntire, Georgia, as well as her outspoken mother June Shannon, a very large woman with a Southern drawl so thick it requires subtitles.

Alana's segment opens with a series of visual cues indicating that race, geography, and class—specifically, working-class Southern whiteness—would remain at the forefront of Alana's *Toddlers & Tiaras* segment. These images include an old railroad crossing sign, a train rumbling past the Shannon-Thompsons' modest rural one-story home, a small unkempt living room, packages of toilet paper stacked on a plastic shelf in the kitchen, and general domestic disarray. Set against Alana and June's white skin and thick Southern accents, these details signal that the occupants of this home also occupy a particular niche in American culture—that of the Southern redneck, more pejoratively known as "white trash."

As Laura Portwood-Stacer explains, this designation of "white trash" distinguishes normative—that is to say, middle- to upper-middle-class—whites from those who embody, or are said to embody, stereotypically "trashy" characteristics, some of which are listed above but which also include trailer parks and their residents, welfare mothers, neglected children, Klan members, truck drivers, and more (Portwood-Stacer 2007, 2). In this way, the term "white trash" asserts and normalizes a hierarchy of whiteness, the bottom rung of which is relegated to those whites deemed economically, culturally, and even racially "other," a point Annalee Newitz (1996) emphasizes in her study of white trash imagery. Laura Grindstaff reiterates this point, noting that, when lobbed by middle-class whites, the label of "white trash" "solidifies for the middle and upper classes a sense of cultural and intellectual superiority" and furthermore indicates that the individuals in question are not "doing whiteness" properly, since, from a middle-class perspective, whiteness is presumed to be inseparable from economic stability (Grindstaff 2002, 263–265).

That, however, is not the only point of racial contention on display. Alana's particular brand of Southern whiteness is made even more conspicuous during her star-turn interview, when the she affects the tone and comportment of a stereotypical "sassy black woman." Helena Andrews of the black culture and politics blog *The Root* has since described this performance as a "no she di'in't finger-waving, eye-rolling and neck twisting" caricature that "belongs to . . . a 90s sketch comedy show" (Andrews 2012). "The other girls must be crazy if they think they're gonna beat me, honey boo boo chiiiillle," Alana asserts, a statement accompanied by an exaggerated neck roll and comic mugging. She goes on to say that she does pageants for the money, and reiterating her earlier catch phrase, claims that "a dolla makes me holla, honey boo boo child!"

Although Alana seems to enjoy the pageant (and certainly enjoys the several bottles of "Go-Go juice," a concoction made of Red Bull energy drink mixed with highly-caffeinated Mountain Dew that June has her drink), she only receives third runner-up. When asked by the producers how she feels about the judges' decision, Alana—who wore a skimpy Daisy Duke outfit for the outfit-of-choice segment—admits to feeling sad she didn't get a big trophy or crown. "I showed my belly to the judges," she says, grabbing at her chubby midsection. "Look at this big thing. They don't know a good thing when they see it" (fig. 12.1). The producers can be heard guffawing in the background. The response to Alana's *Toddlers & Tiaras* appearance was overwhelming, if not exactly positive. As chronicled by the "Honey Boo Boo Child" entry on *Know Your Meme* (2012), a vast database of Internet culture, clips of Alana and her mother were featured as reality TV show monsters of the week on

Figure 12.1. They don't know a good thing when they see it.

VH1's *Best Week Ever* (Collins 2012) and Comedy Central's *Tosh.o* (Hallam 2012) and were posted to feminist *Gawker* imprint *Jezebel* (Morrissey 2012). Because of this coverage, tens of thousands of people who would not normally watch *Toddlers & Tiaras* were talking about and sharing clips from the "Honey Boo Boo" episode, resulting in nearly two-and-a-half million YouTube hits to two separate clip reels from the show (*Know Your Meme* 2012). Clearly, the network executives at TLC were impressed with these numbers, and later that year announced that they would be producing a spinoff program called *Here Comes Honey Boo Boo*, which premiered in the summer of 2012. The program focused on Alana and her mother, of course, but also included Alana's father Mike "Sugar Bear" Thompson and her three sisters: eighteen-year-old Anna Shannon, sixteen-year-old Jessica "Chubbs" Shannon, thirteen-year-old Lauryn "Pumpkin" Shannon, and Anna'a newborn daughter Kaitlyn.[1]

While highly successful during its two-year run—the series aired for four seasons between 2012 and 2014—it was canceled in the fall of 2014 after June, who by then had separated from Alana's father Mike, was accused of dating a convicted child molester. This essay, which was drafted during the second season in 2013, does not engage with that scandal or with any behind-the-scenes insight into what the Shannon-Thompson household was "really" like during filming. Not that these issues aren't worth engaging; rather, this essay is interested in TLC's initial marketing strategy and carnivalesque focus on the "lower stratum" of the Shannon-Thompsons' bodies. The essay also explores ambivalent audience responses to the series. While these responses were often outright antagonistic and counterhegemonic—making them a seemingly textbook case of anti-fandom—they were, simultaneously, implicitly affirmative and hegemonic. In this case, notions of anti-fandom weren't just inaccurate in describing ambivalent audience engagement; they also risked obscuring the cultural significance of this ambivalence—raising questions about the broader applicability of the anti-fandom frame when considering other ambivalent participatory behaviors.

Life Unscripted

The interest TLC's producers lavished on Alana and her unruly Southern family serves as the pinnacle (or nadir, depending on one's perspective) of the network's slow transition from an educational NASA and U.S. Department of Health, Education and Welfare offshoot to what I've described elsewhere as "masterpiece exploitainment theatre" (Phillips 2012). This process took a little over a decade, beginning in the mid 1990s with the network's integration of entertainment—as opposed to purely educational—programming into its lineup, a shift calcified by the network's 1998 decision to shorten its original name, The Learning Channel, to the punchier TLC (Acuna 2012). During this intermediary programming phase, TLC produced and aired multiple series with human-interest angles, including *A Wedding Story* (1996), *A Baby Story* (1998), *A Dating Story* (2000), *Trading Spaces* (2000), and *What Not to Wear* (2003), all of which were undergirded by the tagline "Life Unscripted."

Over time, these more mundane topics (getting married, having a baby, remodeling one's home) were replaced with increasingly outrageous programs, including *I Didn't Know I was Pregnant*, which featured first-person accounts of women who give birth unexpectedly, often while sitting on the toilet (2007), documentary specials about children with rare genetic conditions, including primordial dwarfism and Mermaid Syndrome (2007), and *Jon and Kate Plus 8* (2008) and *19 Kids and*

Counting, both of which chronicle the lives of unusually large families. By 2009, TLC had expanded significantly on its "medical oddity" offerings and featured programs like *Toddlers & Tiaras* (2009) and *Sister Wives*, a show chronicling the lives of a Mormon Fundamentalist polygamist family (2010); *My Strange Addiction*, which profiles individuals with unusual addictions, including one woman's inability to stop eating her dead husband's ashes (2010); *The Virgin Diaries*, a look into the lives of America's adult virgins (2012); *Abby & Brittany*, a show about conjoined teenage twins attached at the torso; and *Extreme Cougar Wives* (2012), a voyeur's-eye view of female octogenarians and their twenty-something boytoys, among others.

It was into this latter programming milieu that *Here Comes Honey Boo Boo* was thrust. Given the network's push to feature people and behaviors regarded by the mainstream as "odd" or otherwise non-normative, it should come as no surprise that, in promotion of *Here Comes Honey Boo Boo*, TLC initiated a branding campaign that can best be described as "promissory rubbernecking" ("Do you want to see something crazy/outrageous/weird? Then check your local listings!"). As evidence of this strategy, consider the following first-season promo:

> Dressed in her glitziest pageant outfit, Alana sashays through a red door on a red soundstage. A title card with the show premiere date zooms into view. "She's the toddler that took the TV world by storm," the announcer begins. The camera jump-cuts to a black-and-white clip of Alana's "dolla makes me holla" quote. "If you thought *she* was crazy," the announcer continues, his statement offset with Alana making a fart noise with her armpit, then an image of the Shannon-Thompson family sitting on their living room sofa as each jiggles their excess stomach fat, "wait till you meet the rest of her family." The camera cuts to a picture of June scratching her head. "Hold on I'm scratchin' my bugs," she says. The camera cuts again to June's daughters Anna and Lauryn. "We're not rednecks," Jessica says. "Yes we are," Mike insists. Jessica shakes her head. "We all have our teef, don't we?" Several quick jump cuts show mama June hollering at her kids to jump belly-first into a mud pit, June getting splashed with mud, middle daughter Lauryn covered in mud saying "I did my family proud," and then back to Alana on the family couch, who rolls her neck as she proclaims "You better Redneck-ognize!" [HoneyBooBoo News 2012]

Figure 12.2. Scratch-and-sniff card. Source: *People Magazine*, July 5, 2012.

The promotional blitz surrounding the second season premiere was even more visceral. Instead of focusing on the mere sight and sound of the Shannon-Thompson family, the network directed its marketing attention to an additional sense. "You've seen them," the 2013 promo begins. "You've heard them. Now you can smell them!" The commercial then encourages viewers to participate in the upcoming "Watch and Sniff event," either by visiting their local Time Warner Cable office and picking up a scratch-and-sniff card or by purchasing the July 5 issue of *People Magazine*, featuring a full-page advertisement and scratch-and-sniff insert (Morrisey 2013; see fig. 12.2).

In another season 2 promo, June explains how to play: "Get your card," she explains, pointing to one of six printed scents. "When you see the number on your TV, scratch the corresponding number, take a big whiff and see what you smell" (Dowd 2013). Given that the show opens with a group shot of the Shannon-Thompsons interrupted by a loud fart and the fact that Mama June confidently proclaimed during a season 1 episode that farting twelve to fifteen times per day helps you lose weight (see Székely Barna Attila 2012), the offer to "see what you smell" was winkingly ominous, particularly when offset with images of the Shannon Thompsons smelling each other's breath, Alana making a fart face, and Anna sniffing Kaitlyn's diapers.[2]

Taken together, the first and second season 2 promos can be distilled to this summary: The Shannon-Thompson family is loud, chaotic, and very entertaining. This is not how a "normal" family behaves; this is how a crazy family behaves. And isn't that funny! As we see in the section below, the episodes themselves more than follow through on the promises set forth in the promos. In fact in, terms of crudeness, ribaldry, and sheer outrageousness, *Here Comes Honey Boo Boo*'s episodes make the promos seems bland in comparison.

"My Asshole Is Raw!"

The above quote is taken from the first episode of *Here Comes Honey Boo Boo*'s second season. It is spoken by twelve-year-old Lauryn ("Pumpkin") after an apparently painful effort in the family's shared bathroom, which is located in June and Mike's ("Sugar Bear's") bedroom. The scene caps off Mike's failed efforts to seduce June, who keeps getting distracted by all the children zipping through the hallways and hurtling themselves onto the master bed. The editors cut to a blueprint of the family's home. "In order to do anything in this house you have to go through our room," Mike explains in a voice-over.

Lauryn's unabashed assertion perfectly captures the spirit and overall tone of *Here Comes Honey Boo Boo*. The Shannon-Thompsons are an outrageous bunch, and at least in relation to bodily functions within a middle- to upper-class milieu, utterly shameless; they belch with aplomb, scratch with abandon, and frequently weaponize their farts (also in the season 2 opener, Alana eagerly explains the family's favorite wrestling move, the "cup-a-fart," in which one participant farts into their hand and smashes the stink onto the other person's face). Whatever family dynamic exists behind closed doors, when the cameras are rolling, the Shannon-Thompsons are quick to laugh at themselves and each other, and, regardless of the circumstance, they appear to have a hell of a good time.

The show thus provides—that is, generates in its audience and features in its subjects—an uncanny analogue to the ambivalent, carnivalesque laughter described by Mikhail Bakhtin in *Rabelais and His World*. As

Bakhtin explains, medieval carnivals were characterized by outrageous, grotesque humor and exaggerated culturally inappropriate behaviors to "incredible and monstrous dimensions" (Bakhtin 1984, 206). The "lower stratum" of the human body, most conspicuously the stomach and anus, was of particular significance within Rabelais's "merry and rich" universe (308). After all, the various orifices of the human body are the source of, and receptacle for, all manner of excess—excessiveness being a fundamental hallmark of carnivalesque humor—but also of life itself, making the medieval carnival as much an affirmation of the world as an inversion of its more conservative mores (303–309).

The Shannon-Thompsons' exploits are nothing if not excessive, fixated on the lower stratum, and fundamentally lively. Consider episode 2 of the first season, "Gonna Be a Glitz Pig." In this episode, the family adopts a teacup pig named Glitzy, after the glitz style of child pageants ("glitz" requires a full face of makeup; a very formal, usually sequined, dress; hairpieces; and false front teeth plates called "flippers"). June then brings in an etiquette coach for Alana, who, according to the judges at their last beauty pageant, could use some refinement (jump cut to Alana pursing her stomach rolls into the shape of a mouth. "Those judges are nuts," she quips). Finally, June and the girls attend a community food auction to bid on overstocked and/or expired snack food, and June takes then seventeen-year-old Anna, who is in her third trimester, to get an ultrasound of her unborn daughter Kaitlyn.

Two scenes in "Gonna Be a Glitz Pig" stand out as being particularly carnivalesque. In the first, etiquette coach Barbara Hickey attempts to instill in Alana and Lauryn proper table manners. After being told never to raise her napkin to her face, Lauryn does so and proceeds to blow her nose into its center. Jump cut to an interview bite (a clip recorded either before or after the featured scene) with Alana. "Picking your nose isn't ladylike because it's not pretty, and it's nasty," she says, a statement directly followed by a clip from that same interview in which Alana is picking her nose. A soft fart can be heard in the background. The scene returns to the family kitchen. Barbara Hickey explains how to excuse oneself from the dinner table. "Like if you gotta take a poo-poo or somethin'?" Lauryn asks. Hickey looks stunned. "Don't . . . say that out loud," she says. "So can you fart at the table?" Lauryn continues. "Is that rude?" Another pause. "That is probably the height of rudeness," Hickey finally answers. Jump cut to an interview bite with the beleaguered etiquette coach. "There's some . . . *habits* they need to break. The bodily functions thing, we don't do that." Back in the kitchen, Lauryn continues: "I could fart like sitting down like this." She clenches her body in the chair. Jump cut to an interview bite with Lauryn. "I'll stop passing gas when I'm dead," she says, defiantly tossing her hair.

The second scene takes place in the First Glimpse ultrasound office, where a very pregnant Anna is having a checkup. "How can you tell that she's a girl?" Alana asks, looking up at the ultrasound monitor. "She has girl parts," the nurse answers. "Look, you see right there?" The nurse gestures at the monitor. "Where's her biscuit?" Alana asks. "Right there," the nurse says. Jump cut to an interview bite with June. "It's called a 'biscuit' cause it looks like a biscuit, you know, when it opens up." She spreads open her hands. "And um . . . [June laughs, as does someone standing off-camera] . . . you know, it does. It looks like a biscuit. If you look at a biscuit, and if it's cooked right, you know like in, like Hardees[3] or something . . . [June is cut off by an off-camera giggle fit. She throws back her head and laughs]."

For those who have internalized the hallmarks of middle-class etiquette, characterized by politeness, discretion, and self-control, this sort of exposure would be unwelcome, if not profoundly embarrassing. But not to the Shannon-Thompsons, as June explained in an interview with *Gawker*'s Rick Juzwiak: "I don't feel like I should be embarrassed about anything. . . . People will say, 'You're white trash.' Whatever. You don't even know me. But it is what it is. You've got critics. You've got people who love you and people who hate you." As for the idea that the audience is laughing at her and her family's exploits? "We're laughing at our asses too," she told Juzwiak (2012).

This "too" indicates, first of all, that June is well aware of the kind of reaction her family inspires. Second, it calls attention to the often-slippery nature of antagonistic laughter, which as the following section will attest, is often equally—and simultaneously—subversive and hegemonic.

Like Gnats to a Forklift Foot

Whatever the producers' motivations might have been for highlighting the "white trash" aspects of June and Alana's life, the fact remains that they *did* highlight—and therefore exploited—white trash stereotypes. Similarly, whatever argument(s) the producers of *Here Comes Honey Boo Boo* intended to make about the Shannon-Thompsons specifically, or so-called rednecks generally, whether good, bad, or indifferent, is less important than the implications of these choices: namely, that the recurring images and themes in *Here Comes Honey Boo Boo*, coupled with TLC's overall marking strategy, were designed to solicit strong audience reactions. Although some of these reactions were explicitly positive and some are explicitly negative, a significant percentage of viewer-generated content associated with the program was an odd, hard-to-define combination of both.

The following is a close textual analysis of the kinds of ambivalent audience engagement practices the program inspired, which I collected on a variety of digital media platforms during the show's four-season run. First, I present a representative example of ambivalent digitally mediated fan art. I then discuss engagement at the blogosphere level, including several representative examples of how paid bloggers on highly trafficked sites engaged with the program. Finally, I forward an example of ambivalent analog fan art that was subsequently reported on and amplified by large corporate media outlets, indicating the "clickability" of such content. As I illustrate, the primary characteristic undergirding each type of engagement—a characteristic that suffused the vast majority of the content I observed from 2012 to 2014—is ambiguity: Even those who created fan art for the show and who spent a great deal of time and energy posting and reposting content related to *Here Comes Honey Boo Boo* did so in a way that could be interpreted as simultaneously mocking and enthusiastic.

Consider participatory user activity on Tumblr, a massive multimedia microblogging platform known for its seemingly infinite and frequently rabid fandoms. During the show's run, Tumblr fans of *Here Comes Honey Boo Boo* regularly posted captioned images and GIFs (short loops of animated visual content popular on Tumblr and other social platforms) that highlighted the most outrageous, unflattering, and absurd moments from the show. They would also create and share countless photoshopped images juxtaposing the show's stars with all sorts of bizarre content. Figure 12.3 shows a screen grab from an animated GIF posted by Tumblr user conversationalconversations that embodies the

Figure 12.3. Mama June rides a cheesy water slide. Source: conversationalconversations, Tumblr, November 24, 2013.

spirit of much of this engagement. The foreground features an animated loop of June in her bathing suit riding down a water slide, while the background is a static image of bright yellow macaroni and cheese (chosen, presumably, because it is a cheap, shelf-stable, and preservative-laden meal with white-trash connotations). The GIF is tagged "macaroni and cheese," "honey boo boo," and "gross."

Despite this last tag—which implies that the poster is, at least to a certain extent, standing in judgment of June's body, diet, fashion sense, and/or some combination thereof—the image is not entirely negative. June appears to be having a great time, and her likeness is jauntily animated (in the GIF, June's figure rocks back and forth to mimic a sliding motion). Whatever the image might be saying about June, it sure looks like fun. Consequently, the image is difficult to categorize. Is it critical? Is it celebratory? The answer to both questions, it seems, is a resounding "yes." Although it is a single image among a sea of GIFs and photoshops, the above image exemplifies the kinds of artifacts that audiences of *Here Comes Honey Boo Boo* were inclined to create and highlights the ambivalent and vaguely antagonistic nature of even the most ostensibly positive ("positive" in the sense of "creative" and "generative") audience engagement. Of course, individual audience members—however they might have felt about the program—were not the only group with ambivalent motives and output; mainstream outlets were just as likely to walk the line between enthusiasm and mockery.

Few blogs embodied the spirit of this engagement—perhaps most accurately described as WTF (Internet slang for "what the fuck") viewing—more purely than *D-Listed*, a popular celebrity gossip blog written by Michael K. The aforementioned blogger was beside himself when June introduced America to her now-infamous recipe for "sketti," pasta noodles covered in a sauce composed of Country Crock imitation butter and Heinz ketchup. "Throw a bag of white bread from the Wonder Bread outlet on the table and dinner is served!" he wrote (2012c). He was even more taken by June's similarly infamous "forklift foot" water park scene, to which the following selection attests:

> Long before Mama June and her fluffy stack of Bisquick chins became the brightest stars in the TLC universe, she worked at a warehouse, and one day a forklift ran over one of her hooves. That's how her infamous *"Forklift Foot"* was created and apparently she never showed it to her kids until last night's episode of **Here Comes Honey Boo Boo**. The family went to a water park (Note: You haven't seen the raw definition of glamour until you've seen Mama June walk around a water park in wet ankle socks) and at the end of the day, her kids begged her to show them her Quasimodotoe.
>
> As the bells of Notre Dame rang, she pulled her wet bootie sock off and there was her mangled, yellowing Forklift Foot in all its gnat-covered glory. It actually wasn't that gross until the camera zoomed in on a bunch of gnats nibbling on her Forklift Foot gunk. Couldn't TLC just lie to us and tell us those gnats were actually tiny, black butterflies fluttering around what they thought was a beautiful, blooming flower? Oh well, at least we now have the phrase: Like gnats to a Forklift Foot . . . [Michael K. 2012b]

When Anna's baby girl Kaitlyn was born with an extra thumb ("I wish I had an extra finger," Alana said in the delivery episode. "Then I could grab more cheese balls"), Michael K. had this to say:

If you're lucky enough to be born into Georgia's reigning redneck royal family, you will eventually have an extra something. **Mama June** has extra chins, **Sugar Bear** has an extra derp gene ["derp" is a catch-all Internet slang term implying one who is cross-eyed or a bit slow], a few of them have extra chromosomes and **Chickadee's** 5-week-old daughter **Kaitlyn** has an extra thumb. That extra thumb will totally come in handy when Baby Kaitlyn will have to hitchhike out of there to get away from the mud bog fuckery. [Michael K. 2012a]

While unquestionably snarky, Michael K.'s coverage of *Honey Boo Boo* betrayed a basic (if backhanded) affinity for the Shannon-Thompson family. After all, Michael K. was not condemning the family for their perceived *shortcomings*. Rather, he was reveling in their *excessiveness*, from June's extra chins to Mike's "extra derp gene" to Kaitlyn's extra thumb. Michael K. was, in other words, echoing the Shannon-Thompsons' carnivalesque laughter with his own.

This is not to say that Michael K. approved of the Shannon-Thompsons; his engagement, like so much audience (and mainstream media) engagement with the show, could be outright insulting, not to mention explicitly classist, sizeist, and ableist. But his coverage gestured toward the family's appeal. From their diet to their body size to their olfactory output, the Shannon-Thompsons were quite literally in excess of middle-class behavioral norms and, for that reason alone, were very difficult to ignore.

It is unsurprising, then, that the most popular Halloween costumes in 2012 were Honey Boo Boo related. *Time Magazine* ranked Alana as the third best costume and offered a few choice (and mean-spirited) words of advice for prospective costume wearers: "Add to the effect by throwing around words like 'sketti' and other gibberish—though keep in mind that in real life, you won't get subtitled. You may have trouble convincing friends to go as her parents June and Mike (Sugar Bear), but it's worth a try. Just remember not to think about anything too much" (Pous 2012).

Of course, not everyone was so reluctant to dress up as June. Halle Kiefer (2012) devoted an entire article on VH1.com to her June costume, about which she expressed some ambivalence: "To be honest, I hesitated to suggest a budget Mama costume, as I didn't want it to be insulting towards a human I genuinely like and respect," she explained. "I want to pay her homage, not make her feel bad. You know what I mean?" She then offered a step-by-step guide on how to make oneself look fat on a budget, poorly styled on a budget, and neckless on a budget and, most important, how to maintain an "unflagging sense of self worth," with bonus accessories of ketchup and butter ("only pennies on the dollar!"). Once again, excess was the underlying theme of Kiefer's costume. It's not just that June is an extra-large woman, it's not just that she eats too much cheap junk food, it's that she has an excessive amount of self-confidence—apparently the punchline of the costume.

Artist Jason Mecier's "junk portrait" of Alana provides another striking example of ambivalent engagement with the Shannon-Thompsons' perceived excesses (see fig. 12.4). Using twenty-five pounds of trash, including the lid to a tub of I Can't Believe It's Not Butter, a label from a jar of pig's feet, the discarded torso of a Cabbage Patch Doll, a plastic bloody severed finger, a corncob holder, a flattened box of white sugar, and myriad other bits of obsolescent Americana, Mecier, who describes himself as a fan of the show, created an image of Alana giving a peace sign and making what is often derisively referred to as "duck face," a half-smile marked by a cocked head and pursed lips.

Figure 12.4. Honey Boo Boo trash portrait. Source: Lauren Moraski, "Honey Boo Boo Turned into a Trash Art Masterpiece," *CBS News*, November 21, 2012, www.cbsnews.com.

Figure 12.5. The pageant moms are taught a lesson. Source: Rheana Murray, "*Toddlers & Tiaras*' Moms Get Their Own Makeovers on Anderson Cooper's Show," *New York Daily News*, February 16, 2012, www.nydailynews.com.

The photo on which Mecier's junk portrait was based was taken February 16, 2012, during a segment for CNN anchorman Anderson Cooper's short-lived daytime talk show *Anderson* (Murray 2012). This particular segment of *Anderson* featured June and Alana as well as several other pageant girls and their mothers. Each mother was given a pageant "makeover" to show the moms exactly what they were doing to their daughters (essentially giving the mothers a lesson in exploitation). In the full image, Alana flashes a peace sign and serves her best duckface, while June stands behind her, her large body swaddled in pink ruffles. A hint of irony flashing behind her overly made-up eyes, June blows the camera a kiss (fig. 12.5).

Like many of the audience-generated artifacts surrounding *Here Comes Honey Boo Boo*, Mecier's portrait—which uses piles of trash to pay tribute to a family routinely accused of being white trash—is difficult to characterize. It certainly conveys affinity for Alana (at the very least, the amount of time and effort required to complete such a project suggests a basic investment in its subject), but does so via the most humble of mediums (discarded plastic crap) and by highlighting the perceived excesses of the Shannon-Thompson family. The question is, how might one describe this kind of engagement? The following section addresses this question and suggests that existing binaries—particularly the fan/anti-fan binary—are only so helpful when considering the kind of ambivalent audience responses *Here Comes Honey Boo Boo* was so adept at generating.

The Limitations of the Anti-Fan Frame

Initially, the above examples of ambivalent (and at times outright antagonistic) engagement with *Here Comes Honey Boo Boo* seem like clear-cut examples of anti-fandom. But upon closer inspection, the term "anti-fandom" doesn't quite fit. Not only does the concept fail to adequately describe the kinds of ambivalent audience play exhibited by fans of *Here Comes Honey Boo Boo*, it privileges the oppositional and downplays the hegemonic—a serious problem when attempting to place the program in the appropriate cultural and political context.

These limitations are underscored by the rigid affective and behavioral binaries the term tends to reify, most conspicuously evidenced by the oppositional prefix "anti-." This is not to say that theories that utilize the term are themselves rigid. As evidenced by the breadth of studies included in this volume, theories surrounding the concept of anti-fandom afford a broad and nuanced spectrum of behaviors, motivations, and meanings. Further, they concede that anti-fan engagement is not always necessarily antithetical to the interests of the content producers (see Click 2007; Gray 2005; Hill 2015; and Strong 2012).

That said, and again harkening to the "anti-" prefix, the basic demarcation in these theories between positive viewing practices (liking, appreciating, or adding value to a text) and negative viewing practices (disliking, ridiculing, and denigrating a text) are, more often than not, ultimately upheld. Anti-fans might derive pleasure, amusement, or entertainment from actively disliking a particular text, but the behaviors are still (presumed to be) animated by a distinctly negative charge, one predicated on tearing something down, rejecting someone's work, being antagonistic, and taking pleasure in the real or perceived shortcomings of others—a point of divergence Jonathan Gray underscores, even as he carefully contextualizes the full range of anti-fan participation (Gray, in this volume).

It is here that the concept of anti-fandom breaks down in relation to *Here Comes Honey Boo Boo*, since like and dislike of the show, and furthermore hegemonic and counterhegemonic engagement with its stars, cannot—and in my opinion should not—so easily be parsed. First, even the most antagonistic and derisive engagement with the Shannon-Thompsons lined up almost seamlessly with the network's branding strategy. Recall the first season promo, in which the Shannon-Thompsons argued over being rednecks, rolled around in a mud pit (shot at the Redneck Games, no less), and jiggled their stomach rolls for the camera. Recall the second season premiere scratch-and-sniff event, which spotlighted the Shannon-Thompsons' well-established proclivity for bodily emissions and all but asserted that the Shannon-Thompsons stink.

Again, what messages the network executives and show producers intended to convey about the Shannon-Thompson family is less important than the empirically verifiable fact that TLC's promotional materials and editing decisions emphasized the carnivalesque aspects of the Shannon-Thompson family dynamic, as did those who subsequently engaged in WTF viewing. Both camps turned a highly ambivalent eye on their chosen subjects, a point illustrated most conspicuously by Halle Kiefer's (2012) insistence that she "genuinely likes and respects" a woman she simultaneously revels in mocking. Ultimately, then, antagonistic engagement with *Here Comes Honey Boo Boo* challenges the assumption that seemingly negative—namely, mocking or otherwise ambivalent—behaviors and affinities necessarily run counter, or at least represent a negotiated response, to content producers' interests. Not only did such engagement help drive interest in *Here Comes Honey Boo Boo*, it directly echoed the branding strategies employed by TLC as well.

But branding strategies are not the only parallels the concept of anti-fan belies. In addition to mirroring TLC's branding strategy, ambivalent engagement with the Shannon-Thompson family was engaged in a much deeper, if much less conspicuous, form of hegemony. To illustrate how, it will be helpful to revisit Bakhtin's analysis of the political implications of carnivalesque laughter, which, as Bakhtin explains, casts off social hierarchy and conventions, dissolves the boundaries between the object of laughter and he who laughs, and in a nutshell, simply *uncrowns*—that is, it upturns the status quo and replaces it, however briefly, with its opposite (Bakhtin 1984, 10–11, 37).

As I have demonstrated, the Shannon-Thompson family (at least as portrayed on the program) reveled in the act of uncrowning. Anna, Lauryn, Jessica, and Alana regularly broke every rule of middle-class propriety imaginable, including those that seem wildly self-explanatory (e.g., the imperative *Do not lather your hair and bodies with butter and slide around the kitchen for laughs*, which the girls decided to transgress in the first episode of season 2). In each episode, the family unit constantly sought ways to laugh at and with each other, a point to which the very existence of the show attests—recall June's assertion that "we're laughing at our asses too" when confronted with the point that the audience is laughing at them. Furthermore, as television stars, the Shannon-Thompsons provided a living, breathing, excreting counterpoint to the assumption that bodies are pristine objets d'art whose indelicate processes are to be downplayed if not outright denied. Etiquette coach Barbara Hickey's command never to say "poo-poo" out loud and statement that "we don't do" bodily functions provide a perfect example. Hickey can say whatever she wants about what "our" bodies do, but the fact is that all bodies expel waste. By refusing to pretend that their bodies do not, the Shannon-Thompsons handily uncrowned prevailing assumptions about the "appropriate" relationship one should have with one's body, particularly the female body—which, for the record, is every bit the fart machine as its male counterpart.

Laughter directed *at* the Shannon-Thompsons—as opposed to the laughter they themselves initiated—was not so straightforward. In fact, and regardless of the subversive potential that may have echoed throughout the Shannon-Thompson household, ambivalent audience laughter ultimately locked that potential down, further naturalizing the existing social order. Bakhtin's argument indirectly predicts as much. After all, carnival is not an escape from society; rather, it represents "*temporary* liberation from the prevailing truth and from the established order" (Bakhtin 1984, 87; emphasis mine). So, while carnival laughter might uncrown the established order for an institutionally prescribed amount of time and might function as a kind of cultural safety valve, providing a much-needed reprieve from the status quo, the very act of uncrowning is not necessarily an escape from existing hierarchies and conventions. In fact, as anthropologists Max Gluck-man (1956) and Victor Turner (1969, 176–178) argue, carnival and its attendant chaos and licentiousness ultimately reify that which has been uncrowned, just as dressing up on Halloween—while liberating in the moment—serves as an implicit reminder that, on every other day of the year, costumes are not acceptable school and work attire.[4] In this way, the established order functions as an integral component to the existence of carnival. It is what allows carnival to occur and is what remains at its close.

Similarly, while *Here Comes Honey Boo Boo* might have provided some audience members a renewed perspective on the human body, particularly the female body, the program ultimately called attention to, and in fact was dependent upon, a rigid sense of how "normal" (which is often coded to mean "white middle-class") Americans should behave. Without an existing injunction against farting in public, for example, the Shannon-Thompsons' fondness for passing gas on national televi-sion would have gone unnoticed. Without prevailing notions about how "good" young women should behave, Anna, Lauryn, Jessica, and Alana's unruly behavior would have been considered unremarkable. In fact, it would not have been considered at all. Without a standard of beauty that essentially equates a person's worth with their waist size, the Shannon-Thompsons' larger bodies would have made no difference and certainly would not have functioned as jokes unto themselves.

The resulting audience laughter—particularly laughter that was an-tagonistic in nature—thus harkens to anthropologist Mary Douglas's argument that explorations of cultural elements regarded as dirty (i.e., "matter out of place") help one contextualize the elements that are re-garded as clean, that fit, that are *normal* (Douglas 1966). Applied to *Here Comes Honey Boo Boo*, the recognition that the Shannon-Thompson girls were engaging in gross or weird or dirty behaviors (even if these transgressions were ultimately celebrated by viewers) is predicated on viewers' knowledge and basic acceptance of pervasive cultural mores and, further, the viewers' ability to enumerate the Shannon-Thompsons' numerous normative infractions. However oppositional this laughter might have appeared, it was ultimately aligned with dominant ideol-ogy—a fact that calls into immediate question the efficacy of framing such participatory behaviors as being "anti" to anything.

Embedded within, Not Contrary To

As this case study has shown, the term "anti-fandom" isn't universally applicable to all instances of ambivalent fan participation. This isn't to reject the term entirely. Rather, it is to call attention to the fact that anti-fandom, as a function of its binary framing (loosely, anti-fans standing in contrast to unmarked and therefore "normal" fans), easily lends itself to binary thinking. This binary thinking, in turn, risks overlooking the significant slippage between good and bad, social and antagonistic, and positive and negative participatory behaviors, slippage that has quite a lot to say not just about a given community, and not just about a given text, but also about the cultural circumstances out of which both text and community emerge.

Indeed, as Phillips and Milner (2017) argue in their study of ambivalent vernacular play online, the slippage between these (apparent) binaries, including that between presumably normal and presumably aberrational behaviors, provides insight not just into fringe actors and behaviors but into mainstream actors and behaviors as well: the ways ambivalent audience participation is *embedded within* existing systems, even as it runs *counter to* them. The charge, here, one exemplified by ambivalent audience responses to *Here Comes Honey Boo Boo*, is thus to avoid pitting "this" against "that" and instead to embrace both sides of those coins—and, in the process, to help articulate how the periphery connects to, complicates, and even outright animates the center.

NOTES

1   For the sake of clarity, I will refer to the cast by their given names as opposed to their nicknames. When necessary, I will place an individual cast member's nickname in parentheses to remind readers which nickname is associated with which person.

2   To the relief of some and disappointment of others, only one of the scratch 'n sniff scents evoked the bouquet of flatulence; the rest were relatively inoffensive, including flowers, baby powder, gasoline and Mama June's now-infamous spaghetti, butter, and ketchup recipe known as "sketti."

3   An American fast food chain known for its so-called "thickburgers."

4   I am indebted to Lisa Gilman, Director of the University of Oregon's Folklore program, for introducing me to this concept in her "Theories of Performance Studies" course.

REFERENCES

Acuna, Kirsten. 2012. "The 40-Year Transformation of How TLC Went from the Learning Channel to Home of Honey Boo Boo." *Business Insider*, November 28. www.businessinsider.com.

Andrews, Helena. 2012. "Honey Boo Boo? Honey Please." *The Root*, August 15. www.theroot.com.

Bakhtin, Mikhail. 1984. *Rabelais and His World*. Bloomington: Indiana University Press.

Click, Melissa A. 2007. "Untidy: Fan Responses to the Soiling of Martha Stewart's Spotless Image." In *Fandom: Identities and Communities Within a Mediated World*, edited by J. Gray, C. Sandvoss, and C. L. Harrington, 301–315. New York: New York University Press.

Collins, Michelle. 2012. "Meet Alana, the Most Spectacular *Toddlers & Tiaras* Contestant Ever." *VH1.com*, January 5. www.vh1.com.

Douglas, Mary. 1966. *Purity and Danger: An Analysis of the Concepts of Pollution and Taboo*. New York: Routledge.

Dowd, Kathy Ehrich. 2013. "*Here Comes Honey Boo Boo* Premiere Will Be a 'Watch 'n Sniff' Event." *People*, June 19. www.people.com.

Gluckman, Max. 1956. "The License in Ritual." In *Custom and Conflict in Africa*, 109–136. Oxford: Basil Blackwell.

Gray, Jonathan. 2005. "Antifandom and the Moral Text: *Television Without Pity* and Textual Dislike." *American Behavioral Scientist* 48:840–858.

———. In this volume. "How Do I Dislike Thee? Let Me Count the Ways."

Grindstaff, Laura. 2002. "Trash, Class, and Cultural Hierarchy." In *The Money Shot: Trash, Class, and the Making of TV Talk Shows*, 242–275. Chicago: University of Chicago Press.

Hallam, Carly. 2012. "This Child Should Win Every Pageant Ever." *Tosh.o Blog*, January 6. www.comedycentral.com.

Hill, Annette. 2015. "Spectacle of Excess: The Passion Work of Professional Wrestlers, Fans and Anti-Fans." *European Journal of Cultural Studies* 18, no. 2:174–189. doi: 10.1177/1367549414563300.

HoneyBooBoo News. 2012. "Here Comes Honey Boo Boo—TLC Promo." YouTube, August 8. www.youtube.com/watch?v=11T59SdqguQ.

Juzwiak, Rich. 2012. "A Portrait of a Portrait of an American Family." *Gawker*, September 26. http://gawker.com.

Kiefer, Halle. 2012. "In a World of Honey Boo Boos, Be a Mama . . . for $20 or Less: A Celebrity Halloween How-To." *VH1.com*, October 25. www.vh1.com.

Know Your Meme. 2012. "Honey Boo Boo Child." http://knowyourmeme.com.

Michael K. 2012a. "FYI: Honey Boo Boo Chile's Newborn Niece Was Born with Three Thumbs." *D-Listed*, August 29. http://dlisted.com.

———.2012b. "Hot Slut of the Day: Mama June's Forklift Foot." *D-Listed*, August 30. http://dlisted.com.

———. 2012c. "Hot Slut of the Day: Mama June's Signature Sketti Sauce." *D-Listed*, September 13. http://dlisted.com.

Moraski, Lauren. 2012. "Honey Boo Boo Turned into a Trash Art Masterpiece." *CBS News*, November 21. www.cbsnews.com.

Morrissey, Tracie Egan. 2012. "Pageant Kid Succinctly Sums Up Our Feelings about Alcohol." *Jezebel*, January 5. http://jezebel.com.

———. 2013. "Now You Will Be Able to Smell 'Here Comes Honey Boo Boo.'" *Jezebel*, June 13. http://jezebel.com.

Murray, Rheana. 2012. "*Toddlers & Tiaras*' Moms Get Their Own Makeovers on Anderson Cooper's Show." *New York Daily News*, February 16. www.nydailynews.com.

Newitz, Annalee. 1996. "White Savagery and Humiliation, or A New Racial Consciousness in the Media." In *White Trash: Race and Class in America*, edited by Matt Wray and Annalee Newitz, 131–155. New York: Routledge.

Phillips, Whitney. 2012. "TLC: A Retrospective." *Modern Primate* (category), at *A Sandwich, with Words???*(blog), August 25. https://billions-and-billions.com.

Phillips, Whitney, and Ryan Milner. 2017. *The Ambivalent Internet: Mischief, Oddity, and Antagonism Online*. Cambridge: Polity Press.

Portwood-Stacer, Laura. 2007. "Consuming 'Trash': Representations of Poor Whites in U.S. Popular Culture." Paper presented at the annual meeting of the International Communication Association, San Francisco, May 23. www.allacademic.com.

Pous, Terri. 2012. "The 14 Best (Topical) Halloween Costumes of 2012: Honey Boo Boo." *Time Magazine*, October 24. http://time.com.

Strong, Catherine. 2009. "'. . . It Sucked Because It Was Written for *Teenage Girls*': *Twilight*, Anti-Fans and Symbolic Violence." Paper presented at the Australian Sociological Association conference, December. https://tasa.org.au.

Székely Barna Attila. 2012. "Honey Boo Boo's Mama 'Farting 12–15 Times a Day Helps You Lose Weight.'" YouTube, August 12. www.youtube.com/watch?v=JHw9kvArS3g.

Turner, Victor. 1969. *The Ritual Process: Structure and Anti-structure*. Chicago: Aldine.

13

"If Even One Person Gets Hurt Because of Those Books, That's Too Many"

Fifty Shades Anti-Fandom, Lived Experience, and the Role of the Subcultural Gatekeeper

BETHAN JONES

Introduction

In the summer of 2012, a trilogy of romance novels featuring a billionaire CEO and a virginal college student featured on bestseller lists across the United Kingdom and beyond and sparked a series of discussions about fan fiction, domestic abuse, and BDSM.[1] E. L. James's *Fifty Shades* novels (*Fifty Shades of Grey, Fifty Shades Darker* and *Fifty Shades Freed*; see James 2012a, 2012b, and 2012c) dominated media platforms, the British mainstream press alone publishing more than one thousand stories about the books (Deller and Smith 2013), with the series variously credited for the increase in sales of handcuffs and paddles (Berrill 2012) and decried for being "abominably written trash" (Kilpatrick 2012). Criticism of the series did not just come from professional quarters, however. Many members of fannish communities, particularly within *Twilight* fandom, accused James of exploiting her fans and bringing fandom into disrepute by pulling the fan fiction *Fifty Shades* was based on from the Internet and publishing it as original fiction.[2] But the fannish community was not the only one that reacted negatively to the books. Anti-fans of romance and erotic fiction criticized the novels for their poor writing while anti-fans of *Twilight* drew on gendered readings of the source fandom to criticize the derivative content. In a display of what Matt Hills (2012) calls "inter-fandom," *Twilight* fans criticized *Fifty Shades* fans. More pertinent to this chapter, however, is that members of the BDSM community similarly responded with anger, this time at the way in which the series depicted a BDSM relationship as abusive and individuals interested in kink as psychologically damaged. Posts discussing the books and their portrayal of BDSM were published to a variety of blogs and websites, their tones ranging from hostility to exasperation to education (see Click, in this volume, for an analysis of how digital media has made increasingly visible fans' negative affective evaluations of media texts). It is these posts that I examine in this chapter, assessing how the posters' experiences as members of the BDSM community have affected their readings of, and responses to, *Fifty Shades,* and examining how the subcultural capital these anti-fans have accrued owing to their experiences of BDSM, positions them as subcultural gatekeepers. I suggest that anti-fans' lived experiences within the BDSM community enable them to voice cultural concerns over *Fifty Shades* rather than voicing moral or ethical concerns that sections of other fandoms have predominantly focused on. My focus on the BDSM community also, however, draws attention to the fact that their critique of the text is made while trying to police the boundaries of their community, which is also under threat from the mainstream.

The bloggers whose work I cite have all written extensively on BDSM and abuse in the United Kingdom and the United States, and they have all been frequently cited in Internet discussions. Each of the bloggers also has a wide knowledge of the Anglo-American BDSM community, and the points they make in relation to BDSM, consent, and *Fifty Shades* have implications for how the media and the public understand both kink and the novels. In addition, many (though not all) of the bloggers are academics or have been invited to talk about their experiences of BDSM in academic contexts. While some may argue that this means that these bloggers are not indicative of the BDSM community at large, I suggest that they are taking up themes found within the wider community and giving them a more public platform while safeguarding the identities of community members who may not be able to talk publicly about their interest in BDSM. I also acknowledge here that BDSM communities outside of the Anglo-American context may have a different opinion of the novels, and while an examination of this is outside the scope of this work, I suggest that a broad analysis of anti-fans of *Fifty Shades* in a variety of languages would help our understanding of the social and cultural contexts in which anti-fandom is performed.

One strand of work in fan studies has involved reassessing the audiences we examine as fan studies scholars, asking whether we can fully understand what it means to interact with media texts by only examining fans (Gray 2003; Sandvoss 2005). Jonathan Gray raises an important critique of reception studies, arguing that focusing so intently on the fan distorts our "understanding of the text, the consumer and the interaction between them" (Gray 2003, 68). Gray suggests that anti-fans are not necessarily ignorant of the texts they hate, and anti-fan behaviors can resemble fan behavior. Anti-fans engaging in campaigns opposing a text are reminiscent of fan activism supporting a text, and anti-fans discussing a text at length mirror fans' desire to discuss a text. In this chapter, however, I focus on those anti-fans who have engaged in a close reading of the text and for whom a textuality is born into existence when the content of the text has provoked a reaction based on the anti-fan's lived experience. Gray concludes that

> if we can track exactly how the anti-fan's text . . . has been pieced together, we will take substantial steps forward in understanding textuality and in appreciating the strength of contextuality. [Gray 2005, 845]

The issue of contextuality is one that drives this chapter, and I suggest that it plays an important role in anti-fan reactions to a text. Simply stating that we need to appreciate the strength of contextuality fails to help us theorize the complex relationships that exist between anti-fans and texts and between anti-fans and fans. Melissa A. Click notes that the fan's relationship with a text is "a complex experience affected by the social contexts in which a text exists" (Click 2007, 306), and I argue that the same is true for the anti-fan's relationship with the text. I further argue, however, that the relationship with a text is affected by the social contexts in which the text is read (Jones 2015). The roles that cultural—or subcultural—capital and the lived experience play in anti-fandom thus need to be examined in much more detail than current scholarship allows for. I begin this chapter by outlining the ways in which BDSM and kink are depicted in the *Fifty Shades* novels before moving on to examine the ways anti-fans' lived experiences of BDSM frame their reading of, and responses to, the text. I argue that the role of the lived experience plays an important role in studying anti-fans and suggest that it influences the role of subcultural gatekeeper that anti-fans adopt in writing about *Fifty Shades*. They are not simply responding to a moral or aesthetic text, as Jonathan Gray argues (2005), but are involved in a subcultural reading of the text and respond as gatekeepers of that subculture. Anti-fan activities therefore are much more complex than snarking about a text[3] or warning others of the danger of a text (although these may be ways in which this complexity finds expression): In many cases they are policing the boundaries of a community already misunderstood, where the mainstreaming of a text that portrays a subculture incorrectly has serious implications for members of that community.

"I Will Fuck You, Any Time, Any Way, I Want—Anywhere I Want": Depictions of Kink in the *Fifty Shades* Universe

The *Fifty Shades* series, depicting the BDSM relationship between Christian Gray and Anastasia Steele, has brought BDSM to a far larger audience than any previous media text. Retailers were quick to monopolize on the success of the novels, with adult stores offering *Fifty Shades*–themed evenings and encouraging people to buy in-store the items featured in the novels (Martin 2013). Discussions about the sexual nature of the series ranged from whether the depiction of domination and submission was a "good" thing—especially for women (Arthurs 2012; Flood 2012)—to whether its visibility was "important" in highlighting the pleasure women get from reading erotica (Parker 2012; Wilkinson 2012). Although *Fifty Shades* has been credited with opening discussions about female sexuality, Barker, Gupta, and Iantaffi (2007) note that BDSM is becoming more visible in the "mainstream," and many of the criticisms aimed at *Fifty Shades* suggest that the series conflates BDSM with abuse, rather than being an acceptable, alternative lifestyle. Barker argues that much discussion around nonconsensual behavior within BDSM communities questions the previously accepted line that "BDSM is not (ever) abuse," challenging "simplistic neoliberal notions of consent which were previously prevalent in BDSM communities and are central to the *Fifty Shades* series due to their culturally taken-for-granted status" (Barker 2013, 897). BDSM is placed in a central position within *Fifty Shades of Grey*, the first nod to Christian's dominant side coming just pages into the first chapter when Ana notes that he sounds like a control freak (James 2012a, 10).

More explicit references to BDSM are made, however, in the chapters dealing with the signature of the contract, the play that Christian and Ana engage with, and Christian's personal history. Examining how kink is represented in these sections of the book is pertinent to the arguments I make later in this chapter.

In chapter 7 Ana is introduced to Christian's playroom (which she dubs the "red room of pain") shortly before the issue of the contract is broached. The room contains canes, floggers, a Saint Andrew's cross, a four-poster bed complete with chains and cuffs and spanking bench—in short, the same equipment to be found in playrooms and fetish clubs across the globe. The contract itself details a variety of rules that Ana is expected to follow, including sleeping for at least seven hours each night, not snacking between meals, exercising four times a week, and obeying any instruction provided by the Dominant (Christian). An appendix to the contract sets out the hard and soft limits for both Dom and sub. As Barker (2013) notes, the explicit references to BDSM contracts, safe words, and checklists of activities draw on common understandings and practices from BDSM communities, however the community's attitudes toward these references vary. Andrea Zanin argues that the contract is straightforward and includes plenty of very clear, easy outs for Ana should she dislike anything about her submissive relationship with Christian, although Zanin concedes that asking a virgin with no experience of BDSM to sign a contract is a poor idea (Zanin 2012). Discussion around safe words is more contentious. Veaux notes that talk of negotiation and safe words in BDSM communities can operate as a veneer under which people assume that anything is fine provided the other person enjoys it or does not complain (Veaux 2012). Barker agrees that this is similar to what happens in many of the scenes in *Fifty Shades* and "reflects a wider cultural tendency to evaluate sex on whether it is going well rather than on whether it is consensual" (Barker 2013, 904). Such a position is strongly criticized by many BDSM bloggers, such as Maxine, member of a London-based polyactivist community: "I think of this as Schrödinger-sex. You don't know until you open the box whether it contains an orgasm or a jail sentence. Why on earth would anyone find that attractive??! (E.L. James, I'm looking at you, here.)" (Maxine 2012). The play in which Christian and Ana engage is often depicted as aggressive and nonconsensual: Ana enters scenes about which she is unsure and in which Christian fails to read her body language and stop even though the safe word is never utilized. Furthermore, Ana is often abandoned postscene with no aftercare or discussion about what happened during the sessions. James, according to BDSM bloggers, is unaware of the concept of Safe, Sane and Consensual or the more recent Risk Aware Consensual Kink,[4] which proves problematic in the way in which kink is depicted in the series. Far from presenting a realistic depiction of kink, as understood by the community at large, James instead portrays an abusive, careless relationship. In doing so, members of the BDSM community contend, she perpetuates notions of kink, as understood in the mainstream, as degenerate, perverse, and dangerous.

The depiction of BDSM more broadly, however, is also aligned to mainstream understandings of kink as deviant and morally bankrupt. During the series, the reader discovers that the only sexual relationships Christian initiates as an adult have been with women who are self-identified submissives and that he was "turned" kinky by an older woman referred to by Ana as "Mrs. Robinson" (or occasionally "the child molester"). We further discover that Christian's biological mother was a "crack whore" who was killed in front of him when he was four, leaving him unable to experience normal intimacy and presumably leading to BDSM. As Zanin points out, the book "portrays kink as being an indicator of both mental illness and criminality in all circumstances other than [a] heterosexual relationship heading toward marriage and reproduction" (Zanin 2012). In this way, *Fifty Shades* accurately reflects mainstream understandings of consent and acceptable sexual conduct. For those in the BDSM community, however, this representation is problematic and does not reflect their lived experiences. This lack of representation leads to anti-fandom and anti-fannish behavior, as I discuss in the next section.

"When I See People Making Excuses and Saying That This Sort of Repulsive, Sickening, Criminal Behavior Is Not Only Sexy but Acceptable, I GET SCARED": Anti-Fandom and the Lived Experience

Gray has observed that hatred of a text can be just as powerful as an affective relationship with it and can produce just as much activity and identification or unite and sustain a community (Gray 2005, 841).

Hatred of a text can, indeed, sustain a community—as my analysis of *Fifty Shades* thus far has demonstrated—but a relationship with a text is necessarily affected by the social contexts in which the text is read. In his study of *Television Without Pity* forums, Gray (2005) notes that many expressions of anti-fandom were framed explicitly as moral objections to a text, and he suggests that the commenters' interaction with the text was influenced by their moral or ethical concerns, such as a TV movie taking advantage of a horrible tragedy rather than presenting facts.[5] This engagement with the moral text frequently happens before the aesthetic text has aired, and many of the posters Gray examined did not watch the programs that they derided. They "read" the moral text of the program—they had engaged with paratexts such as newspaper articles, news segments, and blogs—but had no desire to engage with the aesthetic or rational-realistic text.

Gray proposes then that we either "once again have a case of a moral text without an aesthetic text or a case of the moral text wholly subsuming the aesthetic text to the point of erasure and insignificance" (Gray 2005, 848), and I certainly would not argue that some anti-fans of *Fifty Shades* engaged only with the moral text (see the religious backlash against the novels discussed in Whitehead [2013] and the UK charity that called for copies of the book to be burned, referred to by Flood [2012]). Where Gray's posters did engage with the aesthetic text, however, a moral text was also consumed and eventually infringed on some viewers' ability to enjoy the aesthetic. In discussing the anti-Omarosa campaign that resulted from TV show *The Apprentice*, he notes that the "moral text viewers" worried about other people's reception and argues that this demonstrates that reception occurs with an imagined community of others and, thus, "a good deal of what the text means to [viewers] is a reflection of what they believe it will mean to others and what effects it will have on others" (Gray 2005, 851). What Gray fails to account for in his analysis, however, and what forms the basis of this chapter, is what the text means to individual viewers, and the effect that the text can have on viewers and their physical community.

Bloggers Ket Makura and Gehayi, both of whom have experience with BDSM, undertook a close reading of the books to "spork" them, "sporking" being writing and posting mocking and/or critical commentary on a work that is considered extraordinarily bad.[6] The two read each book in the series, pulling out sections of interest and commenting on them online. In the introduction to the sporking, Ket wrote:

> All right, personal history time! Anyone who's read other sporkings I've done will probably not be *shocked* to find out that I'm into BDSM. What you might not know is that I was in the Lifestyle for a while. As a Submissive . . . I know that there are healthy, happy Total Power Exchange relationships. But too often, they're written as abusive, as predatory, and hey, let's call a spade a spade here—as rape. And this . . . this piece of dried-up shit [*Fifty Shades of Grey*] here? Is all three of those things. [Ket, at Geyahi and Ket Makura 2012]

Ket has an investment in the experiences depicted in and meanings attributed to *Fifty Shades* as they contrast directly with her lived experience of being a submissive. A close reading of the text, as well as drawing links to lived experiences, was thus an important part of the sporking. However, the text is also made to matter to Ket, and other members of the BDSM community, because of its popularity and the role it has played in introducing people to kink. As Zanin notes, many members of the community see the spike in interest caused by *Fifty Shades* as a negative thing as this mainstream representation of kink "causes people to show up in our spaces with a really skewed idea of what to expect, and . . . those of us who've been around for a while have to engage in the repetitive and sometimes exhausting work of dismantling stereotypes and setting people straight about what this whole kink thing is really all about" (Zanin 2012). The concerns of bloggers like Ket and Zanin are thus not simply, I would suggest, an engagement with the moral text. Rather, they demonstrate anti-fandom of a *(sub)cultural* text. Zanin, Ket, and the anti-fans I examine later in this chapter criticize *Fifty Shades* for portraying BDSM in a negative and false light, and they do so based on their lived experiences, as Flox does:

> As someone who believes the world could do with a more open-minded approach to people's consensual sexual interests, I initially thought the book was doing bondage and discipline, dominance and submission, and sadomasochism (BDSM) a service by bringing it into the national dialogue through fantasy.

> Before I could make any such statement, of course, I had to read it. I wasn't far into the story when I realized that *Fifty Shades of Grey* not only sets people who live a BDSM lifestyle back decades in terms of being understood by society, but that it eroticizes dangerous practices as well, especially for those who are new to this aspect of sexuality and looking to incorporate it into their lives. [Flox 2012]

The notion of the lived experience within fan studies has primarily focused on the fan, with fans "accumulat[ing] cultural capital of television programs in ways that affect the physicality of their own lived experience" (Todd 2011, 860). Not merely buying mugs or clothing with a favorite series' logo or characters on them, fans copy the hairstyles of much-loved characters and bid on items that appear in a series, thus extending the set from the television into their own homes (861). Writing about TV show *Friends*, Todd notes that "through the accumulation of official and unofficial memorabilia, *Friends* becomes more than a television program, it is the fans' lived experience" (862). The lived experience of fans, however, can be markedly different to that of anti-fans. While the former is developed *because of* a positive affective relationship with a series, the latter *causes* a negative affective relationship (for more on the role that negative fan affect plays in fan culture, see Stein, in this volume). Jenny Trout, writing about her experiences of BDSM, describes her relationship with her husband and the contrast with Ana's relationship with Christian:

> During the entire encounter, I was never afraid that my husband wouldn't stop. I knew that if I used the safe word, it would be okay, we could do something else. He wouldn't blackmail me with his past emotional tragedies to try and shame me for using the safeguard we agreed upon to protect our mutual trust. [Trout 2013]

This lived experience of BDSM is detailed in many of the blog posts discussing the portrayal of kink in *Fifty Shades*, and those involved in the community or in BDSM relationships are quick to refer to their own personal experience of BDSM as evidence of their authority to comment on the books. In writing about fan activity, Henry Jenkins (1992) states that our common narratives no longer originate with the lived experience of the members of a society but are created and distributed by publishing houses and production studios. Fan fiction is thus one way to reclaim agency and participate in the story. I suggest, however, that the narratives created by anti-fans, particularly anti-fans of *Fifty Shades*, do originate with their lived experiences, and these lived experiences are used to counter the experiences created and distributed by those publishing houses and production studios. I further argue that those lived experiences enable anti-fans to accrue a certain kind of subcultural capital, simultaneously allowing them to speak from positions of authority and participate in (retelling) the story by acting as subcultural gatekeepers.

"Fans Are NOT Bad People for Liking This Series. They Just Aren't CAREFUL Readers": Anti-Fandom and the Role of the Subcultural Gatekeeper

In his 2005 article on anti-fans, Gray argues that in engaging with the moral text we see a hallmark of much anti-fandom: "the interest, or even sense of responsibility, in sharing one's reading and, thus, encouraging an avoidance of the aesthetic text in others too" (Gray 2005, 848). Gray suggests that these desires to warn others are a result of readings of the moral text, but I would suggest that anti-fans who engage with the aesthetic text, particularly if they engage in a close reading of it, demonstrate their own subcultural capital while simultaneously leveraging their subcultural capital to encourage others to avoid that text.[7] I should note here that the bloggers discussed in this chapter are not self-described anti-fans, although some of them admit to hating the series—hidingfromsomeone (2012) writes "I am not simply hatin' [*sic*] on 50 Shades for the sake of it. I could, fuck me sideways, I could"—but many more position themselves as being concerned with the books' contents or hating what *Fifty Shades* says about BDSM. The term "anti-fan," therefore, is one that I am applying to these bloggers, developing the theory Jonathan Gray (2003) first espoused, as they clearly demonstrate anti-fannish behavior and practices: They write copious amounts on the text, and they engage in awareness raising (what could be referred to as campaigning). Furthermore, they each engage in close readings of the books to deconstruct the potential messages within them: Jenny Trout undertook a chapter by chapter sporking of the book, writing, "So, as I announced in a delirium of hatred last night, I have begun reading 50 Shades of Grey, and I'm going to share the experience with you" (Trout 2012). Flox noted that before she could state that *Fifty Shades* was doing BDSM a service by bringing it into the mainstream she had to read it (Flox 2012). And Zanin defended her position by saying, "My book club, the Leather Bindings Society, had just finished reading the trilogy for one of our meetings, so it was fresh in my mind. . . . And yes, I did read all three of them, cover to cover" (Zanin 2012). The careful choice of language used by these bloggers in their deconstructions, however, is also interesting for what it says about the nature of their anti-fandom. Significantly, given much of the anti-fandom of, and mainstream criticism leveled at, *Fifty Shades* and other "female" texts, they are rarely antagonistic, preferring instead to educate or disparage through humor rather than by negative stereotyping or pathologizing. This criticism thus avoids much of the gendered language used by those opposed to the text, and it also furthers commentators' own subcultural capital, drawing on their lived experiences and affective relationships with the community rather than using hyperbole and inflammatory language.

These BDSM bloggers thus function as subcultural gatekeepers; however, they fulfil a somewhat different function to that proposed by Sarah Thornton (1995) and Bertha Chin (2010). Subcultural capital within the BDSM community, as I have noted elsewhere (with Sarah Harman), is accumulated "through an engagement with the scene, a knowledge of the nuances of the community, and a distinction between mainstream or 'vanilla' sexual practices" (Harman and Jones 2013, 962). The BDSM community's responses to *Fifty Shades* are thus intended to protect the community from inaccurate representation as well as to educate individuals attracted to the community through reading *Fifty Shades*. I argue, however, that BDSM practitioners' familiarity with the text precludes them from being simply BDSM fans who are protecting their community. hidingfromsomeone (2012), discussing safe BDSM play, writes, "It is something that I rarely discuss other than with those in the community for fear of repercussions—BDSM is fairly misunderstood by the wider public." Given this, many BDSM practitioners are afraid to speak out against misconceptions of the lifestyle, and I suggest this makes BDSM anti-fan response to *Fifty Shades* even more unique.

Furthermore, as Zanin (2012) notes, perverts are jumping on the *Fifty Shades* bandwagon, with BDSM educators and organizers picking up the *Fifty Shades* meme and using it to educate the mainstream and increase the visibility of safe kink. Of course, some of these will use *Fifty Shades'* popularity to make a profit while never having read the book. I do not categorize these as anti-fans in the same way that I categorize the bloggers referred to in this chapter. However, the bloggers I discuss here, many of whom are not BDSM "professionals" but simply members of the community, are engaged in a more complex practice than defending their lifestyle: When anti-fans have familiarity with the subject matter but no real investment in the text under question, they base their arguments about the text in their subcultural knowledge, pointing out how the text (and thus fans) gets it wrong. Simultaneously, however, their critique of the text is made while trying to police the boundaries of their community, a community that, in this case, is also under threat. In this respect, it may be useful to draw on Hills's notion of inter-fandom, although I do have some concerns in comparing a media fandom such as *Fifty Shades* with an alternative lifestyle practice like BDSM.

Inter-fandom examines the relationships between different media fandoms, "whereby one fan culture defines itself against and negatively stereotypes another" (Hills 2012, 122). Hills uses the example of *Twilight* fandom in his work, detailing how its presence at Comic-Con in 2008 and 2009 brought it into proximity with a range of other media fandoms, many of which felt *Twilight* and its fans had no place at a comic convention. I argue that inter-fandom is at work between *Twilight* and *Fifty Shades* fandom, with many *Twilight* fans embarrassed that *Fifty Shades* was responsible for more media attention being turned on the *Twilight* fandom and criticisms aimed at James for pulling her fan fiction to publish it as original work (see Jones 2014). Tensions between *Fifty Shades* fans and BDSM bloggers, however, are much rarer, and when they do exist, they focus on the lack of education of *Fifty Shades* fans, rather than negatively stereotyping or pathologizing them. Jenny Trout writes that

> Ana and Christian are not an example of a healthy BDSM relationship, and when *50 Shades* defenders—whose only exposure to BDSM has come through this single source—frame it as though it is, they're actually harming the image of BDSM more. But that's not something they want to hear.

They want to feel like they're protecting a misunderstood and beautiful people, who do sexy things in expensive high rise apartments. [Trout 2013]

Here, Trout criticizes the lack of awareness of BDSM, rather than *Fifty Shades* fans themselves. *Fifty Shades* fans may want to protect a "misunderstood and beautiful people," but their perception of the BDSM community is skewed, based on *Fifty Shades*, rather than on any lived experience. Given this lack of stereotyping, pathologizing, or devaluing, the *Fifty Shades* anti-fans discussed in this chapter represent a new and different breed to those proposed by Gray and Hills.

I contend, then, that *Fifty Shades* anti-fans are gatekeepers of a specific subculture, BDSM, and they patrol the fringes of the *Fifty Shades* fannish space to protect would-be members from potentially dangerous BDSM practices. Indeed, anti-fan activities such as blogging and writing fan fiction can be seen as trying to appeal to an audience beyond those in their cultural sphere. Gehayi notes:

As we have said multiple times, the fans are NOT bad people for liking this series. We're saying that they aren't CAREFUL readers. . . . We worry about those messages [the novels send] and the possibility of someone picking up on them—consciously or subconsciously—and getting hurt. If even one person gets hurt because of those books, that's too many. . . . I don't know how many people we're reaching, but we have to say something. *But we do not pass judgment on the readers.* If they decide to get into BDSM, we want them to be fully informed. If they decide to consent to participate in a BDSM scene, we want them to understand what they're consenting to. [Gehayi, email to the author, 2013]

While many of Gehayi's posts are humorous, the intention behind them is to educate. Gehayi is therefore aware of the paratextual nature of her blog and the role it plays in affecting readings of the novels. The exhortations that many other bloggers make in their posts also demonstrate an awareness of the role that *Fifty Shades* may play in an individual's desire to become involved in BDSM, as well as their responsibility as bloggers and members of the community to ensure newcomers are aware of Safe, Sane, and Consensual kink. Zanin ends her blog entry with the caution, "If you wanted to, you could use the physical techniques described in

Fifty Shades to get up to some pretty safe sexy fun. But please, please do not ever use *Fifty Shades* as a relationship model. On that front it is outright dangerous" (Zanin 2012). The tone of these anti-fans is markedly different from those *Twilight* anti-fans who see the fan base as culturally dismissible (Pinkowitz 2011) or who discuss female fans using "Victorian era gendered words" (Click 2009), and are also different from those *Fifty Shades* anti-fans who condemn the series for its sexual content. I have already noted the careful language used in the blog posts, but the refusal of bloggers to condemn readers of *Fifty Shades* along with the books is unique within anti-fandom. I suggest that there are two prime reasons for this, tied up with Jonathan Gray's notion of anti-fannish "responsibility" and the position of BDSM within mainstream culture. First, hidingfromsomeone writes, "I feel like it is my responsibility as one of the people who bridges the gap between the BDSM community and the *Fifty Shades* readership to speak out against the practices shown in the series," echoing Gray's argument that the "sense of responsibility, in sharing one's reading" is a consequence of readings of the moral text surrounding the object of anti-fandom (Gray 2005, 848). This sense of responsibility results in a more conciliatory tone being taken by these anti-fans. Rather than criticize fans of *Fifty Shades* in the same way as *Twilight* fans have been critiqued, resulting in the creation of a defensive barrier around the fandom, by taking on the role of educator these *Fifty Shades* anti-fans are more likely to be heard by fans of *Fifty Shades*.

Second, BDSM has often been misrepresented in mainstream culture. Zanin, discussing the portrayal of kink in the books as an indicator of both mental illness and criminality, writes,

> The message is twofold: if you're kinky and you're not partnered in a heterosexual, monogamous fashion, you are mentally ill and criminally dangerous; and if you're heterosexual and monogamous, then jealousy, stalking and control are indications of love, and playing with kink a little bit is hot as long as you don't do it too much and you keep it in the bedroom. [Zanin 2012]

BDSM practitioners' awareness of the ways the culture is represented in the mainstream press and the criminalization of some practices puts them in a vulnerable position, like that of some media fandoms that have been pathologized. *Twilight* fandom, for example, is negatively stereotyped by the mainstream media, its female fans described as rabid, ravenous, and frenzied (Hills 2012). But inter-fandom relationships with *Twilight* are also strained, with the "profoundly ironic" result that "fan cultures who may themselves historically have been victims of pathologizing stereotypes are now in some instances turning those patterns of stereotyping onto other, younger fans and fandoms" (Hills 2012, 123; see also Jones 2016). I suggest, however, that the BDSM community consciously moved away from this stereotyping of *Fifty Shades* fans, precisely because of their lived experiences within a pathologized subculture. That female desire—of *Twilight* fans particularly—has been attacked by cultural commentators and that *Fifty Shades*—described condescendingly as "mommy porn"—is attacked for bringing female sexuality into the mainstream also plays a role in these anti-fan responses. Condemning female fans who have discovered alternative sexuality through reading *Fifty Shades* is antithetical to the alternative lifestyle adopted by the BDSM anti-fans of *Fifty Shades.*

The anti-fans I have discussed in this chapter do not "snark" about the text,[8] as the anti-fans Francesca Haig (2014) studied do, nor do they pathologize other fans. Rather, they engage in close readings of the text, drawing on their own lived experiences to educate others about the perceived dangers inherent in James's trilogy.

Conclusion

Throughout the course of this chapter I have argued that anti-fan activity is far more complex and nuanced than current academic analysis acknowledges. *Fifty Shades* anti-fans are certainly recognizable in some aspects of Gray's definition but not in others, and this opens anti-fandom to further analysis. Opponents to *Fifty Shades*, such as those discussed here, often spend considerable time discussing why the text has made them angry, and some may campaign against it, but that campaigning more often takes the form of blog posts than the activism normally associated with fandom (such as letter writing). Indeed, Zanin argues against a book-burning campaign allegedly begun by a British domestic abuse charity, writing that "it is an approach that self-justifies abuse in the name of stopping abuse, and that self-justifies censorship in the dubious name of protection" (Zanin 2012). Similarly, many anti-fans do not attempt to prevent people from reading *Fifty Shades*; rather, they point out the problematic nature of the book and signpost interested readers to better BDSM resources. However, a far more significant difference lies in the way in which *Fifty Shades* anti-fans draw on their own lived experiences of BDSM to reinforce their positions as subcultural authorities and secure their social hierarchy (Ahmed 2004).

Anti-fan commentary thus plays an important role not only in enforcing taste but also in negotiating the meaning found in *Fifty Shades*. The analysis found in Gehayi and Ket Makura's sporking of the series, or the experiences of BDSM described by hidingfromsomeone and Jenny Trout serve a similar function to meta, which is written by fans for an object of fandom but subverts the meaning of the text by bringing it into conversation with other topics.[9] The anti-fans I have examined throughout this chapter therefore complicate current notions of anti-fandom as well as the role that lived experience plays in anti-fannish engagement with a text. Anti-fans' lived experiences enable them to accrue subcultural capital that affects their anti-fandom by enabling them to recognize the inconsistencies or inaccuracies within a text, and this subcultural capital further positions these anti-fans as subcultural gatekeepers. Bloggers involved in the BDSM community thus create compelling considerations for the future of anti-fan activity and its position within fan studies scholarship: We need to consider more carefully the role of the lived experience in relation to anti-fandom as well as the different texts that anti-fans may be responding to. (Sub)cultural texts can be read as easily as can moral texts, aesthetic texts, or rational-realistic texts, and in some cases, such as the examples I have discussed here, they play a far more important role in the performance of anti-fandom.

I noted at the beginning of this chapter that anti-fan scholarship needs to do more work to understand the complex ways in which contextuality affects audience-text relationships and that more attention needs to be paid to the social contexts in which the text is read and the roles that affect and cultural—or subcultural—capital play. My analysis of *Fifty Shades* anti-fans demonstrates the importance that lived experience has on the reading of and relationship to the text. Furthermore, I suggest that future research into anti-fandom should also examine the ways that anti-fans' social contexts influence their affective relationship with the texts and the way in which fannish spaces are encroached on by anti-fans to police the boundaries of their own, threatened communities. Work has been done in audience studies on the importance of context to audience research (Bury 2005; Fiske 1992; Morley 1980), but little has yet been done to utilize this in the study of anti-fandom. Similarly, the affective relationship fans have with their object of fandom has also been discussed (Grossberg 1992), but the role that affect plays in anti-fan responses to a text has been sidelined within fan studies, as Melissa Click points out (in this volume). I suggest that these are both important areas for consideration in future anti-fan studies, but I further argue that work on anti-fandom must consider communities that are viewed as occupying a lower cultural status than the fannish community they critique. While fandom is becoming more visible in the mainstream, BDSM is still considered degenerate and dangerous. Anti-fans from within the BDSM community who thus use their subcultural capital to police their own community and raise awareness of the dangers of *Fifty Shades* are working in a far less privileged environment than, for example, white, straight, male anti-fans of *Fifty Shades* who approach it from a position of "high culture" and privilege. Those of us working in fan studies must acknowledge our own privileges, in addition to stating and theorizing our own positions as fans, and pay more attention to those who do not share those same positions.

NOTES

1 A compound acronym, which encompasses bondage and discipline, domination and submission, sadism and masochism.

2 Originally published under the title *Master of the Universe*, a piece of *Twilight* fan fiction in which Edward Cullen was a rich CEO and Bella Swan a college student, the fic was well known within *Twilight* fandom, and James, writing under the name Snowqueens Icedragon, had amassed her own fan following. When James contracted with The Writer's Coffee Shop to publish *Master of the Universe* as an original work, the fan fiction was pulled offline, and the *Twilight*-specific details were removed. When the series was subsequently picked up by Vintage, its fan fiction origins were acknowledged but downplayed.

3 "Snark" is defined by the *Urban Dictionary* as a combination of "snide" and "remark" (see Tootybug47 2004).

4 Safe, Sane and Consensual advocates emphasize that BDSM activities should be safe, sane, and consensual, while those who advocate Risk Aware Consensual Kink argue that notions of "safe" and "sane" vary depending on the individuals involved. Therefore, given that no sexual activity is totally safe, members of the

BDSM community must ensure that their partners acknowledge the risk and still consent to the activity (see Veaux 2012).

5 Gray does acknowledge that it would be wrong to regard anti-fandom as always moral, and there are examples of anti-fandom provoked by poor levels of realism or sense. However, he limits his discussion of these to commercials and talk shows, noting that many adverts were criticized by *Television Without Pity* posters for making no sense and lacking in logic and that the host of *The O'Reilly Factor* fails to support his assertions with evidence (Gray 2005, 853).

6 "Sporking" is closely linked to "hatereading," in which a text is read for the express purpose of ridiculing it or indulging the reader's disdain for the author and/or the content, but sporking is generally more humorous. The term takes it name from the utensil, the spork, which is the right size and shape to dig out an eye.

7 Gray's discussion of "bad object" anti-fandom goes some way to analyzing anti-fan reactions to *Fifty Shades*, noting that, "in a patriarchal society, female figures and texts aimed at or otherwise coded as designed for women will prove easy default bad objects" (Gray, in this volume). For further discussion of this, see Harman and Jones (2013).

8 See Tootybug47 (2004) for the definition of "snark."

9 The website *Fanlore* notes that "meta" is a term used in fandom to describe a discussion of fan works, fan works in relation to the source text, fan fiction characters and their motivation and psychology, fan behavior, or fandom itself (*Fanlore*, n.d.). Meta or a meta essay can also be a fan-authored piece of non-fiction writing that discusses any of the above topics.

REFERENCES

Ahmed, S. 2004. *The Cultural Politics of Emotion*. New York: Routledge.

Arthurs, D. 2012. "Samantha Brick Slams *Fifty Shades of Grey* on This Morning as 'Badly Written Porn That Is Demeaning to Women.'" *Daily Mail*, July 2. www.dailymail.co.uk.

Barker, M. 2013. "Consent Is A Grey Area? A Comparison of Understandings of Consent in Fifty Shades of Grey and on the BDSM Blogosphere." *Sexualities* 16, no. 8:896–914.

Barker, M., C. Gupta, and A. Iantaffi. 2007. "The Power of Play: The Potentials and Pitfalls in Healing Narratives of BDSM." In *Safe, Sane and Consensual: Contemporary Perspectives on Sadomasochism*, edited by D. Langdridge and M. Barker, 197–216. Basingstoke: Palgrave Macmillan.

Berrill, A. 2012. "*Fifty Shades* Phenomenon Gives Ann Summers a Boost as 'Mummy Porn' Trend Sends Sales of Handcuffs and Blindfolds Soaring." *Daily Mail*, December 10. www.dailymail.co.uk.

Bury, Rhiannon. 2005. *Cyberspaces of Their Own: Female Fandoms Online*. New York: Peter Lang Publishing.

Chin, B. 2010. "From Textual Poachers to Textual Gifters: Exploring Fan Community and Celebrity in the Field of Fan Cultural Production." Ph.D. thesis, Cardiff University.

Click, M. A. 2007. "Untidy: Fan Response to the Soiling of Martha Stewart's Spotless Image." In *Fandom: Identities and Communities in a Mediated World*, edited by J.

Gray, C. Sandvoss, and C. L. Harrington, 301–315. New York: New York University Press.

———. 2009. "'Rabid', 'Obsessed', and 'Frenzied': Understanding Twilight Fangirls and the Gendered Politics of Fandom." *Flow*, November 4.www.flowjournal.org.

———. In this volume. "Introduction: Haters Gonna Hate."

Deller, R., and C. Smith. 2013. "Reading the BDSM Romance: Reader Responses to *Fifty Shades*." *Sexualities*, 16, no. 8:932–950.

Fanlore. n.d. "Meta." http://fanlore.org.

Fiske, J. 1992. "The Cultural Economy of Fandom." In *The Adoring Audience: Fan Culture and Popular Media*, edited by L. A. Lewis, 30–49. New York: Routledge.

Flood, A. 2012. "*Fifty Shades of Grey* Condemned as 'Manual for Sexual Torture.'" *Guardian*, August 24. www.theguardian.com.

Flox, A. V. 2012. "The Troubling Message in Fifty Shades of Grey." *Blogher*, April23. www.blogher.com.

Gehayi and Ket Makura. 2012. "Chapter One." *Das Sporking*, April 6. Hosted at *Livejournal*. www.livejournal.com.

Gray, J. 2003. "New Audiences, New Textualities: Anti-Fans and Non-Fans." *International Journal of Cultural Studies* 6:64–81. doi: 10.1177/1367877903006001004.

———. 2005. "Antifandom and the Moral Text: *Television Without Pity* and Textual Dislike." *American Behavioral Scientist* 48:840–858.

———. In this volume. "How Do I Dislike Thee? Let Me Count the Ways."

Grossberg, L. 1992. "Is There a Fan in The House? The Affective Sensibility of Fandom." In *The Adoring Audience: Fan Culture and Popular Media*, edited by L. A. Lewis, 50–65. New York: Routledge.

Haig, F. 2014. "Guilty Pleasures: *Twilight*, Snark and Critical Fandom." In *Screening Twilight: Critical Approaches to a Cinematic Phenomenon*, edited by W. Clayton and S. Harman, 11–25. London: I. B. Tauris.

Harman, S., and B. Jones. 2013. "Fifty Shades of Ghey: Snark Fandom and the Figure of the Anti-Fan." *Sexualities* 16, no. 8:951–968.

hidingfromsomeone. 2012. "Fifty Shades and the 'Philadelphia Incident.'" Tumblr. http://hidingfromsomeone.tumblr.com/post/22270527450/ fifty-shades-the-philadelphia-incident-im-not.

Hills, M. 2012. "'Twilight' Fans Represented in Commercial Paratexts and Inter-Fandoms: Resisting and Repurposing Negative Fan Stereotypes. In *Genre, Reception, and Adaptation in the "Twilight" Series*, edited by A. Morey, 113–129. Burlington, VT: Ashgate.

James, E. L. 2012a. *Fifty Shades of Grey*. London: Random House.

———. 2012b. *Fifty Shades Darker*. London: Random House.

———. 2012c. *Fifty Shades Freed*. London: Random House.

Jenkins, H. 1992. *Textual Poachers: Television Fans and Participatory Culture*. New York: Routledge.

Jones, B. 2014. "Fifty Shades of Exploitation: Fan Labor and *Fifty Shades of Grey*." In "Fandom and/as Labor," special issue, edited by Mel Stanfill and Megan Condis. *Transformative Works and Cultures*, no. 15. doi: 10.3983/twc.2014.0501.

———. 2015. "Antifan Activism as a Response to MTV's *The Valleys.*" In "European Fans and European Fan Objects: Localization and Translation," special issue, edited by Anne Kustritz. *Transformative Works and Cultures*, no. 19. doi: 10.3983/twc.2015.0585.

———. 2016. "'I Will Throw You off Your Ship and You Will Drown and Die': Death Threats, Intra-Fandom Hate, and the Performance of Fangirling." In *Seeing Fans: Representations of Fandom in Media and Popular Culture*, edited by L. Bennett and P. Booth, 53–66. New York: Bloomsbury.

Kilpatrick, C. 2012. "Forget *Fifty Shades of Grey* . . . Try Reading Bible Instead." *Belfast Telegraph*, August 21. www.belfasttelegraph.co.uk.

Martin, A. 2013. "Fifty Shades of Sex Shop: Sexual Fantasy for Sale." *Sexualities* 16, no. 8:980–984.

Maxine. 2012. "Getting Away with It: How You Are Probably a Sex Criminal Too." *Emanix*, October 17. Hosted at *Livejournal*. www.livejournal.com.

Morley, David. 1980. *The Nationwide Audience: Structure and Decoding*. London: British Film Institute.

Parker, J. 2012. "Bad Romance: What the *Fifty Shades of Grey* Phenomenon Says about the Modern Sexual Condition." *Atlantic*, October. www.theatlantic.com.

Pinkowitz, J. M. 2011. "'The Rabid Fans That Take [*Twilight*] Too Seriously': The Construction and Rejection of Excess in *Twilight* Antifandom." *Transformative Works and Cultures*, no. 7. doi: 10.3983/twc.2011.0247.

Sandvoss, C. 2005. *Fans: The Mirror of Consumption*. Cambridge: Polity Press.

Stein, L. In this volume. "Dissatisfaction and *Glee*: On Emotional Range in Fandom and Feels Culture."

Thornton, S. 1995. *Club Cultures: Music, Media and Subcultural Capital*. Cambridge: Polity Press.

Todd, A. M. 2011. "Saying Goodbye to Friends: Fan Culture as Lived Experience." *Journal of Popular Culture* 44, no. 4:854–871.

Tootybug47. 2004. "Snark." *Urban Dictionary*, February 9. www.urbandictionary.com.

Trout, J. 2012. "50 Shades of Grey, Chapter One, or Why Ana Is the Shittiest Friend Ever." *Trout Nation* (blog), April 18. http://jennytrout.com.

———. 2013. "Dear 50 Shades fan: BDSM Doesn't Need or Want Your Defense." *Sweaters for Days* (blog), April 21. www.blogger.com.

Veaux, F. 2012. "Some Thoughts on Ethics, Safety, and Conduct in BDSM: Part 1." *Tacit*, July 14. Hosted at *Livejournal*. www.livejournal.com.

Whitehead, D. 2013. "When Religious 'Mommy Bloggers' Met 'Mommy Porn': Evangelical Christian and Mormon Women's Responses to *Fifty Shades.*" *Sexualities* 16, no. 8:915–931.

Wilkinson, M. 2012. "We Love Porn, Admit Nine out of Ten Girls." *Sun*, July 1. www.thesun.co.uk.

Zanin, A. 2012. "Crazy and Criminal: On Those Damn Books, and Why They Matter." *Sex Geek* (blog), September 20. https://wordpress.com.

14

When Hated Characters Talk Back

Twitter, Hate, and Fan/Celebrity Interactions

BERTHA CHIN

Fans have been celebrated for their activism (Bennett 2012; Jenkins and Shresthova 2012), banding together for save-the-show campaigns when a TV show is threatened with cancellation (Savage 2014) or raising money to donate to a charity supported by a favorite celebrity (Jones 2012). The bulk of fan studies research has extolled the creativity, productivity, and collaborative spirit of fandom, centered on the concept of love for, and protectiveness of, the source text. Lately, the notion of the anti-fan (Gray 2003)—individuals who consider a text or genre stupid or inane but would engage with the text to criticize and hate it—has gained prominence. The *Twilight* franchise, for instance, has been the subject of anti-fandom studies (Pinkowitz 2011; Sheffield and Merlo 2010; Williams 2013), reflecting the taste cultures of anti-fans in which *Twilight* fans are presented as "rabid" and "excessive" and the source text inferior, while scholars such as Harman and Jones observed that *Fifty Shades of Grey*—originally a *Twilight* fan fiction—is considered "bad literature [and] bad eroticism" (Harman and Jones 2013, 952). Gray's seminal work positions anti-fans as "fans' Other" (Gray 2003, 71), who construct a notion of the hated text as undesirable and substandard and thus deserving of their hate and condemnation—a definition he has since reexamined (Gray, in this volume), exploring the myriad contexts in which anti-fandom can occur.

However, Gray's early theorization does not account for fans' hateful and toxic practices, in which discussions are centered on hatred for a character and the actor who plays the despised character (even when these fans remain invested in a television show), campaigns are waged to get actors fired from TV shows, and conflicts are played out between fans, as well as with cast and crew members, in public forums and social media networks like Twitter. Under Gray's new taxonomy, this would be classified as "disappointed anti-fandom" (Gray, in this volume). Sentiments of hate often manifests from fans' frustrations with the shows and are often exacerbated by the showrunners' and actors' presence and responses to fans (and anti-fans) who publicly express their feelings of frustration and hatred on social media. I suggest, in this chapter, that fandom and anti-fandom are intricately related by exploring how fans' frustrations with a text may prompt them to behave like anti-fans and that, much like Emma Jane argues (in this volume), fans' sense of entitlement is leading them to abuse celebrities who are active on social media.

Early fan studies research, such as Bacon-Smith's *Enterprising Women* (1992), was careful to stress the positive—and communal—aspects of fandom to avoid further pathologizing fans as "obsessed," "scandalous," or "weird." But Dunlap and Wolf have called for fan scholars to acknowledge the less positive facets of fandom as well. They argue that, while certain fan practices "might not be pretty or always leave us feeling positive about fan culture, . . . these are invaluable studies into the reality of [fans'] lived experiences" (Dunlap and Wolf 2010). In short, fandom is not necessarily always beautiful, as some have claimed (Coppa 2014), and hate and dislike are as much a part of the complex makeup of the fan identity and fan affect as are the emotions of love and support. The expression of these negative emotions and toxic behaviors are now further complicated and facilitated by social media networks like Twitter, where both fans and industry professionals, including actors, interact publicly. It also evokes new ethical considerations, as Emma Jane reflects, where continuing to categorize death threats as an extreme form of anti-fandom could "leave us exposed to accusations that we are exculpating those people issuing threats and underplaying the suffering of those who receive them" (Jane, in this volume). However, I argue that the case studies presented in this chapter differ from those presented by Jane in that the fans/anti-fans in this chapter are effectively "powerless" to affect change (e.g., removing actors from shows) and that there is always pushback, either from the celebrities themselves (through their management or the industry) or other fans.

Jonathan Gray reminds us that "the fan cannot and should not serve as textuality's default magic charm" (Gray 2003, 78) and that we should also look at anti-fans and non-fans in order to broaden the field. I would also like to propose, by way of Gray's anti-fandom treatise, and following Dunlap and Wolf, that we should look at how fans' frustration with their favorite television shows, and their dislike of certain characters, can manifest into hate and to "anti-fandom" directed toward the actors portraying hated characters. As such, my approach is closer to Vivi Theodoropoulou's concept of anti-fandom, which is "caused and triggered by fandom" (Theodoropoulou 2007, 318).

In this chapter, I look at how fans' frustrations with the addition of new characters to their favorite television series, *Supernatural* and *Hawaii Five-o* (*H50*), have manifested in how they interact online with the actors who portray the hated characters, especially on Twitter. I begin by examining the literature surrounding anti-fandom (Gray 2003) and fan-tagonism (Johnson 2007) before looking, first, at *Supernatural* fans who organized campaigns to have the character of Castiel (and by extension, the actor Misha Collins) removed from the show and, second, at the criticism directed at Michelle Borth, an actress on *H50* (who plays the character Catherine Rollins) who had publicly engaged in antagonistic exchanges with those who were critical of her inclusion as a regular to the show. Essentially, this chapter proposes not only to expand the discussions of anti-fandom and hate but also to engage critically with fan practices that are normally overlooked in fan studies. These practices may not necessarily portray fandom in a positive light, such as when fans make actors the target of their hate and frustrations with the TV series on public forums like Twitter. For the anti-fans of Castiel, their actions are justified by their professed love for *Supernatural* and the desire to see its quality return to the way they deem worthy. On *H50*, Borth's inclusion is seen by some fans as an intervention of the slash relationship between the lead characters[1]—a pairing which fans argue is often teased by the show's producers but never fulfilled—thus preventing the show from becoming socially progressive for featuring lead queer characters.

In essence, one could argue that these anti-fandom emotions are derived out of love for the text and its characters but expressed in ways that can be seen as negative as the hate is directed toward actors, intimating the complex relationship between fandom and anti-fandom. The chapter also proposes that fans' shipping of their favorite characters[2]—slash or otherwise—creates antagonism among different fan groups that mirror the fandom/anti-fandom divisions Theodoropoulou observed among fans of competing sports teams. In this case, fans who ship different pairings are campaigning for their voice to be heard and for their favorite pairing to be acknowledged and recognized by producers and actors. Concurrently, this discussion also brings to mind how social media networks like Twitter have changed fans' interactions with actors and media producers. The seemingly direct access to industry insiders enables fans to voice their grievances to media producers as well as to actors, making fan hate and anti-fandom more public and direct, with the potential to spread and escalate quickly when, and if, actors engage with anti-fans in defense of their characters.

Anti-Fandom and Hate

Jonathan Gray reflects in a 2003 essay that, in fan scholars' fervor to present the many positive facets of fan culture, an important section of the audience is often overlooked. Gray argues that this section of the audience openly dislikes a text or a specific genre but nevertheless engages with the texts critically and passionately through surrounding paratexts such as trailers, magazine and news articles, and word-of-mouth from various sources in order to condemn the hated texts. Identifying these audiences as anti-fans, Gray observes that these individuals impose conditions of morality, value, and quality on texts and are very specific as to what they consider "a text should be like, of what is a waste of media time and space, of what morality or aesthetics texts should adopt, and of what [they] would like to see others watch or read" (Gray 2003, 73).

Gray's concept of anti-fandom posits an indirect engagement with the text, as anti-fans construct their knowledge and criticism of the text, either "from paratextual fragments" (Sheffield and Merlo 2010, 209) or by not engaging with the text at all (Gray 2005). This positioning situates anti-fandom in direct opposition to fandom, contrasting hate (anti-fandom) with love (fandom), displeasure with pleasure. However, Gray does concede in a followup article that fandom and anti-fandom should not exist on opposite ends of the spectrum; rather, "they perhaps more accurately exist on a Möbius strip, with many fan and antifan behaviors and performances resembling, if not replicating, each other" (Gray 2005, 845). This suggests that anti-fandom and fandom are more intricately linked and that fans assign notions of value, morality, and quality to the texts they love, just as anti-fans do to texts they hate. When fan expectations (e.g., for the text to be more sexually and/or culturally progressive, for the couples they ship to be canon, etc.) are not met, or when fans feel that their concerns are not being addressed or taken seriously, their love can shift to hate, with those frustrations directed toward showrunners and actors through letter-writing campaigns and in public spaces like fan discussion forums and LiveJournal, Tumblr, and Twitter posts. In his 2005 piece, Gray's observation on various TV forums on the website *Television Without Pity* prompted him to remark that "angry or upset fan discussion often bordered on antifandom" (Gray 2005, 847).

Vivi Theodoropoulou maintains that the anti-fan can exist within the fan, arguing that "fandom is a precondition of anti-fandom [whereby] a fan becomes an anti-fan of the object that 'threatens' his/her own, and of that object's fans" (Theodoropoulou 2007, 316). But rather than suggesting that fans' passionate engagement with a beloved text can turn into anti-fandom when, for instance, fans disagree with a particular storyline or with an addition of a new character, Theodoropoulou situates anti-fandom of one text in clear opposition to another, such as when two fan objects like rival sports teams are positioned against one another. Matt Hills contends that Theodoropoulou's hypothesis, while valid for sports fandom, may not necessarily be transferable to media fandom as "anti-fandoms are neither as fixed nor as strongly learned as those surrounding rival sports teams" (Hills 2012, 122). Furthermore, sports fandom (and anti-fandom) are often more explicitly communal (see, e.g., Gilbert, in this volume, on hatewatching), whereas media fandom's expression of hate may only be explicitly expressed as such as a reaction to a specific event (such as a fan campaign or celebrities responding directly to their anti-fans).

However, the actions of the anti-fans I explore in the next section did not originally derive from hate or ridicule of the texts, unlike what is commonly observed of *Twilight* and *Fifty Shades of Grey* anti-fans. Rather, these are fans who become frustrated and disillusioned with the texts, performing what Gray (in this volume) identifies as "hopeful hatewatching," in the hopes that things will get better. Rather than merely hatewatching though, these anti-fans go further by going on social media networks and directly targeting actors to voice their hate, transferring their frustrations with the text and characters onto those who portray them on-screen.

At this point, it is also crucial to remember that anti-fans' dislike of certain texts is also predicated on what these anti-fans consider to be inferior texts. In their exploration of *Fifty Shades of Grey* anti-fandom, Sarah Harman and Bethan Jones state that "anti-fans . . . position themselves as gatekeepers . . . performing a service for the good of fandom (or the public)" (Harman and Jones 2013, 959). Harman and Jones note that anti-fans' close reading and analysis of *Fifty Shades* as an inferior text is a demonstration of their cultural capital performed through gatekeeping (i.e. indicating why the trilogy counts as inferior). Likewise, it can be argued that fans' hate of a character that results in anti-fandom behavior (likewise with fans' defense of a character hated by others) is a form of gatekeeping when the inclusion of a character interferes with a storyline fans see as the main draw or theme of a TV show and when a character interferes with a popular shipped pairing. The hated characters are seen as obstacles to the shows becoming better (or returning to their former glory), to being more progressive in their representations.

Anti-fandom is not performed independently from fandom either, especially when hate and frustrations are directed at an actor's social media networks such as Facebook pages and Twitter's @replies. Unlike letter-writing campaigns directed at studios and networks, these hate messages on social media are visible to the public, prompting fans (of the actors and those who ship different character pairings) to defend the show or its actors and/or to start alternative social media campaigns to counter the hate. This often results in arguments and wank between the different groups of fans/anti-fans,[3] prompting what Derek Johnson calls "fan-tagonism," an "ongoing, competitive [struggle] between both internal factions and external institutions" (Johnson 2007, 287).

Johnson argues that media producers' inability to satisfy the interests of all the various fan groups and their readings of the text creates a constant struggle in different fan groups/factions, and "antagonisms external and internal to fandom structure its practices, with fan and institutional interests competing to establish dominant meta-textual interpretative discourses while legitimizing specific audience relationships to the industrial production of the hyperdiegetic text" (Johnson 2007, 287). In other words, there is a constant struggle in fandom to establish a dominant reading of the text, to legitimize the pairing fans support, or to rid the show of a hated character and/or storyline. The struggle between the different fan factions, as I demonstrate in the next section, can also include the antagonisms between fandom and anti-fandom practices.

The works of these scholars indicate the necessity for fan studies to move beyond a homogenous, unified view—often one that is positive—of fandom. Henry Jenkins reminds us that "fandom . . . is born of a balance between fascination and frustration" (Jenkins 2006, 247) with media content. Often, this frustration is illustrated through fan transformative works such as fan fiction, videos, and artworks, in which fans employ their creative and technical skills, as well as knowledge of the texts, to instill a different reading of the text (such as slash or shipping a pairing that may have little to no interaction with one another in the source text) than that originally intended by the content creators. In a call to fan scholars to interrogate and challenge our own blind spots, Katherine Larsen and Lynn Zubernis remark that "certain fan practices are over-valued and rendered canonical, while the rest are 'othered'" (Larsen and Zubernis 2012, 4), suggesting that, in focusing on some fan practices, others are disregarded, particularly those that potentially situate fandom in a less than positive light.

What would fan studies gain by exploring and acknowledging fan emotions of hate and dislike, particularly in a digital age where fans, media producers, and actors are all utilizing the same social media networks and where fans are making their frustrations with the text publicly known to media producers and actors, holding them accountable for their frustrations? Indeed, exploring fan emotions of hate and dislike opens the field to exploration of other fan practices (not necessarily just anti-fandom, but also transcultural fan practices, for instance), allowing for diversification from, thus far, a tendency for the field to portray fandom as (socially, culturally, and/or nationally) homogenous. It also allows for explorations into other modes of fandom, such as fans who consider themselves "mainstream fans" (Stein 2014), fans who don't necessarily participate in in-depth discussions or produce transformative works but who engage with actors and showrunners on social media and in convention spaces. In the next section, I look more specifically at how fans express these feelings of hatred and dislike, directed at "media producers [and actors] whom [fans] feel threaten their meta-textual interests" (Johnson 2007, 298), and how, in public spaces like Twitter, targeted celebrities may respond in ways that are beyond or contrary to fans' expectations. These interactions also serve as a reminder that disappointed and frustrated fans react like anti-fans, and these declarations of hatred often become organized campaigns that target actors and those involved in the production of the TV shows, suggesting that anti-fandom and fandom are affectively interrelated.

Supernatural's "Silent Majority" and Hating Misha Collins

New characters are commonly introduced to long-running shows for a variety of reasons: to tell additional stories (e.g., when a lead actor leaves prior to the show's end or when stories are too dependent on a small group of characters) or to introduce a love interest for a lead character. These additions and changes sometimes divide fandoms, splintering fan groups into those who love, and those who hate, the changes.

Supernatural debuted on the CW network in 2005. In its fourteenth season at the time of this writing, the show tells the story of Dean Winchester (played by Jensen Ackles) and Sam Winchester (played by Jared Padalecki), brothers who were trained by their father to hunt and kill supernatural beings after their mother was brutally murdered by a demon. Supporting characters in the form of love interests, other hunters, and demons have dropped in and out of the Winchester brothers' nomadic lives, but it is their relationship with one another that drives the show's main storyline. In the season 4 (2008) premiere, a new character in the form of an angel, Castiel (played by Misha Collins), was introduced and subsequently added to the main cast,[4] thus introducing a storyline featuring the battle between angels and demons, which became deeply embedded into *Supernatural's* overarching mythology.

The show's online fandom is largely based on the website LiveJournal, which hosts numerous communities for episodic discussions and the archival coverage of fan-creative works like icons, fan videos, and fan fiction.[5] Tumblr has also become a popular platform for the fandom, particularly for image-based posts such as GIFsets. Aside from LiveJournal and Tumblr, a collaborative website in the format of Wikipedia known as *Super-Wiki* (hosted at www.supernaturalwiki.com) is also popular, documenting news and information on the show, the cast and crew, convention reports, as well as the norms, culture, and practices of the fandom.

As the show features a predominantly male cast, slash pairings—particularly that of Sam/Dean (known collectively as "Wincest") and Dean/Castiel ("Destiel")—are popular with fans.[6] The two fan groups often have a publicly antagonistic relationship, with fans competing for each pairing's popularity on Internet polls and for legitimization from producers. On the one hand, Destiel supporters argue that writers and producers imbue Dean and Castiel's interactions with innuendo, which are then not followed through in the show. While Collins (Castiel) has openly engaged in conversations with fans about Destiel at numerous fan conventions and events, others (including the producers and Jensen Ackles, who plays Dean) appear to be less receptive of this fan reading, with Ackles frequently refusing to answer any questions related to the pairing or Dean's sexuality at conventions.[7]

On the other hand, some fans see Wincest as the accepted pairing in canon, as episodes such as the fourth season "The Monster at the End of the Book" (airdate April 2, 2009) addressed the show's fandom directly, making tongue-in-cheek references to Wincest. Fans have been divided by the episode, according to Laura Felschow (2010, para. 1.2), with some viewing it as "playful and inclusive" while others see its representation of slash (Wincest) fans as "harsh and demeaning." The show's various nods to Wincest, and the producers' continual tease on Destiel, led to fans' constant struggle for their reading of the text to be legitimated by producers and thus recognized as canon.[8] Castiel is often credited by the popular press as a fan favorite, but some fans, however, view the inclusion of Castiel as an impediment to the development of Sam's storyline and to the Wincest pairing,[9] particularly when Destiel supporters frequently campaign for the recognition of the pairing online and during conventions, confronting producers on their refusal to embrace the Destiel pairing but continuing to tease fans with homoerotic subtext anyway.[10] This often results in ire, not just directed at Destiel shippers but also at Castiel (and by extension, Misha Collins, the actor). This character hate has seen the formation of groups such as the "SPN Silent Majority," established at the end of the show's seventh season in 2012 by fans who felt that the writing quality on *Supernatural* had declined and that the addition of Castiel (as well as other supporting characters) robbed "the emotional resonance and the quality" (SPN Silent Majority 2012a) of the show. These Castiel anti-fans believe the show should be grounded in the relationship between the Winchester brothers, rather than those with other supporting characters (in particular, Castiel, whose friendship with Dean forms an integral part of the show's story arc in later seasons). Although SPN Silent Majority's strategy involved writing to the show's producers, studio, and network, as well as directly tweeting *Supernatural*'s executive producers and writers, the campaign was linked to a "I hate Misha Collins Day" movement. Anonymous messages were left on *Supernatural* fans' Tumblr blogs announcing an organized effort to vocalize and share the hate by tweeting the CW, the network's publicist, and the show's producers, calling for Collins (Castiel) to be removed permanently from the show. In retaliation, the actor's fans organized a "We Love Misha" countermovement and reported a suspected Twitter account for spreading hate speech.[11] As the Twitter hate campaign caught the attention of several Internet-based entertainment websites,[12] SPN Silent Majority, who was accused of organizing the actions, declared the campaign to be a hoax spread by Destiel shippers to subvert their campaign to restore the show to its original focus on the brothers:

> We've seen over and over again how determined one group of fans on one side of the ship war is trying to pull us into their trenches. . . . After a week of these attacks, our theory that a handful of fans are trying to hold parts of fandom in a chokehold have been proven true. These are very dirty tactics and have no place in a community. [SPN Silent Majority 2012b]

The attention to the "I Hate Misha Collins Day" brought on by the reports on Internet-based entertainment sites and fans tweeting the actors directly also caught the attention of several cast members, such as Jim Beaver (Bobby Singer) and Richard Speight, Jr. (The Trickster/Gabriel), who, along with Collins, tweeted in response to the fans' action of spreading hate (see fig. 14.1).

Alice Marwick and danah boyd argue that part of Twitter's appeal for fans is the perception that fans get direct access to celebrities and are able to interact with them: "Famous people mention fans to perform

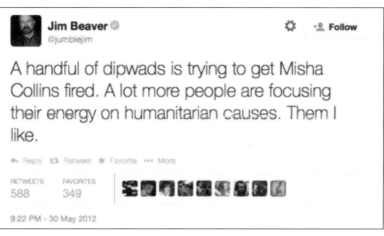

Figure 14.1. *Supernatural* cast members responding to the "I Hate Misha Collins Day" campaign.

connection and availability, give back to loyal followers, and manage their popularity" (Marwick and boyd 2011, 145). The proliferation and immediacy of the medium also makes it a good tool for fans to organize campaigns, as both the "I Hate Misha Collins" and "We Love Misha" movements make Twitter their main platform for spreading the hate (and love). The media industry's presence on the platform—the CW network, its publicity department, *Supernatural*'s producers, and many of the show's regular and recurring cast members—makes Twitter a convenient space in which frustrated fans can air their grievances. In this case, Twitter is also used to counteract the anti-fan campaign to have Collins (Castiel) fired, as well as to call out the fan faction that is unhappy about his inclusion to the cast.

By tweeting the cast members directly and informing them of the hate some fan factions were determined to spread, fans were highlighting the hate to others who may have had no knowledge of the campaign previously, potentially inciting interfactional hate within the *Supernatural* fandom as fans rushed to defend the show, its producers, and cast members. The hate campaign directed toward Misha Collins (Castiel) exemplifies the complex makeup of fan identity, whereby hate is very intricately linked to love. SPN Silent Majority's campaign, it can be argued, stems from altruism: to return the show to its original emphasis (i.e., the brothers), thus calling for the exclusion of, or reduced screen time for, other characters whom they see as a threat and impediment to the advancement of the original storyline and. more important, the brothers' relationship. In this case, it can be argued that fans adopted the strategies of anti-fandom to try and sway media producers to support their readings of the text. The actions of the Castiel haters resemble the definition of anti-fans advanced by Theodoropoulou (2007), whereby the fan becomes an anti-fan of the object (in this case, the character and, by extension, the actor) that threatens their love of the source text.

Collins's tweet above could be interpreted as a way of telling anti-fans that his position in the show is secure and that the hate campaigns would not affect him in any way (i.e., the fans are powerless). Having said that, despite the public rebuttal of the hate campaign by the actors, none of the fans involved were individually named or tagged (on Twitter) by the actors who commented on the issue. This is in contrast to the case of *Hawaii Five-0*, which I explore in the following section, in which the actor who is the subject of fan hate engaged directly with fan criticism through her Twitter account. Accusations of unprofessional behavior and bullying ensued, whereby petitions were made to the network to have the actor fired for her behavior.

Hawaii Five-o: The Case of Catherine Rollins

The character of Catherine Rollins, played by Michelle Borth, was introduced to the reimagined *Hawaii Five-o* (hereafter *H50*) on CBS early in the show's first season in 2010. Rollins, a recurring character, flitted in and out of the weekly storyline as a potential love interest for the lead character, Steve McGarrett, until she was promoted to a series regular in the show's third season in 2012. In the *H50* fandom, the pairing of McGarrett and his partner, Danny Williams (known collectively in fandom as the McDanno pairing), in the elite Hawaiian law enforcement team, Five-o, is the most popular. It has inspired countless fan discussions in LiveJournal communities, and fan transformative works are shared and archived at the *Archive of Our Own* and Tumblr websites.[13]

The announcement of Borth's inclusion as a regular cast member was met with fan resistance, as fans argue that the inclusion of a love interest is an attempt at heteronormalizing McGarrett. Fans further argue that they are constantly teased with McDanno's homoerotic subtext on the show and in promotional material from CBS that appears to tease the queer subtextual reading with tweets such as: "Are Danny & McGarrett going on a man date?" (*Hawaii Five-o* 2013). Not only does Catherine threaten fans' interpretive reading of McDanno's relationship, but she is also condemned for taking attention and screen time away from the four original cast members. Such complaints about the direction of a show "have been the prerogative of fans since time immemorial and will continue to be so as long as there are professional storytellers and people to listen" (Schmidt 2010, para. 2.16). As with the *Supernatural* case study I discussed in the previous section, in this case fans are not merely voicing their dissatisfaction with the show's direction to writers and producers; cast and crew members active on social media also become targets of fans' ire, specifically those actors who portray the hated characters.

As Catherine's role became more prominent on the show, fans took to Twitter to express their dislike of her, appropriating the #H50 hashtag that CBS is still promoting as part of their social media campaign for the show.[14] After the airing of a Catherine-centered season 3 episode, "Olelo Pa'a" (airdate April 15, 2013), a fan, Erin, took to Twitter to comment about how Catherine has become a central focus on the show, mockingly calling her the "heart of the show." Borth saw the tweet and dismissed the fan by directly responding to her comment (see fig. 14.2).[15] After a series of Twitter exchanges, Borth engaged with another fan, this time tweeting her support for the McDanno pairing, writing: "I kinda secretly ship McDanno too . . . if the show would ever dare to really go there I'd be the first to champion it" (2013a).

This declaration prompted fans to then accuse her of using "queer-baiting" tactics to divert attention away from being called out on her callous behavior when responding to Erin (by first claiming her dog had gotten into her Twitter account, and then later deleting the tweet). In a matter of days, as the story spread throughout the *H50* fandom, other fans unfollowed Borth on Twitter as a show of solidarity to Erin. Meanwhile Borth's supporters started to attack those who had tweeted in support of Erin, accusing them of spreading hate. As these antagonistic exchanges spread, Erin's friends and supporters began to document Borth's various Twitter exchanges with *H50* fans on Tumblr and Live-Journal, creating timelines complete with screenshots as evidence of her alleged "mistreatment" of fans.[16]

Karen Hellekson asserts that the practice of fan documentation during conflicts is important, where "the goal is to construct a persuasive document that revolves around coming to a consensus about the events' believability. A piece of evidence . . . that results in extensive commentary, is presented, examined, discussed and judged" (Hellekson 2010, 59). In compiling and screencapping Borth's responses to fans and anti-fans on Twitter, *H50* fans use their collected documentation to convince others about Borth's bullying tactics and to chronicle the sequence of events that led to the antagonistic exchanges among Borth, her fans, and those who have criticized her and her character. This documentation is shared and commented upon on sites like Tumblr and acts as the evidence upon which Borth's actions are judged by the *H50* fandom. As the exchanges between Borth and her anti-fans continued, Borth was labeled a bully and criticized for being ungrateful for the success that *H50*'s fans have bestowed on the show by tuning in loyally every week.

Figure 14.2. Twitter exchange between Michelle Borth and *H50* fan.

Borth's response—in which she tweets, "I keep reading that the 'fans' dictate my success as an actor . . . hmmm i've been working for the last 15yrs [*sic*] just fine on merit alone, not fans" (Borth 2013b)—led one fan to declare on Tumblr that

> what most celebs tend to forget is that no matter how good the show is, without fans it becomes NOTHING. . . . Ugly fact: We fans are your boss. . . . It's fully within our rights to judge and comment/critic. It's within our right to speak our mind—no matter how nonsense you think our opinions are. It's our right to like or hate you and no, we don't need to give you excuses. We could hate you just because. [CriZz Universe 2013]

By engaging directly with fan criticism and hate (of her character), Borth directed the frustrations fans had been expressing to *H50* producers and CBS on the inclusion of Catherine onto herself. As a result of the exchanges between Borth and her character's anti-fans, *H50* fans began to compile contact details of various CBS personnel, urging those who had allegedly been attacked by Borth (and her supporters) to share their experiences with the fandom and report her to CBS for misconduct. The fans who recorded the timeline of events argued that, while Borth claimed her Twitter account is "personal" (Borth 2013c), she is under the employment of a multinational corporation and therefore subject to the social media policy in place for CBS employees.

Furthermore, CriZz Universe's statement—that fans "could hate [the character/actor] just because"—is interesting here. Is Borth expected to remain silent, even when fans are criticizing her acting and the character she portrays? She is not merely a text, as Jane argues, despite fan and anti-fan scholarship's tendencies to portray human subjects that are "intimately connected with . . . media texts which are the target of antifan activities" as such (Jane 2014, 177–178). While Borth's initial response to Erin, and her subsequent belligerent tweets, tagging and engaging directly with those who had been spreading hate about her character, could admittedly have been handled with more grace,[17] it could also be argued that because Twitter is a public—and social—forum, Borth has every right to defend herself as well as the character she portrays weekly on television. Even if Borth was not directly tagged in the original tweet, Erin had used the #H50 hashtag, thus making the tweet visible to anyone and arguably rendering it as an official criticism of the episode. Marwick and boyd argue that Twitter offers the "possibility of interaction" (Marwick and boyd 2011, 144) between fan and celebrity, as well as other media industry insiders. As this case demonstrates, Twitter enabled fans to voice their displeasure with actors who portray hated characters, tagging them directly or using official hashtags to criticize the characters.

However, Twitter also renders true the prospect of accountability for the criticism and hate fans spread, especially when media producers and celebrities now have access to the same platform, reading hashtags or mentions of their names to gauge fan—as well as anti-fan—reception. As Marwick and boyd argue that, while gossiping about celebrities is a common practice that creates social bonds and provides a frame for discussion of larger issues . . . , participants on Twitter run the risk of being publicly shamed by the individual they are discussing. . . . [However], this . . . may backfire. There are plenty who seek attention and will settle for negative attention. . . . Twitter gossip may be silenced through direct acknowledgement from celebrity practitioners. At the same time, it may also be ignited. [Marwick and boyd 2011, 146]

Borth has constantly defended her Twitter account as a personal space, and she has argued that she is within her rights to defend herself and the character she portrays against those who are critical and hateful. However, her direct engagement with anti-fans (or at the very least, her character's anti-fans) has provided a way in which her anti-fans can further construct and document instances of her persona as evidence for why she (not just her character) should be hated.

Derek Johnson asserts that "fans attack and criticize media producers whom they feel threaten their meta-textual interests" (Johnson 2007, 298), but I argue that through social media, fan frustrations can also manifest toward actors who portray characters whom they hate and feel are taking attention away from other beloved characters or pose a threat to fans' favorite pairings. With the proliferation of social media networks like Twitter, fans are increasingly taking their frustrations with storylines and characterizations directly to media producers and actors on the platform, utilizing official hashtags as well as organizing hate campaigns to make their feelings known.

But just as hate campaigns such as *Supernatural* fandom's "I Hate Misha Collins Day" can be organized, or anti-fans of *H50*'s Catherine Rollins can appropriate the show's hashtag to criticize her character, fans opposed to the hate can likewise bring the actors' attention to the hate, as *Supernatural* fans did when they alerted the show's actors active on Twitter to the Misha Collins hate campaign. Likewise, the actors can choose to respond directly (in the case of Michelle Borth) or indirectly (as in Misha Collins). Both cases show that fandom can very often shift into anti-fandom when fans feel that their concerns and opinions about the show and its direction are not being taken seriously by those involved in the production. This isn't to say that fans' shifting emotions toward their favorite shows are anything new; rather, the case studies above indicate that social media networks like Twitter and Tumblr have enabled fans to organize hate and counterhate (as well as save-the-show) campaigns, and just as much as Twitter is used by fans to express their love toward a show, character, or actor, social media networks are also used to express frustration, dislike, and hate toward actors and producers. What is also distinct is that social media like Twitter provide a platform with which actors and producers can directly respond to these expressions of hate and love.

Furthermore, while the case of *Supernatural* and *H50* focused on slash pairings, this by no means indicates that anti-fandom shipping only centers on slash. Shows like *Arrow* (CW, 2012–present), for instance, with popular heterosexual pairings commonly known in fandom as Olicity and Lauriver, encounter similar expressions of frustrations from fans, suggesting the importance of affect in fandom. And while this isn't to the point of campaigning for the removal of an actor from the show, it nevertheless illustrates that fan attachment to their favorite pairing—slash or otherwise—is an emotional one.

Conclusion

Dunlap and Wolf surmise that "the future of fan culture studies must be prepared to look at realistic fan practices," and that includes *both* "good" and "bad," "positive" and "negative" emotions (Dunlap and Wolf 2010). To this end, many works on anti-fandom have focused on how certain texts are derided, and the fandom devalued, because these fans' engagements are considered to be inauthentic and usually, problematically gendered female. However, as Theodoropoulou (2007) has explored, the line between being a fan and an anti-fan is less distinct than originally assumed, and anti-fandom extends beyond just audiences who dislike a particular text through their encounter with said text via surrounding paratexts.

Fans who become disillusioned with a text and want it returned to its original storyline employ anti-fandom tactics to show media producers and actors their displeasure, as displayed by the practices of SPN Silent Majority of *Supernatural* fandom. Shippers of popular slash pairings, where the homoerotic subtext is always teased but never truly acknowledged by the producers, can turn their ire and frustrations to actors who play characters they view as an obstacle to the pairing being realized. Furthermore, while Twitter serves as a convenient tool to voice fan hate, it also leaves anti-fans accountable for their criticism, especially if the targeted actors respond directly, like Michelle Borth did.

The manner in which anti-fans appropriate hashtags to criticize hated characters and then target the actors directly by starting campaigns to get actors fired presents a less positive practice of fandom—an aspect that fan studies has been reluctant to explore thus far, an aspect, too, that Jane (2014) has criticized for not having taken the well-being of the human subjects into account, when anti-fandom rhetoric targets actors and producers. Nonetheless, fan hate and dislike are not separate from fan identity and affect, and as Dunlap and Wolf (2010), as well as Larsen and Zubernis (2012) have reminded us, it is important for the field to acknowledge that these fan practices are equally productive and important. While this chapter doesn't afford me the space to explore further, the targets of the anti-fans and, in particular, their connection to slash pairings in the two case studies examined here adds a complexity to fan studies' often straightforward conceptualization of gender (in that gender is often associated with building a safe and nurturing space for fans rather than one that might incite notions of hate and dislike). More important, fan hate and dislike serve as a reminder that fandom is not homogenous and that love and affect are not necessarily the only emotions at play when a fan embraces his or her fan identity.

Rather, anti-fandom and hate are equally essential in giving us a complex and multifaceted view of fan identity, which remains undertheorized in fan studies. Much has been written about how fans are quick to adopt new technology to suit their fannish needs, usually for building communities and the sharing of texts and transformative works. But the case studies in this chapter show that social media networks are also utilized to express dislike and hate, as opposed to merely being used to express fans' love for a text, as the media industry undoubtedly prefers, which also complicates ethical considerations when those under attack are not merely texts.

The perceived intimacy of interactions on social media networks like Twitter has often been noted as a marked change in how interactions occur between fans and celebrities, as they are seemingly communicating without the traditional gatekeepers of publicists and entertainment news media. However, it is also enabling fans to voice their frustrations, dislike, and hate directly to actors and media producers active on social media, thus rendering declarations of anti-fandom more public, accessible, and often intermixed with messages of love directed toward the show itself or other actors on it. To echo Dunlap and Wolf's call, we need to start acknowledging and investigating anti-fandom and fan hate as intricately linked to fandom and love in order to illustrate a more comprehensive view of fans' lived experiences.

NOTES

1 "Slash" is used to indicate homoerotic pairings in fandom.

2 "Shippers" is used to identify fans who support a romantic pairing between specific characters; "shipping" would be the act of supporting those relationships.

3 "Wank" is often the term used to describe hostile disagreements between different fan groups.

4 For some fans, the inclusion of Castiel intervenes with the family dynamics of Sam and Dean, and as Castiel was introduced as Dean's savior, fans felt Sam was sidelined to develop Dean and Castiel's connection and friendship.

5 The show also has an active offline fandom that centers on conventions (with the first *Supernatural*-centered convention occurring in Chicago in 2007) in various cities across North America, as well as in Europe, Australia, and South America. These conventions occur throughout the year and often have cast attendance. A collection of some *Supernatural* fan fiction also moved to the website *Archive of Our Own* (https://archiveofourown.org) which, as of May 2014, stores close to seventy thousand stories (with over twenty-five thousand of those stories featuring the slash pairing Destiel), while the website *Fanfiction* (www.fanfiction.net) has around ninety-four thousand stories.

6 Catherine Tosenberger argues that *Supernatural*'s format alludes to classic male buddy series like *Starsky and Hutch*, and "the fact that Sam and Dean are brothers in no way detracts from the slashy vibe. In fact, as brothers, they are given a pass for displays of emotion that masculinity in our culture usually forbids, which intensifies the potential for queer readings" (Tosenberger 2008, para. 1.2).

7 *Supernatural Wiki* (n.d.) has documented some of the earlier exchanges in the show that comment on the relationship between Dean and Castiel, including the reception of the pairing among producers and the cast. Misha Collins (Castiel) has also spoken at length in an interview about why he engages with fans on the topic with Katherine Larsen and Lynn Zubernis (2014). Fans who want the pairing acknowledged as canon have accused producers of "queerbaiting"—a term, as described by the website *Fanlore*, used by fans to describe the "perceived attempt by canon creators . . . to woo queer fans by introducing a character whose sexual-

ity seems, early on, to be coded as something other than one hundred percent heterosexual" (*Fanlore*, n.d.). For an example of this kind of discussion, which is a complicated issue that I do not have space to get into here, see Veronika K. (2013).

8 "The Monster at the End of the Book" is by no means the only episode that features a representation of *Supernatural*'s fandom. In the course of the show's airing history, six other episodes have referred to, or commented on, the show's fanbase, represented through the recurring character of Becky.

9 I'm not suggesting here that fans who hate Castiel are immediately supporters of Wincest. Rather, there are also fans who felt that the inclusion of Castiel intervenes with the brothers' story, specifically, that Sam's characterization is often sacrificed for the development of Dean and Castiel.

10 A recent public confrontation among fans, anti-fans, and the producers can be seen during CW's *Supernatural* promotion for the 2014 San Diego Comic-Con, which resulted in CW having to cancel the #AskSupernatural hashtag on Twitter. The incident was reported by Cruz (2014) and Romano (2014).

11 See, e.g., Sup3ernatural (n.d.) for an example of a "We Hate Misha Collins Day" declaration. Also see r/Supernatural (n.d.); and Wilken (2012).

12 In a possible separate lead-up to these events, threats toward Misha Collins were sent anonymously to various Castiel fans and Destiel shippers, intimating that the actor be set on fire. See r/Supernatural (n.d.); and Wilken (2012).

13 For example, out of the 7,589 works of fan fiction (as of May 2014) archived at *Archive of Our Own*, 5,631 of them features the McDanno pairing.

14 CBS has been promoting the use of the #H50 Twitter hashtag since 2011 (Warren 2011), although there is no clear indication as to whether fans were the ones who used #H50 to symbolize their fandom first before it was officially appropriated by CBS during promotions, or vice versa.

15 Borth was not tagged in the fan's original tweet, although her character's name was mentioned and the show's hashtag was used. It was unclear if Borth was reading the hashtagged tweets to see responses to the episode or if her attention was brought to it by another person.

16 An example of an extensive compilation of the timeline of events can be found at the blog *Unconditional Love* (2013).

17 See, e.g., Borth (2017d, 2017e).

REFERENCES

Bacon-Smith, C. 1992. *Enterprising Women: Television Fandom and the Creation of Popular Myth*. Philadelphia: University of Pennsylvania Press.

Bennett, L. 2012. "Fan Activism for Social Mobilization: A Critical Review of the Literature." In "Transformative Works and Fan Activism," special issue, edited by H. Jenkins and S. Shresthova, *Transformative Works and Cultures*, no. 10. doi: 10.3983/twc.2012.0346.

Borth, M. 2013a. "@Andie_Louise_ i kinda secretly ship McDanno too . . . ," February 24. Twitter. https://twitter.com/michelleborth/status/305583826950828032.

———. 2013b. "I keep reading that . . . ," April 8. Twitter. https://twitter.com/ michelleborth/status/321369853388812288.

———. 2013c. "yes this is MY personal twitter account . . . ," April 17. Twitter. https:// twitter.com/michelleborth/status/324619516380340224.

———. 2013d. "Apparently there are experts . . . ," April 27. Twitter. https://twitter.com/ michelleborth/statuses/328325158454579201.

———. 2013e. "You hate me because . . . ," Apeil 27. Twitter. https://twitter.com/ michelleborth/statuses/328326181332086785.

Coppa, F. 2014. "Fuck Yeah, Fandom Is Beautiful." *Journal of Fandom Studies* 2, no. 1:73–82.

CriZz Universe. 2013. "Urgh . . . Y Is This My Fandom?" Tumblr. http://changhomin. tumblr.com/post/49150867914/urgh-y-is-this-my-fandom.

Cruz, E. 2014. "Fans Take *Supernatural* to Task for 'Queer Baiting.'" *Advocate*, July 17. www.advocate.com.

Dunlap, K., and C. Wolf. 2010. "Fans Behaving Badly: Anime Metafandom, Brutal Criticism, and the Intellectual Fan." In "Fanthropologies," *Mechademia* 5:267–283.

Fanlore. n.d. "Queer Batiting." http://fanlore.org.

Felschow, L. 2010. "'Hey, Check It Out, There's Actually Fans': (Dis)Empowerment and (Mis)Representation of Cult Fandom in *Supernatural*." *Transformative Works and Cultures*, no. 4. doi: 10.3983/twc.2010.0134.

Gilbert, A. In this volume. "Hatewatch with Me: Anti-Fandom as Social Performance."

Gray, J. 2003. "New Audiences, New Textualities: Anti-Fans and Non-Fans." *International Journal of Cultural Studies* 6:64–81.

———. 2005. "Antifandom and the Moral Text: *Television Without Pity* and Textual Dislike." *American Behavioral Scientist* 48:840–858.

———. In this volume. "How Do I Dislike Thee? Let Me Count the Ways."

Harman, S., and B. Jones. 2013. "Fifty Shades of Ghey: Snark Fandom and the Figure of the Anti-Fan." *Sexualities* 16, no. 8:951–968.

Hawaii Five-o. 2013. "Are Danny & McGarrett going on a man date? . . . ," February 18. Twitter. https://twitter.com/HawaiiFiveoCBS/status/303519535493963776.

Hellekson, K. 2010. "History, the Trace, and *Fandom Wank*." In *Writing and the Digital Generation: Essays on New Media Rhetoric*, edited by H. Urbanski, 58–69. Jefferson, NC: McFarland.

Hills, Matt. 2012. "'Twilight' Fans Represented in Commercial Paratexts and Inter-Fandoms: Resisting and Repurposing Negative Fan Stereotypes." In *Genre, Reception, and Adaptation in the Twilight Series*, edited by Anne Morey, 113–129. Burlington, VT: Ashgate Publishing, Ltd.

Jane, E. 2014. "Beyond Antifandom: Cheerleading, Textual Hate and New Media Ethics." *International Journal of Cultural Studies* 17, no. 2:175–190.

———. In this volume. "Hating 3.0: Should Anti-Fan Studies Be Renewed for Another Season?"

Jenkins, H. 2006. *Convergence Culture: Where Old and New Media Collide*. New York: New York University Press.

Jenkins, H., and S. Shresthova. 2012. "Up, Up, and Away! The Power and Potential of Fan Activism." *Transformative Works and Cultures*, no. 10. doi: 10.3983/twc.2012.0435.

Johnson, D. 2007. "Fan-tagonism: Factions, Institutions, and Constitutive Hegemonies of Fandom." In *Fandom: Identities and Communities in a Mediated World*, edited by J. Gray, C. Sandvoss, and C. L. Harrington, 285–300. New York: New York University Press.

Jones, Bethan. 2012. "Being of Service: *X-Files* Fans and Social Engagement." In "Transformative Works and Fan Activism," special issue, edited by Henry Jenkins and Sangita Shresthova, *Transformative Works and Cultures*, no. 10. doi: 10.3983/twc.2012.0309.

Larsen, K., and L. S. Zubernis. 2012. "Introduction." In *Fan Culture: Theory/Practice*, edited by K. Larsen and L. S. Zubernis, 1–13. Newcastle upon Tyne: Cambridge Scholars.

———. 2014. "Fandom, Passion and Supernatural: A Chat with Misha Collins." *Fangasm* (blog), April 7. https://wordpress.com.

Marwick, A. E., and danah boyd. 2011. "To See and Be Seen: Celebrity Practice on Twitter." *Convergence: The International Journal of Research into New Media Technologies* 17, no. 2:139–158.

Pinkowitz, J. 2011. "'The Rabid Fans That Take [*Twilight*] Much Too Seriously': The Construction and Rejection of Excess in *Twilight* Antifandom." *Transformative Works and Cultures*, no. 7. doi: 10.3983/twc.2011.0247.

Romano, A. 2014. "'Supernatural' fandom gives the CW a lesson in Twitter PR." *Daily Dot*, July 17. www.dailydot.com.

r/Supernatural. n.d. "Misha Hate Day!?" Reddit. www.reddit.com.

Savage, Christina. 2014. "*Chuck* versus the Ratings: Savvy Fans and 'Save Our Show' Campaigns." In "Fandom and/as Labor," special issue, edited by Mel Stanfill and Megan Condis. *Transformative Works and Cultures*, no. 15. doi: 10.3983/twc.2014.0497.

Schmidt, L. 2010. "Monstrous Melodrama: Expanding the Scope of Melodramatic Identification to Interpret Negative Fan Responses to *Supernatural*." *Transformative Works and Cultures*, no. 4. doi: 10.3983/twc.2010.0152.

Sheffield, J., and E. Merlo. 2010. "Biting Back: Twilight Anti-Fandom and the Rhetoric of Superiority." In *Bitten by Twilight: Youth Culture, Media and the Vampire Franchise*, edited by Melissa A. Click, Jennifer Stevens Aubrey, and Elizabeth Behm-Morawitz, 207–222. New York: Peter Lang.

SPN Silent Majority. 2012a. "Our Platform: A Message from Long-Time Supernatural Fans." *Scribd*. www.scribd.com.

———. 2012b. "A Statement a/b the Misha Hate." Tumblr. http://spnsilentmajority-mod.tumblr.com/post/24138858125/statement-on-misha-hate.

Sup3rnatural. n.d. "We're declaring Thursday May 31st as 'I HATE MISHA COLLINS DAY' . . ." Tumblr, May 30. www.tumblr.com.

Stein, Louisa, moderator. 2014. "Spreadable Media: Creating Value and Meaning in a Networked Culture." Roundtable, participants Paul Booth, Kristina Busse, Melissa

Click, Sam Ford, Henry Jenkins, Xiaochang Li, and Sharon Ross. *Transformative Works and Cultures*, no. 17. doi: 10.3983/twc.2014.0633.

Supernatual Wiki. n.d. "Dean/Castiel." www.supernaturalwiki.com.

Theodoropoulou, V. 2007. "The Anti-Fan within the Fan: Awe and Envy in Sport Fandom." In *Fandom: Identities and Communities in a Mediated World*, edited by J. Gray, C. Sandvoss, and C. L. Harrington, 316–327. New York: New York University Press.

Tosenberger, C. 2008. "'The Epic Love Story of Sam and Dean': *Supernatural*, Queer Readings, and the Romance of Incestuous Fan Fiction." *Transformative Works and Cultures*, no. 1. doi: /10.3983/twc.2008.0030.

Unconditional Love. 2013. "Rough Draft Timeline List (in Progress)," May 13. Blog entry. https://wanderlustlover.dreamwidth.org.

Veronika K. 2013. "*Supernatural*—9.07—Dean and Castiel's Reunion and Queerbaiting." *SpoilerTV*, September 20. www.spoilertv.com.

Warren, C. 2011. "CBS Embraces Social Media for Fall TV Launch." *Mashable*, September 12. https://mashable.com.

Wilken, Selina. 2012. "Spiteful 'Supernatural' Fans Try to Get Misha Collins Fired, Fail Epically." *Hypable*, May 31. www.hypable.com.

Williams, R. 2013. "'Anyone Who Calls Muse a Twilight Band Will Be Shot on Sight': Music, Distinction, and the 'Interloping Fan' in the Twilight Franchise. *Popular Music and Society* 36, no. 3:327–342.

15

"Putting the Show out of Its Misery"

Textual Endings, Anti-Fandom, and the "Rejection Discourse"

REBECCA WILLIAMS

Jonathan Gray describes anti-fans as those who "strongly dislike a given text or genre, considering it inane, stupid, morally bankrupt and/ or aesthetic drivel" (Gray 2003, 70). He also acknowledges that "fans can become anti-fans of a sort when an episode or part of a text is perceived as harming a text as a whole" (73). However, as his contribution to this collection discusses, anti-fan practices are varied and take a number of different forms. This chapter considers how fans of a television series employ discourses of anti-fandom, often based on disliking or rejecting specific elements of the text, when their favored fan objects cease production, a form of what Gray refers to as "disappointed anti-fandom" (Gray, in this volume). As my discussion demonstrates, fans' use of a "rejection discourse" (Williams 2015) often sees them adopting a critically defensive posture, articulating that shows have "jumped the shark" and are past their best. This "allows fans to distance themselves from a show discursively positioning themselves as critical and non-emotionally involved and suggesting that a program is past its best period and deserves to end" (Williams 2015, 103).

Although television studies has a "preoccupation with examples that are themselves 'current'" (Hastie 2007, 79), my concern with how forms of anti-fandom operate around the period of a television show's cessation means that my case study focuses on an older show that has finished airing. This chapter focuses on *The West Wing*, a political drama that aired on the NBC network in the United States between 1999 and 2006 and which was created by Aaron Sorkin, who had enjoyed previous critical acclaim with his TV series *Sports Night* (ABC, 1998–2000) and, subsequently, with *The Newsroom* (HBO, 2012–2014). *The West Wing* was considered a "textbook case" of "television's mainstream of quality drama" (Feuer 2007, 148) owing to its narrative storytelling, its ensemble of talented actors, and its willingness to deal with complex political and social issues such as the Middle East peace process, 9/11, and social security in the United States. It attracted popular and critical acclaim, and much of this success was linked to Sorkin's creative control over the show (he wrote or co-wrote eighty-five of the first eighty-eight episodes) before his departure at the end of the fourth season in 2003. After Sorkin's exit, producer John Wells took over as executive producer, leading to critiques from some fans and reviewers that the show had begun to focus on more sensationalist story-lines (including the bombing of a presidential delegation in the Middle East) at the expense of the more nuanced political narratives that Sorkin had emphasized. Ratings slowly declined across the final three seasons of the show, from an average of 12.88 million to 8.08 million (ABC Television Network 2004, 2006).

The discussion here focuses on three ways in which modes of anti-fandom were articulated as the political drama series *The West Wing* drew to a close. First, fans discussed the apparent overall decline of the series, which was linked to a focus on newer characters at the expense of established ones, particularly in the fifth, sixth, and seventh seasons after creator Aaron Sorkin's departure. Second, fans offered often vitriolic comments about those involved in producing the show, particularly Sorkin's replacement as executive producer, John Wells. Finally, and linked to these previous two fan arguments, fans implicitly suggested that their anti-fan feelings at the show's cessation had undermined their previously positive attitudes and enjoyment of the series and declared that they were happy to see the end of show. The chapter thus considers three various modalities of anti-fandom that share overlapping anti-fan sentiments while revealing different strands of anti-fandom through affective ties (via blame, via detachment, via rejection). This chapter thus argues that the invocation of forms of anti-fandom offers opportunities for some fans to cope with, and renarrate, possible ruptures to a sense of identity or self-narrative that the cancellation of a series may provoke. In so doing, it draws on the work of sociologist Anthony Giddens which, as Matt Hills argues, has potential for understanding fandom and the "(psychical as well as social) uses that can be made of television and its texts; and . . . how a medium such as television . . . can be embedded into the 'ontological security' or object-constancy of trusted, ritualised daily life and its everyday creativity" (Hills 2013, 80).

Television and fan studies have recently begun to explore the concept of endings in more detail. For example, Levine and Parks (2007) discuss the "afterlife" of *Buffy the Vampire Slayer*; C. Lee Harrington (2013) has considered what makes a "good" or "appropriate" end for a series; and Jason Mittell (2015) has sought to sketch out the range of different endings that may befall a television show. Greater attention has also been paid to close analysis of the aesthetics and narrative of textual endings of television series such as *Seinfeld* (Morreale 2003), *The Sopranos* (Corrigan and Corrigan 2012), and *Lost* (Morreale 2010). There is also work on fan practices after programs end, including Chin's (2013) discussion of fan/producer relationships after the end of the original series of *The X-Files*, Bore and Hickman's (2013) analysis of how fans of *The West Wing* used Twitter to portray the characters and continue the diegetic world of the series online, and several studies of the sitcom *Friends* (Eyal and Cohen 2006; Lather and Moyer-Guse 2011; Todd 2011). However, the majority of studies assume that fans are sad to see the endings of favored shows and that their reactions are ones of upset, disappointment, or grief. In relation to *Friends*, Todd notes that "fans were not just watching the end of a show, they were saying goodbye to *Friends* along with millions of other viewers, experiencing the sadness that the characters expressed" (Todd 2011, 859). This chapter challenges this, arguing that fans often articulate anti-fan sentiments when their favorite shows cease airing. Considering the moments when television shows move from being active and ongoing to canceled allows discussion of responses to the cessation of fan objects, especially how forms of anti-fandom are articulated as a "rejection discourse" (Williams 2015) by fans of a series.

Using a dormant show such as *The West Wing* allows examination of discourses of anti-fandom and dislike when the series ended. In exploring the fan comments shortly before the final episodes, as the episodes aired, and in the immediate aftermath, we can understand how anti-fandom operates as television programs draw to a close and why a "discourse of rejection" is mobilized. This chapter thus contributes to understandings of fan responses to the ending of television series and to conceptualizations of how anti-fandom is invoked to discuss or cope with the transition to a dormant text. As work continues to develop on fan reactions to the ending of favorite fan objects, it is important to look beyond reactions of sadness and grief and the concept of "textual mourning" (Harrington 2013, 580). The research presented here offers a new perspective on such reactions, considering both how fans may respond more negatively to the cessation of favorite texts and also how anti-fandom continues to be drawn on across a range of contexts and fandoms. It also considers the limits to the concept of "affective economies," which, as Melissa Click notes, encourage "producers to build networked communities around their media offerings by engaging consumers emotionally" (Click, in this volume). These emotional affective connections can, and obviously do, endure after a favorite fan object "ends." However, when anti-fan discourses are mobilized at the point of an object's cessation and are used to help fans to disentangle themselves from their emotional engagements, their loyalty as brand consumers becomes compromised.

Methods

Data collection for this study was undertaken at the online fan community *Television Without Pity* (*TWoP*), which hosted forums for a variety of U.S.-based television shows. *Television Without Pity* was more likely to offer anti-fandom and criticism than other fan sites, such as the official NBC *West Wing* fansite or other more fan-specific online spaces. This was because of its focus on a range of programs that tended to attract both avid fans and more casual television viewers who watched, and commented on, a range of different shows. *Television Without Pity* members prided themselves on their sense of "snark," referring to their ability to be often scathing about the perceived failings of television shows. This concept endures in fandoms, as noted in studies of the anti-fan communities surrounding *Twilight* (Haig 2014) and *Fifty Shades of Grey* (Harman and Jones 2013) and the practice of "hatewatching"—watching a series that one does not actually like (Falero 2016). As Andrejevic (2008) has noted, and as Click expands on in the introduction to this collection, sites like *TWoP* have led to the increased "visibility of fans' negative affective evaluations of media texts" (Click, in this volume). Originally an independent site, *TWoP* was bought in 2007 by the American cable and satellite channel Bravo (owned by NBCUniversal), which led to some critique that the site became less independent and more commercial (Donaghy 2007). As a site that actively encouraged "snark" and modes of anti-fandom, it offered a chance to view the range of discourses that fans deploy to discuss programs that they were once fans of. Thus, while not all posters at *TWoP* were anti-fans, the site was "renowned for its sarcastic and at times brutal honesty, encouraging play with and criticism of television. . . . *TWoP* simultaneously create[d] ample room for networking textual disappointment, dislike, disapproval, distaste, and disgust" (Gray 2005, 841). *Television Without Pity* provided opportunities for considering more positive and approving fan commentary alongside "clusters and even communities of antifandom" (841). As such, *TWoP* was a prolific site that has attracted substantive academic attention (see Andrejevic 2008; Falero 2016; Gray 2005; Peters 2006; Williams 2015).

Once a show ceased airing, posts about it were archived in the *TWoP* forum. While users could not then post to *West Wing* threads, posts were accessible online until May 2014, when NBCUniversal shut the website down. To gather data for this research, I archived threads about each new episode of the final season, from the first episode on September 25, 2005, to the finale on May 14, 2006. There were twenty-two threads to examine, as well as a thread dedicated to the cancellation entitled "It's Official—West Wing to Conclude Sunday, May 14" and a thread entitled "The Reflecting Pool: A Look Back at the Show." Across these threads, all comments directly related to the cancellation or ending of the show were archived, and quotes included below were chosen to demonstrate commonalities in fan discussion or to highlight occasions in which dissenting views were heard. Posters at *TWoP* were "aware of speaking potentially to thousands and [are] already reasonably anonymous; and the performative nature of much *TWoP* commentary itself belies an awareness of (or even a desire for) a considerable audience" (Gray 2005, 847). Such performativity, size, and openness rendered privacy at *TWoP* impossible and, as such, all postings made at the site were widely considered to be in the public domain. Despite this, in keeping with the ethical framework of my research, when citing online quotes I refer to the thread name and post number only. However, in March 2014 the closure of both the site and the forums was announced, highlighting how, "as fan objects end, so too do the spaces where fans [and anti-fans] can discuss them" (Williams 2015, 10; also see Falero 2016, 151–166).

Anti-Fandom, Post-Object Fandom, and Ontological Security

This chapter draws on two key concepts: anti-fandom and post-object fandom. Anti-fandom can often result from oppositions between media texts or objects, such as sports team rivalries (see Theodoropoulou 2007). It can also occur when seemingly disparate and unconnected fandoms clash, such as the *Twilight* franchise and the rock band Muse, who were forced into antagonistic "accidental anti-fandom" in which "seemingly contingent intertextual associations can prompt discourses and practices of anti-fandom" (Williams 2013, 238). Furthermore, scholars such as Jane (2014) have criticized approaches to anti-fandom that focus solely on texts or audiences, arguing instead that anti-fandom clearly overlaps with other forms of hate and prejudice such as sexism, homophobia, and racism since "human texts are likely to suffer from the circulation of vitriolic antifan discourse in a way that inanimate texts . . . do not" (Jane 2014, 177). Academics working in fan studies have argued that "a further elaboration of such a notion of the anti-fan is certainly needed, so that we might better conceptualize and theorize it. Pursuing such a task can lead to a better understanding not only of the role of anti-fandom to the identity positions of the fan, but more generally of fandom's expression and appropriation" (Theodoropoulou 2007, 326). This chapter contributes to such elaboration by focusing upon anti-fandom within a singular fan community when the object of fandom comes to a close. Fandom of television series can clearly continue post series through rewatching, maintaining connections with other fans, and/or attending conventions and other fan events. Similarly, "Fans may move into or out of periods of anti-fandom across time—for example, a one-time fan of a television show or band may 'grow out' of them and move from a position of dedication to dislike or hatred" (Williams 2015, 105). However, here I specifically explore how discourses of anti-fandom are utilized at the point of a show's cessation. As Gray notes, such "disappointed anti-fandom" allows consideration of fans who like a particular text "to a point" but who take umbrage with certain aspects of that text (e.g., problematic representations of gender; see Gray, in this volume). *The West Wing* fans discussed here are examples of fans who have become dissatisfied with certain aspects of the show (e.g., the writers, the storylines) and who have chosen to occupy positions of anti-fandom that are, as Gray explains, "performed with close knowledge of the text and yet [are] devoid of the interpretive and diegetic pleasures that are usually assumed to be a staple of almost all media consumption" (Gray 2005, 842). Such fans allow consideration of the fact that, as noted above, "fans can become anti-fans of a sort when an episode or part of a text is perceived as harming a text as a whole" (Gray 2003, 73). However, this discussion explores this explicitly through the broader lens of furthering our knowledge and understanding of how fans respond when favorite fan objects "end."

The second concept drawn on here is "post-object fandom" (Williams 2011, 2015). This term refers to the situation in which a fan object ceases to offer any new official texts or installments and, "although fans can re-watch DVDs or re-runs and new audiences might find the show through these means, their fandom enters a period of *post-object fandom* in which fan practices and interactions inevitably change" (Williams 2011, 269) as individuals and fan communities find new ways to engage with a series and to maintain or, in some cases, abandon their fandom. Fans can often feel a sense of anxiety as objects of adoration cease to produce new installments, and they can negotiate this anxiety in a number of ways, for example, by playing down their attachment to a favored series. This is linked to what sociologist Anthony Giddens terms "ontological security," which offers an "emotional inoculation against existential anxieties—a protection against future threats and dangers which allows the individual to sustain hope and courage in the face of whatever debilitating circumstances she or he might later confront" (Giddens 1991, 40). Ontological security is a reward gained from relationships with other people or with important fan objects, but, once a sense of trust in that relationship is undermined, ontological security can be threatened. Furthermore, since "self-identity is one dimension of ontological security, and for Giddens this is narratively based" (Hills 2012, 113), an individual's self-narrative must be reworked in order to cope with this disruption. For example, a fan may need to negotiate and deal with changes to an object of fandom if, for example, a celebrity dies, a band splits up or changes musical direction, or a footballer leaves a particular club and moves to another. This can be particularly acute in television fandom since ontological security often relies on familiarity, routine, and repetition, such as TV's "schedules, genres, and narratives" (Silverstone 1994, 15). If something that has been part of the "fixed schedules, in which the same program is put on at the same time of the day" (Moores 2005, 20) is no longer available, fan audiences need to come to terms with this loss of the presence of the fan object. Such feelings of loss will then need to be negotiated to cope with this period of mourning before refashioning fan self-identities to deal with this rupture. This chapter considers how fans cope with the loss of a fan object that provides such a sense of security and how forms of anti-fan discussion and performance allow this coping to take place. For, although fans can gain comfort from the routine of their fandom (such as anticipating the scheduling of *The West Wing* in a regular time slot and knowing that it will return in each new television season), ontological security is not solely dependent upon such repetitions and expectations. It cannot offer some form of magical "emotional inoculation" (Giddens 1990, 94) against disruption or distress. Rather, ontological security allows people to cope with rupture or change and to continue their lives afterward, even if this is a long process of renegotiation since self-identity is found "in the capacity to keep a particular narrative going. . . . The individual's biography . . . must continually integrate events which occur in the external world, and sort them into the ongoing 'story' about the self" (Giddens 1992, 54). It is essential for individuals to deal with the loss of the beloved object (whether a person, a text, and so on) and to incorporate this demise into their self-narratives and to necessitate a "coming to terms with the psychological past, and a rewriting of the narrative of the self" (Giddens 1992, 103). Such issues have been examined in Hills's (2007) work on DVD box sets and ontological security and his study of spoilers (2012), Garner's (2013) discussion of fans of *Doctor Who* and *Sarah Jane Adventures* actress Elisabeth Sladen, and my own prior work on more positive responses of *West Wing* fans at the show's cessation (Williams 2011, 2015). This chapter now turns to the words of fans themselves, considering threats to fan ontological security when fan objects end and how anti-fan discourses are utilized to help fans deal with these ruptures and changes.

Quality, Authorship and Anti-Fandom at the End of
The West Wing

The cancellation of *The West Wing* was announced in January 2006. Many of the fans I observed online at the end of the show in 2006 were disappointed and upset both at news of the cancellation and as the series aired its final episodes (Williams 2011, 2015). This chapter builds upon my previous discussions of the positive and negative reactions of fans to the series' ending, considering how some fans were more critical of the show's decline and took up positions more in line with anti-fans than grieving viewers. This chapter now explores the three interlinking ways in which anti-fan sentiment was displayed toward the ending of *The West Wing*. These were discussions of decline of the series, evaluation of the writers and producers involved in the shows and critique of their abilities, and the associated response that fandom of the show had lessened. In using these often overlapping discourses of rejection, fans of the show utilized anti-fandom as it drew to a close, an aspect of anti-fandom that has not yet been examined in academic scholarship of anti-fans and television endings more widely.

Across *The West Wing* fans studied, many adopted a critical or defensive posture, articulating that the show was past its "golden age" (Tulloch and Jenkins 1995) and that they were glad to see its demise. Fan campaigns to save shows (Abbott 2005; Menon 2007; Paproth 2013) are relatively common while efforts by former fans turned anti-fans to have a series canceled are more unusual. However, in the case of *The West Wing*, some had actively called for the show to be cancelled via the "Don't Save Our Show" campaign (Tucker 2004). Other posters at the *Television Without Pity* forum reacted by using discourses of euthanasia, alluding to "putting the show out of its misery" (*Television Without Pity*, n.d.-d, post #124, "The Last Hurrah") or lamenting that "it's sad watching my favorite show die. I know the patient is on life support and not expected to live much longer, but I can't help watching it wither away" (*Television Without Pity*, n.d.-c, post #298, "Two Weeks Out"). Here, genuine fan affective attachment operates alongside more negative expressions about the series; there is a sense of mercy in ending a show that these fans feel is "dying" but to which they cannot help remaining attached. Such declarations allow these posters to protect themselves and to attempt to ward off any emotional upset when the show ends as they rationalize their affective ties away via the suggestion that the show had ceased to be worthy of their attention.

These discussions over the perceived demise in quality relate to *West Wing* fan debates over what constituted the "true" show. Such discussions were also commonplace within the *Television Without Pity* community before the cancellation of the show was announced, demonstrating that some online posters continue to view programs they "no longer really liked because they want to participate in the ongoing online dissection of the program, its characters and its writers" (Andrejevic 2008, 44). In these discussions, posters often debated what constituted the "real" *West Wing*, espousing anti-fan readings of the show. For instance, some fans felt that episodes focusing upon the presidential campaign between the Democrat and Republican candidates to replace President Bartlet were not "proper" episodes of the show. For these fans, episodes that sidelined the original cast of characters were seen as examples of what Gray refers to when he describes forms of anti-fandom as being dissatisfied when a specific "episode or part of a text is perceived as harming a text as a whole" (Gray 2003, 73):

> [I totally agree] about the need to re-name this show. Out of all of those folks who were on the screen tonight, only TWO of them were created by Aaron Sorkin, and only ONE of them had even ever worked in the West Wing. [*Television Without Pity*, n.d.-a, post #9, "Message of the Week"]

> An okay ep. But not the West Wing. It was New Wing. Purely. [*Television Without Pity*, n.d.-a, post #15, "Message of the Week"]

> It just isn't the same show without all of our original characters. It might not be a bad spin off but, it simply isn't *TWW*. [*Television Without Pity*, n.d.-a, post #57, "Message of the Week]

These fans work to bracket off their idea of the "true" show. Such idealization is common across fandoms. As Matt Hills notes in relation to *Doctor Who*, there are debates over "what counts as 'authentic' *Who*. This argument is never far away in . . . comparisons between different stories or eras of the program, for by praising or condemning certain

moments of the show, fans assert their model for 'proper' *Doctor Who*"
(Hills 2010, 5). However, in the case of *The West Wing*, such declarations
intensified and occurred with increasing regularity as the final episode
approached since there was only a short amount of time in which the
preferred aspects of the narrative could be resolved. When the ante-
penultimate episode "The Last Hurrah" was screened, many fans were
disappointed about the neglect of long-term characters and the episode's
focus on newer figures who had been introduced in the later seasons:

> I realize its not quite over as I'm posting this but its a commercial. I only
> have three episodes left and they have NOTHING to do with my regular
> cast members? Nothing to do with characters I'm seven years invested
> in? Or a returning rob lowe? Santos is pretty to look at but I'm incred-
> ibly wounded by this. [*Television Without Pity*, n.d.-d, post #3, "The Last
> Hurrah"]

> What a total WASTE of one of the final episodes. They've got three weeks—
> what is that, something like 132 minutes of actual screen time?—to wrap
> up seven years worth of characters and plotlines. So they devote an entire
> episode to characters we barely know, and useless sub-plots . . . all involv-
> ing AN ADMINISTRATION WE'RE NEVER GOING TO SEE. [*Television
> Without Pity*, n.d.-d, post #12, "The Last Hurrah"]

> Dear John Wells, Thank you for living up to my exceptionally low expec-
> tations of you. I now know that saying goodbye to this show will be easier
> than I had originally anticipated. Now give me back the last hour of my
> life. Sincerely, One of a Million Disappointed Fans. [*Television Without
> Pity*, n.d.-d, post #19, "The Last Hurrah"]

Such vitriolic statements indicate the level of fans' attachment to the
original characters and premise of the show and the sense of disappointment and betrayal that they feel regarding such episodes, demonstrating
a producer-focused anti-fandom that blames those in charge of *The West
Wing* for these perceived failings.

The emphasis upon the fact that there are only a few episodes of the
show left also demonstrates an anxiety that the narrative can never fully
sate their need for resolution of events. These anti-fan statements further

indicate a level of blame toward the writers and producers, suggesting that they are incapable of writing satisfactory conclusions to the story and are deliberately antagonizing fans in their insistence that storylines involving new characters are what the audience wants. This is not to say that John Wells or the other writers were actually behaving in this fashion. Here, anti-fandom is articulated in terms of "quality" television, and these discursive fan strategies must be read as symptomatic of their debates and struggles over what constitutes *The West Wing* and what types of episodes are "good" or "bad." Although these fan discussions are not performing political work by calling attention to issues such as racism, homophobia, or sexism (Jane 2014), they still have a role to play in helping establish and discursively police ideas over what forms of media are valued and what are not. Anti-fan discourses are employed to single out aspects of the show that are seen to be inadequate, offering insight into one example of how fans make value judgments about text and allowing, as Gray puts it, "meaningful re-entry points to discussing quality, values and expectations, allowing us to focus on the range of everyday viewers' values, and on how they interact with media consumption, use and meaning" (Gray 2003, 73).

However, such distinctions do not merely result from the impending demise of the show. One poster sarcastically notes, "Yay, we've gone back to a year ago this time. Because those episodes were so great" (*Television Without Pity*, n.d.-d, post #27, "The Last Hurrah"), indicating that episodes in prior seasons that focused upon the newer characters were equally unpopular and perceived as "inauthentic" *West Wing*. Here, in order to protect their fan/object relationships (and their ontological security and sense of self-identity), some fans refute any potential threat caused by the ending of the series by reiterating that they foresaw that the fan object was decreasing in quality. This suggests that such discursive manoeuvres are a way for fans to protect themselves against threats to their fan identities. Some fans claim that such flaws led them to be relieved that the show was ending, commenting that "it's episodes like this that make me remember why this show just can't go on" (*Television Without Pity*, n.d.-d, post #12, "The Last Hurrah") or, after the final episode, "Dissenting here. I thought it was just dull. They clearly had nothing more to do or say. Such a boring finale helps me get over my sadness that the show was ending" (*Television Without Pity*, n.d.-e, post #86, "Tomorrow").

However, these types of anti-fan sentiment allow fans to make defensive statements that enable them to deal with the loss of a previously valued fan object. If episodes such as "The Last Hurrah" or "Tomorrow" are dismissed as violating or denigrating what a fan initially liked about the show in the first place, then its "textual death" (Harrington 2013) can be rearticulated as a welcome relief. Fans' self-identities can thus be protected from any possible threat or upset when the series ends. Related to this is the fact that discourses of good/bad episodes and the "proper" show are often related to issues of authorship and production (Tulloch and Jenkins 1995, 151–153). *West Wing* fans commonly distinguish between the show's earlier seasons, which were overseen by show creator Aaron Sorkin and seasons 4–7, which were led by John Wells (see Williams 2015, 111–112). Wells was thus cast as a negative force who had run the show into the ground while Sorkin continued to be elevated and revered by many fans since, as the original creator of the series, he functioned as its author and offered a guarantee of "quality" (Hills 2002, 133). Again, such anti-fan discussions demonstrate that, "behind dislike, after all, there are always expectations—of what a text should be like, of what is a waste of media time and space, of what morality or aesthetics texts should adopt, and of what we would like to see others watch or read" (Gray 2003, 73). In the case of *The West Wing*, episodes were expected to focus on familiar and beloved characters and to offer fans a version of the show that they recognized. However, such distinctions became more pronounced as the series neared its end, with fans frequently bemoaning the opportunities wasted by John Wells and his emphasis on emotionality and "gimmicky" writing:

Ya know, I do believe I could have figured it all out without the song to inform me how the characters were feeling (Cold & Lonely). Sort of sums up the Wells era for me. [*Television Without Pity*, n.d.-b, post #56, "The Cold"]

I didn't want this feeling of being manipulated by John Wells—he just went for the sucker punch again and again and again. There was no story here—just endless manipulation of my emotions as I watched the finest series that has ever graced American Television come to an end. [*Television Without Pity*, n.d.-e, post #20, "Tomorrow"]

> John Wells . . . well I know not to seek out anything that you had a hand
> in making! I know you tried, but it just didn't work. [*Television Without
> Pity*, n.d.-e, post #198, "Tomorrow"]

These distinctions between Sorkin and Wells suggest an anxiety that
the show will never fully resolve all of its narratives, leaving the fan
unfulfilled once the final episode airs. The "hyperdiegesis"—the "vast
and detailed narrative space, only a fraction of which is ever directly
seen or encountered within the text" (Hills 2002,137)—of *The West Wing*
does enable fans to imagine a narrative world beyond the final frame.
However,

> Events which are not rendered canonical in the final few episodes will
> never be realised, undermining fans' sense of ontological security since
> their readings of the show, and their points of attachment and affective
> connection, are not validated by the show's producers. Furthermore,
> berating the writers for unpopular episodes also shifts the fault for the
> threats to fans' ontological security and self-identity onto outside sources,
> allowing fans to deal with their potential feelings of loss by apportioning
> blame. [Williams 2015, 112]

For these fans of *The West Wing*, aspects of anti-fandom are used to
articulate a discourse of rejection at the end of the series. These are fans
who have, at other times, been appreciative and positive fans, highlighting that "anti-fans must find cause for their dislike in *something*. This
something may vary from having previously watched the show and having found it intolerable; to having a dislike for its genre, director or stars;
to having seen previews or ads, or seen or heard unfavourable reviews"
(Gray 2003, 71, emphasis in original).

Conclusion

As anti-fandom continues to be studied scholars must pay attention
to how it is deployed at different points in fans' attachments to objects
and at various points across the trajectory of the objects themselves. As
argued here, anti-fandom is often displayed in fan reactions to the endings of television series. Drawing on the work of Anthony Giddens, this

chapter has considered how threats to fan ontological security and identity can be dealt with via discourses of rejection and anti-fandom as a series ends. It urges continued study of the impact when the cessation of "a favorite program creates an emotional void and forced detachment from the program narrative" (Costello and Moore 2007, 135), in particular when "a textual death [is] roundly rejected by fans" (Harrington 2013, 591).

During its life, *Television Without Pity*'s emphasis on "snark" and humorous critique of television shows led to arguments that it was more likely to engender anti-fan sentiment than other online fan spaces. However, such modes of snarky or outright hateful engagement are becoming commonplace in contemporary digital and convergence culture (see Falero 2016; Haig 2014; Harman and Jones 2013; Jane 2014), and, as Gray and Murray argue, study of hate and dislike helps extend "the reach of audience analysis when what is represented is neither what is desired nor hoped for" (Gray and Murray 2016, 370). Exploring how anti-fan attitudes are articulated as favorite fan objects draw to a close enables a better understanding of the range of discourses anti-fans draw on and the reasons why, as well as how, fans respond when textual endings are not what they wanted nor hoped for. In the case of *The West Wing* fans studied here, possible threats to their fan identities were warded off by their active creation and maintenance of a defensive system to neutralize those threats. They used a range of discourses to devalue the program and suggested their disengagement with it. By highlighting flaws in the narrative and characterization, and by apportioning blame for these faults on the writers and producers—particularly by comparing John Wells to Aaron Sorkin—these fans drew on well-established anti-fan tactics to suggest that the show was no longer worthy of their attachment. These two discourses contribute to the idea, often more implicitly expressed by these fans, that their fandom of the series was finished owing to these perceived shortcomings.

Furthermore, studying anti-fandom "is to study what expectations and what values structure media consumption" (Gray 2003, 73) and "to understand both how citizens make sense of the media's role in their everyday lives, and what they want from media" (Gray and Murray 2016, 358). This discussion of *West Wing* fans offers knowledge of the expectations that certain fans had at the end of the series and on what the show's narrative should focus. Considering how some fans demonstrate relief and even pleasure, rather than sadness or grief, at the end of once-beloved television shows and how they work to distance themselves from their fan objects, this chapter broadens our understanding of anti-fandom and how it operates across fandoms at different times. Fans' reactions at the ending—or beginning—of their fandom can be hugely varied, suggesting the "nuances of viewership and fanship" (Harrington and Bielby 1995, 113). We should pay attention to the different stages of fan attachment, and their intersections with modes of anti-fan discourse, to allow greater understanding of how fans' relationships with fan objects ebb and flow across the lifespan of the fan object and, in many cases, of the fans themselves.

REFERENCES

Abbott, S. 2005. "'We'll follow Angel to Hell . . . or Another Network': Fan Response to the End of *Angel*." In *Reading Angel: The TV Spin-off with a Soul*, edited by S. Abbott, 230–233. London: I. B. Tauris.

ABC Television Network. 2004. "I.T.R.S Ranking Report: 01 through 210 (Out of 210 Programs). Daypart: Primetime Monday to Sunday," June 2. www.abcmedianet.com. Hosted at the *Internet Archive Wayback Machine*. http://web.archive.org.

———. 2006. "Season Program Rankings: Part One, 1–100," May 31. www.abcmedianet.com. Hosted at the *Internet Archive Wayback Machine*. http://web.archive.org.

Andrejevic, M. 2008. "Watching *Television Without Pity*: The Productivity of Online Fans." *Television and New Media* 9, no. 1:24–46.

Bore, I. L., and J. Hickman. 2013. "Continuing *The West Wing* in 140 Characters or Less: Improvised Simulation on Twitter." *Journal of Fandom Studies* 1, no. 2:219–230.

Chin, B. 2013. "The Fan–Media Producer Collaboration: How Fan Relationships Are Managed in a Post-Series *X-Files* Fandom." *Science Fiction Film and Television* 6, no. 1:87–99.

Click, Melissa A. In this volume. "Introduction: Haters Gonna Hate."

Corrigan, J. M., and M. Corrigan. 2012. "Disrupting Flow: *Seinfeld*, *Sopranos* Series Finale and the Aesthetic of Anxiety." *Television and New Media* 13, no. 2: 91–102.

Costello, V., and B. Moore. 2007. "Cultural Outlaws: an Examination of Audience Activity and Online Television Fandom." *Television and New Media* 8, no. 2:124–143.

Donaghy, J. 2007. "Help Me Save *Television Without Pity*." *Guardian*, April 4. www.theguardian.com.

Eyal, K., and J. Cohen. 2006. "When Good *Friends* Say Goodbye: A Parasocial Breakup Study." *Journal of Broadcasting and Electronic Media* 50, no. 3:502–523.

Falero, S. M. 2016. *Digital Participatory Culture and the TV Audience: Everyone's a Critic*. London: Palgrave Macmillan.

Feuer, J. 2007. "HBO and the Concept of Quality TV." In *Quality TV: Contemporary American Television and Beyond*, edited by J. McCabe and K. Akass, 145–157. London: I. B.Tauris.

Garner, R. P. 2013. "Remembering Sarah Jane: Intradiegetic Allusions, Embodied Presence/Absence and Nostalgia." In *New Dimensions of Doctor Who: Exploring Space, Time and Television*, edited by M. Hills, 192–215. London: I. B. Tauris.

Giddens, A. 1990. *The Consequences of Modernity*. Cambridge: Polity Press.

———. Giddens, A. 1991. *Modernity and Self-Identity: Self and Society in the Late Modern Age*. Cambridge: Polity Press.

———. Giddens, A. 1992. *The Transformation of Intimacy: Sexuality, Love, and Eroticism in Modern Societies*. Stanford, CA: Stanford University Press.

Gray, J. 2003. "New Audiences, New Textualities: Anti-Fans and Non-Fans." *International Journal of Cultural Studies* 6, no. 1:64–81.

———. 2005. "Anti Fandom and the Moral Text: *Television Without Pity* and Textual Dislike." *American Behavioral Scientist* 48, no. 7:840–858.

———. In this volume. "How Do I Dislike Thee? Let Me Count the Ways."

Gray, J., and S. Murray. 2016. "Hidden: Studying Media Dislike and Its Meaning." *International Journal of Cultural Studies* 19, no. 4:357–372.

Haig, F. 2014. "Guilty Pleasures: *Twilight*, Snark and Critical Fandom." In *Screening Twilight: Critical Approaches to a Cinematic Phenomenon*, edited by W. Clayton and S. Harman,11–25. London: I. B. Tauris.

Harman, S. and B. Jones. 2013. "Fifty Shades of Ghey: Snark Fandom and the Figure of the Anti-Fan." *Sexualities* 16, no. 8:951–968.

Harrington, C. L. 2013. "The *ars moriendi* of US Serial Television: Towards a Good Textual Death." *International Journal of Cultural Studies* 16, no. 6:579–595.

Harrington, C. L., and D. B. Bielby. 1995. *Soap Fans: Pursuing Pleasure and Making Meaning in Everyday Life*. Philadelphia: Temple University Press.

Hastie, A. 2007. "The Epistemological Stakes of *Buffy the Vampire Slayer*: Television Criticism and Marketing Demands." In *Undead TV: Essays on Buffy the Vampire Slayer*, edited by E. Levine and L. Parks,74–95. Durham, NC: Duke University Press.

Hills, M. 2002. *Fan Cultures*. London: Routledge.

———. 2007. "From the Box in the Corner to the Box Set on the Shelf." *New Review of Film and Television Studies* 5, no. 1:41–60.

———. 2010. *Triumph of a Time Lord: Regenerating Doctor Who in the Twenty-First Century*. London: I. B. Tauris.

———. 2012. "Psychoanalysis and Digital Fandom: Theorizing Spoilers and Fans' Self-Narratives." In *Producing Theory in a Digital World: The Intersection of Audiences and Production In Contemporary Theory*, edited by R. A. Lind, 105–122. New York: Peter Lang.

———.2013. "Media Users: An Introduction." In *Little Madnesses: Winnicottian Film Studies*, edited by A. Kuhn, 79–86. London: I. B. Tauris.

Jane, E. A. 2014. "Beyond Antifandom: Cheerleading, Textual Hate and New Media Ethics." *International Journal of Cultural Studies* 17:175–190.

Lather, J., and E. Moyer-Guse. 2011. "How Do We React When Our Favourite Characters Are Taken Away? An Examination of a Temporary Parasocial Breakup. *Mass Communication and Society* 14, no. 2:196–215.

Levine, L., and L. Parks. 2007. "Introduction." In *Undead TV: Essays on Buffy the Vampire Slayer*, edited by E. Levine and L. Parks, 1–15. Durham, NC: Duke University Press.

Menon, S. 2007. "A Participation Observation Analysis Of the *Once and Again* Internet Message Bulletin Boards." *Television and New Media* 8, no. 4:341–374.

Mittell, Jason. 2015. *Complex TV: The Poetics of Contemporary Television Storytelling.* New York: New York University Press.

Moores, S. 2005. *Media/Theory.* London: Routledge.

Morreale, J. 2003. "Sitcoms Say Good-Bye: The Cultural Spectacle of *Seinfeld*'s Last Episode." In *Critiquing the Sitcom: A Reader*, edited by J. Morreale, 274–285. Syracuse, NY: Syracuse University Press.

———. 2010." *Lost, The Prisoner*, and the End of the Story." *Journal of Popular Film and Television* 38, no. 4:176–185.

Paproth, M. 2013. "'Best. Show. Ever.': Who Killed *Veronica Mars*? *Journal of Popular Television* 1, no. 1:39–52.

Peters, M. 2006. "Getting A Wiggins and Being A Bitca: How Two Items of Slayer Slang Survive on the *Television Without Pity* Message Boards." *Slayage: The Online International Journal of Buffy Studies*, vol. 20. www.whedonstudies.tv.

Silverstone, R. 1994. *Television and Everyday Life.* London: Routledge.

Television Without Pity. n.d.-a. "Message of the Week." www.televisionwithoutpity.com.

———. n.d.-b. "The Cold." www.televisionwithoutpity.com.

———. n.d.-c. "Two Weeks Out." www.televisionwithoutpity.com.

———. n.d.-d. "The Last Hurrah." www.televisionwithoutpity.com.

———. n.d.-e. "Tomorrow." www.televisionwithoutpity.com.

Theodoropoulou, V. 2007. "The Anti-Fan within the Fan: Awe and Envy in Sport Fandom." In *Fandom: Identity and Communities in a Mediated World*, edited by J. Gray, C. Sandvoss, and C. L. Harrington, 316–327. New York: New York University Press.

Todd, A. M. 2011. "Saying Goodbye to *Friends*: Fan Culture as Lived Experience." *Journal of Popular Culture* 44, no. 4: 854–871.

Tucker, K. 2004. "Broken Wing." *Entertainment Weekly*, April 30. www.dontsaveourshow.org/eweekly.jpg. Hosted at the *Internet Archive Wayback Machine.* http://web.archive.org.

Tulloch, J., and H. Jenkins 1995. *Science-Fiction Audiences: Watching "Doctor Who" and "Star Trek."* London: Routledge.

Williams, R. 2011. "'This Is The Night TV Died': Television Post-Object Fandom and the Demise of *The West Wing*." *Popular Communication* 8, no. 4:266–279.

———. 2013. "'Anyone Who Calls Muse a *Twilight* Band Will Be Shot on Sight': Music, Distinction, and the 'Interloping Fan' in the *Twilight* Franchise." *Popular Music and Society* 36, no. 3:327–342.

———. 2015. *Post-Object Fandom: Television, Identity and Self-Narrative.* London: Bloomsbury.

ACKNOWLEDGMENTS

My interest in dislike and hatred of media figures and texts emerged through my research on Martha Stewart at the height of her popularity in the late 1990s. I struggled to name and understand fans' love/hate relationships with Stewart until I met Jonathan Gray in 2002 on a panel at the Crossroads in Cultural Studies conference in Tampere, Finland, and heard his conceptualization of "anti-fandom." Much of my work on fandom and digital culture since has grappled with issues of hatred and anti-fandom.

I am grateful to the scholars featured in this collection for many conversations over the last few years about issues of dislike and hatred and also for the incredible chapters they have contributed to this project. This book, which aims to set a course for future research on anti-fandom, would not have been possible without the enthusiasm, support, and guidance of Henry Jenkins, Karen Tongson, Lisha Nadkarni, and Eric Zinner. Thank you also to our reviewers.

When I conceptualized this project, I had no idea that I would ever encounter firsthand the kind of hate that this book explores. The experience offered me a chance to understand more fully the ways digital tools and networks amplify the force and speed with which hate circulates in our contemporary culture. Fortunately, I also learned how fan cultures support and protect beloved targets. I am humbled by and grateful for the love and kindness expressed to me over the last few years. Specifically, I need to shout out to my personal Scorpio fan squad—Chip Callahan, Nina Huntemann, and Jennifer Stevens Aubrey. Your unfaltering support has helped me transform the hate into motivation. #laterhaters

So keep calm, honey, I'ma stick around
For more than a minute, get used to it
—Katy Perry

ABOUT THE CONTRIBUTORS

Bertha Chin is Communications and Social Media Lecturer at Swinburne University of Technology (Sarawak). She has published extensively, is a board member of the Fan Studies Network, and is co-editor of *Crowdfunding the Future: Media Industries, Ethics and Digital Society* (2015).

Melissa A. Click is Assistant Professor of Communication Studies at Gonzaga University. Her work on fans, audiences, and popular culture has been published in *Television and New Media*, the *International Journal of Cultural Studies*, *Popular Communication*, *Popular Music and Society*, *Transformative Works and Cultures* and in the anthologies *Fandom: Identities and Communities in a Mediated World* and *Cupcakes, Pinterest, and Ladyporn: Feminized Popular Culture in the Early 21st Century*. She is co-editor of *The Routledge Companion to Media Fandom* and *Bitten by Twilight*.

Anne Gilbert is Assistant Professor of Entertainment and Media Studies at the University of Georgia. She researches media audiences, industries, and technologies and is writing a book on San Diego Comic-Con and its position in contemporary participatory culture.

Jonathan Gray is Professor of Media and Cultural Studies at University of Wisconsin–Madison. He is the author of four books, including *Television Entertainment* and *Show Sold Separately: Promos, Spoilers, and Other Media Paratexts*, and co-editor of seven collections, including *Keywords in Media Studies* (with Laurie Ouellette), *The Companion to Media Authorship* (with Derek Johnson), and *Fandom: Identities and Communities in a Mediated World*, 2nd ed. (with Cornel Sandvoss and C. Lee Harrington).

Matt Hills is Professor of Media and Film at the University of Huddersfield and co-director of the Centre for Participatory Culture based

335

there. He has published widely on media fandom, including *Fan Cultures* (2002) and *Doctor Who: The Unfolding Event* (2015).

Holly Willson Holladay is Assistant Professor of Media, Journalism and Film at Missouri State University. She has published essays in *Television and New Media*, the *International Journal of Cultural Studies*, *Popular Music and Society*, and *Participations: Journal of Audience and Reception Studies*, as well as a number of edited collections.

Emma A. Jane (formerly Emma Tom) is Senior Lecturer at the University of New South Wales in Sydney, Australia. Her ninth book—*Misogyny Online: A Short (and Brutish) History*—was published in 2017. Over the course of her career, she has received multiple national and international awards for her investigative reporting, her fiction writing, and her scholarship.

Bethan Jones is a Ph.D. candidate at the University of Huddersfield. Bethan has published extensively on fandom, gender, and new media in both academic and popular publications. Her work has appeared in the journals *Sexualities*, *Transformative Works and Cultures*, and *New Media and Society*, as well as in edited collections. She has also co-edited the collection *Crowdfunding the Future: Media Industries, Ethics, and Digital Society* (2015). She is a board member of the Fan Studies Network and a principal researcher in the World Star Wars Project.

Alfred L. Martin, Jr., is Assistant Professor in the Department of Communication Studies at the University of Iowa. Martin has published essays in *Feminist Media Studies*, *Communication, Culture and Critique*, *Popular Communication*, *Television and New Media*, the *Journal of Black Masculinity*, and *Spectator*. His forthcoming book, *The Queer Politics of Black-Cast Sitcoms*, examines the production, reception, ideology, and industrial context of black gay characters in black-cast sitcoms and will be published in 2019.

Richard McCulloch is Lecturer in Film and Cultural Studies at the Centre for Participatory Culture, University of Huddersfield. He is co-director of the World Star Wars Project, co-editor of *Disney's Star Wars:*

Forces of Production, Promotion and Participation (2019) and *The Scandinavian Invasion: The Nordic Noir Phenomenon and Beyond* (2018), and he sits on the board of the Fan Studies Network. His current book project is a monograph on unfolding reputations and the Pixar animation brand.

Roberta Pearson is Professor of Film and Television Studies at the University of Nottingham. Among her most recent publications are the co-authored *Star Trek and American Television* (2014) and the co-edited *Many More Lives of the Batman* (2015) and *Storytelling in the Media Convergence Age: Exploring Screen Narratives* (2015). The co-edited collection *Contemporary Transatlantic Television Drama* is forthcoming in 2018. She is in total the author, co-author, editor, or co-editor of fourteen books and author or co-author of over eighty journal articles and book chapters.

Whitney Phillips is Assistant Professor of Communication, Culture, and Digital Technologies at Syracuse University. She is the author of *This Is Why We Can't Have Nice Things: Mapping the Relationship between Online Trolling and Mainstream Culture* and the co-author of *The Ambivalent Internet: Mischief, Oddity, and Antagonism Online* with Ryan M. Milner. Across her books, numerous journal articles, book chapters, and popular press pieces in outlets like the *New York Times*, the *Atlantic*, and *Slate*, her work explores antagonism and identity-based harassment; the reciprocal relationship between public expression, corporate and state institutions, and technological affordances; political memes and other forms of ambivalent civic participation; and digital ethics, including journalistic ethics and the ethics of everyday social media use.

Michelle M. Rivera is a Mellon/American Council of Learned Societies (ACLS) Public Fellow (2017–2019) and currently the Public Engagement Manager for Diversity and Inclusion at the Field Museum in Chicago, Illinois. Her published work on global Latin pop culture and digital fandom also appears in *50 Events That Shaped Latino History: An Encyclopedia of the American Mosaic*, *The Routledge Companion to Latina/o Media*, and *Seeing in Spanish: From Don Quixote to Daddy Yankee*. She is currently writing a book that will comprise her research on anti-fandom and the global crossover of reggaetón music.

Cornel Sandvoss is Professor of Media and Journalism and co-founder of the Centre for Participatory Culture at the University of Huddersfield. His work focuses on forms of fandom across the spectrum of popular culture from sports to music, art, and politics. His books include *Fans: The Mirror of Consumption.*

Louisa Stein is Associate Professor of Film and Media Culture at Middlebury College, where she teaches classes on remix culture, youth media, YouTube, and gender and sexuality media. She is the author of *Millennial Fandom: Television Audiences in the Transmedia Age* and co-editor of *Sherlock and Transmedia Fandom* and *Teen Television: Programming and Fandom.* She is book review editor for *Transformative Works and Cultures,* and she is co-editing *A Tumblr Book* with Allison McCracken, Alexander Cho, and Indira Neill and a special issue of *Transformative Works and Cultures* on *Tumblr and Fandom* with Lori Morimoto.

Rebecca Williams is Senior Lecturer in Communication, Culture and Media Studies at the University of South Wales. She is the author of *Post-Object Fandom: Television, Identity and Self-Narrative* (2015) and *Theme Park Fandom* (forthcoming), and she is the editor of *Torchwood Declassified* (2013) and *Transitions, Endings, and Resurrections in Fandom* (2018). She is a member of the Board of the Fan Studies Network, and her work on fandom and media audiences has been published in journals including *Participations, Cinema Journal, Continuum, Popular Communication, Celebrity Studies, Transformative Works and Cultures,* and *Television and New Media.*

INDEX

activism. *See* campaigns

Adorno, Theodor, 210, 215, 217

affect: and ante-fandom, 105, 111, 115, 118–19; and "bad objects," 29, 39, 72, 166, 197; and community, 68–69, 107–8, 110, 118, 219, 245, 289, 318; economy, 8–9, 13–14, 318; and fan generations, 103, 116; and fan objects, 3, 133–37, 230–31, 242, 276, 286–87, 323–24, 328; growth of scholarship on, 6–7, 12–15; and identity, 25, 68–69, 71, 105, 114, 133–34, 171, 197, 219, 230–31, 245, 279, 292, 308–9, 316; individualized, 107, 110–11, 118; theory, 13–14, 40, 245n3, 264; value to fan studies, 1, 3, 12–15, 119, 228. *See also* ambivalence; dissatisfaction; fantipathy; feels culture

age/generation: discrimination, 129, 163, 167; and fan identity, 18, 30, 32, 75, 103–6, 108, 112–16, 119, 133; Latin youth market, 184; marginalization of youth, 32–33, 108–10, 191–193, 206; millennial fans, 67–68, 81–98; millennials on television, 67–68, 74–75, 81–98; multi-generational fandom, 102–19; of Radio 3 listeners, 206; of study participants, 156, 169; teens on television, 86–90; and transgressive femininity, 249–67. *See also* ante-fandom; identity

agency: collective, 132, 140; individual, 17, 45–46, 56–57, 159; as paradox in media scholarship, 57; reclaiming, 280; and spreadable media, 30

Ahmed, Sara, 13–15, 17, 68, 83, 107, 111, 164, 286

alienation: classical radio listeners, 205, 215–21; fangirls, 12; political, 138; reggaetón fans, 184, 200; teens, 86–88; textual, 31–32, 87–88

ambivalence: in "anti-fandom within the fan" discourse, 117; and fan behaviors, 252, 258–68; and interplay with positive emotion, 83, 96–97, 231–32, 252. *See also* affect; dissatisfaction; fantipathy

Andrejevic, Mark, 9–11, 50, 76, 138, 245n4, 245n5, 318, 319, 324

Ang, Ien, 4, 231–32

antagonism: in (anti-)fan/celebrity interaction, 49, 56, 147–151, 161–63, 293, 296–97, 299–303, 304–6; between (anti-)fan groups, 11–14, 188, 231, 293, 296–97, 299–303, 304–6; political, 135–36, 139–40; racial, 188–89; as structural to fandom, 296; targeting "ordinary" people, 16, 43–56, 155; as unifier, 135; within (anti-)fan groups, 75, 82, 106, 110–11, 115, 228, 231, 237–38, 241–42, 299–306. *See also* affect; competitive anti-fandoms; hatewatching; online forums

ante-fandom: 102–19; key attributes of, 107; as individualized affect, 107, 111. *See also* age/generation; *Doctor Who* fans

anti-fan community. *See* community/communities